Lecture Notes in Artificial Intelligence   1374

Subseries of Lecture Notes in Computer Science
Edited by J. G. Carbonell and J. Siekmann

Lecture Notes in Computer Science

Edited by G. Goos, J. Hartmanis and J. van Leeuwen

Springer

Berlin
Heidelberg
New York
Barcelona
Budapest
Hong Kong
London
Milan
Paris
Santa Clara
Singapore
Tokyo

Harry Bunt   Robbert-Jan Beun
Tijn Borghuis (Eds.)

Multimodal Human-Computer Communication

Systems, Techniques, and Experiments

 Springer

Series Editors
Jaime G. Carbonell, Carnegie Mellon University, Pittsburgh, PA, USA
Jörg Siekmann, University of Saarland, Saarbrücken, Germany

Volume Editors

Harry Bunt
Tilburg University
Warandelaan 2, 5000 LE Tilburg, The Netherlands
E-mail: bunt@kub.nl

Robbert-Jan Beun
Center for Research on User-System Interaction (IPO)
P.O. Box 513, 5600 MB Eindhoven, The Netherlands
E-mail: rjbeun@ipo.tue.nl

Tijn Borghuis
Eindhoven University of Technology
P.O. Box 513, 5600 MB Eindhoven, The Netherlands
E-mail: tijn@win.tue.nl

Cataloging-in-Publication Data applied for

Die Deutsche Bibliothek - CIP-Einheitsaufnahme

Multimodal human computer communication : systems,
techniques, and experiments / Harry Bunt ... (ed.). - Berlin ;
Heidelberg ; New York ; Barcelona ; Budapest ; Hong Kong ;
London ; Milan ; Paris ; Santa Clara ; Singapore ; Tokyo : Springer,
1998
  (Lecture notes in computer science ; Vol. 1374 : Lecture notes in
  artificial intelligence)
  ISBN 3-540-64380-X

CR Subject Classification (1991): I.2, H.5.1-2, I.3.6, D.2.2, K.4.2

ISSN 0302-9743
ISBN 3-540-64380-X Springer-Verlag Berlin Heidelberg New York

© Springer-Verlag Berlin Heidelberg 1998
Printed in Germany

Typesetting: Camera ready by author
SPIN 10631926   06/3142 – 5 4 3 2 1 0   Printed on acid-free paper

Preface

This volume contains revised versions of seventeen selected papers from the First International Conference on Cooperative Multimodal Communication (CMC/95), held in Eindhoven, the Netherlands, in May 1995. This was the first conference in a series, of which the second one was held in Tilburg, The Netherlands, in January 1998. Three of these papers were presented by invited speakers; those by Mark Maybury, Bonnie Webber, and Kent Wittenburg. From the submitted papers that were accepted by the CMC/95 program committee, thirteen were selected for publication in this volume, after revision.

We thank the program committee for their excellent and timely feedback to authors of submitted papers, and at a later stage for advising on the contents of this volume and for providing additional suggestions for improving the selected contributions. The program committee consisted of Norman Badler, Harry Bunt, Jeroen Groenendijk, Walther von Hahn, Dieter Huber, Hans Kamp, John Lee, Joseph Mariani, Mark Maybury, Paul Mc Kevitt, Rob Nederpelt, Kees van Overveld, Ray Perrault, Donia Scott, Wolfgang Wahlster, Bonnie Webber, and Kent Wittenburg. We thank the Royal Dutch Academy of Sciences (KNAW) and the Organization for Cooperation among Universities in Brabant (SOBU) for their grants that made the conference possible.

January 1998

Harry Bunt
Robbert-Jan Beun
Tijn Borghuis

Table of Contents

Issues in Multimodal Human-Computer Communication

Harry Bunt

Computational Linguistics and Artificial Intelligence Group
Tilburg University
5000 LE Tilburg, The Netherlands
bunt@kub.nl

1 Introduction

Human communication is inherently multimodal in nature. People naturally communicate by means of spoken language in combination with gestures, mimics, and nonlinguistic sounds (laughs, coughs, sniffs,..). They thereby use several communicative systems (*'modalities'*), and several physical 'carriers' of the messages of these systems, such as vocal sounds and visible hand movements, (*'multimedia'*), the use of which involves several perceptual channels. The various modalities are moreover not used independent of each other, but in such a way that the information communicated using one modality depends on that for which another modality is used more or less simultaneously.

Many modalities have originally developed in combination with a particular medium, but have in time become used also in combination with other media. For instance, natural language originally developed in combination with speech but later also with print and Braille, and gestures and mimics, like pointing, winks and smiles, originally developed using visible movements and facial expressions (involving the haptic-kinesthetic and visual channels), but have recently found new expression with the medium of computer screens as '=>', ';-)' and ':-('. The development of new media, in particular of digital media, has contributed much to the insight that communicative systems should be conceptually distinguished from the physical carriers they use, thus leading to the distinction between (multi)modality and (multi)media. Multimodal communication usually involves several media, but may also derive its multimodal character from the use of several communicative systems that make use of the same medium, e.g. text and graphics.

When the communicative situation precludes the use of certain media or modalities, the degree of multimodality and multimedia obviously decreases; for instance, two people who speak totally different languages can only communicate by means of gestures and mimics. It seems, though, that people naturally exploit all the available communicative resources, communicating according to what we might call the Multimax Principle: *In natural communication, the participants use all the modalities and media that are available in the communicative situation.* Natural communication is thus maximally multimodal and multimedia.

It seems quite clear why this should be so: the maximal use of modalities and media gives a maximal bandwith for communication, allowing communication to be maximally effective, by exploiting redundancy, and efficient, by using different media/modalities simultaneously for different aspects of the information to be exchanged. Widening the communication bandwith by arbitrary adding more and more modalities and media is of course not the way to optimize communication, however; the success of adding modalities depends on whether the cognitive processes operating on the messages conveyed in these modalities are capable of handling the information flow allowed by the bandwith. Human cognitive processes are well-attuned to the forms of multimodality and multimedia of natural communication between people, but for new, technology-driven modalities and media, this is not always the case; the design and evaluation of new forms of multimodal human-computer communication which are well-suited to human cognitive and perceptual processing therefore forms an important area of research. The same goes for new forms of human-human communication mediated by new modalities and media. In computers, the relation between input information and internal ('cognitive') processing is a well-known bottleneck from the point of view of information flow (see e.g. Thimbleby, 1990), which stands in the way of developing powerful user interfaces.

2   Interaction and Human-Computer Communication

When using a computer, one interacts with it in two fundamentally different ways. On the one hand, one formulates instructions or queries, typically by typing commands and by clicking on menu items. On the other hand, one adjusts the window size, the font size in a window, and the brightness of the monitor; this is typically done not by typing commands, but by physically manipulating switches or by mouse clicks (again!) on a window edge or on items in a pop-up menu. Activities of the latter type are similar to adjusting the colours or the volume of a TV, and are not *communicative* in nature; instead, in these activities the user treats the computer as a physical object, comparable to a TV, a washer, or a kitchen machine. One does not 'communicate' with such objects, but 'interacts' with them as with other physical objects. By contrast, when one inputs a query or a command, one is treating the computer as an agent that tries to find answers to queries and to carry out commands, i.e. one treats the computer as a conversational partner: one *communicates* with the machine.

Communicating with computers is often a rather frustrating business, because computers don't live up to the expectations created by the 'conversation metaphor' (Hutchins, 1989). A conversational interface by its very nature offers a mode of interaction that has certain similarities with natural human communication; there is an implicit suggestion that the main difference is one of syntax: if only one could type English instead of Unix commands, one would essentially be able to communicate in a similar way as when talking to an assistant. Computer experts know that this is not true, that there are fundamental limitations behind the syntactic obscurities and constraints of most user interfaces, but they can't easily say what these limitations are, unless they are communication experts as well.

One important limitation of human-computer interfaces is that they do not obey the Multimax Principle: not all the modalities that the human partner naturally uses in a face-to-face situation can be used when facing a computer; one cannot speak in a normal way, one cannot use ordinary gestures, and one cannot use facial expression (smiles, frowns,..); in fact, *none* of the natural modalities can be used! Users therefore have to be trained to learn the limited modalities that are offered, and only people who use computers regularly and over an extended period of time, gradually learn to live comfortably with the limited interactive possibilities. In fact, they learn that the interaction with the machine is not *really* like ordinary communication at all. What is it that makes interacting with a computer on the one hand somewhat similar to communication, and why is it, most of the time, not really like communication after all, or at best an extremely primitive form of communication?

To answer this question, we may consider again the two fundamentally different ways of interacting with a computer, mentioned above: the communication-like formulation of instructions and queries, and the 'physical' adjustment of window size, font size, or screen brightness. In the 'physical' mode of interaction, one treats a computer as a physical object, which is inherently *passive*: a physical object cannot do anything which is not fully and directly under the control of a human operator. In the 'communicative' mode of interaction, by contrast, the computer is assumed to *understand* instructions and queries, and to decide, on the basis of this understanding, what to do. The computer is thus viewed as *active*: it performs such activities as interpreting inputs, evaluating the interpretation, and computing a reaction to an input, and these activities are not fully, and certainly not directly, under the user's control. In this respect the situation parallels that of human communication, and gives rise to the idea that interacting with a computer is indeed like communicating. Why then is communicating with a computer at best an extremely primitive form of communication, if it at all? This is, apart from the violation of the Multimax Principle, because present-day computers do not or only in an extremely primitive form possess certain basic qualities that are required of the participants in full-blown communication.

Full-blown communication requires two (or more) agents who can take turns at playing sender and receiver roles, and perform at least the following activities:

1. understand messages from the agent in the sender role w.r.t. content and function (*What does the sender intend to achieve with this message?*);

2. evaluate the result of understanding in the light of background knowledge, i.e., answer questions like *Can I accept the information offered?* and other such questions, depending on the type of communicative act performed by the sender;

3. choose and perform appropriate (noncommunicative) actions to be carried out, like updating one's state of information, or performing some physical activity to fulfill a request;
4. generate communicative acts to continue the interaction.

In order to be able to perform these activities, a communicative agent must possess the following qualities:

1. Be knowledgeable as a communicative agent, i.e., be competent in the use of the various available modalities and their combinations. This requirement includes knowing what types of communicative actions can be performed, what action is appropriate to perform under what conditions, and what is an appropriate form of an intended action in a given context, when a particular modality is used.
2. Be informed about the domain of discourse and the current dialogue context. Knowledge of the domain of discourse is indispensable for understanding the user, since understanding involves relating the elements of an input message to semantic concepts. Knowledge of the current dialogue context can be divided into the following categories (Bunt, 1997a; 1997b):
   (a) *linguistic context*, most importantly the recent dialogue history;
   (b) *semantic context*, i.e. the current state of the domain of discourse (or 'task domain');
   (c) *cognitive context*, including the current beliefs about the dialogue partner (or 'user model', in a dialogue system), and information about the current status of cognitive processes, such as the information that the interpretation process of the last input message needs additional information to resolve an ambiguity;
   (d) *physical and perceptual*, relating to the physical conditions of the interaction and the perceptual availability of information;
   (e) *social*, describing current 'pressures' to perform certain communicative actions (such as returning a greeting, or giving feedback on carrying out an instruction).
3. Have reasoning capacities. To apply his knowledge of communication, of the domain of discourse, and of the current dialogue context, an agent has to be able to combine pieces of information in a logically correct way. Understanding and evaluating the content and function of messages involves making such combinations, and thus involves reasoning, as do the planning and generation of noncommunicative as well as communicative acts.
4. Be rational. Being able to reason is not sufficient. The ability to draw correct inferences should be used in a rational way, to compute for instance the intentions and other relevant conditions of (communicative or other) actions that are instrumental to achieving a certain goal or purpose, or to infer subgoals that are on the way to a higher goal. Rationality directs the use of reasoning power.
5. Be social. Knowing the rules and conventions of using a communicative system (in a certain type of interactive situation within a community) is not

sufficient: one must also have the *disposition* to act accordingly. An important aspect of this is that a social agent takes other participants' goals, desires, beliefs, and other properties into account, in particular so as to help others to achieve their goals - which is commonly called *being cooperative* (Bunt, 1997b; see also Allwood, 1997).

In short, a communicative agent must be *pragmatically and semantically knowledgeable, intelligent, rational,* and *social,* where the latter property includes being *cooperative.*

Building an artificial communicative agent, that possesses these qualities, is to some extent that of 'simply' building an artificial intelligent agent: an agent that is knowledgeable in a certain domain and is able to apply that knowledge in a rational way. The more specific issues in building artificial communicative agents are those that concern the requirements of competence in the use of communicative systems (multimodal ones included), of being able to maintain and use knowledge of the dialogue context, and that of being 'social', in particular: cooperative. The contributions in this book all relate to one or more of these issues.

3   Systems, Techniques and Experiments in Multimodal User Interfaces

The chapters in this book relate to the above issues in designing user interfaces that allow multimodal human-computer communication, in one of three ways:

1. in terms of design aspects of experimental cooperative multimodal systems or systems under development;
2. in terms of formal or computational techniques that may be useful for certain aspects of multimodal and multimedia systems;
3. in terms of experiments that explore the feasibility or usefulness of particular features of multimodal systems.

Chapter 2, *Toward Cooperative Multimedia Interaction* by Mark Maybury, is concerned both with multimodal techniques and with system aspects of multimodal interfaces. Maybury uses the term 'media' in a broad sense, as "the object through which communication occurs, either physically (e.g., ink and paper, keyboard and graphical display) or logically (e.g., natural language, graphical languages);" his use of the term 'multimedia' thus corresponds with the use of 'multimodality' in a number of other chapters and in the title of this book. (Maybury uses 'modality' in a perceptual sense, as referring to an agent's visual, auditory, or tactile system.) Maybury argues that efficient and effective interaction with complex information in large quantities requires communication forms which are both cooperative and multimedia, and illustrates this with several applications that aim to enhance interaction with complex systems or information sources. After overviewing the key processes in the generation of multimedia, Maybury describes a visionary system for information access. The chapter concludes with a description of recent efforts toward providing content-based browsing and search of video.

This chapter is followed by a group of six chapters (3–8) which are all concerned primarily with 'system aspects' of multimodal human-computer communication, describing system architectures, theoretical foundations of systems, or the use of systems in the study of specific phenomena in communication.

3.1 Multimodal Systems

Chapter 3, *Multimodal Communication and Cooperation with the* DENK *System*, describes and motivates the architecture of a 'generic' cooperative multimodal human-computer interface, with particular attention to the representation of dialogue contexts. The architecture is 'generic' in the sense that it capitalizes on the incorporation of fundamental principles of (multimodal) communication, and could be applied equally to other modalities than the ones currently implemented. The authors, Harry Bunt, René Ahn, Robbert-Jan Beun, Tijn Borghuis, and Kees van Overveld argue for an 'inside-out' approach to system development, starting from a global overall design based on a 'triangle view' of the relation between a user, an application as modeled in the system, and a 'cooperative assistant' module that has expert knowledge of the application and has built-in principles of communication and cooperation. The 'inside-out' development of the system means that first a formal model of communication as context change is implemented, where dialogue contexts are represented in a powerful logical formalism based on typed lambda calculus. The internal interfaces to this central component are defined, and from there on the design of the other system components is developed. The chapter describes the approaches to context representation, to communication modeling, to natural language interpretation, and to the visual representation of the application domain by means of object-oriented animation, and outlines the first preliminary prototype of the DENK system.

Chapters 4 and 5 are both concerned with research on animated simulation of virtual human agents, which display naturalistic linguistic and motion behaviour, modeling in particular the form of multimodality that we find in natural human communication (see Badler et al., 1993).

In *Synthesizing Cooperative Conversation*, Catherine Pelachaud, Justine Cassell, Norman Badler, Mark Steedman, Scott Prevost, and Matthew Stone describe an implemented system which automatically generates and animates conversations between human-like agents. These agents use appropriate and synchronized speech, intonation, facial expressions, and hand gestures. The research reported in this chapter is particularly interesting for the way information relating to different modalities is used in an integrated fashion in the generation of multimodal messages. In people, speech, facial expressions, and gestures are all the reflection of a single system of meaning. The experimental system described automatically generates multimodal communicative behaviour by synchronizing the behaviour produced by several modality-specific generators that all work on the basis of the same dialogue planner (and world and agent model, used by this planner).

Bonnie Webber in chapter 5, *Instructing Animated Agents: Viewing Language in Behavioral Terms* presents research on the instruction of animated human-like agents in natural language. She demonstrates the possibility of analyzing linguistic constructs in terms of behavioural specifications and constraints by treating instructions containing *until* clauses in terms of the perceptual activities and the conditions they are used to address. She shows how the resulting analysis contributes to understanding how an agent is supposed to carry these instructions out.

The following two chapters both describe (prototypical) multimodal systems that combine natural language input with graphics, in both cases applied to geographical information.

Jacques Siroux, Marc Guyomard, Franck Multon and Christophe Remondeau describe in chapter 6, *Modeling and Processing of Oral and Tactile Activities in the GEORAL System*, how speech input is combined with touching an pointing at locations on a map, or drawing lines to indicate regions. They consider the different ways in which the two kinds of inputs can be semantically related and indicate how the inputs are merged in the system. To this end they analyze the various interactive activities in terms of communicative acts (Bunt, 1989; Maybury, 1992). Modeling communicative acts in the implementation by means of planning operators with constraints and preconditions is argued to lead to an architecture that allows great flexibility in adapting the system to the user's behaviour and to other modalities.

Adam Cheyer and Luc Julia in their chapter *Multimodal Maps: An Agent-Based Approach* address the question of what input modalities are comfortable for humans, and how a synergistic combination of modalities can lead to natural user interfaces. (See Nigay and Coutaz, 1993, for the notion of synergistic modality combination, and other types of combination.) They use the TAPAGE system for multimodal design and correction of tables (Faure and Julia, 1994) as a building block. By adding concepts for the synergistic combination of input modalities to an existing architecture with heterogeneous software agents, they claim to have developed an approach that is quite general and that allows rapid prototyping. Their prototype system for travel planning is one of the first that accepts commands made of synergistic combinations of spoken language, handwriting, and gestural input.

In the last chapter of this group, Yi Han and Ingrid Zukerman present their multimodal presentation planning system MAGPIE (Multi-Agent Generation of Presentations In Physics Education). They give a detailed account of a multi-agent planning mechanism based on the blackboard architecture, that takes into consideration the overall structure of the discourse as well as restrictions imposed by partial plans generated in early stages of the planning process. They describe the facilities used by agents to communicate with each other in this architecture, and discuss the planning processes used by the agents in MAG-PIE. Their approach has been used for generating multimodal presentations for several discourse plans, which require the activation of up to 32 agents. Their results clearly demonstrate the flexibility of the approach.

3.2   Techniques

The next group of chapters is not so much about complete prototype systems, but about formal and software techniques for developing such systems.

Jean-Claude Martin, Remko Veldman and Dominique Béroule discuss the use of two techniques. In their chapter, entitled *Developing Multimodal Interfaces: A Theoretical Framework and Guided Propagation Networks* (chapter 9), they present first a framework for analyzing combinations of modalities, distinguishing different goals of the combination of modalities, and defining a formal language for the specification of input modality combinations. (A similar way to specify output modality combinations is described in (Martin, in press)). They demonstrate the use of this specification technique with the help of COMIT, a multimodal test application. The second technique described in this chapter is that of Guided Propagation Networks, a connectionist memory model that is used for organizing the cooperation between modalities in combination with an architecture which implements synchrony coding.

In chapter 10, *Cooperation between Reactive 3D Objects and a Multimodal X Window Kernel for CAD*, Patrick Bourdot, Mike Krus and Rachid Gherbi discuss the use and implementation of multimodality for computer-aided design tasks. In a CAD task, the user is designing objects to perform graphical and spatial simulations in order to find solutions for the constraints on the objects to be designed. Existing CAD systems are rather uncooperative in the simulation steps of object design. To improve this situation, Bourdot, Krus and Gherbi have developed a system, called MIX 3D, where objects can be built that have reactive behaviour, and with which the user can interact with a combination of graphical actions and vocal commands. The authors give a fairly detailed description and illustration of their system, and claim that the architecture they have developed can be used as a basis for a complete multimodal user interface system, with multimodal output as well as input. MIX 3D is shown to have a realistic implementation with a distributed architecture based on the X Window system, and to be able to provide most of the services required by multimodal fusion systems.

Fergal McCaffery, Michael McTear and Maureen Murphy in chapter 11, *Designing a Multimedia Interface for Operators Assembling Circuit Boards*, describe the design of a multimodal interface that incorporates coordinated graphics, text, verbal and audio input, and composes multimedia output for use by circuit board assembly operators in a telecom company. The approach taken is that of bringing the Multimax principle in practice, allowing the system to be as human-like as possible in allowing input from eyes, hands and ears. On the output side, the system is to automatically compose and generate, on the basis of a user model and a domain knowledge base, relevant output messages in coordinated multimedia using both canned text and frames as generation techniques. The activities to be supported by the system are, moreover, modeled by means of task analysis techniques. The user model, containing information about the user's preferences and level of technical expertise, is used to provide adaptation in input as well as in output mode and is the main source of 'intelligence' in the system.

Chapter 12, by Kent Wittenburg, is devoted to a discussion of formal linguistic modeling techniques for the representation and processing of two-dimensional structures. In this chapter, *Visual Language Parsing: If I Had a Hammer...*, Wittenburg considers how higher-level grammars and parsing techniques might contribute to visual modes of human-computer communication. It is argued that visual parsing is perhaps not the best approach to interpreting visual language expressions under the control of a GUI, although there are potential benefits if only some agreement would be reached on standardization of input representations. On the other hand, Wittenburg argues that higher-dimensional parsing techniques are promising when applied to graphical expressions that are not so much a means of communication, but that are the goal of a creative or engineering enterprise. Design assistance, generation-as-parsing for multimedia documents, and visual focusing are examples of such applications.

Multimodal dialogues can be regarded as generalizations of linguistic discourses, and the question may thus arise to what extent the concepts of linguistic discourse analysis generalize to the multimodal case. John Lee and Keith Stenning address this question, focusing on the concept of anaphoric reference, in chapter 13, *Anaphora in Multimodal Discourse*. In linguistic discourse analysis, anaphora are 'reduced' expressions, like pronouns, that take their meaning (reference or sense) from another, fuller expression. Singer (1990) has suggested that anaphora exist in graphical form in purely graphical interaction, and Wahlster et al. (1991) have suggested that anaphoric relations can also exist between graphics and language. Lee and Stenning provide a theoretical analysis which leads them to conclude that 'graphical anaphora' is not a meaningful notion, and that anaphora is an essentially linguistic phenomenon. They do argue, however, supported by examples, that a deeper application of the semantic concepts of linguistic discourse analysis can have practical significance for practical analyses of graphical interaction.

3.3 Experiments

The final group of chapters in this book (14–18) describes and discusses experimental studies of multimodal communication.

The first of these, by Laurel Fais, Kyung-ho Loken-Kim, and Young-Duk Park, is inspired by the uncertainty of the nature of speech behaviour in multimedia speech processing systems, and more specifically by the question how different media may be used to support spoken human-computer communication. When input is allowed in spoken form, the need for the system to request and process clarifications of users' utterances will be evident. Fais, Kim and Park therefore investigate the way people react to clarification requests. They study the linguistic and modal aspects of responses given by subjects in a Wizard-of-Oz experiment to repetition requests by the 'Wizard.' In their contribution,

Speakers' Responses for Repetition in a Multimedia Language Processing Environment, they report on these experiments, where English-speaking 'clients' participating in a task-oriented cooperative dialogue with Japanese-speaking 'agents' were asked to clarify utterances that were complex or lengthy. Their results indicate that people adjust to the constraints of the interactive situation in making various types of linguistic reductions that would lessen the burden on automatic speech processing. They also tend to converge to a more consistent linguistic behaviour after difficulties in communication are encountered. Media use in these responses does not exhibit a clear pattern. The chapter concludes with a discussion of the implications of the results for the design of multimodal systems including speech, in particular w.r.t. constraints on media use.

The next two chapters are both concerned with studies of the way people refer to objects, depending on the availability of interactive modalities. In chapter 15, *Object Reference in Task-Oriented Keyboard Dialogues*, Anita Cremers describes experimental studies of the interactive behaviour of subjects who can use typed natural language and hand gestures, but have no face-to-face contact. The use of natural language expressions and gestures in these conditions is analyzed and compared to that where spoken language can be used instead of typed language (a condition that was studied in previous experiments with the same task). The results are related to the so-called *principle of minimal cooperative total effort*, which says that, within the limitations of the available modalities, the participants aim at spending as little total effort as possible on referring to a certain object on the other hand, and on identifying the object on the other hand. This principle is shown to offer a basis for understanding both the preferred choice of properties in referring expressions, and the differences in referential behaviour between the typed and the spoken modality, in view of the different effort in using language, gesturing, and inspecting the application domain in the different conditions.

Referent identification also occupies center stage in the study by Tsuneaki Kato and Yukiko Nakano reported in chapter 16, *Referent Identification Requests in Multi-Modal Dialogues*. They have conducted experiments in which experts explain the installation of a telephone in four situations: spoken-mode monologue, spoken-mode dialogue, multimodal monologue, and multimodal dialogue. Referent identification requests were analyzed from two perspectives: information communicated and style of goal achievement. A close relationship is found between the information conveyed via different communicative modes, and a model is sketched that explains this, treating information as a primitive unit that cannot be divided into semantic content conveyed and communicative modes employed. Pointing is considered as information, in this sense.

We argued above that the Multimax principle, regarding the use of available modalities, is a fundamental property of natural human communication, that one would expect to be important also in human-computer communication (though with a caveat concerning the use of modern media and modalities, not necessarily well-attuned to human cognition and perception). Carla Huls and Edwin Bos investigate the usefulness of combining natural language and direct manipulation in chapter 17, *Studies into Full Integration of Language and Action*. They argue that the combination of modalities in multimodal interfaces should be based on empirical studies of their usefulness. They investigated questions of the efficiency, expertise, speed, and errors for multimodal and unimodal interaction forms. The results they present do give support to the widespread presupposition that multimodality is indeed useful.

In the closing chapter, Marie-Christine Bressolle, Bernard Pavard, and Marcel Leroux analyze the interactive behaviour of air traffic controllers, with particular attention to their use of modalities, as a step in the design of software tools to support air traffic control. They give an account of the subtle ways in which the members of a team of air traffic controllers collaborate using not only speech and gestures, but also strips of paper on which information is written and which are placed in particular ways to achieve specific communicative effects. They also show that the team members make use of properties of their working environment, such as the knowledge that a message addressed to one team member can be observed by other team members who may act upon the information they pick up that way, even though it was not primarily aimed at them. They discuss the implications of such findings for the design of future multimodal systems to support the activity air traffic controllers.

References

Allwood, J. (1997), An Activity Based Approach to Pragmatics. In: W.J. Black & H.C. Bunt (eds.) *Abduction, Belief, and Context. Studies in Computational Pragmatics*. London: University College London Press (forthc.)

Badler, N., Phillips, C. and Webber, B. (1993), *Simulating Humans: Computer Graphics, Animation, Control*. Oxford: Oxford University Press.

Bunt, H. (1989) Information dialogues as communicative action in relation to information processing and partner modelling. In: M.M. Taylor, D.G. Bouwhuis and F. Néel (eds.) *The Structure of Multimodal Dialogue*. Amsterdam: North-Holland, 47–73.

Bunt, H. (1997a) Dialogue Context Modeling. In: *Proc. CONTEXT'97, International Interdisciplinary Conference on Modeling and Using Context*, Rio de Janeiro, February 1997, 130–150.

Bunt, H. (1997b) Iterative Context Specification and Dialogue Analysis. In: W.J. Black & H.C. Bunt (eds.) *Abduction, Belief, and Context. Studies in Computational Pragmatics*. London: University College London Press (forthc.)

Hutchins, (1989) Metaphors for Interface Design. In: M.M. Taylor, D.G. Bouwhuis and F. Néel (eds.) *The Structure of Multimodal Dialogue*. Amsterdam: North-Holland, 11–28.

Maybury, M. (1992) Communicative Acts for Explanation Generation. *International Journal of Man-Machine Studies* 37 (2), 135–172.

Nigay, L. and Coutaz, J. (1993) Multifeature systems: from HCI properties to software design. In: J. Lee (ed.) *Pre-Proceedings of the First International Workshop on Intelligence and Multimodality in Multimedia Interfaces: Research and Applications*. University of Edinburgh, 13–14.

Faure, C. & Julia, L. (1994) An agent-based architecture for a multimodal interface. *Working Notes of the AAAI SYmposium on Intelligent Multimedia and Motimodal Systems,* March 1994, Stanford.

Martin, J-C. (1996) Types et buts de coopération entre modalités dans les interfaces multimodales. *Techniques et Science Informatiques* 15 (10) 1996, 1367–1397.

Singer, R. A. (1990) Graphical treatment of anaphora and ellipsis within intelligent tutoring systems. *Journal of Artificial Intelligence in Education,* 2, 79–97.

Thimbleby, H, (1990) *User Interface Design.* Menlo Park (CA): Addison-Wesley/ACM Press.

Wahlster, W., André., E, Finkler, W., Graf, W., and Rist, T. (1991) Designing illustrated text: how language production is influenced by graphic generation. Technical Memo RR-91-05. Saarbrücken: Deutsches Forschungszentrum für Künstliche Intelligenz.

Toward Cooperative Multimedia Interaction

Mark T. Maybury

Artificial Intelligence Center, The MITRE Corporation
202 Burlington Road, Bedford, MA 01730
maybury@mitre.org

Abstract. The proliferation of information and services on our global information highways demands mechanisms to support more effective and efficient interaction. This article claims that efficient and effective interaction requires both cooperative and multimedia communication, illustrating this through several applications developed by our group that aim to enhance interaction with complex systems or information sources. After defining the terms cooperative and multimedia and arguing for their centrality in interfaces, we overview key processes in the automated generation of multimedia. We then illustrate these with implemented examples from several domains including information retrieval, direction providing, mission planning and computer maintenance. After describing a visionary system for information access, we conclude by describing our current efforts toward providing content-based browsing and search of video.

1 Cooperative Multimedia Interaction

Our global information superhighway is continuously populated with new sources, media, and services. Current communication across this infrastructure includes human-human (including multiparty), human-machine, and machine-machine interaction. This communication is increasingly multimedia in content, as evidenced by the rapid growth of the World Wide Web. By media we refer to the object through which communication occurs, either physically (e.g., ink and paper, keyboard and graphical display) or logically (e.g., natural language, graphical languages). Media can be further decomposed, for example, natural language can occur in typed, written, or spoken form. In contrast to media, modalities are communication agent (e.g., user) centered, and refer to environmental sensors/effectors and related perceptual processes (e.g., an agent's visual, auditory, or tactile system). Cooperative interaction is realized via mechanisms that enable agents, human or machine, to perform their task more efficiently or effectively, perhaps by mitigating communication or application complexity, ambiguity, or vagueness. A cooperative multimodal system will likely contain explicit knowledge of the user, task, or situation which it will exploit to provide tailored assistance or completion of tasks. Fundamental to cooperative interaction are mechanisms that support media interpretation, generation, (language and representation) translation, and summarization. Figure 1 illustrates some of the tasks we might expect intelligent multimedia agents to perform in the future, including media analysis (i.e., capture, conversion/ translation, and indexing of media), extraction of information from media, automated generation of multimedia presentations (possibly including summarization of information from the media), visualization of media, and 'intelligent' mechanisms that support user creation of and interaction with media.

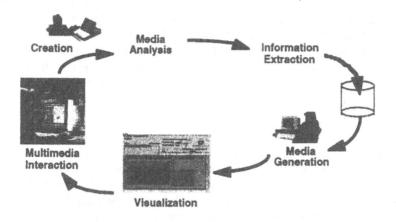

Fig. 1. Multimedia computing

Why do we need intelligence and/or multimedia at all in the interface? In general, knowledge-based interfaces have the potential to move us beyond current direct manipulation interfaces toward agent-based interaction. Systems with explicit knowledge of the user, task, and context can use this knowledge to tailor interaction to the situation (e.g., providing appropriate help, hints, or warnings to the right users at the right time) to facilitate the increased accuracy or speed of task completion (e.g., via automatic script creation). Just as intelligent behavior is critical to human machine interaction, so too the ability to interpret and generate coordinated multimedia can improve interaction by appropriately utilizing an agent's multiple modalities. For example, we have moved from data to information and increasingly to knowledge overload. Tools that have knowledge of language and media can find, filter, extract, and summarize information and knowledge are becoming not only useful but increasingly essential for many human endeavors. Also, media have differing properties, strengths and weaknesses, that make them more or less appropriate for differing kinds of information (e.g., qualitative versus quantitative, two-dimensional versus n-dimensional). By explicitly generating multimedia artefacts from underlying knowledge, we have the ability to engage the user in a much richer interaction than presently afforded by canned presentations. For example, a user can ask follow up questions of media generated from underlying representations, presentation sequences can be tailored to individual or session needs, and common content can be used across multiple presentation languages, physical devices (e.g., paper, CD-ROM, differing displays) and interface styles, thus avoiding expensive custom crafting of presentations or interfaces for all situations.

However, this is not to say that intelligent interfaces or multimedia will necessary improve communication. Indeed, Krause (1993) showed that the poor application of simple graphical display devices such as graying out non-optional menu items can actually reduce user task effectiveness. Sutcliffe et al. (1997) illustrate how performance is degraded when ill-phrased questions lead users to search inappropriate media, how lack of explicit cross references between media can degrade the extraction of information, and that well known information retrieval problems such as null result sets are exacerbated by multimedia. Finally, in one electronic document editing application, allowing the user flexibility to choose among alternative input devices (e.g., speaking vs. typing vs. handwriting comments), (Neuwirth et al., 1995) showed an increased volume but degraded quality of editorial comments.

It is similarly not the case that human-human communication serves as the best communication model. It is often ambiguous, vague, and imprecise. Despite these characteristics, we should learn all we can about how humans communicate well. Central to this is the careful analysis of multimedia communication. For example, Cremers (1995) reports how users exploit available modalities to minimize their effort during object reference and identification (e.g., shortening referring expressions in typed versus spoken communication). However, when Fais et al. (1995) contrasted clarification requests in telephone only versus a multimedia environment, their results were less conclusive. While they found that in both telephone and multimedia interaction speakers repeated words, minimized disfluencies, and slowed speaking rate during clarification subdialogues, they found that subjects exhibited varying use of non-speech media (e.g., typing text, drawing on a map, filling in slots in a form). Careful empirical studies will illuminate how discourse and media modify communication. This should aid us in developing and evaluating principled models of communication (including cooperativity) and multimedia, with the aim of improving human-machine communication and possibly even human-human communication.

This article provides an overview of our group efforts in cooperative multimedia interaction. This remainder of this article is organized as follows. We first outline the central processes of multimedia generation. Next, we describe issues and approaches to allocating information to media. We next describe a system that automatically allocates information to media and sequences this information using multimedia communicative actions to produce multimedia directions. We then describe further communicative actions and associated similarity measures which are used to design and layout multimedia comparisons of entities. We next describe how multimedia presentations can be tailored to support particular cognitive activities and how by appropriately indexing canned media (e.g., video), systems can be more rapidly developed. We discuss tailoring output to particular user information seeking needs. We then describe a tool for graphical visualization of large retrieved documents collections which allows the user to manually manipulate the size, color, and order encoding of document relevancy measures. We show how these various technologies can be integrated to provide a richer interaction with hypertext browsers. Finally, we describe our current work in progress to develop content-based access to multimedia, in particular, to broadcast news video, via analysis of multiple redundant media streams.

2   Media Generation

The most effective means of ensuring cooperative multimodal communication is to manage it from first principles. Since the days of Aristotle's studies of rhetoric, researchers have attempted to characterize the actions underlying communication. A number of articles in this collection focus on computational models of communication, including those by Bunt (1995), Wahlster (1995), and Webber (1995). Our research has been guided by philosophy of language theories which view language as a purposeful endeavor (Austin, 1962). Motivated by Appelt's (1985) seminal speech act research, our approach consists of analyzing human-human communications and formalizing communication actions as plan operators. As human-human communication is multimedia and multimodal in character, this has led us naturally to the need to capture multimedia communicative acts, that include physical, linguistic, and graphical ones (Maybury, 1993). One of the fundamental results of this and related efforts was the formulation of multimedia presentation as a communicative process which entails fundamental processes including content selection (What should we say?), intention/presentation planning and re-planning (Why should we say it and How should we sequence and structure content to achieve particular purposes?), media allocation (In what media should we say it?), media coordination (How should we ensure consistency, cohesion, and coherence across media?), realization (How should we say it?), and media layout (How should we show it?).

These processes are guided by an overall communication management function for both attention and intention management, which includes the initiation, continuation, and termination of dialogue exchanges. An idealized set of cascaded processes shown in Fig. 2 illustrates how multimedia output, guided by communication management, moves from content (e.g., a data or knowledge base) to presentation, where explicit feedback from subsequent processes can modify choices made by proceeding processes. For example, failure to fit a generated piece of text or graphics into a given space on a page could result in a directive to modify the realization of a given piece on content if not to shorten the content itself. This is not to claim that any of these processes should occur sequentially. Indeed, in current implemented presentation systems such as TEXPLAN (Maybury, 1993) and WIP (André et al., 1993), processes such as content selection, media allocation and media layout are assumed to co-constrain. Moreover, a user can interact not only with the resulting artefact but conceivably at all levels of presentation design, from selecting content to laying out information. (In addition to selecting media appropriate to the information, successful presentations must ensure coordination across media. First, the content must be consistent, although not necessarily equivalent, across media. In addition, the resulting form (layout, expression) should be consistent.)

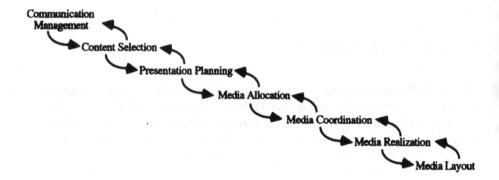

Fig. 2. Multimedia presentation design tasks

Our research has concentrated on the more general problem of communication (as opposed specifically to presentation) which has led us to the use of communicative actions for presentation design and communication management. The intention is that just as a declarative grammar of a language can be used for both interpretation and generation, so too an explicit characterization of communication actions should generalize to handle both input and output in human-machine interaction. To make the processes illustrated in Fig. 2 more concrete, we first detail one of the more studied processes, media allocation. We exemplify single media allocation by describing a tool which involves the user in the process of encoding information in graphical presentation to facilitate information retrieval. We then provide examples of presentations designed automatically from two knowledge bases for two diverse communicative purposes: instruction and comparison.

3   Media Allocation

Media allocation consists of apportioning a given set of semantic propositions or pieces of information to one or possibly multiple media. The first work in media allocation involved the use of coding techniques (e.g., position, size, shape) to convey information characteristics in Mackinlay's (1986) APT system. Subsequent work developed heuristics that map information properties onto classes of media, as in the Integrated Interfaces system (Arens et al., 1991), SAGE (Roth and Mattis, 1991) and COMET (Feiner and McKeown, 1993) systems. For example, in COMET, a system which provided multimedia instructions, media allocation heuristics would

1. realize locational and physical attributes in graphics only,
2. realize abstract actions and connectives among actions (e.g., causality) in text only, and
3. realize simple and compound actions in both text and graphics.

In contrast to these heuristics, the AIMI system (Burger and Marshall 1993), a multimedia question/answer interface for mission planning, utilized design rules which preferred cartographic displays to flat lists to text based on the semantic nature of the query and response. Considerations of query and response included the dimensionality of the answer, if it contained qualitative vs. quantitative information, if it contained cartographic information. For example, a natural language query about airbases might result in the design of a cartographic presentation, one about planes that have certain qualitative characteristics, a list, ones that have certain quantitative characteristics, a bar chart. One interesting notion in AIMI was the use of non-speech audio to convey the speed, stage or duration of processes not visible to the user (e.g., background computations). AIMI also included mechanisms to tailor the design to the output device (e.g., a black and white printer versus a large color monitor). A common language generator for text in the body of an explanation, graphical axes, captions, and data point labels ensured consistency within a mixed multimedia presentation.

Related research in media allocation exploited not only informational properties, but used also the underlying semantics and pragmatics of a presentation plan to guide media selection. For example, the WIP knowledge-based presentation system (André and Rist, 1993) included the following rules for media allocation:

- use text to express temporal overlap, temporal quantification (e.g., *"always"*), temporal shifts (e.g., *"three days later"*) and spatial or temporal layout to encode sequence (e.g., temporal relations between states, events, actions);
- use text to express semantic relations (e.g., cause/effect, action/result, problem/solution, condition, concession) to avoid ambiguity in picture sequences; graphics for rhetorical relations such as condition and concession only if accompanied by verbal comment

Some of these preferences were captured in constraints associated with presentation actions, which were encoded in plan operators, and used feedback from media realizers to influence the selection of content.

Another early lesson lealy lesson learned was the broad range of information sources which could guide media allocation. For example, Hovy and Arens (1993) use a systemic network of interrelated constraints to represent knowledge about the information to be presented, media characteristics, as well as information about the speaker, addressee and communicative situation. For example, information is characterized by properties such as dimensionality, transience, and urgency. Media are characterized by properties such as their dimensionality, temporal endurance, and default detectability. Declarative rules are defined in a systemic framework to capture complex information property to media property dependencies. For example, their rules specify:

1. Present data duples (e.g., locations) on planar media (e.g., graphs, tables, maps).
2. Present data with specific denotations (e.g., spatial) on media with same denotations (e.g., locations on maps).

They represent more complex rules to characterize the use of properties such as information urgency. One important point is that the systemic network (which represents feature choices) can be used for both interpretation and generation.

What remains to be done is to computationally investigate and (with human subjects) evaluate these and other rules in an attempt to make progress toward a set of principles for media allocation. In contrast to automating media choice, the work we describe next involves the user in the process of media selection.

4   Multimedia Directions

Our interest in multimedia communication has been motivated, in part, by the need to communicate spatial and temporal information in the context of geographic information systems. As detailed in Maybury (1991b), supporting linguistic realization in this domain requires extending traditional models of focus to include both temporal and spatial focus. Whereas our point of departure is an underlying object-oriented mapping system with a focus on communicative actions to organize route descriptions, others have focused on translating visual information (e.g., images of traffic scenes or soccer matches) into natural language descriptions (Herzog and Wazinski, 1994), supporting incremental generation of route descriptions (Maass, 1994), or investigating multimedia interfaces to maps (Cheyer and Julia, 1995).

Following a tradition that views language as an action-based endeavor (Austin, 1962; Searle, 1969), researchers have begun to formalize multimedia communication as actions, striving toward a deeper representation of the mechanisms underlying communication. Some systems have gone beyond single media to formalize multimedia actions, attempting to capture both the underlying structure and intent of presentations by formalizing communication actions as plans. For example, WIP (André et al., 1993) designs its picture-text instructions using a speech-act like formalism that includes communicative (e.g., describe), textual (e.g., S-request), and graphical (e.g., depict) actions.

In Maybury (1991a; in press) we detail a taxonomy of communicative acts that includes linguistic, graphical, and physical actions. These are formalized as plan operators with associated constraints, enabling conditions, effects, and subacts and have been evaluated in the TEXPLAN system which has been applied to several applications. Certain classes of actions (e.g., deictic actions) are characterized in a media-independent form, and then specialized for particular media (e.g., pointing or tapping with a gesture device, highlighting a graphic, or utilizing linguistic deixis as in the natural language expressions "this" or "that"). One example of cross-media actions are attention-directing and referent-identification actions. Figure 3 illustrates a communication plan (and a transcription of the resulting multimedia communication) for giving multimedia directions between two German cities in the context of a knowledge-based map. This communication plan (an intentional structure) is generated by a set of multimedia communicative planning operators, including ones that specify actions for explaining routes, controlling the cartographic display (e.g., displaying regions, highlighting objects), describing objects, and instructing the addressee. Each leaf node in the communication plan is a primitive action associated with one or more communication acts in some media (e.g., text, map, label). The example illustrates the distinction made in the planning operators between focus-setting actions (e.g., displaying a region) and referential actions (e.g., identifying and indicating dictically). This builds on Appelt's (1985) KAMP architecture, in which he investigated the formalization as plan operators of both physical (e.g., pointing) and linguistic referential acts.

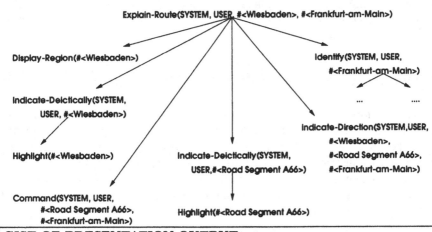

GIST OF PRESENTATION OUTPUT

(Display map region around Wiesbaden) (highlight Wiesbaden) From Wiesbaden take Autobahn A66 Northeast for thirty-one kilometres to Frankfurt-am Main. *highlight Autobahn A66) (indicate direction with blinking arrow) (highlight Frankfurt-am Main)* Frankfurt-am-Main is located at 50.11^0 latitude and 8.66^0 longitude.

Fig. 3. A communication plan and resulting presentation

Media allocation includes selecting particular communicative actions based on the availability and effectiveness of them to achieve a given communication goal. In our example in Fig. 3, as cartographic information is identified, this is accomplished both visually via highlighting objects on the digital map and reenforced linguistically using coordinated natural language narration (indicated below the communication plan in Fig. 3, which is linearized as the text/graphics combination of the graphical action 'Highlight Wiesbaden' and the temporally coordinated text *"From Wiesbaden ..."*). Thus certain, more general, communication actions can occur across media (e.g., focus directing, reference identification) whereas others (e.g., highlighting, spoken or typewritten natural language assertions) are media-specific. This specialization and generalization supports more fault-tolerant communication. Media choices are constrained by a number of factors including communication bandwidth, user needs (e.g., visually or auditorilly impaired users), and the availability of media, e.g. if an object has geospatial properties and there is no map, or these realization components fail, the system may need to use text or speech.

When multiple design and realization choices are possible, preference metrics, which include media preferences, mediate the choice. Given a choice, our preference metric prefers plan operators with fewer subplans (cognitive economy), fewer new variables (limiting the introduction of new entities in the focus space of the discourse), those that satisfy all preconditions (to avoid backward chaining for efficiency), and those plan operators that are more common or preferred in naturally-occurring explanations (e.g., certain kinds of communicative acts occur more frequently in human-produced presentations or are preferred by rhetoricians over other methods).

5   Media/Multimedia Comparisons

The physical format and layout of a presentation often conveys the structure, intention, and significance of the underlying information and plays an important role in the presentation coherency. There have been a range of previous investigations into multimedia layout, most notably Graf's (1992) LayLab system which maps semantic and pragmatic relations (e.g., 'sequence', 'contrast' relations) onto geometrical/topological/temporal constraints (e.g., horizontal and vertical layout, alignment, and symmetry).

In our work, layout is also guided by the intentional structure of the underlying communication plan and is influenced by content selection. For example, when comparing two entities, our system uses a similarity metric to measure the most typical and unique characteristics of an entity in a knowledge base (Maybury, 1995a) to determine the most discriminating attributes and values of that entity. This is analogous to interclass similarity and intraclass similarity measures used in case-based reasoning. First, let us consider comparisons in general; we will then show some results of our system for generating multimedia comparisons.

Humans use at least three rhetorical strategies to compare and contrast entities:

1. describing their similarities and differences,
2. comparing and contrasting the entities point by point (i.e., feature by feature),
3. describing each entity in turn.

We have formalized these three methods as communicative acts and represented them as a series of hierarchically related plan operators, each with headers, preconditions, constraints, effects, and decomposition as reported in (Maybury, 1990; 1992).

The choice between these three techniques is based on the relation of the two entities. For example, the first technique, compare-similarities-differences, is preferred if the two entities share more than one common attribute with the same value and more than one common attribute with different values. In contrast, the second technique, compare-point-by-point, is preferred if the two entities have similar attributes but different values. The third technique is chosen by the text planner when the first two are not selected. In actual operation our explanation generator, TEXPLAN, selects only the most promising of these. Maybury (1995a) details the object similarity metric, for example, indicating how qualitative features (e.g., offensive and defensive capability in our examples) can be mapped onto quantitative scales to support numeric computations of similarity.

Table 1. Discriminatory power of attribute-value pairs of a TR-1 and an RF-4.

Attribute	TR-1	RF-41
offensive-capability	1.0	0.4
max-fuel	0.78	0.13
defensive-capability	0.6	0.11
cruise-speed	0.4	0.07

Table 1 illustrates the application of the similarity metric to compare two classes of reconnaissance aircraft in a military expert system.[1] As each object can have many features (attribute-value pairs), only those features with the highest measure of distinction from features of other objects in the database are used for comparison. The top four discriminatory features of the two classes (TR-1 and RF-4) are listed in the table. Figure 4 illustrates the results of the multimedia explanation prototype developed by Judy Sider at MITRE which allocates information to modalities using a probabilistic model that maps sources of evidence (e.g., the desired speed or accuracy of presentation, the characteristics of the information, the stereotypical level of expertise of the user, the role of that information in the communication plan) onto media choices (e.g., text versus graphics) for each 'proposition' of information (in this case, each selected attribute value pair). Selecting content for these comparisons is based on an empirical threshold of discriminatory power so only those most distinctive features

---

[1] Whereas the TR-1 has only one superclass (the class, reconnaissance aircraft), the RF-4 has two superclasses (the classes, reconnaissance aircraft and F-4 aircraft), and so, in general, the RF-4's attributes are significantly less discriminatory than those of the TR-1 because the RF-4 has more siblings with similar attribute-value pairs.

are used in the comparison. In Fig. 4, the system has decided to use the compare-similarities-differences strategy because the compared classes share more than one common attribute with the same value and more than one common attribute with different values.

After indicating the overall class similarity and specific attribute similarity in the first two sentences, the system uses a cross-media reference in the text to redirect the user's attention to the graphic window panes below, which contrast differing attributes of highest discriminatory power. Each of the two window panes actually contains multiple graphics (navigable via the label, which is a mousable menu, below the pane). The presentation of these graphics is ordered by discriminatory power, that is, when the explanation first is presented to the user, the offensive-capability and max-fuel capability attributes are the first to appear in the window panes.

Whereas the similarity metric is used to guide both content selection and layout in multimedia comparisons, it has also proven valuable in selecting content for referring expressions and term definitions. We have found the resulting explanations are both more precise, containing only the most significant information about a particular entity in an underlying knowledge base, and more comprehensive, containing all the significant information about the entity. Extensions to these comparisons could include adding a temporal dimension (e.g., controlling the display of panes over time, highlighting the most discriminatory attributes or values within window panes during comparison, highlighting the text and graphics to indicate cross media connections). Moreover, in addition to comparing two classes, we could consider a three-way, in general, an N-way comparison, possibly resulting in more information conveyed in tabular form.

Figure 5 exemplifies the value of re-ordering to improve the presentation. Figure 5a shows the original presentation. Figure 5a displays a textual comparison in the text pane, offensive capabilities in graphics pane 1, and cruising speeds in graphics pane 2. Unfortunately, there is only a minor difference in cruise speeds, despite the prominent graphical position this acquires in the resulting mixed text/graphics. In contrast, Fig. 5b changes which items are shown in pane 1 vs. pane 2 (originally cruise speeds and defensive capabilities in pane 1; nick names and offensive capabilities in pane 2). That is, in Fig. 5b the order of the panes and the order of elements in the panes is changed. The result is that 'capabilities', which are most distinctive, are contrasted first in window pane 1, then cruising speeds, which are less distinctive, are shown in pane 2.

While the re-ordering appears to improve upon the original by ensuring the most distinguishing features are contrasted, user studies measuring, for example, the time to perform information discovery or extraction tasks are required to validate this claim.

6 Re-use of Multimedia Artifacts: Video Repair

One of the problems identified by early research in presentation generation we shall term here the media acquisition bottleneck. For example, in order to au-

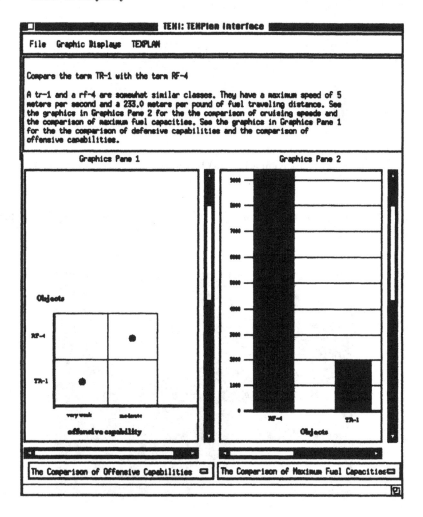

Fig. 4. Multimedia comparison

tomatically generate mixed text-picture operation instructions for an expresso machine, André et al. (1993) needed to represent significant amounts of knowledge about the domain, objects and actions therein, presentation plans, user and discourse models. Generating even basic wireframe diagrams required representing and reasoning about spatial relations, for example, to support effective layout. A significant advantage of generating these presentations from underlying representations is that this enables more sophisticated manipulations of the presentations (e.g., zooming, panning, part explosion), including tailoring them to individual users and contexts. Of course a significant drawback is the time and expense of creating such a system. Wahlster (1995) estimates the overall WIP project constitutes approximately 30 person-years worth of effort. While acquisition of some of this knowledge from existing databases or computer aided

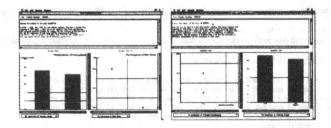

Fig. 5. Multimedia comparison (a) before and (b) after re-ordering

design files might mitigate part of the problem, generating pictures from first principles will remain a difficult task in the near future.

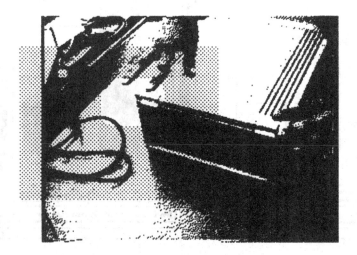

Fig. 6. Graphic overlay on legacy video. From Goodman (1993)

One alternative approach is exemplified by Goodman's (1993) Video Repair system which directly addressed the media acquisition problem in his Apple Macintosh IIcx^{TM} repair tutor. After acquiring and representing knowledge about standard maintenance and repair actions from manuals and experts, Goodman filmed expert repair technicians performing typical repair steps (e.g., open, unscrew, remove). Sequences of frames illustrating particular repair actions were identified and catalogued. Individual video frames within these sequences were then annotated to identify specific objects and their location within each frame. This enables the presentation planner, for example in Fig. 6, to describe how to remove a fan not only using spoken language but also by focusing the user's visual attention. In Fig. 6, presentation of the original video is temporally and spatially coordinated with a graphical overlay and spoken language output to simultaneously focus the user's attention to facilitate referent identification by the user *"You see the tab on the left side of the case top ..."*. Figure 7 illustrates how each of these channels of output was coordinated by an explanation generation component. Each communication channel (video, speech, or text) represents a sequence of communicative acts (much like those described in previous sections) such as displaying an object or action, identifying it with spoken language, describing what action is occurring, or labeling the parts or overall image via labels and captions.

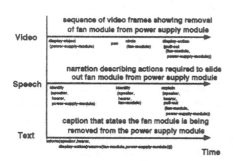
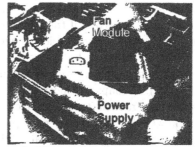

Fig. 7. Multimedia communicative acts for video repair (Goodman, 1993)

The focusing aspect illustrated in Fig. 6 is inversely related to Koons et al. (1993) research in eye tracking, with exploits multiple input channels (speech, gaze, gesture) to interpret ambiguous or imprecise referent identification by the user in one input stream (e.g., gesture). While we have illustrated the explanation generation aspects of Goodman's system, in fact, it was built for interactive training sessions. Given a simulated problem, the user would first specify a repair plan via a direct manipulation interface (e.g., selecting and sequencing actions with associated objects). The user could then visualize the plan via a video dynamically created from pre-existing video (as above) and have the system compare this to known correct plans and provide a critique. The result is an innovative cooperative multimedia system. What is perhaps most impressive about Goodman's work, underscoring the value of media re-use, is that the system was created in one person-month.

7   Tailoring Multimedia Output

In addition to selecting and coordinating output, it is important to design presentations that are suited to a particular user's abilities and task. Presentation tailoring needs to go beyond pre-canned presentations that have simple distinctions (e.g., short vs. long, simple vs. complex) to encompass personalized presentations which adapt media to the user's task, strengths, and preferences.

In their research with SAGE, (Roth and Mattis, 1991) characterize a range of information-seeking goals for viewing quantitative and relational information. These purposes included accurate value-lookup (e.g., train table times, phone numbers), value-scanning (approximate computations of, e.g., the mean, range, or sum of a data set), counting, n-wise comparison (e.g., product prices, stock performances), judging correlation (e.g., estimating covariance of variables), and locating data (e.g., finding data indexed by attribute values). Each of these goals may be supported by different presentations. As Fig. 8 illustrates, Burger and Marshall (1993) capture this task-tailoring when they contrast two (fictional) responses to one natural language query, *"When do trains leave for New York from Washington?"*. If the addressee is interested in trend detection, a bar chart presentation is preferred; if they are interested in exact quantities (e.g., to support further calculations), a table is preferred.

Presentations can be tailored to other factors, such as properties of the task, context (e.g., previously generated media), and user (e.g., visual ability, level of expertise). Perhaps the most successful (and practical) efforts in this area is the use of user models to interactively adapt hypertext to a user's changing skill and knowledge. Several user adapted hypertext investigations (e.g. Boyle and Encarnacion, 1994; Kobsa et al., 1994; Kaplan et al., 1993), including sometimes rather modest representations of the user, have demonstrated both timeliness and quality improvements in searching for information.

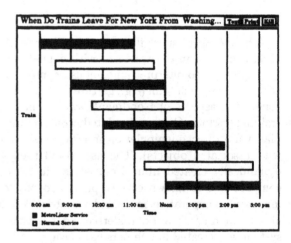

Fig. 8. Tailoring media output to the user's task (Burger and Marshall, 1993)

8   Toward Cooperative Multimedia Interfaces

In order to provide cooperative multimedia interaction, future human-machine interfaces must incorporate both the automated understanding and generation of multimedia. Effective multimedia dialogue requires both the ability to integrate multimedia input and generate coordinated, user- and situation-tailored multimedia output. Cooperative interaction thus relies upon explicit models of the user, task, and discourse as well as models of media, such as those exemplified in previous sections.

Multimedia dialogue prototypes have been developed in several application domains including CUBRICON for a mission planning domain (Neal and Shapiro, 1991), XTRA: tax-form preparation (Wahlster, 1991), AIMI: air mission planning (Burger and Marshall, 1993), and AlFresco: art history information exploration (Stock et al., 1993). Typically, these systems parse mixed (typically asynchronous) multimedia input and generate coordinated multimedia output. They also attempt to maintain coherency, cohesion, and consistency across both multimedia input and output. For example, these systems typically support integrated language and deixis for both input and output. They extend research in discourse and user modeling (Kobsa and Wahlster, 1989) by incorporating representations of media to enable media (cross) reference and reuse over the course of a session with a user. These enhanced representations support the exploitation of user perceptual abilities and media preferences as well as the resolution of multimedia references (e.g., *"Send this plane there"* articulated with synchronous gestures on a map). The details of discourse models in these systems, however, differ significantly. For example, CUBRICON represents a global focus space ordered by recency whereas AIMI represents a focus space segmented by the intentional structure of the discourse (i.e., a model of the domain tasks to be completed).

While intelligent multimedia interfaces promise natural and personalized interaction, they remain complicated and require specialized expertise to build. One practical approach to achieving some of the benefits of these more sophisticated systems without the expense of developing full multimedia interpretation and generation components, was achieved in AlFresco (Stock et al., 1993), a multimedia information kiosk for Italian art exploration. By adding natural language processing to a traditional hypermedia system, AlFresco achieved the benefits of hypermedia (e.g., organization of heterogeneous and unstructured information via hyperlinks, direct manipulation to facilitate exploration) together with the benefits of natural language parsing (e.g., direct query of nodes, links, and subnetworks which provides rapid navigation). Providing a user with natural language within a hypertext system helps overcome the indirectness of the hypermedia web as well as disorientation and cognitive overhead caused by large amounts of typically semantically heterogeneous links representing relations as diverse as part-of, class-of, instance-of or ellaboration-of. Also, as in other systems previously described (e.g., CUBRICON, TACTILUS), ambiguous gesture and language can yield a unique referent through mutual constraint. Finally, AlFresco incorporates simple natural language generation which can be combined with more complex canned text (e.g., art critiques) and images. Reiter, Mellish, and Levine (1992) also integrated traditional language generation with hypertext to produce hypertext technical manuals.

While practical systems are possible today, the multimedia interface of the future may have facilities that are much more sophisticated. These interfaces may include human-like agents that converse naturally with users, monitoring their interaction with the interface (e.g., key strokes, gestures, facial expressions) and the properties of those (e.g., conversational syntax and semantics, dialogue structure) over time and for different tasks and contexts. Equally, future interfaces will likely incorporate more sophisticated presentation mechanisms. For example, Pelachaud (1992) characterizes spoken language intonation and associated emotions (anger, disgust, fear, happiness, sadness, and surprise) and from these uses rules to compute facial expressions, including lip shapes, head movements, eye and eyebrow movements, and blinks. Finally, future multimedia interfaces should support richer interactions, including user and session adaptation, dialogue interruptions, follow-up questions, and management of focus of attention.

9   Visualizing Text with Graphics: FISH

Just as we discussed in Section 3 the processing of allocating information to particular media to support generation of more effective mixed media, so too we can also exploit the properties of information and associated media to support other kinds of tasks, such as design or information retrieval ones. One application of information encoding using graphical devices is used in a tool called *Forager for Information on the Super Highway* (FISH) (Smotroff et al., 1995; Mitchell, 1996).

FISH supports the visualization of large, physically or logically distributed document collections. Figure 9 illustrates the application of FISH to three Wide Area Information Server (WAIS) databases containing information on joint ventures from the Message Understanding Conference (MUC). Figure 9b illustrates the application of FISH to visualize e-mail clustered by topic type for a moderator supporting a National Performance Review electronic town hall. The traditional WAIS interface of a query box and a list of resulting hits is replaced by the interface shown in Figure 9, which includes a query box, a historical list of queries, and a graphically encoded display of resulting hits. Motivated by the University of Maryland's TreeMap research for hierarchical information visualization, FISH encodes the measure of relevance of each document to a given query (or set of compound queries) using both color saturation and size, the latter in an iterative fashion. In WAIS, the relevancy of a document to a given keyword query is measured on a scale from 1-1000, where 1000 is the highest relevancy by the frequency and location of (stems of) query keywords in documents.

In the example presented in Fig. 9a, each database is allocated screen size in proportion to the number of and degree with which documents are relevant to the given query. For example, the MEAD database on the left of the output window is given more space than the PROMT database because it has many more relevant documents. Similarly, individual documents that have higher relevancy measures for a given query are given proportionally more space and a higher color saturation. In this manner, a user can rapidly scan several large lists of documents to find relevant ones by focusing on those with higher color saturation and more space. Compound queries can be formulated via the 'Document Restrictions' menu by selecting the union or intersection of previous queries (in effect an AND or OR Boolean operator across queries). In Fig. 9, the user has selected the union of documents relevant to the query *"japan"* and the query *"automobile"*, which will return all documents which contain the keywords *"japan"* or *"automobile"*. Color coding can be varied on these documents, for example, to keep their color saturation distinct (e.g., blue vs. red) to enable rapid contrast of hits across queries within databases (e.g., hits on Japan vs. hits on automobile) or to mix their saturation so that intersecting keyword hits can be visualized (e.g., bright blue-reds could indicate highly relevant Japanese automobile documents, dark the opposite).

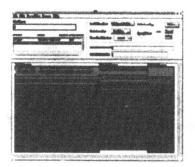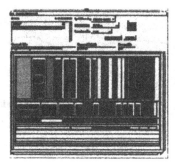

Fig. 9. Information visualization (Smotroff et al., 1995; Mitchell, 1996)

Importantly, the user can select among alternative encoding strategies if not satisfied with the given presentation. For example, by selecting 'YY' from the 'Spatial Encoding' menu the user can allocate variable vertical space for each document base, resulting in a bar-graph like presentation, where the length of each vertical display for each document base is relative to the number of retrieved documents from that source. This might be used to support rapid gross evaluation of the relevancy across sources, with overall size acting as a kind of summary of the relevance of the database, just as the WAIS relevancy measure and its encoding in size and color saturation acts as a kind of summary of the relevance of an individual document. Similarly, the order in which documents appear ('Order Encoding') and the way in which relevance measures are color encoded ('Color Encoding') can be varied. In this manner the user can dynamically vary three presentation dimensions – color, size, and order – to achieve the display which is most effective for the current information discovery purpose.

Since the information to be encoded by FISH is quantitative (the WAIS relevance ranking), a graphical presentation serves well. It is often the case, however, that information to be presented is more complex in character and thus demands more than one media, as discussed in previous sections. Moreover, access may need to occur in the context of a richer set of facilities. In fact, we next describe a visionary prototype representing an integration of FISH with several other technologies to enable a more powerful form of information access.

10   Intelligent Multimedia Browsing

An important element of future interaction are intelligent and intuitive interfaces to complex information spaces. For example, consider a visionary demonstration of interaction on the internet prototyped for ARPA by MITRE, whose architecture is illustrated in Fig. 10 (Smotroff, Hirschman, and Bayer, 1994). The prototype addressed some limitations of Mosaic: disorientation in a web of hypertext, poor indexing of document collections, and untailored information presentation.

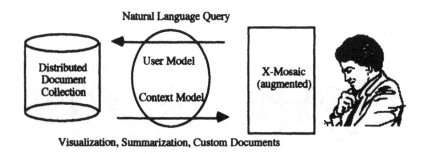

Fig. 10. Intelligent Mosaic

The MITRE team augmented the existing X-Mosaic infrastructure with an event queue to manage interactions. More significantly, they adapted and integrated natural language processing and distributed document visualization capabilities to support the process of information exploration and retrieval from a database of joint venture documents representing different sources on joint ventures (e.g., Mead, Prompt, Wall Street Journal). First, a natural language understanding system for full-text understanding was applied to the document collection to generate database templates representing the joint venture objects and relationships represented in the content of the documents.[2] MITRE further integrated CMU's Phoenix natural language parser to provide a natural language front-end to the document collection. Successful hits against a user query were then displayed in a visualization tool, essentially a matrix, with columns representing different information sources and rows representing a rank-ordered set of

---

[2] As current information extraction techniques have low precision and recall, this was simulated in the prototype by using the templates manually generated by domain experts to be used as answer keys in the Message Understanding Conference evaluation.

the most relevant documents. Color and size were used to emphasize individual document relevance. This adaptation of University of Maryland's TREEMAP visualization software further enabled the user to interatively refine their query, resulting in an updated color and size encoded visualization of the distributed document space. The user could either retrieve the full text of the document or request a summary of the document, generated automatically from the underlying database templates by MITRE's TEXPLAN system for natural language generation. A user model adapted output to user characteristics (e.g., their age, preferred language) and a discourse model interpreted queries in the context of their use (e.g., anaphoric expressions such as *"the ones that are from Japan"* are resolved automatically). Custom collections of documents could be generated on the fly based on a user query along with custom views (e.g., a table of contents page resulting from an ad-hoc collection of documents). A visionary facility for converting sources from one media to another (e.g., from a full-text article to a multimedia presentation) was also simulated.

An important aspect of the above demonstration was the ability to search on the content of the information, that is on the people, places, organizations, relationships, events and so on, mentioned in the document. Because automating this remains difficult, it was actually simulated by searching on the object-oriented answer keys developed for the Message Understanding Conference, which is focused on automated information extraction technology. Both automated extraction and machine translation of foreign documents remain important needs. Also important is the ability to perform content-based search on multimedia sources (e.g. text, video, audio). In the demonstration, the user was able to retrieve video by simple keyword search of associated closed-captions. While this interface was primarily passive, other researchers are investigating more active, agent-based systems that engage the user in a mixed-initiative dialogue.

11   Content-Based Multimedia Access

The explosion of multimedia information on our world wide information web is demanding more sophisticated tools to segment, browse, retrieve, extract, summarize and customize information captured in natural language text (written or typed), spoken language, graphics, imagery, and video or some combination thereof. One principal advantage of the automatically generated presentations described above is that they include explicit representations of the underlying presentation semantics and intention. This enables users to access the underlying content directly or via the presentations. In contrast, most existing electronic documents exist as media such as text, graphics, or video with at best document structure relations (e.g., a directive language such as TeX or a mark-up language such as SGML to encode document elements such as header, section, subsection). Even given a richer document markup semantics, manually indexing materials remains time consuming and error-prone. Document markup may be as straightforward as typing hyperlinks (e.g., part-of, example-of, elaboration-of) or as detailed as identifying the entities and relations in text or images (e.g., objects, attributes, events, states, processes) to support detailed information extraction and query. For example, in navigating the World Wide Web, one cannot pose a query such as *"Find me all video clips in the last six months from foreign broadcasts of no longer than 20 seconds long that show Boris Yeltsin and detail his heart condition"*.

Given increased volumes of information and knowledge, tools to mine this information, detecting correlations and trends, will be necessary. Several research groups are now investigating the content-based access of non-textual media such as sound, graphics, imagery, and video (Maybury, forthcoming). Commercial products exist already for content-based still imagery access, supporting image search by visual features such as color, texture, and shape (Flickner et al., 1995). With more complex artefacts, such as video, key problems include the need to segment, summarize, and support interaction with these complex artefacts. Within the video stream, techniques performing in the ninety plus percent accuracy range have been developed to index video based on transitions (e.g., dissolve, fade, cut) and shot classification (e.g., anchor versus story shots (Zhang et al., 1995), however, this still results in far too many shots for browsing or search. Researchers have recognized that more sophisticated single and multi-stream analysis will be required to support more fine grained analysis of the content and to provide access to higher-level structure for browsing and search (Aigraine, 1995).

Our group is endeavoring to create speech and language analysis capabilities that might address the segmentation, summarization, and visualization of video (Mani et al., in press). Figure 11 illustrates the overview of our Video Analysis and Library $(VAL)^{TM}$ system and our associated video viewer, Broadcast News Navigator $(BNN)^{TM}$. Analysis tools process the imagery, audio and textual streams and store the gathered information in a relational and a video database management system.

For the imagery stream associated with video, we use commercial scene transition detection hardware/software (Scene Stealer^{TM} (Dubner, 1996)) together with keyframe selection heuristics we have engineered based on the structure of individual video programs (e.g., keyframes for stories in the Jim Lehrer News Hour are selected from the news summary at the beginning of the news hour as these are more effective as a graphical summary of the story). For audio analysis, we are experimenting with speaker change detection algorithms created at Lincoln Laboratory. For the textual stream, created from closed caption, we create named entities, story segments, and detect commercials. Named entity tags improve standard keyword-based text retrieval by detecting people, organizations, locations, dates and moneys in free text using message understanding technology (Aberdeen et al., 1995). We use the story segmentation algorithms based on discourse cues, details and results of which we present in Mani et al. (in press).

BNN enables a user to view a visualization of proper names (e.g. people, organizations, locations) extracted from closed captions associated with a broadcast video. Having analyzed these charts for patterns or trends, a researcher can browse the related news segments, which are segmented using linguistic processing of discourse cues (e.g. anchor/reporter handoffs) and other non-textual indicators (e.g., changes in speaker, scene changes). A user can thus, interactively browse and query the video document collection using techniques similar to those used for text information retrieval. Potential applications include video mail, radio and television broadcast indexing, video teleconference archiving.

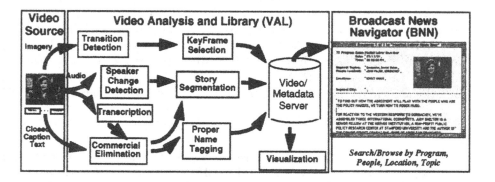

Fig. 11. Content-based access to video

As systems become more sophisticated in their ability to extract content from multimedia sources, this will enable the application of user and discourse models to tailor this output to the user, both in terms of selecting content, realizing it (e.g., choosing shading and shape encoding versus colors for color blind users), and ensuring appropriate cross media coordination (e.g., between audio descriptions and labels in a related graphic).

12   Conclusion

We have outlined key processes in multimedia generation, some efforts focused on media allocation, communicative-act based multimedia comparison, direction, and instruction generation. We have discussed tailoring output to particular information-seeking tasks, and illustrated how natural language access, visualization tools, information extraction, and summarization can be integrated to provide richer web-based intelligent multimedia information access. Finally we have pointed to our recent efforts to provide content-based access to video.

A key area for future work is the increasing need for personalized interaction on our global information infrastructure. Tools that can support information and knowledge creation, access, summarization, sharing, and visualization will become increasingly important. Enabling this interaction will be discourse models which explicitly track and manage interaction, task models that monitor the performance of user actions to enable error detection, correction, and prevention, user models that support interaction tailored to the knowledge, skills, and abilities of individuals, and group models that facilitate collaboration and effective work flow.

Acknowledgments

Judy Sider designed and implemented the multimedia comparison system described herein. John Burger and Ralph Marshall developed the AIMI system. Brad Goodman designed the video repair system. I thank all the referenced authors for their ideas, which I have attempted to faithfully represent herein. Rich Mitchell and colleagues created FISH. Ira Smotroff, Lynette Hirschman, Sam Bayer and colleagues created the visionary information access system briefly described in Section 10. I thank Wolfgang Wahlster, Harry Bunt, and the anonymous CMC/95 reviewers for their comments on multimedia and multimodal issues. Apple^{TM} and Macintosh IIcx^{TM} are registered trademarks of Apple Computer, Inc. Cupertino, CA. CNN is a registered trademark of Cable News Network. Scene Stealer^{TM} is a registered trademark of Dubner International.

References

Aberdeen, J., Burger, J., Day, D., Hirschman, L., Robinson, P., and Vilain, M. (1995) Description of the Alembic System Used for MUC-6. *Proc. Sixth Message Understanding Conference.* Columbia, MD: Advanced Research Projects Agency, Information Technology Office.

Aigraine, P., Joly, P. and Longueville, V. (1995) Medium Knowledge-based Macro-Segmentation of Video into Sequences. In M. Maybury (ed.) *Working notes of IJCAI-95 Workshop on Intelligent Multimedia Information Retrieval,* 5–16. To appear in (Maybury, 1997)

André, E., Finkler, W., Graf, W., Rist, T., Schauder, A., and Wahlster, W. (1993) WIP: The Automatic Synthesis of Multimodal Presentations. In M. Maybury (ed.) *Intelligent Multimedia Interfaces,* Menlo Park: AAAI/MIT Press, 73-90. Also DFKI Research Report RR-92-46, Saarbrücken.

Appelt, D. (1985) *Planning English Sentences.* Cambridge, UK: Cambridge University Press.

Arens, Y., Miller, L., and Sondheimer, N. K. (1991) Presentation Design Using an Integrated Knowledge Base. In J. W. Sullivan, and S. W. Tyler (eds) *Intelligent User Interfaces.* New York: ACM Press, 241-258.

Austin, J. (1962) *How to do Things with Words,* edited by J. O. Urmson. Oxford, UK: Oxford University Press.

Boyle, C. and Encarnacion, A. O. (1994) MetaDoc: An Adaptive Hypertext Reading System. *User Modeling and User-Adapted Interaction* 4(1), 1–19.

Bunt, H., R. Ahn, R.-J. Beun, T. Borghuis and C. van Overveld (1995) Cooperative Multimodal Communication in the DenK Project. In H. Bunt, R.-J. Beun and T. Borghuis (eds.) *Proc. International Conference on Cooperative Multimodal Communication CMC/95).* Eindhoven: IPO, 79-102.

Burger, J., and Marshall, R. (1993) The Application of Natural Language Models to Intelligent Multimedia. In (Maybury, 1993), 167-187.

Catarci, T., Costabile, M. F., and Levialdi, S. (eds) (1992) *Advanced Visual Interfaces: Proceedings of the International Workshop AVI'92* Singapore: World Scientific Series in Computer Science, Vol 36.

Cheyer, A. and Julia, L. (1995) Multimodal Maps: An Agent-based Approach. In H. Bunt, R.-J. Beun and T. Borghuis (eds.) *Proc. International Conference on Cooperative Multimodal Communication CMC/95).* Eindhoven: IPO, 103-113. Reprinted in this volume.

Cremers, A. 1995. Object Reference During task-related Terminal Dialogues. In H. Bunt, R.-J. Beun and T. Borghuis (eds.) *Proc. International Conference on Cooperative Multimodal Communication CMC/95).* Eindhoven: IPO, 115-128. Reprinted in this volume.

Dubner, B. (1996) *Automatic Scene Detector and Videotape logging system, User Guide.* Dubner International, Inc., Copyright 1995.

Fais, L. Loken-Kim, K., Park, Y. (1995) Speaker's Responses to Requests for Repetition in a Multimedia Language Processing Environment. In H. Bunt, R.-J. Beun and T. Borghuis (eds.) *Proc. International Conference on Cooperative Multimodal Communication CMC/95).* Eindhoven: IPO, 129-143. See also Fais et al., this volume.

Feiner, S. K. and McKeown, K. R. (1993) Automating the Generation of Coordinated Multimedia Explanations. In M. Maybury (ed.) *Intelligent Multimedia Information Retrieval.* Menlo Park: AAAI/MIT Press, 113-134.

Flickner, M., Sawhney, H., Niblack, W., Ashley, J., Huang, Q., Dom, B., Gorkani, M., Hafner, J., Lee, D., Petkovic, D., Steele, D. and Yanker, P. (1995) Query by Image and Video Content: The QBIC System. IEEE Computer.

Goodman, B. A. (1993) Multimedia Explanations for Intelligent Training Systems. In M. Maybury (ed.) *Intelligent Multimedia Information Retrieval.* Menlo Park: AAAI/MIT Press, 148-171

Graf, W. (1992) Constraint-based Graphical Layout of Multimodal Presentations. In Catarci, Costabile, and Levialdi (1992), 365-385. Also available as DFKI Report RR-92-15.

Herzog, G. and Wazinski, P. (1994) VIsual TRAnslator: Linking Perceptions and Natural Language Descriptions. *Artificial Intelligence Review* 8, 175-187.

Hovy, E. H. and Arens, Y. (1993) On the Knowledge Underlying Multimedia Presentations. In M. Maybury (ed.) *Intelligent Multimedia Information Retrieval.* Menlo Park: AAAI/MIT Press, 280-306.

Kaplan, C., Fenwick, J. and Chen, J. (1993) Adaptive Hypertext Navigation Based on User Goals and Context. *User Modeling and User-Adapted Interaction* 3(3), 193-220.

Kobsa, A., Nill, A. and Fink, J. (1994) KN-AHS: An Adaptive Hypertext Client of the User Modeling System BGP-MS. *Proc. First International Conference on User Modeling (UM-94),* Cape Cod, MA.

Kobsa, A. and Wahlster, W. (eds.) (1989) *User Models in Dialogue Systems.* Berlin: Springer Verlag.

Koons, D. B., Sparrell, C. J., and Thorisson, K. R. (1993) Integrating Simultaneous Output from Speech, Gaze, and Hand Gestures. In M. Maybury (ed.) *Intelligent Multimedia Information Retrieval.* Menlo Park: AAAI/MIT Press, 243-261.

Mackinlay, J. D. (1986) Automating the Design of Graphical Presentations of Relational Information. *ACM Transactions on Graphics* 5(2), 110-141.

Mani I., House, D., Maybury, M. and Green, M. (in press) Toward Content-based Browsing of Broadcast News Video. In (Maybury, forth.)

Maass, W. (1994) From Vision to Multimodal Communication: Incremental Route Descriptions. *Artificial Intelligence Review* 8, 159-174.

Maybury, M. T. (1991a) Planning Multimedia Explanations Using Communicative Acts. In *Proc. Ninth National Conference on Artificial Intelligence.* Anaheim, CA: AAAI, 61-66.

Maybury, M. T. (1991b) Topical, Temporal and Spatial Constraints on Linguistic Realization. *Computational Intelligence: Special Issue on Natural Language Generation* 7(4), 266-275.

Maybury, M. T. (ed.) (1993) Intelligent Multimedia Interfaces. Menlo Park: AAAI/MIT Press.
(http://www.aaai.org:80/Press/Books/Maybury-1/maybury.html)

Maybury, M. T. (1994) Automated Explanation and Natural Language Generation. In C. Sabourin (ed) *A Bibliography of Natural Language Generation*. Montreal: Infolingua, 1–88.

Maybury, M. T. (1995a) Using Similarity Metrics to Determine Content for Explanation Generation. *International Journal of Expert Systems with Applications. Special issue on Explanation*, 8(4), 513–525.

Maybury, M. T. (1995b) Research in Multimedia Parsing and Generation. In P. McKevitt (ed.) *Artificial Intelligence Review: Special Issue on on the Integration of Natural Language and Vision Processing* 9(2-3), 103–127.

Maybury, M. T. (ed.) (1997) *Intelligent Multimedia Information Retrieval*. Menlo Park: AAAI/MIT Press.
(http://www.aaai.org:80/Press/Books/Maybury-2)

Maybury, M. T. (in press) Communicative Acts for Multimedia and Multimodal Dialogue. In M. M. Taylor, F. Néel, and D. G. Bouwhuis (eds.) (in press) *The Structure of Multimodal Dialogue II*.

Michell, R. (1996) *Forager for Information on the Super Highway* (FISH). Unpublished Manuscript.

Neal, J. G. and Shapiro, S. C. (1991) Intelligent Multi-Media Interface Technology. In Sullivan and Tyler (1991), 11–43.

Neuwirth, C., Chandhok, R., Chamey, D., Wojahn, P. and Kim, L. (1994) Distributed Collaborative Writing: A Comparison of Spoken and Written Modalities for Reviewing and Revising Documents. In *Proc. Human Factors inCOmputing Systems (CHI'94)*, Boston, 51–57.

Pelachaud, C. (1992) Functional Decomposition of Facial Expressions for an Animation System. In Catarci, Costabile, and Levialdi (1992), 26–49.

Reiter, E., Mellish, C. and Levine, J. (1992) Automatic Generation of on-line Documentation in the IDAS Project. *Proc. 3rd Conference on Applied Natural Language Processing*. Morristown: ACL.

Roth, S. F., and Mattis, J. (1991) Automating the Presentation of Information. In *Proc. IEEE Conference on AI Applications*, Miami Beach, FL., 90–97.

Searle, J. R. (1969) *Speech Acts: An Essay in the Philosophy of Language*. Cambridge, UK: Cambridge University Press.

Smotroff, I., Hirschman, L., and Bayer, S. (1995) Integrating Natural Language with Large DataspaceVisualization. To appear in N. Adam and B. Bhargava (eds), *Advances in Digital Libraries*. Lecture Notes in Computer Science, Berlin: Springer Verlag.

Stock, O. and the ALFRESCO Project Team (1993) ALFRESCO: Enjoying the Combination of Natural Language Processing and Hypermedia for Information Exploration. In M. Maybury (ed.) *Intelligent Multimedia Information Retrieval*. Menlo Park: AAAI/MIT Press, 197–224.

Sullivan, J. W., and Tyler, S. W. (eds) (1991) *Intelligent User Interfaces*. New York: ACM Press, Frontier Series.

Sutcliffe, A., Hare, M., Doubleday, A. and Ryan, M. (1997) Empirical Studies in Multimedia Information Retrieval. In M. Maybury (ed.) *Intelligent Multimedia Information Retrieval*. Menlo Park: AAAI/MIT Press, 449–472.

Wahlster, W. (1991) User and Discourse Models for Multimodal Communication. In Sullivan and Tyler (1991), 45–67.

Wahlster, W. (1996) Intellimedia. Invited Talk at the International Workshop on Cooperative Multimodal Communication CMC/95, May 1995, Eindhoven, the Netherlands.

Webber, B. (1995) Instructing Animated Agents: Viewing Language in Behavioral Terms. Invited Talk at the International Conference on Cooperative Multimodal Communication CMC/95, May 1995, Eindhoven, the Netherlands. Reprinted in this volume.

Zhang, H. J., Low, C. Y., Smoliar, S. W. and Zhong, D. (1995) Video Parsing, Retrieval, and Browsing: An Integrated and Content-Based Solution. *Proc. of ACM Multimedia '95*. To appear in Maybury, 1997)

Multimodal Cooperation with the DENK System

Harry Bunt[1], René Ahn[1], Robbert-Jan Beun[2], Tijn Borghuis[3], and
Kees van Overveld[3]

[1] Computational Linguistics and Artificial Intelligence Group, Tilburg University,
P.O. Box 90153, 5000 LE Tilburg, The Netherlands,
{bunt,ahn}@kub.nl
[2] Center for Research on User-System Interaction (IPO)
P.O. Box 513, 5600 MB Eindhoven, The Netherlands
rjbeun@ipo.tue.nl
[3] Department of Mathematics and Computing Science, Eindhoven University of
Technology, P.O. Box 513, 5600 MB Eindhoven, The Netherlands
{tijn, wsinkvo}@win.tue.nl

Abstract. In this chapter we present the DENK project, a long-term
effort where the aim is to build a generic cooperative human-computer
interface combining multiple input and output modalities. We discuss the
view on human-computer interaction that underlies the project and the
emerging DENK system. The project integrates results from fundamental
research in knowledge representation, communication, natural language
semantics and pragmatics, and object-oriented animation. Central stage
in the project is occupied by the design of a cooperative and knowledgeable electronic assistant that communicates in natural language and that
has internal access to an application domain which is presented visually
to the user. The assistant, that we call the *Cooperative Assistant*, has
an information state that is represented in a rich form of type theory,
a formalism that enables us to model the inherent cognitive dynamics
of a dialogue participant. This formalism is used both for modeling domain knowledge, for representing the current dialogue context, and for
implementing a context-change theory of communication.

1 Introduction

The DENK project is long-term collaborative research activity of the universities of Tilburg and Eindhoven that aims at the exploration, formalization and
application of fundamental principles of communication from a computational
perspective, in order to build advanced cooperative human-computer interfaces.[1]
The project combines fundamental research in knowledge representation, communication, natural language semantics and pragmatics, and object-oriented animation.

---

[1] 'DENK' is an abbreviation of 'Dialoogvoering en Kennisopbouw', which means 'Dialogue Management and Knowledge Acquisition'. The word *denk* in Dutch means
think.

Point of departure in the DENK project is that, from a user's point of view, a computer should ideally present itself as an intelligent 'electronic assistant' who is knowledgeable about the task and the domain of the application and interacts in an intelligent and cooperative way with the user, using natural language and other modalities as appropriate. The DENK system, that should instantiate this ideal, is intended to be *generic* in that its architecture, as well as the techniques developed and incorporated in the various modules and interfaces, should be applicable over a wide range of application domains and tasks.

In this chapter we first discuss the motivation and the fundamental principles that underlie the architecture and functionality of the DENK system. In subsequent sections we discuss the research concerned with knowledge representation and reasoning, natural language interpretation, pragmatics and dialogue management, and visual domain representation. We describe the design of the major components in a first, preliminary prototype of the system to be developed. In conclusion, we consider some of the main results obtained thus far, and outline the research agenda for the near future.

2   Human-Computer Interaction and Communication

The DENK project takes an approach to communication according to which communicative behaviour is analysed in terms of actions, motivated by a goal, purpose, or function. This is the general idea of speech act theory (Austin, 1962; Searle, 1969) as well as of more recent approaches to dialogue analysis such as *Dynamic Interpretation Theory* (Bunt, 1991; 1994; 1997) and *Communicative Activity Analysis* (Allwood, 1976; 1997). The motivation for communicating may in the case of human-human interaction be either of a social character, such as being friendly, seeking support, or courting; or it may concern a specific task such as solving a planning problem. In the case of human-computer communication, social motivations do not arise, so we may assume that the user communicates with a computer in order to accomplish a certain task - what is often called an *application*. Many kinds of application, for instance in areas such as process control and computer-aided design, involve real-world objects or models of such objects. The interaction with such objects is physical, in the form of such actions as picking up, turning around, or fastening, and perceptual, in terms of seeing, feeling, hearing, or smelling. Interaction with other *agents*, by contrast, is in symbolic form, using signalling systems such as natural language, gestures, and facial expressions. Symbolic actions, like speech acts, require an interpreter to bridge the gap between symbols and their actual meaning and purpose, before they can produce changes in the domain of physical objects, or can provide information about these objects. Physical acts, by contrast, directly change the application domain, while perceptual acts directly provide information about the domain (see also Hutchins, 1989; de Souza, 1993)

The distinction of two types of interaction, direct and indirect, is clearly reflected in the design of the DENK system, with two components playing distinct roles in the user-system interaction:

a. the *Cooperative Assistant*, which supports symbolic interaction; it interprets messages in natural language from the user, is capable of reasoning about various aspects of the domain and the user, and produces communicative behaviour adequate with respect to (its model of) the user's beliefs and goals;

b. the *Application Domain Model*, implemented by means of an animation system which incorporates spatio-temporal components and graphical tools for the representation and visualization of the domain. The user can visually observe the domain, in particular see the events that take place, and can operate directly on domain objects with graphical actions.

The user of the DENK system can thus interact with the application domain both (not: *either*) indirectly, through linguistic communication with the Cooperative Assistant who has internal access to the domain, and (not: *or*) directly, through graphical operations. We emphasize *both .. and* instead of *either .. or*, since the user can also interact by using these two modalities in combination, for instance by using a deictic expression and grasping an object on the screen. This is depicted in the *'triangle view'* of interaction, depicted in Fig. 1, where we have three interacting components: the User, the Cooperative Assistant, and the Domain Model. We will see below that the overall design of the DENK system is based on this triangle view.

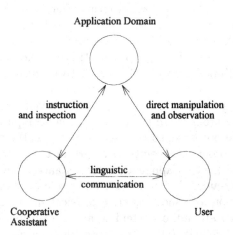

Fig. 1. The DENK *'triangle view'* of interaction: User, Cooperative Assistant, and Application Domain.

It may be noted that the overall architecture of the DENK system, in reflecting the triangle view, differs from that of other intelligent multimedia systems, such as AIMI (Burger & Marshall, 1993), WIP (Wahlster et al., 1993), MMI² (Wilson et al., 1991) and CUBRICON (Neal & Shapiro, 1991), in which there is no direct link between the user and the application domain. An advantage of our approach is that certain particularly complex aspects of the interaction, such as the visualization of autonomous motion behaviour of objects, do not have to be considered by the Cooperative Assistant and can be left to the interactive component of the application domain model.

In order to be able to act as the ideal electronic cooperative assistant, the DENK system's Cooperative Assistant should have the properties required of a communicative agent, as laid out in (Bunt, 1997b):

1. Be a knowledgeable communicative agent, i.e., be competent in the use of the available modalities and their combinations. This requirement includes knowing what types of communicative actions van be performed, what action is appropriate to perform under what conditions, and what is an appropriate form of an action in a given context.

2. Be informed about the domain of discourse and the current dialogue context. Knowledge of the domain of discourse is indispensable for understanding the user, since understanding involves relating the elements of an input message to the semantic concepts that make up their meanings. Knowledge of the current dialogue context can be divided into the following categories (Bunt, 1997a):

   (a) *linguistic context*, most importantly the recent dialogue history;

   (b) *semantic context*, i.e. the current state of the domain of discourse;

   (c) *cognitive context*, including the current beliefs about the user, and information about the current status of cognitive processes (such as the information that the interpretation of the last input message needs additional information to resolve an ambiguity);

   (d) *physical and perceptual*, relating to the physical conditions of the interaction and the perceptual availability of information;

   (e) *social*, describing current 'pressures' to perform particular communicative actions (such as making an apology, or providing feedback on the result of carrying out an instruction).[2]

3. Have reasoning capacities. To apply his knowledge of communication, of the application domain, and of the current dialogue context, an agent has to be able to combine pieces of information in logically correct ways. Understanding and evaluating the content and function of messages involves making such combinations, and thus involves reasoning, as do the planning and generation of noncommunicative as well as communicative acts.

4. Be rational. Being able to reason is not sufficient. The ability to draw correct inferences should be used in a rational way, to compute for instance the intentions and other relevant conditions of (communicative or other) actions that are instrumental to achieving a certain goal or purpose, or to infer subgoals that are on the way to a higher goal. Rationality directs the use of reasoning power.

---

[2] Social aspects of context do not only play a role in human-human communication, but also in human-computer interaction. Acknowledgements and apologies, for instance, help to make clear to the user to what extent the communication is proceeding successfully.

5. Be social. Knowing the rules and conventions of using a communicative system (in a certain type of interactive situation, within a community) is not sufficient: one must also have the *disposition* to act accordingly. An important aspect of this is that a social agents takes other participants' goals, desires, beliefs, and other properties into account, in particular so as to help others to achieve their goals - which is commonly called *being cooperative*.

In projects that aim at building multimodal communication systems, there is a tendency to start working on the processing of inputs from several modalities, or on the use of modalities for output presentation; this may be explained by the fact that the forms of inputs and outputs are conspicuous aspects of multimodal systems. As a consequence, many of the requirements just listed tend to receive relatively little attention. In the DENK project, we decided to work the other way round, in an 'inside-out' fashion, developing first (a) a powerful representation of dialogue contexts, and (b) a model of the mechanisms for context change under the influence of interaction with the user, as well as (c) a model of the way changing contexts give rise to communicative activity. This approach can be viewed as implementing the context-change view of communication in a system-internal knowledge representation formalism, using an architecture that allows multiple input and output modalities for the expression of communicative action, and adding a number of modalities in a later stage.

In the presentation in this chapter we follow the same approach, paying attention first to the use of the powerful representation formalism that was chosen and extended in the DENK project for context representation and communication modeling. We then outline the overall system architecture, and we briefly consider the visual domain modeling in the Application Domain Model component and the approach to adding natural language as input and output modality for the Cooperative Assistant.

3 The DENK System

As mentioned above, the DENK system is intended to be *generic* in that its architecture, as well as many of the techniques developed and incorporated in the various modules and interfaces, should be applicable over a wide range of application domains and tasks. To demonstrate the generic character of the system, several applications are envisaged, the most important one being a training simulator for the use of a modern electron microscope as developed by Philips Electron Optics. This is an important instrument for materials research in physics, as well as for medical research in pathology. The device is very complex, and uninitiated users have to go through an intensive training period in order to learn how to use it. This is primarily due to the difficulty that users have in forming an adequate picture of the internal workings of the device (the relevant parts, their functions, and their relations), that manifests itself to users essentially as a black box. Offering trainees the possibility to exercise with an interactive training simulator is expected to considerably shorten the training period. We will refer to this application of the DENK system under construction as the *'DK-2 system'*.

For experimental purposes, a preliminary partial prototype of the DENK system has been implemented, from now on referred to as the *'DK-1 System'*, where the application domain is a blocks world, with toy blocks of different shapes, sizes and colours, with specifiable autonomous movements in 3D space such as rotating, moving to or from a distance, etc. The blocks world has a 3D representation on the screen by means of an animation system described below. This DK-1 prototype does not allow direct manipulation of objects by the user, and supports only simple dialogue behaviour and a toy fragment of natural language. The DK-1 system can execute simple commands to act on the domain and answer questions about its current state.

A simple way in which the current system uses context information is that, when answering questions, it takes the preceding dialogue into account and supplies only information which, according to its context information, is not shared with the user. The system also uses context information (viz. domain knowledge) to detect presupposition violations. If the user gives a command that is impossible to perform, the system will detect and report this.

The project's 'inside-out' strategy, concentrating first on developing the formalisms and techniques for context representation, reasoning and domain modeling, has resulted in the availability in the DK-1 prototype of the Application Domain Model component, and in the representation-, reasoning-, evaluation-, and visualization systems that form the backbone of the system.

4   Knowledge Representation and Reasoning

4.1   Type Theory

For modeling the information state of the Cooperative Assistant and the way it changes under the influence of the communication, we use Constructive Type Theory (CTT), a versatile and powerful logical formalism for knowledge representation and reasoning, based on typed lambda calculus. The language of (explicitly) typed lambda calculus consists of statements of the general form $V : T$, expressing that an object V has type T. Type-theoretical statements '$V : T$' should be read: 'V is an object of type T', or 'V is an inhabitant of T'. Such expressions are called 'entries' or 'introductions'. The subexpressions 'V' at the left-hand side of an introduction are variables, those at the right-hand side are types. Entries can be grouped into sequences, which in type theory are called *contexts*.

Types are atomic or complex. Atomic types come in two varieties: constants and variables. A variable x may be used as a type, provided that it has been introduced in the context in which occurs (i.e., there is an introduction of the form $V : T$ earlier in the sequence that forms the current context, where an expression of the form $A : V$ occurs). Constant atomic types can be used at any point in a context, and are also called *'sorts'*. Among the sorts is *prop*, for propositions, and *class*, for objects of any other kind. Two complex types of importance here are function types, formed by means of 'Π-*abstraction*' (also called 'Π-*formation*'), and the types formed by function application.

Function types are defined as follows. If t_i and t_j are types and x is a variable then $\Pi x{:}t_i.t_j(x)$ is a function type. If f is a function of this type, and y is an inhabitant of type t_i, then f(y) is an inhabitant of the type $t_j(y)$. A special case is that where the variable x does not occur in $t_j(y)$, in that case we use the simpler notation $t_i \rightarrow t_j$, instead of $\Pi x{:}t_i.t_j(x)$.

A *context* can now be defined more precisely as a well-formed sequence of introductions, well-formed in that every type occurring in the right-hand side of an introduction is either a sort or is the left-hand side of an introduction earlier in the sequence.

Whether a type-theoretical statement V : T is true has to be decided on the basis of the context in which it occurs: the preceding sequence of statements should either already contain that expression, or it should be possible to obtain the expression from the preceding context by means of the type inference rules of the logic.

Typed lambda calculi have been applied in foundational mathematical research, which was their original motivation, as well as in the mathematical study of programming languages and the semantics of natural language. Barendregt (1991) noticed that many existing systems of typed lambda calculus can be uniformly represented using the format of *Pure Type Systems* (see also Barendregt, 1992). Formalisms within this class include *Automath* (de Bruijn, 1980) and the *Calculus of Constructions* (Coquand, 1985); closely related is also *intuitionistic type theory* (Martin-Löf, 1984).

A crucial and peculiar point of type theory is that *propositions can be treated as types*, and inhabitants of a proposition as proofs of that proposition; a proposition itself has type 'prop'. Propositions thus occur in type-theoretical expressions in the same way as individual concepts, and proofs occur as individual objects. Proofs and other objects may be combined to form new proofs and other objects. The inference rules of the type system restrict the way in which this can be done, and guarantee that all reasoning is sound.[3] Type theory thus takes proofs to be first-class citizens: proofs are considered as abstract objects, have representations in the language, and are fully integrated within the formalism. This means that in type theory we can represent not only *what* an agent believes, but also *how* he comes to believe it, by having explicit representations of the proofs that justify his beliefs.

The proof-theoretical nature of type theory does not mean that *truth* is the central notion of the framework, however. Central to type theory is the recording of information (in type-theoretical contexts) and of what has been shown to follow from this information. An agent whose beliefs are represented type-theoretically, is regarded as *explicitly* believing those propositions that are present in the type-theoretical context, and *implicitly* believing those proposi-

---

[3] This ingenious idea is known as the *Curry-Howard-De Bruijn isomorphism* (Curry & Feys, 1958).

tions that are not explicitly present but for which he can effectively construct a proof, given the available axioms, deduction rules and proof-construction strategies. (Once the agent has constructed such a proof, he can record it in his context, the belief then becomes explicit.) The framework is thus *constructivist* in the sense that effective constructability of a proof is central, rather than truth.

The total set of the agent's beliefs is thus determined by what the agent is able to deduce from the (type-theoretical) context. For some propositions p, the agent will not be able to construct a proof, nor will he be able to construct a proof of not p, hence this framework constitutes an inherently *partial* approach to belief modelling.

In recent years, research in the DENK-project has shown the great potential of type-theoretical contexts as formalizations of context information, provided the expressive capabilities and proof methods of standard type theory are extended in order to model states of information and intention of agents participating in a dialogue (Borghuis, 1994; Ahn, 1995a; Jaspars, 1993; Beun & Kievit, 1996). An extension with epistemic modalities has been defined by Borghuis (1994), which allows the formal modelling of beliefs with different degrees of certainty, and of distinguishing 'private' beliefs from assumed shared beliefs. Further extensions are required for the type-theoretical representation of the time-dependent aspects of the behaviour of objects in the application domain, and also for the representation of and the reasoning about the temporal aspects of natural language utterances (see Ahn, 1996; Ahn & Borghuis, 1996).

In the DENK-project, CTT is used for implementing the semantic representation of the utterances exchanged by the user and the system; for implementing representations of the system's knowledge of the task domain (the global semantic context, which is assumed to be shared with the user); and for representing the shared beliefs of user and system derived from the dialogue, (i.e. the system's view of the 'local semantic context'). The representation of local semantic context is implemented in a simple way by dividing a CTT context into two parts, 'Common' and 'Private'. Common is defined as the part where the system stores the information it believes to be shared with the user; Private contains the beliefs the system does not believe to be shared with the user. The two subcontexts are taken as primitives, which means that modalities are not modelled in the CTT-language itself; the CTT-language does not contain operators like C, P or B (for common, private and belief).[4]

In the following section we show, by means of a simple example, how the information state of the Cooperative Assistant can be represented by a type-theoretical context.

---

[4] The incorporation of epistemic operators into the object language of CTT is not excluded; Borghuis (1994) shows how modalities can be modelled explicitly in CTT, extending CTT with deduction rules for entering and exiting subcontexts. The implementation with contexts separated into parts is computationally simpler, however, and adequate for the purposes of the DENK-project.

4.2   Information States as Type-theoretical Contexts

We consider the blocks world domain of the DK-1 prototype system, where we have pyramids, cubes and the like, which can move around and have properties like colour and size. In this example we assume the Cooperative Assistant to have the following information:

- there may be pyramids and colours in the domain (the Cooperative Assistant is familiar with the notions 'pyramid' and 'colour'; see below);
- 'small' is a predicate applicable to pyramids, and 'bright' is a predicate applicable to colours;
- there is actually a pyramid, which is small;
- all pyramids have a colour, and all pyramids have a bright colour.

To describe the Cooperative Assistant's information state, we begin with an empty context and gradually introduce the information listed above. First, we have to introduce the necessary types corresponding to the concepts we assumed, i.e. 'pyramid' and 'colour'. In type theory, new types may be introduced as inhabitants of one of the sorts, or of one of the types already introduced. So we construct the following context:[5]

[pyramid : class , colour : class]

Once a type has been introduced, inhabitants of that type can be introduced. The knowledge that there actually is a pyramid in the (current state of the) domain is expressed in CTT by introducing an individual of that type, so we extend the context with the entry:

p_{38} : pyramid

(using the variable 'p_{38}' as an arbitrary name for this individual).

Predicates are represented in CTT as functions to propositions, so the predicate 'bright' is a function that, applied to a colour, yields a proposition like: 'Yellow is bright'. Propositions are treated as types, as mentioned above, and occur in CTT expressions in the same way as the types 'pyramid' and 'colour' in the present example. We thus introduce the predicate 'small' as a function from pyramids to propositions, and the predicate 'bright' as a function from colours to propositions (objects of type 'prop'). These are added to the example context by extending it with the entries:

small : pyramid $\rightarrow$ prop
bright : colour $\rightarrow$ prop

---

[5] The entries making up a context are separated by commas; beginning and end of a context are marked by '[' and ']', respectively.

The knowledge that the particular pyramid 'p_{38}' is small is expressed type-theoretically by saying that there is a proof of this fact. This corresponds to adding the entry:

pr_1 : small(p_{38})

(where 'pr_1' is an (arbitrary) name of the proof). We can now express the Cooperative Assistant's knowledge that pyramids have a colour, and that all pyramids have bright colours. We first extend the context with an entry representing a function, 'col', that associates colours to pyramids:

col : pyramid $\rightarrow$ colour

To represent that the colour of a pyramid is always bright type-theoretically, we have to express that for every pyramid we have a proof that its colour is bright. To this end we introduce a function f that, given a pyramid x, returns a proof that the colour of x is bright. In other words, f(x) is an object of type bright(col(x)). The following introduction achieves this:

f : Πx:pyramid.bright(col(x))

Combining all the above entries results in the following context, which represents the beliefs of the Cooperative Assistant about the domain:

[pyramid : entity , colour : entity ,
  p_{38} : pyramid ,
  small : pyramid $\rightarrow$ prop, bright : colour $\rightarrow$ prop ,
  pr_1 : small(p_{38}) ,
  col : pyramid $\rightarrow$ colour ,
  f : Πx:pyramid.bright(col(x))]

Once the information is represented in the form of a type-theoretical context, the Cooperative Assistant can make inferences by constructing new objects using the entries in the context. In fact, this representation can be used to support an effective proof construction method for type theory, combining resolution style proofs with natural deduction (Helmink & Ahn, 1991). The Cooperative Assistant incorporates a theorem prover based on this method.

4.3 Communication in Type Theory

The Cooperative Assistant is responsible for the communication with the user, i.e. it has to interpret the user's utterances and to generate appropriate responses. We mentioned above that the DENK system is based on a view of communication as change of local context change, where *local context* is viewed, following Dynamic Interpretation Theory, as the totality of information that may change through communication (Bunt, 1994). The full context that is relevant for the interpretation and generation of communicative behaviour has, besides this local part, also a *global part*, consisting of information that is not changed through communication. The DENK system, or rather the Cooperative Assistant, is viewed as an expert w.r.t. the application, so its beliefs about the application cannot be changed by the user; it forms part of the global context. The only possible change in application-related information is that the system comes to know that the user shares some belief with the system. This is then represented in Common, the CTT-subcontext containing the 'shared beliefs', In the current design of the DENK system, we therefore restrict the notion of 'local context' to the shared beliefs about the application domain, and represent this as a type-theoretical context. (Other kinds of local context information, such as information about the status of perceptual, interpretive and inferential processes, could in principle also be represented in type-theoretical form; see Bunt, 1997b.)

In order to interpret the user's utterances as context-changing actions, the Cooperative Assistant incorporates components for analysing utterances and representing their meanings in CTT. These are discussed in Sections 5 and 7. In the present section we consider the user-system communication at the formal level of type theory, i.e. for the moment we take the conversions between linguistic (and gestural) form and type theory for granted.

We consider three cases in which the Cooperative Assistant generates a pragmatically correct reply to an utterance of the user, using contextual information. In the first case the user makes a statement, in the second he asks a question; in both cases, we assume the information state of the Cooperative Assistant to be the one represented above, and we assume that all beliefs of the Cooperative Assistant are shared with the user, except for the constraint that every pyramid has a bright colour, which is a 'private' belief of the Cooperative Assistant. Note that the Cooperative Assistant is assumed to be an expert about the domain and that all declarative utterances about the domain contributed by the user are therefore interpreted not as statements but as verification questions.

Having inspected the visual representation of the state of the application domain on the screen, the user might produce the utterance:

"The pyramid is small."

In order to interpret this utterance, the Cooperative Assistant has to figure out which pyramid is meant. In view of the definiteness of the noun phrase, the Cooperative Assistant may consult both the application domain and shared beliefs. The Cooperative Assistant's private beliefs are irrelevant here, because the user cannot be aware of those, and hence cannot take them into account when producing a definite reference. The Cooperative Assistant will therefore assume that the user refers to the pyramid about which a shared belief is stored in his common context ('p_{38} : pyramid'). He will interpret the user's utterance as saying that there is evidence that $small(p_{38})$ holds. After checking the truth of this proposition in the application domain, the Cooperative Assistant extends his Common subcontext with the following entry;

e_5 : small(p_{38})

where e_5 labels the evidence the Cooperative Assistant has found for the proposition small(p_{38}). The Cooperative Assistant will give the answer *"yes"*, to indicate that he agrees. The proposition the pyramid is small becomes a shared belief of Cooperative Assistant and user. If, on the other hand, the Assistant can prove the proposition to be false, a *"no"* answer will be generated; if the Assistant cannot establish the truth of the proposition, for instance because no referent can be found for *"The pyramid"*, then this will be reported to the user.

Suppose that the next utterance of the user is:

"Is the colour of the pyramid bright?"

The communicative function of the utterance is a YES/NO-QUESTION; the user signals that he wants to know whether the proposition the pyramid is bright holds. The Cooperative Assistant complies with this wish by trying to construct an object for the proposition (bright(col(p_{38})). Using the theorem prover, the Cooperative Assistant succeeds in constructing such an object from the entries in his Private subcontext:

$f(p_{38})$: bright(col(p_{38}))

Because the question was a YES/NO-QUESTION, only the *existence* of a proof object matters. The Cooperative Assistant has found a proof object, hence the question will be answered affirmatively.

Had the user asked:

"Why is the colour of the pyramid bright?"

then the Cooperative Assistant would have been under the obligation to communicate how he came to believe bright(p_{38}). This is recorded in the proof object $f(p_{38})$; by the Gricean maxim of quantity the Cooperative Assistant should communicate only those ingredients of the proof that he does not believe to be already among the user's beliefs. By checking the Common context, the Cooperative Assistant can find out that the user already believes that there exists a pyramid (p_{38} : pyramid), and that it is small (e_5 : small(p_{38})). Hence, the Cooperative Assistant generates an answer from the only ingredient in his proof that is not in the Common context, viz. f : Πx:pyramid.bright(col(x)):

"Because every pyramid has a bright colour."

This answer is satisfactory since it provides the user with only the *new* information needed to infer how the Cooperative Assistant came to believe that the pyramid was bright.

In answering WH-QUESTIONS, other complications also occur. It may be particularly difficult to communicate the identity of an object, even if it occurs in the Common subcontext, because the message to the user should use the properties of the object to find a description that identifies the object unambiguously for the user. Which description is actually most appropriate is a complicated matter, depending on aspects such as the difference in salience of the properties of the objects, previous utterances, and domain focus (see Cremers, 1995; 1997). We have not yet implemented the generation of such answers; in the current implementation the Cooperative Assistant will simply 'point out' the desired object by highlighting it in the graphical domain representation on the screen.

5 Linguistic Interpretation and Dialogue Management

The user of the DeNK system communicates in natural language with the Cooperative Assistant, who is responsible for the analysis of the user's dialogue contributions and the decision of what actions (domain actions and communicative actions) to perform. The design of the Assistant is based on the view that dialogue participants use language to perform communicative acts, aimed at changing the addressee's cognitive state in certain ways. Two basic aspects of a communicative act are its *semantic content*, describing the information the speaker[6] introduces into the dialogue, and its *communicative function*, describing the particular way in which the addressee's cognitive state is to be updated with the semantic content.[7] The communicative function determines, together with the semantic content, the effects of the communicative act on the Cooperative Assistant's information state.

The Assistant thus has to interpret the user's utterances in terms of their communicative function(s) and semantic contents, has to consider updating its information state accordingly, and has to generate communicative acts and/or domain acts on the basis of its updated information state.

5.1 Syntactic and Semantic Analysis

In linguistic analysis, a distinction is traditionally made between morphosyntactic, semantic and pragmatic analysis. Syntactic analysis is aimed at decomposing a complex expression into its constituent parts; this is the typical job of a parser

---

[6] We use 'speaker' in a general sense here, to designate the participant whose contribution to the dialogue we are considering.

[7] The notions of 'semantic content' and 'communicative function' are obviously related to what in speech act theory are called 'propositional content' and 'illocutionary force'. For a definition of the concepts of 'communicative function' and 'semantic content' and a discussion of the difference with standard speech act concepts see Bunt (1997b).

(see e.g. Bunt and Tomita, 1996). Semantic analysis is concerned with the semantic consequences of the syntactic analysis in combination with the meanings of lexical items, and pragmatic analysis ties semantic analysis to aspects of the context of use. In the DENK project we have adopted the framework of *Head-driven Phrase Structure Grammar, HPSG* (Pollard & Sag, 1994) for linguistic analysis. This framework emphasizes the *integration* rather than the separation of these aspects of analysis; an HPSG parser does not build purely syntactic structures, but typed feature matrices which incorporate both syntactic, semantic, and pragmatic information.

Although HPSG presents an integrated approach to the representation of syntactic, semantic, and pragmatic information, the approach has been worked out primarily for syntactic analysis. Existing grammars in HPSG format have been developed to give detailed accounts of syntactic phenomena; for semantic phenomena this is much less so, and HPSG grammars that provide detailed treatments of pragmatic phenomena, i.e. give an account of how syntactic and semantic phenomena depend on context information, have hardly been developed at all. We have added semantic and pragmatic interpretation components to the standard form of HPSG analysis that are well suited to the DENK system, in particular to the maintenance of formal representations of dynamic information states.

The interpretation of a natural language expression depends, in general, not only on the syntactic structure of the expression and the meanings of the constituent lexical items, but also on the context of use. While acknowledging this, formal theories of natural language interpretation are unable to take context information into account in a substantial way, in the absence of articulate representations of context. In the DENK system we have such a representation, in the form of (a) a structured type-theoretical context recording the Cooperative Assistant's beliefs and the beliefs the Assistant takes to be shared with the user; (b) the visual display of objects and events in the application domain, as observable by the user and internally accessible by the Cooperative Assistant. The DENK system therefore provides an excellent basis for context-driven interpretation (and generation) of natural language utterances. We have designed such an interpretation process as consisting of two main stages:

1. A stage of context-independent interpretation, where the semantic consequences of morphosyntactic structure are made explicit;
2. A stage of context-dependent interpretation, where contextual information is taken into account in order to obtain contextually appropriate interpretations.

The first stage of this interpretation process produces representations in a format that is convenient for the second stage, which results in a type-theoretical representation (a CTT context). The intermediate format is called *'Underspecified Logical Form'*. ULF representations are allowed to be 'underspecified' in that they may leave open various aspects of the meaning of the natural language expression under consideration, such as the relative scopes of scope-bearing elements, the logical interpretation of natural language quantifiers, or the intended referents of anaphoric pronouns. (In fact, ULF representations leave open any aspect of meaning that cannot be decided on the basis of the syntactic evidence available in the utterance.) The ULF language has been designed by Kievit (1996), based on the representation language developed in the projects PLUS (Geurts & Rentier, 1993) and ΔELTA (see Rentier, 1993; Bunt, 1995b), and inspired in its general ideas by the Quasi-Logical Form language of the Core Language Engine (Alshawi, 1992).

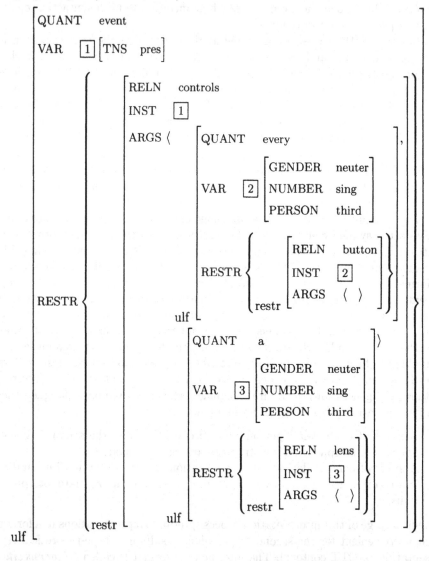

Feature structures of type ulf introduce three features: *quant, var,* and *descr.* The value of *quant* is a quantifier which we take to represent quantification over an event or an object. Such events and objects correspond to a variable, the value of *var,* which intuitively also corresponds to a discourse referent in the sense of

DRT. *Restr* takes as its values feature structures which have the features *reln* and *inst*, indicating a relation and an instance of this relation (the value of *inst* is token-identical to that of *var*). If the relation involves thematical dependents, then these are represented on a list called *args*, for 'arguments'. Since *args* takes values of type ulf, these typed feature structures are recursively defined.

The ULF for this utterance linearizes this feature structure as follows:

```
ulf(event,X,[tense:pres],[control(X,[
    ulf(every,Y,[pers:3d,num:sg,gend:neuter],[button(Y,[])]),
    ulf(a,Z,[pers:3d,num:sg,gend:neuter],[lens(Z,[])]) ])])
```

It may be noted that all the words of the original sentence occur in this representation: not just the content words (*button, control, lens*), but also the quantifiers *every, a*. None of these words have been interpreted in this stage, and the relative scopes of the two quantifiers is not specified. The second stage of the interpretation process uses a (heuristically strengthened) variant of the Hobbs-Shieber (1987) scoping algorithm to take into account the syntactic restrictions on possible relative scopes.

5.2   Pragmatics and Dialogue Management

The second, context-dependent stage of interpreting user utterances, has the aim to compute 'contextually appropriate' interpretations, relating content words to the concepts of the application domain, relating pronominal anaphors and definite descriptions to the objects the user intended to refer to, interpreting natural language quantifiers in terms of logical relations appropriate for the application task and domain, etc. To be 'appropriate', a contextual interpretation should in general be compatible with all the context information available to the interpreter. Note that this does not imply that a contextually appropriate interpretation is necessarily unambiguous. The Cooperative Assistant is assumed to be able to perform appropriate actions on the basis of its understanding of the user's utterance (or rather, on the basis of the change of its information state that resulted from this understanding), so the essential requirement with respect to ambiguity is that the Assistant should construct interpretations that are specific enough to enable it to act. If the interpretation process is unable to construct such an interpretation, it will engage in a subdialogue with the user in order to interactively disambiguate the user's utterance.

The end result of interpretation is the construction of a representation in type-theoretical form, which in itself is unambiguous. Still, such a representation may cover more than one reading of a sentence. For instance, suppose the user asks: *"Every button controls a lens?"*. Besides the intuitively more plausible reading where *"every"* has scope over *"a"*, there is also a reading which can be paraphrased as: *"Is there a lens such that every button controls it?"*. The latter reading is a special case of the former: also in this case does every button control one or more lenses; it just so happens that the buttons all share the control of one of these lenses. This reading can thus be viewed as 'narrowing' the more general former reading; in logical terms, the latter ('stronger') reading implies the ('weaker') former. Both readings can be represented in CTT; in the DENK system, when a ULF representation allows several readings, one of which is more general than the others, we transform the ULF into the CTT representation of that reading - unless contextual evidence calls for a narrower reading (see Ahn et al., 1995).

Type-theoretical representations, as constructed by the context-dependent stage of the interpretation process, bear some resemblance to the representations of Discourse Representation Theory (Kamp & Reyle, 1993). The variable x in an introduction x: t can be seen as corresponding to a discourse referent in DRT, and the type as corresponding to a predicate in a DRT condition. The following example illustrates the possible use of CTT for semantic representation.

Consider the sentence *"A farmer laughs"*. The NP gives rise to an introduction of the form x: farmer, but farmer has to be introduced first to obtain a well-formed context. So we get, initially:

[farmer : class, x : farmer]

The VP corresponds to a predicate, applicable to farmers, and must be introduced as such, i.e. as a function from farmers to propositions:[8]

laugh : farmer → prop

We can now complete the CTT representation of the sentence by adding the statement that corresponds to the condition laugh(x) in DRT, to obtain the context:

[farmer : class, x : farmer, laugh : farmer → prop, e : laugh(x)]

This can be read as: farmers are objects (as opposed to propositions); x is a farmer; laughing is a property that farmers may have; there is evidence that x laughs. A CTT analysis of a sentence or a discourse thus introduces objects of various kinds and adds them to the context that grows incrementally as the discourse proceeds, similar to what happens in DRT. In fact, Ahn & Kolb (1991) have shown that CTT-contexts can be regarded as generalizations of DRSs.

During the contextual interpretation of utterances, one of the important things the Cooperative Assistant has to do is to link objects mentioned by the user to entities in the application domain. In the case of a definite reference, like *"the red block"*, the Cooperative Assistant looks for a specific red block that has

---

[8] For a systematic translation between DRT and CTT it is more convenient to construct somewhat more complex CTT representations, treating both nominal predicates (like *farmer*) and verbal predicates (like *laugh*) as function types (from *class* to *prop*). This would give rise to a CTT context like: [f_1 : class, farmer: Πx:class.prop, laugh: Πx:class.prop, pr_1: farmer(f_1), pr_2: laugh(f_1)].

been introduced in the dialogue before and therefore belongs to the Assistant's shared beliefs, or that can be detected in an unambiguous way in the current state of the discourse domain by inspecting its visual representation. In the case of an indirect reference, as in *"Move a red block"*, no specific object needs to be identified, and the choice of the object is left to the Assistant.

New variables that arise from the introduction of definite and indefinite objects in the discourse are linked to entities in the domain by means of so-called 'satisfying assignments (Ahn & Kolb, 1991). For instance, the variable that results from interpreting *"the red block"* has to be linked to a suitable object in the Cooperative Assistant's shared beliefs; if the link can be established, the user can refer anaphorically to the object in subsequent utterances. If no such link can be established for instance because there is no such object, the Cooperative Assistant generates feedback to signal this.

Another crucial aspect of context-dependent interpretation concerns the assignment of communicative functions to user utterances. Formally, the interpretation of a user utterance results not just in a CTT expression, but in a pair of two expressions, each belonging to a well-defined formal language. Such pairs are called *annotated segments* (Piwek, 1995). The CTT expression in an annotated segment is a so-called 'CTT segment' and is defined as follows: if a nonempty CTT context Γ is split into two parts, Γ_1 and Γ_2, where Γ_1 is a legal context, then Γ_2 is a CTT segment. In other words, a segment represents certain information that is meaningful with regard to a given context. Annotations are sets of feature-value pairs that tell the system what to do with the information represented in the CTT segment. An annotation contains, for instance, the information whether the user's utterance is an assertion, a command, or a question. (This depends on syntactic properties of the utterance, as represented in its ULF, but also on the knowledge of the user's information state; see Beun, 1989.) Other information represented in an annotation is that certain variables, originating from anaphoric expressions, need to be bound. Using annotated segments, Beun and Kievit (1996) have developed a powerful algorithm for the contextual resolution of definite descriptions, taking into account the referential behaviour of participants in DENK-like situations as observed by Cremers (1995), which uses both the contextual information available in the CTT representation of the current information state and that available in the visual representation of the domain.

Having decided what to do with the semantic content of the user utterance, and extended its current information state accordingly, the Cooperative Assistant has to generate an adequate reaction. For that purpose, we consider the user's goals as established in the form of the communicative functions and the semantic content of the users's utterance. In the implemented DK-1 prototype we have assumed a simple and straightforward relation between an utterance's communicative functions and the underlying user goals: commands are used to change the state of the application domain and questions are used to obtain certain information about the domain. The eventual DK-system will incorporate more sophisticated pragmatic rules that take multifunctionality, indirectness, and dialogue control phenomena into account (cf. Beun, 1991; Bunt, 1994; 1995a).

The Cooperative Assistant considers two types of action in response to the user's communicative behaviour:

- domain acts, that are directed towards a change in the state of the domain;
- communicative acts, that are directed towards a change in the information state of the user (represented as the Cooperative Assistant's shared beliefs).

Domain acts are generated in reaction to a user command, such as *"Remove the blue block"*. In those cases, the Cooperative Assistant has to find the procedure that corresponds to the given command and that can be executed by the domain application.

The interpretation process can only be executed successfully if certain conditions are fulfilled. For instance, all content words in the user's utterances should be interpretable in terms of elements in that part of the Cooperative Assistant's information state that represents shared beliefs. If the user makes assumptions that are not part of the Assistant's beliefs (private or shared), these will be corrected by the Assistant, by means of corrective dialogue acts. For instance, to answer the question *"Why is the red block rotating?"* the Cooperative Assistant looks for a uniquely identifiable red block in the shared beliefs or in the visual domain model before the answer can be provided. If no such object is available, the Assistant generates a correction action. If the interpretation process is successful, this means in practice that the Cooperative Assistant can try to provide an answer to a user question, or to execute certain domain actions.

6   Visual Domain Modeling

In order to support multimodal interaction, an animation system that presents a convincing real-time view of the application domain must meet the following requirements:

1. interrogation of the domain status has to be allowed at any time, i.e. asynchronously with respect to the time evolution of the animation;
2. the display image has to be refreshed continuously, so that the user receives visual feedback irrespective of the state of the dialogue;
3. the user can at any time refer to elements of the visual model both via the Cooperative Assistant and via direct manipulation;
4. for generic support for a large variety of application domains:
   (a) instructions should be available to create objects[9] (both their geometrical shape and their autonomous motion behaviour) and to pass messages to

---

[9] We use terminology from object-oriented programming here. An 'object' is a variable containing data (its 'attributes') and optionally some program fragments (its 'methods'). Calling a method of an object is referred to as passing a 'message' to that object. An object is an instantiation of a 'class'; the class definition lists all available attributes and methods for objects in this class.

objects to alter their properties and behaviour; objects also have to be able to pass messages to each other;

(b) to facilitate programming complex behaviour, e.g., the motions of mechanical devices, of grasping an object, a library of versatile built-in motion methods must be available.

In order to meet these requirements, we have developed an architecture called the *Generalized Display Processor, GDP* (van Overveld, 1991); see below, Section 7.2.

For programming the GDP, i.e. for defining the classes of objects inhabiting a domain, for creating such objects, for programming motion methods, for passing messages, etc. the language LOOKS (Language for Object Oriented Kinematic Simulations) has been defined and implemented (Peeters, 1994). LOOKS supports a variety of object-oriented features, such as data hiding, abstract data types, strong typing, genericity and multiple repeated inheritance; it also implements (quasi-)parallellism to facilitate the specification of concurrent motions. See further below, Section 7.2.

7   DENK System Architecture

According to the DENK 'triangle view', the DK-1 prototype system consists of two relatively independent components: the Cooperative Assistant and the Application Model. We outline the design each of these components in the next two sections. The architecture of the eventual DK-2 system will be an elaboration of this design.

7.1   The Cooperative Assistant

The heart of the DK-1 system is formed by the software components implementing the Cooperative Assistant, shown in Fig. 2. These are the following:

Parser: A parser for natural language, with an implemented natural language fragment.[10] After considering a number of alternatives, the publicly available *Attribute Logic Engine (ALE)* (Carpenter, 1994) was chosen for HPSG-based analysis. The standard HPSG analysis was modified so that the parser delivers underspecified logical form representations. This is only a modification in representation *format*; the 'Semantics Principle' of HPSG, that accounts for the construction of semantic representations during constraint-based parsing, has only been modified so as to work with the modified representations, but has otherwise remained unchanged.

---

[10] In the DK-1 system, the implemented natural language fragment is a toy fragment of Dutch. For the DK-system under construction, the form of natural language is typed English with certain syntactic, semantic and pragmatic limitations reflecting the properties of the tasks and the domain of the application (see Verlinden, 1996).

The implemented ULF language forms the interface between the parser and the Pragmatic Rule Interpreter.

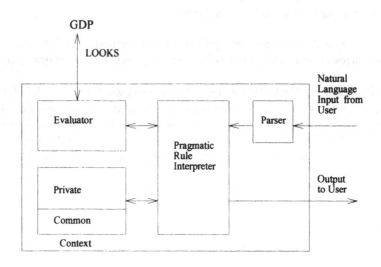

Fig. 2. Architecture of the Cooperative Assistant in the DK-1 system.

Pragmatic Rule Interpreter: A variety of 'pragmatic' rules of various kinds for aspects of context-dependent interpretation (quantifier scoping, referent determination, etc.), for updating the system's information state, and for generating appropriate (re-)actions, needed by the Cooperative Assistant for its operation. In the DK-1 prototype system, only very small sets of rules have been implemented, and the application of these rules is performed in a rather ad hoc manner by the '**Pragmatic Rules Interpreter**' component (see also below, the section Conclusions and Future Work).

For using and updating context information, represented in CTT, and handling information extracted from user utterances and expressed in CTT, a proof checker and a reasoning system for type theory have been implemented. The proof checker checks whether a type-theoretical context is well-formed, in particular whether all expressions in the context under consideration are correctly typed. This checker is based on theoretical work in type theory; see e.g. Barendregt, 1991. The reasoning system for type theory, based on the work of Helmink and Ahn (1991), incorporates strategies for combining type-theoretical deduction steps in order to facilitate effective reasoning with modal information. (In the DK-1 system, only the epistemic modalities of (simple) belief and believed shared belief are considered; in the DK-2 system, temporal modalities will also be handled.)

An implemented 'Conceptual Lexicon' relates ULF predicates to the predicates and types defined in the CTT model of the DK-1 domain. ULF predicates have a straightforward correspondence to natural language content words; the Conceptual Lexicon indirectly relates these words to the concepts of the application domain.

Context: A representation of the Cooperative Assistant's information state in the form of a CTT context. Two epistemic modalities are distinguished in this representation, involving two agents: belief and assumed shared beliefs. The CTT context as a whole represents the beliefs of the Cooperative Assistant; those beliefs that the Assistant believes to be shared with the user form the subcontext Common; the other beliefs form the subcontext Private. This representation is based on theoretical work in type theory by Borghuis (1994).

A model of the DK-1 blocks world has been formalized in Constructive Type Theory and implemented. This model specifies the classes of objects in the domain (pyramids, cubes, colours,..), the predicates that apply to these objects (colour, size, motion, brightness,..), and the constraints that hold in the domain, e.g. the fact that all pyramids have bright colours (see the example context in Section 4.2). This model cannot be changed in a dialogue, and since the user is assumed to know the application domain, it forms a static part of Common. It also seems plausible to assume that the user knows the concepts (object classes, predicates) of the application, hence this information forms part of Common.

Evaluator: An evaluator for converting an expression in type theory into LOOKS (see the next section) and for accessing the visual domain model in order to compute the values of these expressions, given the current state of the domain as represented by the GDP. This involves translating type-theoretical expressions into combinations of the application domain primitives used by the GDP.

The Cooperative Assistant's communicative behaviour is controlled by the Pragmatic Rule Interpreter, which produces a simple form of cooperative behaviour using three types of contextual information:

1. the information state represented in Context;
2. the most recent (communicative) action performed by the user (this act is kept on a local stack, accessible to the Pragmatic Rule Interpreter);
3. the current state of the application domain as represented by the GDP.

First, the interpreter analyses the user's utterance within the current dialogue context and, if no communication failures are noted, it updates Context with the new information in a way determined by the communicative function of the utterance. If the communicative function of the utterance is a command, a domain-related action is performed; if the function is a question, the question is answered, or appropriately responded to if no straight answer can be given. Since the Cooperative Assistant is considered to be an expert about the domain, he does not accept new domain information from the user, and interprets declarative statements about the domain as (verification) questions (see Beun, 1989).

7.2   The Generalized Display Processor (GDP)

The GDP, implementing the Application Model, is a generic emulator for visual domain representation, which is capable of simulating a domain given a formal definition in LOOKS. For its architecture, the GDP can be viewed as a virtual processor consisting of a parser, an interpreter, rendering support, and a database.

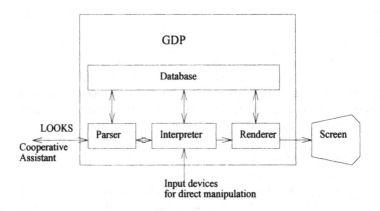

Fig. 3. The Generalized Display Processor.

The parser provides for the communication with the Cooperative Assistant; it checks the incoming information and, if necessary, sends messages back from the interpreter to the Cooperative Assistant. The interpreter calculates the values of the attributes of the objects (e.g. position, speed) in order to generate a new frame of animation, which is displayed on screen by means of the renderer.[11] The behaviour of the objects may be autonomous, or dictated by the Cooperative Assistant or by input devices for direct manipulation (e.g. the mouse).

At any discrete time, a complete description of all geometrical attributes of a moving scene is stored in the database. The database consists of two tables: the class table and the object table. The class table contains the class definitions that state which attributes exist for a particular class as well as which methods

---

[11] Provided the time granularity of the animation is sufficiently small and the renderer is sufficiently fast, the impression of a moving display results.

it may execute.[12] The object table contains the actual objects in the application domain, i.e. instantiations of existing classes.

At any time, fragments of LOOKS may be passed to the parser. Such a fragment can be either a class definition, an object definition or a message. If this fragment is successfully parsed, and if it was a

class definition, then an entry is created in the class table. Apart from the user-defined classes, LOOKS supports a variety of pre-defined classes, including integers, reals, vectors, movable geometric objects, cameras, (coloured) light sources, windows, etc.;

object definition, then an entry is created in the object table;

message to an object, then the corresponding method is handed to the interpreter to be executed.

To enable interaction between the Cooperative Assistant and the GDP via LOOKS (see Fig. 4), a close relation must be established between LOOKS and the type-theoretical formalism used by the Assistant. Type-theoretical expressions are virtually semantically grounded in LOOKS, and the translation from CTT to LOOKS comes down to a standard evaluation process,[13] where complex type-theoretical expressions are expanded into basic expressions that can be interpreted in LOOKS.

In order to generate a frame of animation, the interpreter installs a method it receives from the parser into the list of active methods and executes the methods it encounters. Most active methods can be fully executed (e.g. assignments, expression evaluations, object transformations), after which they are removed from the list.

Methods may, however, also contain a 'synchronize' statement (typically within the body of an (infinite) loop). Execution of an active method proceeds until it is either fully executed, or until a 'synchronize' is encountered. In the latter case, execution stops, but the method is kept in the list; it will again receive the interpreter's attention when preparing the next frame. Since several methods may contain a 'synchronize', several of which may be kept in the active method list simultaneously, the synchronize mechanism may serve to achieve quasi-parallelism.

Also, the execution of a method, due to passing an asynchronous message, may invoke the execution of another method by calling this method. The latter method is also put into the list of active methods, and it will be executed as well during the preparation of the frame.

If no more active methods can proceed any further, the preparation of the frame is complete, and a snapshot of the objects is rendered into the active

---

[12] A class may be defined from 'scratch' or it may inherit attributes and/or methods from other classes. The types of its attributes, as well as the types of the formal parameters in its method headings and the return types of its methods may either be earlier defined classes or generic types.

[13] See also the 'Evaluator' in Fig. 2.

window(s) with respect to the active virtual camera(s), making use of the active light sources and simulated material properties (colour, shininess, etc.).

Part of the preparation of each frame is also the taking into account of user interaction. Via mouse events and appropriate LOOKS system methods, the user may interact with the ongoing animation (e.g. selecting an object and calling the mouse notifier method that has been assigned to this object).

The current GDP-implementation is designed to run on a high-end graphics workstation where it produces a flicker-free display of shaded images, illuminated by simulated light sources, consisting of several hundreds of polygons with a frame update rate between 15 and 20 frames/sec. It covers most of the requirements and functionality as described above; direct manipulation interaction tools and versatile built-in motion methods are presently under construction.

8   Conclusions and Future Work

Following an 'inside-out' strategy, the DENK project has first developed a formal model of communication in terms of changing cognitive states and an implementation of this model in a first prototype system. The formalization in constructive type theory of the context-change model of communication, of which the conceptual basis is provided by Dynamic Interpretation Theory, opens up a way to make progress in dealing with context as one of the major factors contributing to the determination of the meaning of communicative behaviour.

The DENK-approach to user interface design enables one to formulate and to implement rules for cooperative behaviour, independent of a particular application domain or a particular mix of communicative modalities. The DENK design originates from the desire to establish *natural communication* between the application domain and its user, largely independent of the surface structures forms of messages. Well-known phenomena in natural language semantics and pragmatics, such as the context dependence of messages, the use of definite and indefinite reference, the Gricean maxims for cooperative linguistic behaviour, and the use of deixis, can be shown to follow naturally from the fundamental properties of communication viewed as intended change of context. Even the relatively simple model of communication and context implemented in the DK-1 prototype system, presented in this chapter, can be useful in dealing with such phenomena, as the work on resolving definite expressions by Beun & Kievit (1996) demonstrates.

The DK-1 system is primarily interesting as the implementation of a formal backbone of a generic cooperative communication system, with its powerful approach to context modeling in type theory connected to representation formalisms for natural language semantics and visual domain representation. Future (and current) work building on this basis goes in three directions:

Continuation of the inside-out strategy. Moving more to the outer sides of interaction, a substantial and useful fragment of English, based on empirical studies (such as Cremers, 1995) will be defined with corresponding ULF extensions. A set of direct manipulation acts will be specified to allow the user to act directly on the (visual representation of the) application domain, with consequences that the Cooperative Assistant notes by internal inspection of the domain.

Perhaps the most crucial step in outward direction to be taken, to achieve a basis of truly cooperative multimodal interaction, is the development of the pragmatic rules and procedures for their application in the Cooperative Assistant. This is in particular the case with the rules used the Assistant to generate communicative acts, and with the rules and procedures for interpreting combined use of input modalities by the user. The work by Beun and Kievit on reference resolution (Beun & Kievit, 1996) forms a first step in this direction. Continued work in this area is expected to result in a structuring of the Pragmatic Rule Interpreter into several submodules, interacting using annotated segments as interface language.

Inward refinement. The CTT, ULF, and LOOKS formalisms provide a solid basis for developing cooperative human-computer interfaces, but are still in need of improvement. The CTT formalism as developed in the DENK project extends standard type theory with two epistemic modalities associated with two agents (simple belief and believed shared belief), which is the minimal epistemic variation needed to account for context-driven information exchange. To account for more subtle forms of information exchange, additional epistemic modalities have to be considered. Perhaps more urgently, the time dependence of elements in belief contexts will be taken into account in an enhanced version of CTT.

Continued implementation of the inside-out strategy. The extensions of CTT just mentioned (as well as some others) will be implemented in the DK-2 system, affecting Context as well as the reasoning and proof checking procedures used by the Cooperative Assistant.

The domain of electron microscope operation will be formalized in CTT and implemented both in the Context and Evaluator components in the Cooperative Assistant, as in LOOKS and the GDP.

Implementation of the fragment of English defined for this domain (both for user input and for Cooperative Assistant output), in combination with the direct manipulation possibilities offered to the user, will give the system and the user the interactive modalities required for making full use of the implementation of the 'triangle view' of natural interaction with a simulated application domain.

Acknowledgements

We would like to thank the organization for inter-university cooperation between the universities of Tilburg and Eindhoven ("Samenwerkingsorgaan Brabantse Universiteiten") for providing funds to make the DENK project possible. The research reported here is carried out in the Language Technology and Artificial Intelligence Group of the Faculty of Arts at Tilburg University, in the Department of Mathematics and Computer Science at Eindhoven University of Technology, and at the Center for User-System Research IPO in Eindhoven. The participating institutions have all supported the DENK project financially and in other ways.

The following people have contributed to the DENK project: René Ahn, Robbert-Jan Beun, Gino van den Bergen, Tijn Borghuis, Anita Cremers, Frens Dols, Jan Jaspars, Leen Kievit, Paul Piwek, Eric Peeters, Gerrit Rentier, and Margriet Verlinden (mostly in PhD projects), and Rita Roelfs and Liesbeth Melby in providing programming support. Supervision of parts of the project has been given by Jos Baeten, Don Bouwhuis, Rob Nederpelt, and Kees van Overveld; Harry Bunt is overall project leader.

A word of special thanks goes to Hugo van Leeuwen from Philips Electron Optics, for most valuable support in developing the electron microscope training simulation application of the DENK system.

References

Ahn, R. (1995a) Communicating Contexts, a Pragmatic Approach to Information Exchange. In: P. Dybjer, B. Nordström, & J. Smith (eds.) *Types for Proofs and Programs: Selected Papers*. Berlin: Springer, 1–13.

Ahn, R. (1995b) Logical Model of the Electron Microscope. *DenK Report* 95/15, Tilburg University.

Ahn, R. (1996) Monotonic description of dynamic worlds. In: *Proc. NIAC'96 Conference* (forthc.)

Ahn, R. & Kolb, H.P. (1990) Discourse Representation meets Constructive Mathematics. In: Kálmán, L. & Pólos, L. (eds.) *Papers from the Second Symposium on Logic and Language*, Akademiai Kiadó, Budapest, 105–124.

Ahn, R., Kievit, L., Rentier, M. Verlinden, M. (1995) Two Levels of Semantic Representation in DENK. In: T. Andernach, M. Moll & A. Nijholt (eds.) *Papers from the Fifth CLIN Meeting*. Universiteit Twente, 35–58.

Ahn, R. & Borghuis, T. (1996) Chronicle. *DenK Report* 96/21, Tilburg University.

Allwood, J. (1976) *Linguistic Communication as Action and Cooperation*. Gothenburg Monographs in Linguistics 2, University of Göteborg.

Allwood, J. (1997) An Activity-Based Approach to Pragmatics. In: Black, W.J. & Bunt, H.C. (eds.) *Abduction, Belief and Context, Studies in Computational Pragmatics*, University College London Press (forthc.)

Alshawi, H. (1992) *The Core Language Engine*, Cambridge: Cambridge University press.

Austin, J.L. (1962) *How to do things with words*. Oxford: Oxford University Press.

Barendregt, H. (1991) Introduction to Generalized Type Systems. *Journal of Functional Programming, 1(2)*. 125-154.

Barendregt, H. (1992) Lambda calculi with types. In: S. Abramsky, D. Gabbay and T. Maibaum (eds.) *Handbook of Logic in Computer Science*. oxford: Oxford University Press.

Beun, R.J. (1989) *The Recognition of Declarative Questions in Information Dialogues*. PhD Dissertation, Tilburg University.

Beun, R.J. (1991) A Framework for Cooperative Dialogues. In: Taylor, M.M., Néel, F. & Bouwhuis, D.G. (eds.) *Proceedings of the Second Venaco Workshop on the Structure of Multimodal Dialogue*. Maratea, Italy.

Beun, R.J. & Kievit, L.A. (1996) Resolving definite expressions in dialogue. In: *Proc. Fifth Int. Conference on Pragmatics*, Mexico City, July 1996.

Borghuis, T. (1993) Interpreting Modal Natural Deduction in type theory. In: de Rijke, M. (ed.) *Diamonds and Defaults*. Kluwer Academic Publishers. 67-102.

Borghuis, T. (1994) *Coming to Terms with Modal Logic: On the Interpretation of Modalities in Typed λ-Calculus*. Ph.D. Dissertation, Eindhoven University of Technology.

De Bruijn, N.G. (1980) A survey of the project Automath. In: Seldin & Hindley (eds.) *To H.B. Curry: Essays on Combinatory Logic, Lambda Calculus and Formalisms*. Academic Press. 579-606.

Bunt, H.C. (1989) Information dialogues as communicative action in relation to partner modeling and information processing. In: Taylor, M.M., Néel, F. & Bouwhuis, D.G. (eds.) *The Structure of Multimodal Dialogue*. North-Holland, Amsterdam. 47-73.

Bunt, H.C. (1991) DIT - Dynamic Interpretation in Text and Dialogue. In: L. Kálm'an & L. Pólos (eds.) *Papers from the Second Symposium on Logic and Language*, Budapest: Akademiai Kiadó, 67-104.

Bunt, H.C. (1994) Context and Dialogue Control. *THINK Quarterly 3(1)*, 19-31.

Bunt, H.C. (1995a) Dialogue Control Functions and Interaction Design. In R.J. Beun, M. Baker, and M. Reiner (eds.) *Dialogue and Instruction: Modelling Interaction in Intelligent Tutoring Systems*. Berlin: Springer, 197-214.

Bunt, H.C. (1995b) Dialogue Semantics and Pragmatics in the ΔELTA Project. In: L. Dybkjaer (ed.) *Proc. of the Second on Spoken Dialogue and Discourse Workshop*, Roskilde University, 1-27.

Bunt, H.C. (1997a) Dialogue Context Modeling. In: *Proc. CONTEXT'97, International Interdisciplinary Conference on Modeling and Using Context*, Rio de Janeiro, February 1997, 130-150.

Bunt, H.C. (1997b) Iterative Context Specification and Dialogue Theory. In: Black, W.J. & Bunt, H.C. (eds.) *Abduction, Belief and Context, Studies in Computational Pragmatics*, University College London Press (forthc.)

Burger, J.D. & Marshall, R.J. (1993) The application of natural language models to intelligent multimedia. In: Mayburry, M. (ed.) *Intelligent Multimedia Interfaces*. Massachusetts: MIT Press, 174-196.

Carpenter, R. (1982) *The Logic of Typed Feature Structures*. Cambridge: Cambridge University Press.

Coquand, T. (1985) *Une théorie des constructions*. Thèse de troisième cycle. Paris: Université de Paris VII.

Cremers, A.H.M. (1995) *Reference to Objects: An Empirical Investigation of Task-oriented dialogues*. PhD Dissertation, Eindhoven University of Technology.

Cremers, A.H.M. (1997) Object Reference in Task-oriented Keyboard Dialogues. *This volume*.

Curry, H.B. & Feys R. (1958) *Combinatory Logic, Vol. 1*, North Holland Publishing Company.

Geurts, B. & Rentier, G. (1993) The PLUS Grammar. Internal Report ESPRIT Project PLUS, Institute for Language Technology and Artificial Intelligence ITK, Tilburg.

Helmink, L. & Ahn, R. (1991) Goal-oriented proof construction in type theory. In: Huet, G. and Plotkin, G. (eds.) *Logical Frameworks.* Cambridge: Cambridge University Press, 120–148.

Hobbs, J.R. & Shieber, S.M. (1987) An algorithm for generating quantifier scopings. *Computational Linguistics* 13 (1–2), 47–63.

Hutchins, E. (1989) Metaphors for Interface Design. In: Taylor, M.M., Néel, F. & Bouwhuis, D.G. (eds.) *The Structure of Multimodal Dialogue.* Amsterdam: North-Holland, 11–28.

Jaspars, J.O.M. (1993) *Calculi for Constructive Communication.* Ph.D. Dissertation, Institute for Language Technology and Artificial Intelligence ITK, Tilburg.

Kamp, J.A.W. & Reyle, U. (1993) From Discourse to Logic: Introduction to Modeltheoretic Semantics of Natural Language, Formal Logic and Discourse Representation Theory. Dordrecht: Kluwer Academic Publishers.

Kievit, L.A. (1996) ULF. DenK Report 96/27, Tilburg University.

Martin-Löf P. (1984) *Intuitionistic Type Theory.* Naples: Bibliopolis.

Neal, J.G. & Shapiro, S.C. (1991) Intelligent multimedia interface technology. In: Sullivan, J.W. & Taylor, S.W. (eds.) *Intelligent User Interfaces.* Reading, MA: Addison-Wesley, 11–43.

Overveld, C.W.A.M. van (1991) The Generalized Display Processor as an approach to real time interactive 3-D computer animation. *The Journal of Visualisation and Computer Animation, 2(1),* 16–21.

Peeters, E.A.J. (1994) *Design of an object-oriented interactive animation system.* PhD Dissertation, Eindhoven University of Technology.

Pollard, C. & Sag, I. (1994) *Head-driven Phrase Structure Grammar.* University of Chicago Press.

Rentier, G. (1993) ULF. ΔELTA *Working Paper, May 1994,* ITK, Tilburg University.

Searle, J.R. (1969) *Speech Acts.* Cambridge: Cambridge University Press.

de Souza, C.S. (1993) The semiotic engineering of user interface languages. *International Journal of Man-Machine Studies, 39,* 753–774.

Verlinden, M. (1996) Development of the cores syntax for DENK. DENK Report 96/22, Tilburg University.

Wahlster, W., André, E., Finkler, W., Profitlich, H.-J. & Rist, T. (1993) Plan-based integration of natural language and graphics generation. *Artificial Intelligence, 63,* 387–427.

Wilson, M.D., Sedlock, D., Binot, J-L. & Falzon, P. (1991) An architecture for multimodal dialogue. In: Taylor, M.M., Néel, F. & Bouwhuis, D.G. (eds.) *Proceedings of the Second Venaco Workshop on the Structure of Multimodal Dialogue.* Maratea, Italy.

Synthesizing Cooperative Conversation

Catherine Pelachaud[1][*], Justine Cassell[2], Norman Badler[1], Mark Steedman[1], Scott Prevost[1], and Matthew Stone[1]

[1] Department of Computer and Information Science, University of Pennsylvania,
200 S. 33rd street, Philadelphia, PA 19104.
`Pelachau@graphics.cis.upenn.edu`
[2] M.I.T. Media Lab, 20 Ames Street, Cambridge, MA 02139.

Abstract. We describe an implemented system which *automatically* generates and animates conversations between multiple human-like agents with appropriate and synchronized speech, intonation, facial expressions, and hand gestures. Conversations are created by a dialogue planner that produces the text as well as the intonation of the utterances. The speaker/listener relationship, the text, and the intonation in turn drive facial expressions, lip motions, eye gaze, head motion, and arm gesture generators.

1 Introduction

Conversation is an interaction between agents, who cooperate to achieve mutual goal using spoken language (words and contextually appropriate intonation marking topic and focus), facial movements (lip shapes, emotions, gaze direction, head motion), and hand gestures (handshapes, points, beats, and motions representing the topic of accompanying speech). Without being able to deploy all of these verbal and non-verbal behaviors, a virtual agent cannot be realistic, believable. To limit the problems (such as voice and face recognition, and conversational inference) that arise from the involvement of a real human conversant we have developed a dialogue generation system in which two copies of an identical program, differing only in their specific knowledge of the world, must cooperate to accomplish a goal. Both agents of the conversation collaborate via the dialogue to construct a simple plan of action. They interact with each other to propose goals, exchange information, and ask questions.

The work presented builds on a considerable body of research on the relation between gesture, facial expression, discourse meaning and intonation. Most of this research has been purely descriptive lacking any formal theory relating form to discourse meaning. We present a fragment of a theory which allows us to control and verify the communicative models. The development of such a formal theory is as central a goal of the research as is its exploitation in animation. We have used it to develop a high-level programming language for 3D animation,

---

[*] The original version of the paper was written while this author was working at the Università di Roma "La Sapienza".

which we view as a tool to investigate gestural and facial behavior together with spoken intonation, within the context of a dialog.

This language allows users to *automatically animate conversations between multiple human-like agents with appropriate and synchronized speech, intonation, facial expressions, and hand gestures.* In people, speech, facial expressions, and gestures are all the reflection of a single system of meaning. While an expert animator may realize this unconsciously in the "look" of a properly animated character, a program to automatically generate motions must embed this knowledge in a system of rules. A fuller report of some aspects of this work appears in Cassell et al. (1994a) and Cassell et al. (1994b).

1.1   Literature on Facial Animation

Various systems have been proposed for facial animation. Since animating faces manually is very tedious and requires the skill of a talented animator, parameterized, rule-based or analysis-based approaches have been studied.

The set of parameters from Parke's (1982) model distinguished conformation parameters from expression parameters. This set was then extended by adding speech parameters to include lip synchronization (Hill, Pearce, and Wyvill, 1988; Pearce, Wyvill, and Hill, 1986; Nahas, Huitric, and Saintourens, 1988). Cohen and Massaro (1993) use overlapping dominance functions to consider coarticulation phenomenon.

Rule-based systems are based on a set of rules to drive automatically the animation. Multi level structures offer a higher level animation language (Kalra et al., 1991; Patel and Willis, 1991). At the lower level the deformation controller simulates muscle actions by moving some control points. At the higher level the expression controller defines facial expression and lip shape for sentences.

Greater realism at the expense of synthetic control comes from analysis-based techniques which extract information from live-animation. The computed movement information is interpreted as muscle contractions and is given as input to the animation system (Essai and Pentland, 1994; Terzopoulos and Waters, 1993).

Takeuchi and Nagao (1993) propose a categorization of facial expressions depending on their communicative meaning, and implement this framework in a user-interface where a 3D synthetic actor recognizes the words pronounced by a user and generates a response with the appropriate facial displays.

1.2   Literature on Gesture Animation

A "Key-framing" technique is commonly used to create arm and hand motions. Rijpkema and Girard (1991) created handshapes automatically based on the object being gripped. The Thalmanns (Gourret, Magnenat-Thalmann, and Thalmann, 1989; Magnenat-Thalmann and Thalmann, 1991) improved on the hand model to include much better skin models and deformations of the finger tips and the gripped object. Lee and Kunii (1992) built a system that includes handshapes and simple pre-stored facial expressions for American Sign Language (ASL) synthesis. Dynamics of arm gestures in ASL have been studied by Loomis et al. (1983). Chen et al. (1993) constructed a virtual human that can shake hands with an interactive participant. Lee et al. (1990) automatically generate lifting gestures by considering strength and comfort measures. Moravec and Calvert (1991) constructed a system that portrays the gestural interaction between two agents as they pass and greet one another. Behavioral parameters were set by personality attribute "sliders" though the interaction sequence was itself predetermined and limited to just one type of non-verbal encounter.

1.3   Literature on Dialog and Intonation Generation

Generation of natural language is an active area of current research, comprising several independent subproblems. In a high-level phase, generation systems typically identify, organize and sequence material to be presented to determine the overall structure of a contribution to discourse (e.g., Hovy, 1988; Moore and Paris,1989). An intermediate process then structures ideas into sentence-sized units and determines words and referring expressions to use (e.g., Dale, 1989; Meteer, 1991). A final phase realizes the resulting structures as sentences using linguistic knowledge (e.g. Shieber et al., 1990). A good survey of how these tasks are performed in a several recent systems can be found in Reiter (1994).

A few other researchers have attempted to automatically generate both sides of a dialogue (Power, 1977; Houghton, 1986; Biermann et al., 1993; Guinn, 1993; Walker 1993) and to generate communication in the form of text and illustration presented simultaneously (Feiner and McKeown, 1990; Wahlster et al., 1991). Generating speech and gesture for conversations between two animated agents requires a synthesis of techniques in both areas.

A number of researchers have investigated the problem of automatically generating intonational contours in natural language generation systems. Early work by Terken (1984) is concerned with determining relative levels of givenness for discourse entities and applying pitch accents accordingly. The Direction Assistance program, designed by Davis and Hirschberg (1988) determines a route and provides spoken directions for traveling between two points on a map, assigning pitch accent in the synthesized speech based on semantic notions of givenness. Work by Houghton, Isard and Pearson (1987;1988) undertakes the similar task of assigning intonation to computer-generated, goal-directed dialogues. More recently, Zacharski et al. (1993) have proposed a system for generating utterances and appropriate intonation in map-task dialogues.

1.4   Example

In this section of the paper we present a fragment of dialogue (the complete dialogue has been synthesized and animated), in which intonation, gesture, head and lip movements, and their inter-synchronization were automatically generated. This example will serve to demonstrate the phenomena described here, and in subsequent sections we will return to each phenomenon to explain how rule-generation and synchronization are carried out.

In the following dialogue, imagine that Gilbert is a bank teller, and George has asked Gilbert for help in obtaining $50. The dialogue is unnaturally repetitive and explicit in its goals because the dialogue generation program that produced it has none of the conversational inferences that allow human conversationalists to follow leaps of reasoning. Therefore, the two agents have to specify in advance each of the goals they are working towards and steps they are following (see Sect. 2.1).

> Gilbert: Do you have a blank check?
> George: Yes, I have a blank check.
> Gilbert: Do you have an account for the check?
> George: Yes, I have an account for the check.
> Gilbert: Does the account contain at least fifty dollars?
> George: Yes, the account contains eighty dollars.
> Gilbert: Get the check made out to you for fifty dollars
>   and then I can withdraw fifty dollars for you.
> George: All right, let's get the check made out to me
>   for fifty dollars.

When Gilbert asks a question, his voice rises. When George replies to a question, his voice falls. When Gilbert asks George whether he has a blank check, he stresses the word "check". When he asks George whether he has an account for the check, he stresses the word "account".

Every time Gilbert replies affirmatively ("yes"), or turns the floor over to Gilbert ("all right"), he nods his head, and raises his eyebrows. George and Gilbert look at each other when Gilbert asks a question, but at the end of each question, Gilbert looks up slightly. During the brief pause at the end of affirmative statements the speaker (always George, in this fragment) blinks. To mark the end of the questions, Gilbert raises his eyebrows.

In saying the word "check", Gilbert sketches the outlines of a check in the air between him and his listener. In saying "account", Gilbert forms a kind of box in front of him with his hands: a metaphorical representation of a bank account in which one keeps money. When he says the phrase "withdraw fifty dollars," Gilbert withdraws his hand towards his chest.

1.5   Communicative Significance of the Face

Movements of the head and facial expressions can be characterized by their placement with respect to the linguistic utterance and their significance in transmitting information (Scherer, 1980). The set of facial movement clusters contains: *syntactic functions* accompany the flow of speech and are synchronized at the verbal level. Facial movement can appear on accented syllable or a pause (like raising the eyebrows while saying "Do you have a blank CHECK?"); *semantic functions* can emphasize what is being said, substitute for a word or refer to an emotion (like smiling when remembering a happy event "It was such a NICE DAY"); *dialogic functions* regulate the flow of speech and depend on the relationship between two people (smooth turns[1] are often co-occurrent with mutual gaze). These three functions are modulated by various parameters: *speaker and listener characteristic functions* convey information about the speaker's social identity, emotion, attitude, age and *listener functions* correspond to the listener's reactions to the speaker's speech; they can be signals of agreement, of attention, of comprehension.

1.6   Communicative Significance of Hand Gestures

We have taken McNeil's (1992) taxonomy of gesture as a working hypothesis. According to this scheme, there are four basic types of gestures during speaking. *Iconics* represent some feature of the accompanying speech, such as sketching a small rectangular space with one's two hands while saying "Did you bring your CHECKBOOK?". *Metaphorics* represent an abstract feature concurrently spoken about, such as forming a jaw-like shape with one hand, and pulling it towards one's body while saying "You must WITHDRAW money.". *Deictics* indicate a point in space. They accompany reference to persons, places and other spatializeable discourse entities. An example is pointing to the ground while saying "Do you have an account at Mellon or at THIS bank?". The system does not make any distinction between these three categories of gesture. They are all in effect lexical. Finally, *Beats* are small formless waves of the hand that occur with heavily emphasized words, occasions of turning over the floor to another speaker, and other kinds of special linguistic work. An example is waving one's left hand briefly up and down along with the stressed words in the phrase "Go AHEAD."

1.7   Synchrony of Gesture, Facial Movements, and Speech

Speech, gesture, facial expressions and gaze are intimately linked. We will assume as a working hypothesis that gestures are generated in synchrony with their semantically parallel linguistic units. The empirical basis for this assumption remains to be established (in future work, in fact, we regard our system partly as a tool for carrying out such investigations.) Depending on their functions, facial movements are synchronized at the phonemic segment, word or utterance levels (Condon and Osgton, 1971; Kendon, 1974) although in cases of hesitations, pauses or syntactically complex speech, it is the gesture which appears first (McNeill, 1992). Facial expression, eye gaze and hand gestures do not do their communicative work only within single utterances, but also have inter-speaker effects. The presence or absence of confirmatory feedback by one conversational participant, via gaze or head movement, for example, affects the behavior of the other. A conversation consists of the exchange of meaningful utterances and of behavior. One person punctuates and reinforces her speech by head nods, smiles, and hand gestures; the other person can smile back, vocalize, or shift gaze to show participation in the conversation.

---

[1] Meaning that the listener does not interrupt or overlap the speaker.

2 Overview of System

In our implemented system, we have attempted to adhere as closely as possible to a model of face-to-face interaction suggested by the results of empirical research described above. In particular, each conversational agent is implemented as an autonomous construct that maintains its own representations of the state of the world and the conversation, and whose behavior is determined by these representations. (For now, the two agents run copies of the same program, initialized with different goals and world knowledge.) The agents communicate with one another only by the symbolic messages whose content is displayed in the resulting animation. The architecture of a conversational agent is shown in Fig. 1.

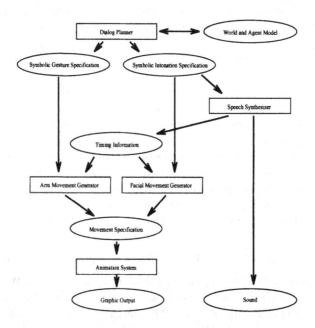

Fig. 1. Architecture of each conversational agent

In this section, we provide an outline of how each agent decides what to say, determines the contribution of this content to the conversation, and uses the resulting representations to accompany speech with contextually appropriate intonation, gesture, facial expression and gaze.

2.1 Dialogue Planner

The selection of content for the dialogue by an agent is performed by two cascaded planners. The first is the domain planner, which manages the plans governing the concrete actions which an agent will execute; the second is the discourse planner, which manages the communicative actions an agent must take in order to agree on a domain plan and in order to remain synchronized while executing a domain plan.

The input to the domain planner is a database of facts describing the way the world works, the goals of an agent, and the beliefs of the agent about the world, including the beliefs of the agent about the other agent in the conversation. The domain planner executes by decomposing an agent's current goals into a series of more specific goals according to the hierarchical relationship between actions specified in the agent's beliefs about the world. Once decomposition resolves a plan into a sequence of actions to performed, the domain planner causes an agent to execute those actions in sequence. As these goal expansions and action executions take place, the domain planner also dictates discourse goals that an agent must adopt in order to maintain and exploit cooperation with their conversational partner.

The domain planner transmits its instructions to take communicative actions to the discourse planner by suspending operation when such instructions are generated and relinquishing control to the discourse planner. Several stages of processing and conversational interaction may occur before these discourse goals are achieved. The discourse planner must identify how the goal submitted by the domain planner relates to other discourse goals that may still be in progress. Then content for a particular utterance is selected on the basis of how the discourse goal is decomposed into sequences of actions that might achieve it.

Following Halliday (1967) and others (Hajičová and Sgall, 1988; Lyons, 1977; Bolinger, 1989; Steedman, 1991), we use the terms *theme* and *rheme* to denote two distinct information structural attributes of an utterance.[2] The theme roughly corresponds to what the utterance is about or the question under discussion. The rheme corresponds to what the speaker has to contribute on that theme. Within information structural constituents, we define the semantic interpretations of certain items as being either *focused* or *background*. Items may be focused for a variety of reasons, including emphasizing their newness in the discourse or making contrastive distinctions among salient discourse entities. We also mark the representation of entities in information structure with their status in the discourse. Entities are considered either new to discourse and hearer (indefinites), new to discourse but not to hearer (definites on first mention), or old (all others) (Prince, 1992).

Distinct intonational tunes have been shown to be associated with the thematic and rhematic parts of an utterance for certain classes of dialogue (Prevost and Steedman, 1993a; 1993b; 1994; Steedman, 1991). In particular, we note that the standard rise-fall intonation generally occurs with the rhematic part of many types of utterances. Thematic elements of an utterance are often marked by a rise-fall-rise intonation.

Text is generated and pitch accents and phrasal melodies are placed on generated text as outlined in Steedman (1991) and Prevost and Steedman (1993a).

---

[2] Although note that we drop Halliday's assumption that themes occur only in sentence–initial position. Functionally similar distinctions in this context are *topic/comment*, *given/new*, and the scale of *communicative dynamism*.

This text is converted automatically to a form suitable for input to the AT&T Bell Laboratories TTS synthesizer (Liberman and Buchsbaum, 1985)[3]. When the dialogue is generated, the following information is saved automatically: (1) the timing of the phonemes and pauses, (2) the type and place of the accents, (3) the type and place of the gestures.

This speech and timing information is critical for synchronizing the facial and gestural animation.

2.2 Symbolic Gesture Specification

The dialogue generation program annotates utterances according to how their semantic content could relate to a spatial expression (literally, metaphorically, spatializeably, or not at all). Further, references to entities are classified according to discourse status as either new to discourse and hearer (indefinites), new to discourse but not to hearer (definites on first mention), or old (all others) (Prince, 1992). According to the following rules, these annotations, together with the earlier ones, determine which concepts will have an associated gesture. Gestures that represent something (iconics and metaphorics) are generated for rhematic verbal elements (roughly, information not yet spoken about) and for hearer new references, provided that the semantic content is of an appropriate class to receive such a gesture: words with literally spatial (or concrete) content get iconics (e.g. "check" as in "do you have a blank check? or "write" as in "you can write the check", first and third frames in Fig. 2); those with metaphorically spatial (or abstract) content get metaphorics (e.g. "help" as in "will you help me?", second frame in Fig. 2); words with physically spatializeable content get deictics (e.g. "this bank"). All of this is done by lexical lookup. Beat gestures are on the other hand generated for such items when the semantic content cannot be represented spatially, and are also produced accompanying discourse new definite references (e.g. "wait for" as in "I will wait for you to withdraw fifty dollars", fourth frame in Fig. 2). If a representational gesture is called for, the system accesses a dictionary of gestures (motion prototypes) that associates semantic representations with possible gestures that might represent them[4] (for further details, see Cassell et al. (1994a)).

After this gestural annotation of all gesture types, and lexicon look-up of appropriate forms for representational gestures, information about the duration of intonational phrases (acquired in speech generation) is used to time gestures. First, all the gestures in each intonational phrase are collected. Because of the relationship between accenting and gesturing, in this dialogue at most one representational gesture occurs in each intonational phrase. If there is a representational gesture, its preparation is set to begin at or before the beginning of

---

[3] We suppressed TTS default intonation assignment algorithm.

[4] This solution is provisional: a richer semantics would include the features relevant for gesture generation, so that the form of the gestures could be generated algorithmically from the semantics. Note also, however, that following Kendon (1980) we are led to believe that gestures may be more standardized in form than previously thought.

Fig. 2. Examples of symbolic gesture specification

the intonational phrase, and to finish at or before the next gesture in the intonational phrase or the nuclear stress of the phrase, whichever comes first. The stroke phase is then set to coincide with the nuclear stress of the phrase. Finally, the relaxation is set to begin no sooner than the end of the stroke or the end of the last beat in the intonational phrase, with the end of relaxation to occur around the end of the intonational phrase. Beats, in contrast, are simply timed to coincide with the stressed syllable of the word that realizes the associated concept. When these timing rules have been applied to each of the intonational phrases in the utterance, the output is a series of symbolic gesture types and the times at which they should be performed. These instructions are used to generate motion files that run the animation system (Badler, Phillips, and Webber, 1993).

2.3 Symbolic Facial Expression Specification

In the current system, facial expression (movement of the lips, eyebrows, etc.) is specified separately from movement of the head and eyes (gaze). In this section we discuss facial expression, and turn to gaze in the next section.

Paul Ekman (1976) and his colleagues characterize facial expressions depending on their function. Many facial functions exist (such as manipulators that correspond to biological needs of the face (wetting the lips); emblems and emotional emblems that are facial expressions replacing a word, an emotion) but only some are directly linked to the intonation of the voice. In this system, facial expressions connected to intonation are automatically generated, while other kinds of expressions (emblems, for example) are specified by hand (Pelachaud, Badler, and Steedman 1991).

We are using **FACS** (Facial Action Coding System (Ekman, 1978)) to define facial expressions.

2.4 Symbolic Gaze Specification

In the current version of the program (as in most of the relevant literature) head and eye behaviors are not differentiated. head and eyes follow the same movement pattern, and gaze is defined in terms of head motion. We identify four primary categories of gaze depending on its role in the conversation (Argyle and Cook, 1976; Collier, 1985). In the following, we give rules of action and the functions for each of these four categories (see Fig. 3).

planning: corresponds to the first phase of a turn when the speaker organizes her thoughts. She has a tendency to look away (possibly in order to prevent an overload of information). On the other hand, during the execution phase, the speaker knows what she is going to say and looks more at the listener. For a short turn (duration less than 1.5 sec.), the speaker and the listener establish eye contact (mutual gaze) (Argyle and Cook, 1976).

comment: accompanies and comments speech, by occurring in parallel with accent and emphasis. Accented or emphasized items are punctuated by head nods; the speaker looks toward the listener. The speaker also gazes at the listener more when she asks a question. She looks up at the end of the question.

control: controls the communication channel and functions as a synchronization signal: responses may be demanded or suppressed by looking at the listener. When the speaker wants to give her turn of speaking to the listener, she gazes at the listener at the end of the utterance. When the listener asks for the turn, she looks up at the speaker.

feedback: is used to collect and seek feedback. The listener can emit different reaction signals to the speaker's speech. Speaker looks toward the listener during grammatical pauses to obtain feedback on how utterances are being received. This is frequently followed by the listener looking at the speaker and nodding. In turn, if the speaker wants to keep her turn, she looks away from the listener. If the speaker does not emit a within-turn signal by gazing at the listener, the listener can still emit a back-channel which in turn may be followed by a continuation signal by the speaker. But the probability of action of the listener varies with the action of the speaker (Duncan, 1974); in particular, it decreases if no signal has occurred from the speaker. In this way the listener reacts to the behavior of the speaker.

3   Parallel Transition Network

Interaction between agents and synchronization of gaze and hand movements to the dialogue for each agent are accomplished using Parallel Transition Net-

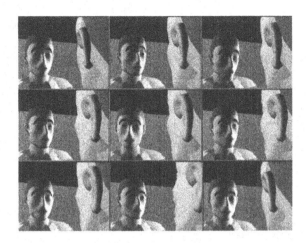

Fig. 3. Facial expressions and gaze behavior corresponding to: "All right. <pause> You can write the check".

works (PaT-Nets), which allow coordination rules to be encoded as simultaneously executing finite state automata (Beckett, 1994). PaT-Nets are a scheduling mechanism. They are able to take a decision, execute an action. They can call for action in the simulation and make state transitions either conditionally or probabilistically. Pat-Nets are scheduled into the simulation with an operating system that allows them to invoke or kill other PaT-Nets, sleep until a desired time or until a desired condition is met, and synchronize with other running nets by waiting for them to finish or by waiting on a shared semaphore.

PaT-Nets are composed of nodes and transitions between these nodes. Each node corresponds to a particular state of the system. Transitions can be conditions or probabilities. When a transition is made the actions specific to the nodes are executed. In addition, the PaT-Net notation is object oriented with each net defined by a *class* with actions and transition conditions as *methods*. The running networks are instances of the PaT-Net class and can take parameters on instantiation. This notation allows PaT-Nets to be hierarchically organized and allows constructing new nets by combining existing nets or making simple modifications to existing nets.

All the behaviors specified above for gestures and gaze are implemented in PaT-Nets. First, a PaT-Net process parses the output of the speech synthesis module, one utterance at a time. Each agent has its own PaT-Net. A PaT-Net instance is created to control each agent: probabilities and other parameters appropriate for each agent given the current role as listener or speaker are set for the PaT-Net at this moment. Then as agents' PaT-Nets synchronize the agents with the dialogue and interact with the unfolding simulation they schedule activity that achieves a complex observed interaction behavior.

PaT-Nets are written in LISP. The input file is a list of lists. Each list has the form: ("George" "Gilbert" "utterance-input" 10.0). The number 10.0 specifies the starting time of the utterance (in seconds). "George" is the speaker, "Gilbert" is the listener and "utterance-input" is the current utterance.

The PaT-Net parses each "utterance-input" and schedules actions when condition are true. It stops when there is no more phoneme. At this point the Gesture and Gaze PaT-Nets send information about timing and type of action to the animation system. The animation itself is carried out by *Jack*™, a program for controlling articulated objects, especially human figures.

The GAZE and GESTURE PaT-Net schedules motions as they are necessary given the current context in semi-real time. All motions do not need to be generated in advance. The animation is performed as the input utterances are scanned. It allows for interactive control and easiness of extension of the system.

4   Gesture PaT-Net

Upon the signaling of a particular gesture, additional PaT-Nets are instantiated; if the gesture is a beat, the finite state machine representing beats ("Beat-Net") will be called, and if a deictic, iconic, or metaphoric, the network representing these types of gestures ("Gest-Net") will be called. The separation in two PaT-Net comes from the fact that beats are superimposed over the other types of gestures; they arise from the underlying rhythmical pulse of speaking, while other gestures arise from meaning representations. Moreover beats are free movements; they are not tied to a particular gestures like the iconic or emblems movements. Beat-Net takes this freedom in consideration when computing beats gestures.

The newly created instances of the gesture and beat PaT-Nets do not exit immediately upon creating their respective gestures; rather, they pause and await further commands from the calling network, in this case, parse-Net. This is to allow for the phenomenon of gesture coarticulation, in which two gestures may occur in an utterance without intermediary relaxation, i.e. without dropping the hands or, in some cases, without relaxing handshape. Once the end of the current utterance is reached, the parser adds another level of control: it forces exit without relaxation of all gestures except the gesture at the top of the stack; this final gesture is followed by a relaxation of the arms, hands, and wrists.

The following example illustrates how gesture PaT-Net acts on a given input. Intonation and gesture streams are specified.

Intonation: do you have@lstar a blank@lstar check@lstarhhs
Gesture: do@st(icon-check-gesture) you have@btpr a blank@bt check@skrxed

"Check" receives a pitch accent ("lstar" stands for low pitch accent) and "blank" a secondary stress. The beat gesture ("bt") begins its preparation phase ('btpr') on 'have'. Its stroke ("sk") falls on "check" and the relaxation phase ("rx") starts afterwards and ends at ("ed"). Since 'blank' receives a secondary stress, the beat gestures falls there and is superimposed over the iconic gesture.

---

† *Jack* is a registered trademark of the University of Pennsylvania.

Gestures are mainly produce by speakers and not by listeners (McNeill, 1992). The timing of a gesture follows the change of speaking turns. The end of a gesture coincides with the end of a turn. In the case a gesture does not have time to finish, it is foreshortened. Another reason for foreshortening is anticipation of the next gesture to be produced in a discourse. In anticipatory co-articulation effects, most often the relaxation phase of the foreshortened iconic, metaphoric or deictic gesture and preparation phase of the next gesture become one.

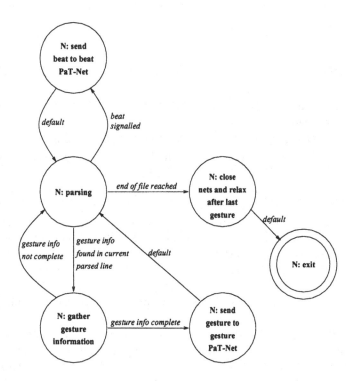

Fig. 4. PaT-Net that synchronizes gestures with the dialogue at the phoneme level.

4.1   Gesture Animation

The gesture system is divided into three parts: hand shape, wrist control, and arm positioning. Each three can be specified independently of the other. The first, hand shape, relies on an extensible library of hand shape primitives based on the American Sign Language Alphabet. It allows also relaxation position. The velocity of handshape changes is limited and allows the modeling of handshape co-articulation. Thus as the speed of the gesture increases, the gestures will 'coarticulate' in a realistic manner.

The wrist motion is specified in terms of the hand direction relative to the figure (e.g. fingers forward and palm up). Joint limits allows the wrists to move in a realistic manner. Beat gestures are a specialized form of wrist motion. The direction of the movement depends on the current wrist position.

The arm motion system accepts general specifications of spatial goals and drives the arms towards those goals within the limits imposed by the arm's range of motion. The arm may be positioned by using general directions like "chest-high, slightly forward, and to the far left".

5   Gaze PaT-Net

Each of the four dialogic functions (planning, comment, control and feedback) appears as a sub-network in the PaT-Net. Each sub-network is represented by a set of nodes, a list of conditions and their associated actions. Moreover each node is characterized by a probability.

Each node of the GAZE PaT-Net is characterized by a probability. The choice of these probabilities is based on evaluation of conversation between two persons. We analyze where and when a person is gazing, smiling and/or nodding. Each of these signals receive binary value: 1 one it happens (gaze is equal to 1 when a person is looking at the other person, 0 when looking away). The conversation is annotated every tenth of a second. Six turn-states are considered, three per agent. When an agent hold the floor she can be speaking while the other agent is pausing (normal turn) or speaking (overlapping talk or occurrence of backchannel), or she can be pausing as well as the listener. For each of these turn-state we compute the co-occurrence of signals: nod, smile and/or gaze. Then probability of occurrence is computed: each node of the PaT-Net corresponds to a particular configuration of a given turn-state and an occurrence of a given signal. E.g. the occurrence of a 'within-turn signal' as we defined it corresponds to the action: agent 1 looks at the agent 2 while having the floor and pausing. Probabilities appropriate for each agent given the current role as listener or speaker are set for the PaT-Net before it executes.

Figure 5 shows the GAZE PaT-Net configuration. Node names are written in bold, actions in italic and conditions are specified on the arcs. Two sub-PaT-Nets are built: Head-Start and Gaze-Start. The differentiation refers only to the type of movements to be performed. As it can be noticed for a same condition different actions can occur. These actions are separated in two: gazing at or away from the other agent, and other head movement (nod, shake...).

Each dialogic function is associated with a set of nodes. A node is entered only if the input condition is true. The corresponding action is occurring only if its probability allows it (this check is done every time; that is when a condition is true, the action is performed only if the probability allows it. Since it is done in each case we are not repeating it). As an example the dialogic function **planning** is defined by the following nodes and conditions: if a short turn is detected then the node G-Short-Turn is entered. The associated action is: the speaker and listener look at each other. The other node corresponds to the first phase of a turn: begin-turn [5] where the speaker looks away. While the function **comment** is represented by: if an accent or a question is detected the corresponding action is executed.

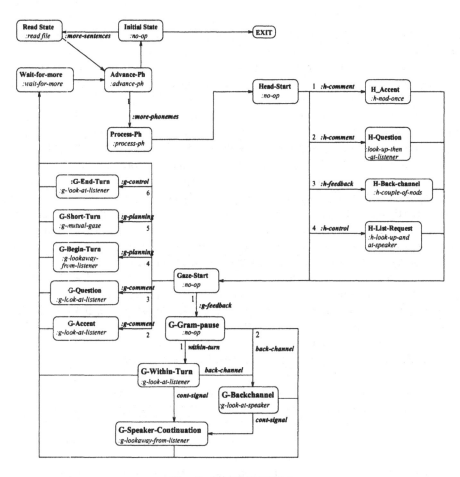

Fig. 5. GAZE PaT-Net

5.1   Gaze Animation

For each phoneme, the GAZE PaT-Net is entered and decides whether or not the head should move. A transition is made on the node whose condition is true. If the probability of the nodes allows it, the action is performed. In such a case no further actions are possible during the duration of the considered action; that

---

[5] A beginning of a turn is defined as all the phonemes between the first one and the first accented segment.

is PaT-Net scheduling is disallowed and delayed until the end of this action. No co-occurrent actions are permitted. If no action is performed on a phoneme the PaT-Net waits for the next available phoneme.

Some actions performed by an agent influence the behavior of the other agent. In the case of the feedback node, different branching is possible depending is the action "looking at the listener" is performed or not by the speaker (corresponding to a within-turn). The probability associated with a back-channel ("listener looking away from speaker") vary. It is smaller if the speaker does not look at the listener (an occurrence of a back-channel has lesser chance to happen) and greater otherwise.

Head motions are performed by tracking an invisible object. The object is placed in the current environment. The head follows the moving object. All swing, nod, turn movements are obtained by giving new coordinates to the object. A head movement is performed by giving the new position of the object, the starting time and duration of the movement. The head velocity has an easy-in/easy-out pattern, that is it accelerates at the beginning and decelerates before stopping. It allows for smoothness of movement. A nod is simulated by moving the invisible object in the vertical plane while swing and turn are executed by moving it in the horizontal plane. Each of these displacements takes as parameters the number of times to perform the move (simulation of multiple nods or swings), and distance (execution of large or small head nods). Varying these parameters allows one to use the same function for different conditions. For example, when punctuating an accent, the speaker's head nod will be of larger amplitude than the feedback head nods emitted by the listener. A gaze direction is sustained until a change is made by another action.

We illustrate a PaT-Net execution with the following example:

```
Gilbert: Get the chEck made OUt to you for fifty dollars
<pause> And thEn <pause> I can withdrAw fifty dollars for you.
```

planning: This utterance is not short so the node **short-turn** is not entered. But for the first few phonemes of the beginning of the example utterance (in our example "Get the ch"), the node **beginning-turn** is entered; the condition of being in a beginning of turn is true but its probability did not allow the action **speaker gazes away** to be applied. Therefore the speaker (Gilbert) keeps his current gaze direction (looking at George).

comment: In our example, on accented items ("chEck", "thEn" and "withdrAw"), the node **accent** of the function **comment** is reached. In the first two cases the probability allows the actions **speaker gazes at the listener** to be performed by Gilbert, while **nod-once** by Gilbert results on "withdraw".

control: At the end of the utterance[6] (corresponding to "fifty dollars for you" here), speaker and listener perform an action: **speaker gazes at listener**

---

[6] End of turn is defined as all the phonemes between the last accented segment and the last phonemes.

from the node **end of turn** and `listener gazes at the speaker` and up
from the node **turn request**.

feedback : The two intonational phrases of our example (*get the check made
out to you for fifty dollars* and *and then*) are separated by a pause; this
corresponds to a within-turn situation. The node **G-feedback** is entered.
If the probability allows it, the action `speaker gazes at the listener`
is performed[7]. After a delay (0.2 sec., as specified by the program), the
probabilities associated with the actions is checked once more. If allowed the
node **back-channel** is reached and the action can happen: `listener gazes
at the speaker`. In either case, the final step corresponds to the reaching
of the node **speaker-continuation** after some delay. The action `speaker
gazes away from the listener` is then performed.

6   Facial Expression Generation

Facial expressions are clustered into functional groups: lip shape, conversational
signal, punctuator, manipulator and emblem (see Sect. 2.3). Each is represented
by two parameters: *its time of occurrence* and *its type*. Our algorithm (Pelachaud,
Badler and Steedman, 1991) embodies rules to automatically generate facial
expressions, following the principle of synchrony. The program scans the input
utterances and computes the different facial expressions corresponding to these
functional groups.

The computation of the lip shape is done in three passes and incorporates
coarticulation effects (Pelachaud, Badler and Steedman, 1991). Phonemes are
characterized by their degree of deformability. For each deformable segment,
the program looks for the nearby segment whose associated lip shapes influence
it. The properties of muscle contractions are taken into account spatially (by
adjusting the sequence of contracting muscles) and temporally (by noticing if a
muscle has enough time to contract or relax).

A conversational signal (movements occurring on accents, like raising of eyebrow) starts and ends with the accented word; while punctuator signals (such
as smiling) coincide with pauses. Blinking (occurring as punctuator or manipulator) is synchronized at the phoneme level. The extent to which the synchronic
assumption holds for real human conversation is a question for future research.
We hope this system and others like it will contribute to this further investigation
by providing a simulation that can be controlled from the linguistic level.

7   Conclusions

Automatically generating information about intonation, facial expression, head
movements and hand gestures allows an interactive dialogue animation to be
created; for a non-real-time animation much guess-work in the construction of

---

[7] In the case the action is not performed, the arc going to the node **back-channel** is
immediately traversed without waiting for the next phonemic segment.

appropriate motions can be avoided. The resulting motions can be used as is, or the actions and timings can be used as a cognitively and physiologically justified guide to further refinement of the conversation and the participants' interactions by a human animator.

Research Acknowledgments

The authors would like to thank Brett Achorn, Tripp Becket and Brett Douville.

This research is partially supported by NSF Grants IRI90-18513, IRI91-17110, CISE Grant CDA88-22719, NSF graduate fellowships, NSF VPW GER-9350179; ARO Grant DAAL03-89-C-0031 including participation by the U.S. Army Research Laboratory (Aberdeen); U.S. Air Force DEPTH contract through Hughes Missile Systems F33615-91-C-000; DMSO through the University of Iowa; National Defense Science and Engineering Graduate Fellowship in Computer Science DAAL03-92-G-0342; and NSF Instrumentation and Laboratory Improvement Program Grant USE-9152503.

References

Argyle, M. and Cook, M., (1976) *Gaze and Mutual gaze*, Cambridge University Press.

Badler, Norman, Phillips, Carry, and Webber, Bonnie (1993) *Simulating Humans: Computer Graphics Animation and Control*, Oxford University Press.

Becket, Tripp M. (1994) *The jack lisp api*, Technical Report MS-CIS-94-01, Graphics Lab 59, University of Pennsylvania.

Biermann, Alan W, Guinn, Curry I., Hipp, Richard and Smith, Ronnie W. (1993) 'Efficient collaborative discourse: A theory and its implementation'. In *Proceedings of the ARPA Human Language Technology Workshop*, 177–181.

Bolinger, Dwight (1989) *Intonation and its uses*, Stanford University Press.

Calvert, Tom (1991) 'Composition of realistic animation sequences for multiple human figures'. In *Making Them Move: Mechanics, Control, and Animation of Articulated Figures*, Badler, Norman I., Barsky, Brian A., and Zeltzer, David (eds.), San Mateo, CA: Morgan-Kaufmann, 35–50.

Cassell, Justine, Pelachaud, Catherine, Badler, Norman, Steedman, Mark, Achorn, Brett, Becket, Tripp, Douville, Brett, Prevost, Scott, and Stone, Matthew (1994) 'Animated conversation:rule-based generation of facial expression, gesture and spoken intonation for multiple conversational agents'. In *Computer Graphics '94*, 413–420.

Cassell, Justine, Stone, Matthew, Douville, Brett, Prevost, Scott, Achorn, Brett, Badler, Norm, Steedman, Mark and Pelachaud, Catherine (1994) 'Modeling the Interaction between Speech and Gesture'. In *Proceedings of the Sixteenth Annual Meeting of the Cognitive Science Society*, Atlanta, GA.

Chen, D. T., Pieper, S. D., Singh, S. K., Rosen, J. M., and Zeltzer, D. (1993) 'The virtual sailor: An implementation of interactive human body modeling'. In *Proc. 1993 Virtual Reality Annual International Symposium*, Seattle, WA:IEEE.

Cohen, M. M. and Massaro, D. W. (1993) 'Modeling coarticulation in synthetic visual speech'. In *Models and Techniques in Computer Animation*, Magnenat-Thalmann, M. and Thalmann, D. (eds.), Tokyo:Springer-Verlag.

Collier, G. (1985) *Emotional Expression*, Lawrence Erlbaum Associates.

Condon, W.S. and Osgton, W.D. (1971) 'Speech and body motion synchrony of the speaker-hearer'. In *The perception of Language*, Horton, D.H. and Jenkins, J.J. (eds.), Academic Press, 150–184.

Dale, Robert (1989) *Generating Referring Expressions in a Domain of Objects and Processes*, PhD thesis, Centre for Cognitive Science, University of Edinburgh.

Davis, James and Hirschberg, Julia (1988) 'Assigning intonational features in synthesized spoken discourse'. In *ACL*, Buffalo, 187–193.

Duncan, S. (1974) 'Some signals and rules for taking speaking turns in conversations'. In *Nonverbal Communication*, Weitz (ed.), Oxford University Press.

Ekman, Paul (1976) Movements with precise meanings, *The Journal of Communication, 26*.

Ekman, P. and Friesen, W. (1978) *Facial Action Coding System*, Consulting Psychologists Press, Inc.

Essai, I.A. and Pentland, A. (1994) 'A vision system for observing and extracting facial action parameters'. In *Proceedings of Computer Vision and Pattern Recognition (CVPR 94)*, 76–83.

Feiner, S. and McKeown, K.R. (1990) 'Generating coordinated multimedia explanations'. In *Proceedings of the Sixth Conference on Artificial Intelligence Applications*, 290–296.

Gourret, Jean-Paul, Magnenat-Thalmann, Nadia, and Thalmann, Daniel (1989) 'Simulation of object and human skin deformations in a grasping task'. In *Computer Graphics, 23(3)*, 21–30.

Guinn, Curry I. (1993) 'A computational model of dialogue initiative in collaborative discourse'. In *Human-Computer Collaboration: Reconciling Theory, Synthesizing Practice, Papers from the 1993 Fall Symposium Series*, AAAI Technical Report FS-93-05.

Hajičová, Eva and Sgall (1988) 'Topic and focus of a sentence and the patterning of a text'. In *Text and Discourse Constitution*, Petofi, János (ed.), Berlin: De Gruyter.

Halliday, Michael (1967) *Intonation and Grammar in British English*, The Hague: Mouton.

Hill, D.R., Pearce, A., and Wyvill, B. (1988) 'Animating speech: an automated approach using speech synthesised by rules'. In *The Visual Computer, 3*, 277–289.

Houghton, George (1986) *The Production of Language in Dialogue: A Computational Model*. PhD thesis, University of Sussex.

Houghton, George and Isard, Stephen (1987) 'Why to speak, what to say and how to say it'. In *Modelling Cognition*, Morris, P. (ed.), Wiley.

Houghton, George and Pearson, M., 'The production of spoken dialogue'. In *Advances in Natural Language Generation: An Interdisciplinary Perspective, Vol. 1*, Zock, M. and Sabah, G. (eds.), London: Pinter Publishers.

Hovy, Eduard H (1988) 'Planning coherent multisentential text'. In *ACL*, 163–169.

Kalra, P., Mangili, A., Magnenat-Thalmann, N., and Thalmann, D. (1991) 'SMILE: A multilayered facial animation system'. In *Modeling in Computer Graphics*, Kunii, T.L. (ed.), Springer-Verlag.

Kendon, Adam (1974) 'Movement coordination in social interaction: some examples described'. In *Nonverbal Communication*, Weitz (ed.), Oxford University Press.

Kendon, Adam (1980) 'Gesticulation and speech: Two aspects of the process of utterance'. In *The Relation between Verbal and Nonverbal Communication*, Key, M.R. (ed.), Mouton, 207–227.

Lee, Jintae and Kunii, Tosiyasu L. (1993) 'Visual translation: From native language to sign language'. In *Workshop on Visual Languages*, Seattle, WA:IEEE.

Lee, Philip, Wei, Susanna, Zhao, Jianmin, and Badler, Norman I. (1990) 'Strength guided motion'. In *Computer Graphics, 24(4)*, 253–262.

Liberman, Mark and Buchsbaum, A. L. (1985) 'Structure and usage of current Bell Labs text to speech programs', Technical Memorandum TM 11225-850731-11, AT&T Bell Laboratories.

Loomis, Jeffrey, Poizner, Howard, Bellugi, Ursula, Blakemore, Alynn, and Hollerbach, John (1983) 'Computer graphic modeling of American Sign Language'. In *Computer Graphics, 17(3)*, 105–114.

Lyons, John (1977) *Semantics (vol II)*, Cambridge University Press.

Magnenat-Thalmann, Nadia and Thalmann, Daniel (1991) 'Human body deformations using joint-dependent local operators and finite-element theory'. In *Making Them Move: Mechanics, Control, and Animation of Articulated Figures*, Badler, Norman I., Barsky, Brian A., and Zeltzer, David (eds.), San Mateo, CA: Morgan-Kaufmann, 243–262.

McNeill, David (1992) *Hand and Mind: What Gestures Reveal about Thought*, University of Chicago.

Meteer, Marie W. (1991) 'Bridging the generation gap between text planning and linguistic realization'. In *Computational Intelligence, 7(4)*, 296–304.

Moore, Johanna D. and Paris, Cécile L. (1989) 'Planning text for advisory dialogues'. In *ACL*, 203–211.

Nahas, M., Huitric, H., and Saintourens, M. (1988) 'Animation of a B-spline figure'. In *The Visual Computer, 3(5)*, 272–276.

Parke, F.I. (1982) 'A parameterized model for facial animation'. In *IEEE Computer Graphics and Applications, 2(9)*, 61–70.

Patel, M. and Willis, P.J. (1991) 'FACES – The facial animation, construction and editing system'. In *Eurographics'91*, 33–45.

Pearce, A., Wyvill, B., and Hill, D.R. (1986) 'Speech and expression: a computer solution to face animation'. In *Graphics and Vision Interface '86*, 136–140.

Pelachaud, Catherine, Badler, Norman I., and Steedman, Marc (1991) 'Linguistic issues in facial animation'. In *Computer Animation '91*, Magnenat-Thalmann, N. and Thalmann, D. (eds.), Springer-Verlag, 15–30.

Power, Richard, (1977) 'The organisation of purposeful dialogues'. In *Linguistics, 17(1/2)*, 107–152.

Prevost, Scott and Steedman, Mark (1993a) 'Generating contextually appropriate intonation'. In *Proceedings of the Sixth Conference of the European Chapter of the Association for Computational Linguistics*, Utrecht, 332–340.

Prevost, Scott and Steedman, Mark (1993b) 'Using context to specify intonation in speech synthesis'. In *Proceedings of the 3rd European Conference of Speech Communication and Technology (EUROSPEECH)*, Berlin, pages 2103–2106.

Prevost, Scott and Steedman, Mark (1994) 'Specifying intonation from context for speech synthesis'. In *Speech Communication, 15(1–2)*, 139–153.

Prince, Ellen F. (1992) 'The ZPG letter: Subjects, definiteness and information status'. In *Discourse description: diverse analyses of a fund raising text*, Thompsoni, S. and Mann, W. (eds.), John Benjamins B.V., 295–325.

Reiter, Ehud (1994) 'Has a consensus NL generation architecture appeared, and is it psycholinguistically plausible?'. In *Seventh International Workshop on Natural Language Generation*, 163–170.

Rijpkema, Hans and Girard, Michael (1991) 'Computer animation of hands and grasping'. In *Computer Graphics, 25(4)*, 339–348.

Scherer, Klaus R. (1980) 'The functions of nonverbal signs in conversation'. In *The Social and Physiological Contexts of Language*, Giles, H. and St. Clair, R. (eds.), Lawrence Erlbaum Associates, 225–243.

Shieber, Stuart, Van Noord, Gertjan, Pereira, Fernando and Moore, Robert (1990) 'Semantic-head-driven generation'. In *Computational Linguistics, 16*, 30–42.

Steedman, Mark (1991) 'Structure and intonation'. In *Language, 67*, 260–296.

Takeuchi, Akikazu and Nagao, Katashi (1993) 'Communicative facial displays as a new conversational modality'. In *ACM/IFIP INTERCHI'93*, Amsterdam.

Terken, Jacques (1984) 'The distribution of accents in instructions as a function of discourse structure'. In *Language and Structure, 27*, 269–289.

Terzopoulos, D. and Waters, K. (1993) 'Analysis and synthesis of facial image sequences using physical and anatomical models'. In *IEEE Transactions on Pattern Analysis and Machine Intelligence, 15(6)*, 569–579.

Wahlster, Wolfgang, André, Elisabeth, Bandyopadhyay, Son, Graf, Winfried, and Rist, Thomas, 'WIP: The coordinated generation of multimodal presentations from a common representation'. In *Computational Theories of Communication and their Applications*, Stock, Oliviero, Slack, John, and Ortony, Andrew (eds.), Berlin: Springer Verlag.

Walker, Lyn (1993) *Informational redundancy and resource bounds in dialogue*, PhD thesis, University of Pennsylvania (Institute for Research in Cognitive Science report IRCS-93-45).

Zacharski, R., Monaghan, A.I.C., Ladd, D.R., and Delin, J., (1993) *BRIDGE: Basic research on intonation in dialogue generation*, Technical report, HCRC: University of Edinburgh, (Unpublished manuscript).

Instructing Animated Agents:
Viewing Language in Behavioral Terms

Bonnie Webber

Department of Computer & Information Science
University of Pennsylvania
Philadelphia PA USA 19104-6389
bonnie@central.cis.upenn.edu

Abstract. One activity of Penn's Center for Human Modelling and Simulation has been the exploration of natural language instructions and other high-level task specifications to create animated simulations of virtual human agents carrying out tasks. The work builds on JACK, an animation system developed at Penn, that provides simulated human models with a growing repertoire of naturalistic behaviors. The value in using high-level task specifications to create animated simulations is that the same specification can be used to produce different animations in different situations, without additional animator or programmer intervention.

But animated simulation driven by natural language instructions can provide another benefit, by forcing us to consider what aspects of language convey information relevant to behavior. What our studies to date have revealed is that more of an utterance conveys such information than its main verb and argument structure.

To demonstrate an analysis of linguistic constructs in terms of behavioral specifications and constraints, I show how instructions containing 'until' clauses can be analysed in terms of perceptual activities and the conditions they are used to assess, and how the resulting analysis contributes to understanding how an agent is supposed to carry these instructions out.

1 Introduction

My group at Penn has been exploring the use of natural language instructions and other high-level task specifications to create realistic animated simulations of virtual human agents carrying out tasks. The work builds on *Jack*™, an animation system developed at the University of Pennsylvania's Center for Human Modelling and Simulation. *Jack* provides biomechanically reasonable and anthropometrically-scaled human models with a growing repertoire of naturalistic behaviors such as walking, stepping, looking, reaching, turning, grasping, strength-based lifting, and both obstacle and self-collision avoidance (Badler, Phillips and Webber, 1993). The value in using high-level task specifications to create animated simulations is that the same specification will produce agent behavior that is appropriate to different environments and/or different conditions, without additional animator or programmer intervention. The resulting simulations thus afford a relatively inexpensive way to carry out human factors studies in computer-aided design or to use in Virtual Reality training, especially in exercises involving multiple agents or a variety of environments.

But animated simulation driven by Natural Language instructions can provide another benefit, by forcing us to consider what aspects of language convey information relevant to behavior. What our studies to date have revealed is that much more of an utterance than its main verb and argument structure help an agent along. Ignoring these other sources of information can lead animated agents to behave in ways that viewers find odd, if not totally bizarre. To avoid this, more research in Natural Language Processing should address relationships between language and behavior.

To demonstrate how linguistic constructs can be analysed in terms of behavioral specifications and constraints, I will show in the main body of the paper how instructions containing 'until' clauses such as

(1)   Squeeze riveter handles **until** rivet stem breaks off.

can be analysed in terms of perceptual activities and the conditions they are used to assess, and how the resulting analysis contributes to understanding what an agent is intended to do in response. Before I begin though, I want to call the reader's attention to our earlier work, as background to this presentation.

In 1990, Barbara Di Eugenio and I did a study of gerundive adjuncts in natural language instructions (Di Eugenio, 1990) such as

(2)   Unroll each strip onto the wall, *smoothing the foil into place vertically (not side to side) to avoid warping and curling at the edges.*
(3)   Sew the head front to back, *leaving the neck edge open.*
(4)   As you work, clean the surface thoroughly each time you change grits, *vacuuming off all the dust and wiping the wood with a rag dampened with turpentine or paint thinner.*

A gerundive adjunct is a type of *free adjunct* – a nonfinite predicative phrase with the function of an adverbial subordinate clause (Stump, 1985). Progressive gerundive adjuncts are fairly common in instructions that specify physical activities. In his analysis of a wide range of free adjuncts in English narrative, Stump (1985) focussed on their truth-conditional properties, distinguishing between *strong* and *weak* adjuncts:

(5)   a. *Having unusually long arms*, John can touch the ceiling.
        b. *Standing on the chair*, John can touch the ceiling.
(6)   a. *Being a businessman*, Bill smokes cigars.
        b. *Lying on the beach*, Bill smokes cigars.

Stump calls the adjuncts in both a sentences *strong*, because their actual truth is uniformly entailed. He calls those in the b sentences *weak*, because their actual truth can fail to be entailed. Stump notes the causal flavor of strong adjuncts:

in the a sentences above, the main clause assertion is true *because* the adjunct is. Weak adjuncts, on the other hand, have a conditional sense: it is (only) when the condition described in the adjunct is true that the main clause assertion is true.

While Stump's observations appear to be both correct and relevant for narrative text, Di Eugenio and I were concerned with the behavioral import of gerundive adjuncts. The main interpretative decision turned out to be whether two separate actions were being specified as in Example 2 (if so, there was a further question as to the specific temporal relationship between the two actions) or only one, as in Example 3 and 4. To determine what action an agent is intended to perform in the latter case, the agent needs to determine whether the adjuct further specifies the action specified in the main clause (e.g., providing information about manner, extent, side effects to avoid, etc.), as in Example 3 or whether the action specifications in the main and adjunct clauses were related by *generation* (Goldman, 1970), as in Example 4. In the latter, the generated action provides a reason for doing the generating action, although we found in subsequent work that the generation relation can convey more information relevant to behavior than just purpose.

Specifically, in her doctoral thesis research, Di Eugenio (1993, see also 1998) focussed on instructions containing 'purpose clauses' of the form

Do α to do β

showing that when they are interpreted as conveying a generation relationship, the relationship may not be between the given α and β, but between a more specific action α' and β. For example, in

(7)   Cut a square in half to make two triangles.

Di Eugenio showed that the action the agent is meant to carry out is not just cutting a square in half (α) but rather the more specific action, cutting a square in half along a diagonal (α'). She then showed how a *description lattice* created in a knowledge representation formalism such as CLASSIC or LOOM can be used to carry out the relevant reasoning. The point I want to emphasize though is that *this systematic inference had gone unnoticed* until utterances were analysed in terms of specifying or constraining behavior.

2   'Until' Clauses

Instructions containing 'until' clauses highlight the rule of perceptual activity in behavior and in behavioral specifications. Obviously, agents use perception when they carry out tasks: if the agent's task is building a brick wall, the agent will use perception to lay the next bed of mortar, to find the next brick to lay, to maneuver the brick to an appropriate place on the mortar bed, to notice and remove excess mortar, etc.

But natural language also uses perceptual tests to *specify* behavior, as I will try to show with 'until' clauses. Now, in a programming language like Pascal, the Boolean condition in an 'until' expression

```
repeat <statement-sequence> until <Boolean-expr>
```

can be assessed by just computing its value. However, for a human agent to comply with an instruction containing an 'until' clause, the agent must

1. understand the *source* of the condition to be checked and the *actions* she must take to assess it;
2. understand what, if any, actions she is assumed to be doing when the condition is to be assessed;
3. determine how to efficiently integrate both sets of actions.

The data on which this analysis is based are drawn from six chapters of two volumes of home repair instructions scanned in by Joseph Rosenzweig, a graduate student at the University of Pennsylvania: Dorling Kindersley's *Home Repair Encyclopedia* (1991) and the *Reader's Digest New Complete Do-It-Yourself Manual* (1991). The data consist of 80 instructions containing 'until clauses', of the form

(Do) α **until** κ.

The chapters were chosen randomly, not because of their subject matter, and all sentences containing 'until' clauses were extracted from them. Some of the instructions concern repair jobs (e.g. fixing broken china, repairing cracked parquet, etc.), and the others concern construction of concrete, asphalt, and/or masonry structures.

While the ideas have not yet been implemented, I am assuming an agent architecture that contains, at the very least:

1. one or more low-level Sense-Control-Act (S-C-A) loops, that can be modified from above by
2. a process-based (as opposed to state-space) task specification such as that recently proposed by Pym, Pryor and Murphy (1995), using process algebra, or the parallel transition network representation (PaT-Net) we have begun to use in much of our animated simulation work (Badler et al., 1996; Becket, 1994).

With respect to such an architecture, a wide class of natural language instructions, including those with 'until' clauses, would be interpreted as process-based representational structures that set the S-C-A loops and interpret both their success and error conditions.

3   Assessing the Specified Condition

The first thing to note is that perception alone may be insufficient to determine whether a condition holds: one or more actions may first be necessary to bring the world into a state in which an appropriate observation can be made. Such actions I will follow Kirsh and Maglio (1994) in calling *epistemic*.[1] That is, in the case of

---

[1] Kirsh and Maglio use the term *pragmatic* action for ones whose purpose is to bring an agent closer to her goal.

(8)   Squeeze riveter handles **until** rivet stem breaks off.

the agent does not have to do anything special to be able to observe the rivet stem breaking off. On the other hand, to determine whether the condition holds in

(9)   Wait for the filler to set and rub it down, first with a needle file and then with glasspaper, **until** it lies flush with the surface.

the agent must assess the condition using tactile perception, which in turn requires her to stop rubbing the filler with glasspaper and feel the filler-surface area with her fingertip(s).

In many cases, as in Example 9 above, the agent is assumed to know how to detect the condition and no explicit guidance is given. In some cases however, explicit guidance is given in the form of relevant epistemic actions and a directly perceivable condition. For example, the instructions below provide guidance in determining whether water contains salt.

(10)   Change the water daily **until** all the salts have gone. To test this, hold a spoonful of the water over a flame so that the water evaporates. There should be no salts left.

One reason for giving such explicit guidance is that, as with other actions, epistemic and perceptual actions can have side effects that the agent might find undesirable. To avoid them, an alternative procedure may be specified in the instructions – e.g.

(11)   Leave this glaze for a short time **until** it becomes 'tacky' (a test strip on an old tile will indicate when it is ready).

'Tacky' is usually assessed through touch, but the assessment leaves fingerprints, which are undesirable on the object being repaired. So an alternative procedure is suggested, where the side effect won't matter.

Of course, it is possible that the specified condition cannot be directly perceived and that no procedure for determining it is provided – e.g.

(12)   Mix the powders a little at a time **until** the proportions look right, ...

The agent is then left to her own devices.

An interesting case is where the condition to be tested for is the agent's ability to perform the next action in the sequence. While the condition may be tested several times and found not to hold, when it *is* found to hold, the next action has effectively been performed – e.g.

(13)   Chip brick with chisel **until** it can be removed.
(14)   After loosening stone with pick and shovel, pry it out with one 2x4, then with the other, **until** you can use one of the levers as a ramp to get stone out of hole.

A more specific form of this condition identifies both the next action α_{next} that the agent is looking to perform and the changes to the world (produced through either her current action or through an independent process – see Sect. 4) that will eventually enable her to perform α_{next}. For example:

(15)   Standard wallpapers are removed by sponging with warm water **until** the paper is **soft enough** to scrape off.

(16)   Continue along the skirting, inserting more wedges as you go, **until** the skirting is **loose enough** to pull away from the wall.

Notice that both 'soft' and 'loose' are vague predicates – there is no definitive test for soft(X) or loose(X), not even tests specific to the type of X (e.g. a soft pudding vs. a soft stomach). As such, an instruction of the form

   (Do) α until Y is soft/loose

is underspecified in a way that could lessen an agent's ability to perform α successfully. On the other hand, if the condition is only specified in terms of the agent's ability to perform α_{next}, she has less information from which to derive the relationship between what is currently happening to the world and when it may be relevant to try to perform α_{next}. Thus having conditions specified in terms of both change and ability can give an agent sufficient information to succeed.

There may, of course, be several ways to assess a condition, and with further experience, an agent may change which one she uses. So in the earlier brick-laying example (repeated here)

(17)   Press it down **until** the mortar is about 3/8 inch thick.

an inexperienced agent may have to interrupt her pressing to measure with a ruler the amount of the mortar still remaining beneath the brick. With experience, the agent may learn to simply eyeball thickness. In creating realistic animations, we can have our agents' skills reflect any degree of experience, as long as it is clear what they are supposed to represent.

4   Determining the Agent's Intended Action

As noted earlier, instructions with 'until' clauses have the general form

   (Do) α until κ

Semantically, α must be interpretable as a Vendlerian 'activity' or a *process* in Moens and Steedman's (1988) terminology – that is, a temporally-extended action with no intrinsic culmination point. If α cannot be directly interpreted as a process, it must be coerced into such an interpretation. Moens and Steedman, for example, note how 'for phrases' such as 'for five minutes', can coerce what they term an *culminated process* – i.e., a temporally-extended action with a culmination point – into a process either through iteration of the basic action or through loss of its intrinsic culmination, as in:

(18) Play the Moonlight Sonata for 1 minute.
(19) Play the Moonlight Sonata for 1 day.

In the first case, the intrinsic culmination point is lost (one stops after a minute, not when one reaches the end of the piece), and in the second, playing the sonata must be repeated until it fills the whole day.

The first thing to note in interpreting instructions with 'until' clauses, is that coercions such as the above can help to determine what the agent is supposed to be doing and what its relationship is to the condition to be assessed. In the most straightforward case, α is the process that affects the world either *cumulatively* until κ is the case

(20) Squeeze riveter handles **until** rivet stem breaks off.

or *nondeterministically* until κ is the case

(21) Try sample specks on the piece **until** you get a get a good match, wiping them away each time **until** you find the right colour.

As the condition-effecting process, α may either be a *simple process* such as in the 'squeeze' example above or in

(22) Rotate the plate **until** the guide fingers touch the rod lightly

or what Moens and Steedman call an *iterated process*

(23) Strike set with fat end of hammer **until** rivet head is rounded off.
(24) Fill in low spots and strike off again **until** concrete is level with the top of the form.

On the other hand, when it is an *independent* process that affects the world either cumulatively or non-deterministically, the agent may not be responsible for doing anything other than actions needed to assess the specified condition κ.

(25) Let poultice stand **until** it dries.
(26) Stop work and wait **until** the water evaporates and the concrete stiffens slightly.

The independent process that produces the specified condition is often one that has been initiated by a previous action taken by the agent. If the process is *cumulative*, the condition to be assessed may either be its *end stage*, as in Example 25, or an *intermediate stage*, as in Example 26, where the process must be interrupted, lest the concrete harden completely. (I speculate that this independent process could alternatively be non-deterministic rather than cumulative, but I do not have any examples yet as evidence.)

An independent process may also be involved in producing the specified condition when the agent is herself engaged in a non-wait process – e.g.,

(27) Place the article in a plastic container and add distilled water .... Change the water daily **until** all the salts have gone.

(28) Heat larger pieces first with a broad flame, otherwise they may distort.
      Heat the joint in the centre **until** it is red hot.

The existence of an independent process can also affect what will happen if the
agent stops her non-wait process – say to check whether the condition holds.

In Example 27, the agent's action of changing the water *enables* the process
of drawing salt out of the article to continue. If the amount of salt in the water
and on the surface of the article are in equilibrium, the process will stop on its
own accord. Thus, if the agent fails to act, the specified condition 'all the salts
have gone' will never be achieved. The agent's action provides, in a sense, the
resources needed for the process to continue.

In Example 28, on the other hand, the agent is not providing additional resources through her action but rather *maintaining* the existing situation, which
in turns *enables* the heating process to continue. If the agent stops her maintenance action – e.g., to check whether the center joint is red hot – the joint will
start to cool.

I noted above two forms of coercion from an activity with a culmination point
to the *process* against which an 'until' clause can be interpreted. I noted such
coercions help to determine what the agent is meant to be doing. Here I want to
suggest a third type of coercion. While I pose it as an alternative to the analysis
given by Moens and Steedman (1988), it adheres to their basic event ontology
and thus provides additional evidence for it. The suggestion is motivated by the
following example:

(29) If solder gets runny or if iron smokes, turn off iron **until** it cools a bit.

I think it is obvious that what the agent is *meant* to do is to turn the soldering
iron off (at which point it will start to cool) and then wait some amount of time
until the iron is cooler and has stopped smoking. The question is what that
interpretation derives from.[2]

Turning off an appliance is a *culmination* in Moens and Steedman's terminology, an activity that gives rise to a change in the world but that a speaker views
as happening instantaneously. Moens and Steedman note that a 'for' adverbial
(which, like an 'until' clause, requires a process) in combination with a culmination seems to denote a time period *following* the culmination. For example

(30) John left the room for a few minutes.

But they deny that such a durative interpretation is correct, suggesting that the
phrase expresses *intention* rather than duration, since the following utterance
would be true even if John is only out of the room for an instance:

(31) John left the room for a half hour, but returned immediately to get his
      umbrella.

I do not believe that the 'until' clause in Example 29 has this property. Consider
the related sentence

---

[2] I thank Joseph Rosenzweig for his contributions to the following analysis.

(32)   John turned off the microphone until his hiccups disappeared.

The inference that the microphone stayed off for the full period until John's hiccups disappeared cannot be denied.[3]

(33)   ?? John turned off the microphone until his hiccups disappeared, but had turn it on again before they disappeared, to get the audience's attention.

I would argue then that the coercion that *seemed* to Moens and Steedman to be the case – that the process in question is a coercion of the *consequent state* that takes hold at the culmination point of 'turn off' and continues until the agent intervenes – is *actually* the case. I believe that such a coercion is only possible if the culmination initiates an independent process, but this needs additional evidence to either support or deny.

There is one more point I want to make about how an agent derives the action she is meant to carry out: being told what condition to check can also convey information as to *how* she must act in order to check it. As such, perceptual conditions can function just like purpose clauses (Di Eugenio, 1993; 1994; 1998, Di Eugenio and Webber, 1992) in guiding an agent to the more specific action she is intended to carry out as well as conveying what perceivable condition should lead her to stop it. Consider, for example:

(34)   Have your helper move the tape side ways **until** the 4-foot mark on the tape coincides with the 5-foot mark on the rule.
(35)   To make sure that all corners are square, measure diagonals AD and BC, and move stake D **until** the diagonals are equal.

Without the 'until' clause , the 'move' verb phrases above are underspecified: they do not tell the agent (or her helper) what *direction* to move in. The 'until' clauses, by indicating the condition to be achieved, conveys direction by implication – whatever direction will most directly lead to the condition becoming true.

5   Integrating Pragmatic and Epistemic Actions

To create a realistic animated simulation, one needs to figure out how an agent's pragmatic and epistemic actions should be integrated. There are two interesting points about this issue:

---

[3] The issue of whether John turned the microphone back on after that is quite separate. The following examples should show that one's belief about what a agent is meant to do *after* a condition holds is strongly influenced by everyday expectations:

(i.)   Slow down your car until you are out of the school zone (at which point you can speed up).
(ii.)   Slow down your car until you reach Mary's house (at which point you should stop).
(iii.)   Slow down your car until you reach the end of the cul-de-sac (at which point you should turn around).

1. Since all actions require resources, the agent must determine whether pragmatic and epistemic actions can be carried out in parallel, or whether they must be interleaved.
2. Even if they can be carried out in parallel, checking a condition has a cost and often undesirable side effects as well, so the agent may prefer to do it as little as possible, without preventing her pragmatic actions from coming to a successful conclusion. This means recognizing *when to start* checking for the specified condition and *how often* to do so.

The impression I get from the instructions I have looked at so far is that lexical semantics can only contribute to the solution of the first problem, in terms of what can be derived from aspectual type and aspectual coercion. For example, when a *culminated process* is coerced to a process through iteration of the basic action, the perceptual condition can be checked at the end of each iteration, as in:

(36)   Strike set with fat end of hammer **until** rivet head is rounded off.
(37)   Fill in low spots and strike off again **until** concrete is level with the top of the form.

On the other hand, I do think the instructions themselves help suggest answers to the questions of *when to start* checking for the specified condition and *how often* to do so. Here I am returning to the notions of *cumulative* effects and *non-deterministic* effects I introduced earlier. First consider a condition that results cumulatively from an on-going process. If the cumulative effect is perceivable, then based on the expected rate of the process, an agent can delay checking the condition until the point that the effect is likely to take hold. For example, in

(38)   Chip brick with chisel **until** it can be removed.

it is not worth the agent's effort to start checking her ability to remove the brick each time she's dislodged another chip. If the cumulative effect is not perceivable, then it is as if the condition were a non-deterministic result of the process. In the case of conditions that arise non-deterministically, then the existence of a reliable probabilistic model of the process might be incorporated into an efficient perceptual strategy.[4]

The examples so far only address the cost of checking conditions and therefore the desirability of a policy that delays them as long as possible and does them as infrequently as possible. I also want to call attention to the danger of starting to check a cumulative condition too soon, a danger that can be avoided by delaying checking:

(39)   Let cement dry **until** kraft paper won't stick to either surface.

Checking too soon can result in kraft paper stuck to the surface.

---

[4] This suggestion is due to Joseph Rosenzweig.

6   Conclusion

I hope to have shown that, by forcing us to consider what aspects of language convey information relevant to behavior, animated simulations of realistic human agents can allow us to better understand language, and by doing so, allow us to better employ such agents for our benefit. Even though we have already shown that following instructions requires attention to more of an utterance than its main verb and argument structure, I believe we have just scratched the surface of what language can provide to agents. I hope that more researchers will now find it of interest to look more into relationships between Natural Language and behavior.

Acknowledgements

The author would like to thank Joseph Rosenzweig and Mark Steedman for comments on earlier drafts of the paper. This research is partially supported by ARO DAAL03-89-C-0031, DMSO DAAH04-94-G-0402 and ARPA DAAH04-94-G-0426.

References

Badler, N., Phillips, C. and Webber, B. (1993), *Simulating Humans: Computer Graphics, Animation, Control*. Oxford: Oxford University Press.

Badler, N., Webber, B., Becket, W., Douville, B., Geib, C., Moore, M., Pelachaud, C., Reich, B., and Stone, M. (1996), Planning for Animation. In *Interactive Computer Animation*, Maginet-Thalmanni, N. and Thalmanni, D. (eds.), Hemel Hampstead: Prentice Hall.

Becket, W. (1994), *The Jack Lisp api*, Technical Report MS-CIS-94-01/Graphics Lab 59, Philadelphia: University of Pennsylvania.

Di Eugenio, B. (1993), *Understanding Natural Language Instructions: a Computational Approach to Purpose Clauses*. PhD Thesis, University of Pennsylvania, Philadelphia (Technical Report MS-CIS-93-91).

Di Eugenio, B. (1994), Action Representation and Natural Language Instructions. In *Proc. 4th Intern. Conference on Principles of Knowledge Representation and Reasoning (KR '94)*, Bonn.

Di Eugenio, B. (1998), An Action Representation Formalism to Interpret Natural Language Instructions. *Computational Intelligence, Vol. 14(1)*, to appear.

Di Eugenio, B. and Webber, B. (1992), Plan Recognition in Understanding Instructions. In *Proc. 1st. Intern. Conference on Artificial Intelligence Planning Systems*, College Park, MD.

Goldman, A. (1970), *A Theory of Human Action*, New York: Prentice-Hall.

Kirsh, D. and Maglio, P. (1994), On Distinguishing Epistemic from Pragmatic Actions. *Cognitive Science 18(4)*, 513-549.

McGowan, J. and DuBern, R. (eds.) (1991), *Home Repair*, London: Dorling Kindersley.

Moens, M. and Steedman, M. (1988), Temporal Ontology and Temporal Reference. *Computational Linguistics, 14(2)*, 15-28.

Pym, D., Pryor, L. and Murphy, D. (1995), Actions as Processes: A position on planning. In *Working Notes, AAAI Spring Symposium on Extending Theories of Action.* Stanford, CA, 169-173.

Reader's Digest New Complete Do-It-Yourself Manual (1991), Pleasantville, NY: The Reader's Digest Association.

Stump, G. (1985), *The Semantic Variability of Absolute Constructions*, Dordrecht: Reidel.

Webber, B. and Di Eugenio, B. (1990), Free Adjuncts in Natural Language Instructions. In *Proc. 13th Intern. Conference on Computational Linguistics* (COLING), Helsinki, 395-400.

Modeling and Processing of Oral and Tactile Activities in the GEORAL System

Jacques Siroux[1], Marc Guyomard[2], Franck Multon[2] and Christophe Remondeau[2]

[1] IRISA, IUT, Lannion, France;
siroux@enssat.fr
[2] IRISA, ENSSAT, Lannion, France

Abstract. This paper presents the processing of tactile and oral multimodal events that occur in inputs of the GEORAL tactile system. First we shall describe the principal results of observations on the behaviour of users in a multimodal interaction environment. These observations, combined with consideration of the technical possibilities and limitations of speech recognition, lead us to proposing a system architecture. The chapter ends with details of the modeling of communicative acts, based on plan operators, and the principal stages of the merging of tactile and oral acts.

1 Introduction

In spite of steady progress in vocal techniques (speech recognition and understanding, as well as speech synthesis), naive users may come up against various difficulties when using such techniques. Such difficulties have to do with the recognition and the understanding of user's utterances and with the quality of synthesized speech, which in certain cases poses understanding problems for the user. One way of resolving these problems is to provide the systems with complementary or redundant input and output means of communication (Lee, 1991; Zancanaro, 1993; Tyler, 1991; Cohen, 1992). For example, for the output we can use a display on the screen of certain utterances pronounced by the computer, or for the input we can use of a mouse or a touch-sensitive screen. In the latter case, new forms and methods of communication appear, and we find ourselves yet again confronted with new problems: how does the user react to such systems, how to model the combination of activities, with which tools, etc. Although partial solutions exist (Bourget, 1992), these problems constitute research domains where answers are still to be found.

This chapter describes how we resolve the integration problem of oral and tactile media for the inputs of an existing system. The integration is based on specific characteristics of the application and the kind of dialogues. We shall first present, in section 2, the observations we have carried out on the linguistic behaviour in interaction with a simulated system. Section 3 is dedicated to the part of the system's architecture which deals with integration problems. Section 4 describes in more detail referential problems that need to be solved, and the modeling of communicative acts used to facilitate processing. Finally, the different stages of processing are presented in section 5.

2   Preliminary Study

2.1   The initial system

In 1992, we developed a dialogue system which was able to provide tourist information about beaches, churches, abbeys, châteaux, etc. for the Trégor region in Brittany (Gavignet, 1991). The user is able to interact with the system in a visual mode by using a map of Trégor displayed on the screen, and in an oral mode via a speech recognition board. The system uses both the oral channel (via a text to speech synthesis board), and graphics, such as the flashing of sites, routes, and localities, and zooming in on subsections of the map, so as to best inform the user. It is important to note that the speech recognition board used considerably reduces the users' linguistic possibilities: the vocabulary is small, sentences are short, and the types of anaphora and ellipsis are limited.

The evaluation of the system shows that errors in the speech recognition can be detrimental to the quality of the interaction. This prompted us to envisage the broadening of input-output media by introducing a touch screen. This would allow a greater flexibility in the wording of utterances, as well as a larger range of wording possibilities, when faced with speech recognition problems.

Today the area of multimodal dialogue is lacking theoretical results as well as corpus data. We therefore decided to set up a simulation (Guyomard, 1995) of the targeted system in a Wizard of Oz mode (see Oviatt, 1992), so as to provide observations which could serve as a foundation for implementation.

The main results of this experiment are the following.

- the presence of the tactile screen modifies the linguistic behaviour of the user: certain deictic terms and syntactic structures appear;
- the use of the tactile screen by the user to overcome recognition problems of the system is not immediate and requires a certain amount of time to adapt to;
- three main possible relationships between oral utterances and tactile gestures have been identified:
  - a *bound* relationship, in which a deictic element of the oral utterance and a touch activity are used together to designate an entity on the map:

      U: Are there any beaches in this locality?
      +
      a touch on a locality.

  - a *confirmative* relationship, where the oral part is sufficient for comprehension but is accompanied by a tactile designation, which is strictly speaking redundant:

U: Are there any beaches in Lannion ?

+

a touch on Lannion.

- a *substitution* relationship, where the tactile designation replaces the linguistic reference:

U: Where are the campsites?

+

a touch on Lannion.

– Finally, concerning the nature of the touch gesture, we notice a pragmatic phenomenon which has already been studied in the area of verbal dialogue. The referential aspect of a touch gesture can only be understood completely if it is considered within the context of the interaction. In other words, the illocutionary gesture can prove to be different from the referential gesture. This manifests itself in two ways according to the nature of the context, either in the complementary oral utterance or in the application:

- The touch gesture can differ in referential specificity from the utterance:

U: Show me the castles in this zone

+

a pointing action.

- The touch gesture must be combined with elements of the map to define a zone:

U: Show me the campsites in this zone

+

drawing a line

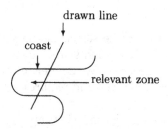

3   Architecture

3.1   General principles

The architecture and the functioning of the GEORAL system are the result of, on the one hand, experimentation exploitation, and on the other hand the use of hardware and software of the pre-existing system. Experimentation has revealed situations in which it is not possible to envisage completely separate processing of tactile and oral inputs. These situations concern in particular tactile gestures that do not provide sufficient information to enable autonomous interpretation.

For example, the trace of a vertical line alone does not enable us to decide whether the zone that the user is interested in is situated to the right or the left of the line. This means that attention needs to be given to speech media, and that the processing of tactile entries should be based on that of spoken entries.

The user's activities in a multimodal environment may occur in an asynchronous or in a synchronous way. The system must therefore deal with the usual problems of parallelism and synchronisation management. In our case the speech recognition board that was used and its management are helpful to solve the problem. The speech recognition board is not in constant use. The user's freedom is limited as he can only act if the system allows him, by displaying a prompt. The user can then speak and touch the screen. Once the end of the input sentence is detected (using a heuristic method, internal to the recognition board) no further tactile activity will be taken into account. Parallelism and synchronisation problems occur only when speech takes place. Taking into account the above observation concerning the dominance of speech, and relying on the fact that in the application the tactile register is limited, we end up using a very simple mechanism for managing the media. In particular, we no longer need time labelling of oral and tactile events. These simplifications seem pragmatically justified as they are not refuted by experimental observations. However, it is clear that these solutions are not universal.

3.2   Architecture

The following diagram shows the principle modules of the system as well as the data flow between the modules. The dialogue module, which manages the user-system interaction using a dialogue grammar (Wachtel, 1985) and algorithms for computing co-operative responses (Guyomard, 1989) and the modules responsible for query evaluation and graphical display are not represented in the diagram.

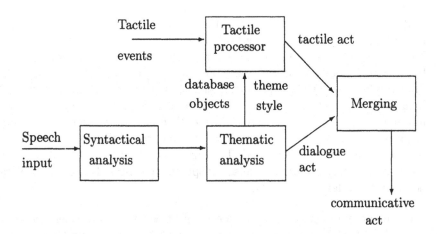

The control flow of the system can be described as follows. The syntactic and thematic analysis are activated after the speech recognition. They produce dialogue acts as well as information necessary for the processing of tactile events. The interpretation of tactile events is made and a tactile act is produced that contains the elements designated by the user. The dialogue and tactile acts are then merged to form a communicative act, the propositional contents of which is completed from a referential point of view. We shall continue by describing the approach we adopt to the modeling of communicative acts, and the principal stages of processing to arrive at communicative acts.

4   Modeling Communicative Acts

4.1   References

Before describing the modeling of communicative acts, it is convenient first to better characterize users' referential behaviour (Cohen, 1984).

The combined tactile and linguistic (oral) activities convey the designation of elements displayed or to be displayed on the screen. A designation can be divided over the use of two media according to the following possibilities:

- without using the tactile screen, either anaphora are used or a new object is introduced in the dialogue;
- both oral and tactile media are used (with confirmative and bound relationships);
- only the tactile medium is used (with the substitution relationship).

In the case of our prototype, the interactive activities present the following characteristics:

- Referents: the user can choose every element displayed on the screen (site or locality). From a pragmatic point of view the referents thus designated are objects that belong to the database and are linked to a locality. This form of designation is simple (Tyler, 1991) and doesn't need complex pragmatic reasoning, such as that suggested by Green (1987).
- Tactile activities: designation can be done either by touching (pointing) or by drawing a zone or a line. Only those zones are handled that are entirely drawn by the user, i.e. without using elements of the map (coast, roads,...).
- Linguistic activities: we note the presence of deictic and anaphoric elements in the utterances (*this area, here, this one, that one*). In general, the dialogic or phrasal contexts alone do not allow us to determine the type of reference (deictic or anaphoric) performed. The number of deictic and anaphoric elements is voluntarily limited because the speech recognition board's capacities do not allow a larger vocabulary.

More generally in person-machine communication situations, other phenomena must also be dealt with: discordance may appear between the oral and tactile activities, speech recognition and understanding errors and faulty tactile activities may arise. The management of these phenomena must be done in such a way that it should be always possible to adapt the processes after having observed new interactions.

4.2 Intermediate Structures

The final representation structures we want to obtain are communicative acts, the propositional content of which is complete from a referential point of view. A communicative act will be construed using two kinds of intermediary acts: dialogue and tactile acts. We have defined 5 dialogue acts which we will need for the application: ASK, ACCORD, ANNULATION, INFORMREF, and SILENCE. In what follows we will be particularly interested in the ASK dialogue act. The form of the act representation that we use is derived from (Allen, citeref:all); the referential elements present in the surface utterances are in the form of a code in the propositional content, without having been resolved. Some examples of ASK acts are:

1. ASK(U, S, INFORMREF(S, U, beach, Q(beach, near(locality (deicphore(zone))))))
   representing *Are there any beaches in the zone?*

2. ASK(U, S, INFORMREF(S, U, beach, Q(beach, locality(deicphore(pointing)))))
   representing *Is there a beach here?*

3. ASK(U, S, INFORMREF(S, U, beach, Q(beach, locality (Lannion))))
   representing *Is there a beach in Lannion?*

The element deicphore(x) indicates that a reference of type x (zone delimitation or pointing) occurred; this reference can be either anaphoric or deictic.

After tactile activities have been treated, they are represented by a tactile act in the following form: DÉSIGNER(U, S, object), where object has one of the following forms (string, type, order, X, Y) or ((string, type, order, X, Y))*, where string represents the object designated in the data base, and type has the value zone or the value pointing; order represents the order of input of the designation, and X and Y are the coordinates of the object.

4.3 Communicative acts

Maybury (1991, 1992) has proposed an approach to communication modeling, the aim of which was to be able to generate answers in a multimedia system. His approach is based on the distinction of three types of acts: rhetorical acts, linguistic acts, and visual acts. Rhetorical acts are the highest-level acts, visual acts the lowest-level ones. A rhetorical act is represented as a planning operator with the usual elements: constraints on current environment, preconditions and effects (in terms of mental states: want, know), and a body. The body contains instances of visual and linguistic acts. For a given illocutionary effect we find a set of rhetorical acts possessing the same header but with different bodies, constraints and preconditions. This makes it possible to choose the correct version of the act taking into account the current environment. Similar principles are found in the work of other authors (Wahlster, 1991; Feiner, 1990), although with differences in implementation and planning.

We have used this representation approach for another purpose, namely that of merging designations, and for recognition rather than generation of acts. The highest level type of act that we will recognize, from tactile and oral inputs is the communicative act. In a way similar to Maybury, we represent a communicative act by means of several models. A model corresponds to a realisation mode of reference (anaphora, completive relationship,...). For example, the communicative act REQUEST has five models:

- REQUEST without anaphora
- REQUEST_completive mode
- REQUEST_confirmative mode
- REQUEST_substitution mode
- REQUEST with anaphora

We detail the first two:

NAME:	REQUEST without anaphora
HEADER:	REQUEST(S, U, ?x, Q(?x,?P)))
BODY:	ASK(U,S, INFORMREF(S, U, ?x, Q(?x, ?P)))
CONSTRAINT:	not(DÉSIGNER(U, ?t, ?y))
PRECONDITION:	none

NAME: REQUEST without anaphora
HEADER: REQUEST(U, S, INFORMREF(S, U, ?x, Q(?x,?P)))
BODY: ASK(U,S, INFORMREF(S, U, ?x, Q(?x, ?P)))
CONSTRAINT: not(DÉSIGNER(U, ?t, ?y))
PRECONDITION: none

NAME: REQUEST_completive mode
HEADER: REQUEST(U, S, INFORMREF(S, U, ?x, Q(?x,?P'(?o'))))
BODY: ASK(U,S, INFORMREF(S, U, ?x, Q(?x, ?P(?D))))
                   DÉSIGNER(U,?t,?o)
CONSTRAINT: none
PRECONDITION: Déictique(?P(?D)), ?o, ?P'(?o'))

The first one corresponds to a REQUEST with neither deictic nor anaphoric phenomena (presence of the item not (DÉSIGNER(U, S, ?o)) in the constraint); the second one corresponds to a REQUEST for which two complementary acts have to be present in the input (this is represented in the body by ASK, in which there is a deicphore, and by the tactile act DÉSIGNER), which must verify the predicate Déictique in the precondition. The predicate Déictique takes care of checking the coherence of coreferences constructing the result that will appear in the propositional content. This predicate is expressed in the form of a set of Prolog rules, for example:

```
Déictique(locality(deicphore(Type)), (Object, pointed, 1, X, Y),
     locality(Object))
  ⇒
```

```
is_pointing(Type),
is_locality(Object).
```

The first two parameters correspond to inputs and the third one is the output if the right part of the rule is true. This form of specification allows a great flexibility in the solution of the merging because we can easily modify the priority assigned to the media and carry out complex coreference verifications (Multon, 1994).

5 Processing

The syntactic analysis has as input a string of words produced by the recognition board (MEDIA50, licence CNET France Telecom)[1] and produces a complete syntactic tree, in which the anaphoric and deictic items are clearly brought to the fore.

The thematic analysis has two principal roles with regard to the tactile function. It determines the possible type (style) of tactile touch (pointing, zone delimitation), as well as the theme of the statement (type of object in question). If the phrase is elliptical, the previous dialogue fragment is taken into account. The transmission of the theme to the tactile processor is accompanied by the transmission of the relevant objects of the database.

The tactile processor receives as input the list of touches performed by the user, the list of objects in the database which it must examine, and the style of touch predicted. It will produce the list of objects effectively designated. This process necessitates the appropriate processing of the tactile events (for example, reconstruction of zones, elimination of duplicate touches), and a verification of the coherence between the predictions produced by the thematic analysis and the observed facts. In case of discrepancies between the predictions and the actual touch, we decided to give priority to the prediction.

The most interesting point of the merging process concerns the determination of the communicative acts coding the user's requests. We determine from the body of actions, constraints and preconditions, which communicative act is suitable (cf. Litman, 1987). The checking of the constraints and preconditions also allows at the same time to instanciate the different elements of the communicative act thanks to the unification process. If the processing doesn't establish propositional contents or a valid communicative act, the dialogue module (that is not represented here) is warned and will calculate an appropriate reaction (e.g., asking for repetition, or computing a co-operative response).

---

[1] The MEDIA50 board uses an overgenerative grammar for recognizing continuous speech and produces a string of words which has to be more deeply analyzed from a linguistic point of view.

6   Conclusion

We have presented the merging of acts resulting from the oral and tactile activities of the user of a multimodal system. The development of the prototype is finished and a first set of experiments has been carried out. The resulting corpus is currently being examined in detail.

The modeling of communicative acts is achieved by using a model of planning operators with constraints and preconditions. This allows a great flexibility for more subtly adapting the system to the user's behaviour as well as for dealing with other types of interaction.

This work is a first step towards a more powerful system. In the future, three points will be investigated. The first one is completing the modeling of communicative acts by adding a representation of mental states. The second is concerned with the modeling of the cartographic context. This will make it possible to take into account a greater number of gestural activities (the ones that use elements of the map), and also to improve the cooperativeness of the system. The third is concerned with improving the processing of the discordances which may arise between the oral and tactile activities. This processing may be based on two scoring functions: for the oral activity, a score can be derived from the speech recognition scoring, while for the tactile activity a score may be defined taking into account characteristics of the user's previous tactile activities. This processing may lead to such decisions as restarting the speech recognition, or favouring one of the two media.

Acknowledgement

This project was partially funded by CNET (France Telecom), contract 92 7B.

References

Allen, J. (1987) *Natural Language Understanding.* Redwood City: Benjamin Cummings.

Bourguet, M. L. (1992) Conception et réalisation d'une interface de dialogue personne-machine multimodale. Thèse de troisième cycle, Institut National Polytechnique de Grenoble.

Cohen, P. R. (1984) The Pragmatics of Referring and the Modality of Communication. *Computational Linguistics* 10 (2), 1984, 97–146.

Cohen, P. R. (1992) The Role of Natural Language in a Multimodal Interface. *Proc. 2nd FRIEND21, International Symposium on Next Generation Human Interface Technology,* Tokyo, November 1991, 143–149.

Feiner, S. K. and McKeown, K. R. (1990) Coordinating Text and Graphics in Explanation Generation. *Proc. AAAI-90,* vol. 1, 442–449.

Gavignet, F., Guyomard, M., Siroux, J. (1991) Implementing an oral and geographic multimodal application: the Géoral project. In *Pre-proceedings of Second Venaco Workshop on the Structure of Multimodal Dialogue,* Acquafredda di Maratea, Italy, September 1991.

Green, G. M. (1987) *Pragmatics and Natural Language Understanding.* Hillsdale, New Jersey: Lawrence Erlbaum.

Guyomard, M., Siroux, J. (1989) Suggestive and corrective answers: a simple mechanism. In M. M. Taylor, D. G. Bouwhuis, and F. Néel (eds) *The Structure of Multimodal Dialog,* Amsterdam: North Holland, 361–374.

Guyomard, M., Le Meur, D., Poignonnec, S., and Siroux, J. (1995) Experimental work for the dual usage of voice and touch screen for a cartographic application. *Proc. ESCA Tutorial and Research Workshop on Spoken Dialogue Systems,* Vigsø, Denmark, May 30-June 2, 1995, 153–156.

Lee, J. (1991) Graphics and Natural Language in Multi-Modal Dialogues. *Preproceedings of Second Venaco Workshop on the Structure of Multimodal Dialogue,* Acquafredda di Maratea, Italy, September, 1991.

Litman, D. J. and Allen, J. A. (1987) A Plan Recognition Model for Subdialogue in Conversations. *Cognitive Science* 11, 163–200.

Maybury, M. T. (1991) Planning Multimedia Explanations Using Communicative Acts. *Proc. Ninth AAAI National Conference on Artificial Intelligence,* Anaheim, CA, July 1991, 61-66.

Maybury, M. T. (1992) Communicative Acts for Explanation Generation. *International Journal of Man-Machine Studies,* 37 (2), 135–172.

Multon, F. (1994) GEORAL tactile un système multimodal. Rapport de DEA, IFSIC, Université de Rennes 1.

Oviatt, S., Cohen, P. R., Fong, M., and Frank, M. (1992) A rapid semi-automatic simulation technique for investigating interactive speech and handwriting. *Proc. 7th International Conference on Spoken Language Processing,* Banff, Canada, October 1992, vol. 2, 1351–1354.

Tyler, S. W., Schlossberg, J. L. and Cook, L. K. (1991) CHORIS: An Intelligent Interface Architecture for Multimodal Interaction. *Proc. AAAI91 Workshop on Intelligent Multimedia Interfaces,* Anaheim, CA, July 1991.

Wachtel, T. (1985) Discourse structure. *LOKI Report NLI1-1.1, Esprit Project 107,* Research Unit for Information Science and Artificial Intelligence, University of Hamburg.

Wahlster, W., André, E., Graf, W., and Rist, T. (1991) Designing Illustrated Texts: How Language Production is Influenced by Graphics Generation. *Proc. EACL 91,* Berlin, April 1991, 8–14.

Zancanaro, M., Stock, O., and Strapparava, C. (1993) Dialog Cohesion Sharing and Adjusting in an Enhanced Multimodal Environment. *Proc. IJCAI 1993,* Chambéry, France, 1230–1235.

Multimodal Maps: An Agent-Based Approach

Adam Cheyer and Luc Julia

SRI International
333 Ravenswood Ave
Menlo Park, CA 94025 - USA

Abstract. In this paper, we discuss how multiple input modalities may be combined to produce more natural user interfaces. To illustrate this technique, we present a prototype map-based application for a travel planning domain. The application is distinguished by a synergistic combination of handwriting, gesture and speech modalities; access to existing data sources including the World Wide Web; and a mobile handheld interface. To implement the described application, a hierarchical distributed network of heterogeneous software agents was augmented by appropriate functionality for developing synergistic multimodal applications.

1   Introduction

As computer systems become more powerful and complex, efforts to make computer interfaces more simple and natural become increasingly important. Natural interfaces should be designed to facilitate communication in ways people are already accustomed to using. Such interfaces allow users to concentrate on the tasks they are trying to accomplish, not worry about what they must do to control the interface.

In this paper, we begin by discussing what input modalities humans are comfortable using when interacting with computers, and how these modalities should best be combined in order to produce natural interfaces. In Sect. 3, we present a prototype map-based application for the travel planning domain which uses a synergistic combination of several input modalities. Section 4 describes the agent-based approach we used to implement the application and the work on which it is based. In Sect. 5, we summarize our conclusions and future directions.

2   Natural Input

2.1   Input Modalities

Direct manipulation interface technologies are currently the most widely used techniques for creating user interfaces. Through the use of menus and a graphical user interface, users are presented with sets of discrete actions and the objects on which to perform them. Pointing devices such as a mouse facilitate selection of an object or action, and drag and drop techniques allow items to be moved or combined with other entities or actions.

With the addition of electronic pen devices, gestural drawings add a new dimension direct manipulation interfaces. Gestures allow users to communicate a surprisingly wide range of meaningful requests with a few simple strokes. Research has shown that multiple gestures can be combined to form dialog, with rules of temporal grouping overriding temporal sequencing (Rhyne, 1987). Gestural commands are particularly applicable to graphical or editing type tasks.

Direct manipulation interactions possess many desirable qualities: communication is generally fast and concise; input techniques are easy to learn and remember; the user has a good idea about what can be accomplished, as the visual presentation of the available actions is generally easily accessible. However, direct manipulation suffers from limitations when trying to access or describe entities which are not or can not be visualized by the user.

Limitations of direct manipulation style interfaces can be addressed by another interface technology, that of natural language interfaces. Natural language interfaces excel in describing entities that are not currently displayed on the monitor, in specifying temporal relations between entities or actions, and in identifying members of sets. These strengths are exactly the weaknesses of direct manipulation interfaces, and concurrently, the weaknesses of natural language interfaces (ambiguity, conceptual coverage, etc.) can be overcome by the strengths of direct manipulation.

Natural language content can be entered through different input modalities, including typing, handwriting, and speech. It is important to note that, while the same textual content can be provided by the three modalities, each modality has widely varying properties.

- Spoken language is the modality used first and foremost in human-human interactive problem solving (Cohen et al., 1990). Speech is an extremely fast medium, several times faster than typing or handwriting. In addition, speech input contains content that is not present in other forms of natural language input, such as prosidy, tone and characteristics of the speaker (age, sex, accent).

- Typing is the most common way of entering information into a computer, because it is reasonably fast, very accurate, and requires no computational resources.

- Handwriting has been shown to be useful for certain types of tasks, such as performing numerical calculations and manipulating names which are difficult to pronounce (Oviatt, 1994; Oviatt and Olson, 1994). Because of its relatively slow production rate, handwriting may induce users to produce different types of input than is generated by spoken language; abbreviations, symbols and non-grammatical patterns may be expected to be more prevalent amid written input.

2.2   Combination of Modalities

As noted in the previous section, direct manipulation and natural language seem to be very complementary modalities. It is therefore not surprising that a number of multimodal systems combine the two.

Notable among such systems is the Cohen's Shoptalk system (Cohen, 1992), a prototype manufacturing and decision-support system that aids in tasks such as quality assurance monitoring, and production scheduling. The natural language module of Shoptalk is based on the Chat-85 natural language system (Warren and Perreira, 1982) and is particularly good at handling time, tense, and temporal reasoning.

A number of systems have focused on combining the speed of speech with the reference provided by direct manipulation of a mouse pointer. Such systems include the XTRA system (Allegayer et al, 1989), CUBRICON (Neal and Shapiro, 1991), the PAC-Amodeus model (Nigay and Coutaz, 1993), and TAPAGE (Faure and Julia, 1994).

XTRA and CUBRICON are both systems that combine complex spoken input with mouse clicks, using several knowledge sources for reference identification. CUBRICON's domain is a map-based task, making it similar to the application developed in this paper. However, the two are different in that CUBRICON can only use direct manipulation to indicate a specific item, whereas our system produces a richer mixing of modalities by adding both gestural and written language as input modalities.

The PAC-Amodeus systems such as VoicePaint and Notebook allow the user to synergistically combine vocal or mouse-click commands when interacting with notes or graphical objects. However, due to the selected domains, the natural language input is very simple, generally of the style "Insert a note here".

TAPAGE is another system that allows true synergistic combination of spoken input with direct manipulation. Like PAC-Amodeus, TAPAGE's domain provides only simple linguistic input. However, TAPAGE uses a pen-based interface instead of a mouse, allowing gestural commands. TAPAGE, selected as a building block for our map application, will be described more in detail in Sect. 4.2.

Other interesting work regarding the simultaneous combination of handgestures and gaze can be found in Bolt (1980) and Koons, Sparrell and Thorisson (1993).

3   A Multimodal Map Application

In this section, we will describe a prototype map-based application for a travel planning domain. In order to provide the most natural user interface possible, the system permits the user to simultaneously combine direct manipulation, gestural drawings, handwritten, typed and spoken natural language. When designing the system, other criteria were considered as well:

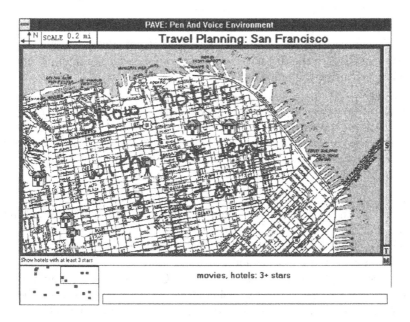

Fig. 1. Multimodal application for travel planning

- The user interface must be light and fast enough to run on a handheld PDA while able to access applications and data that may require a more powerful machine.
- Existing commercial or research natural language and speech recognition systems should be used.
- Through the multimodal interface, a user must be able to transparently access a wide variety of data sources, including information stored in HTML form on the World Wide Web.

As illustrated in Fig. 1, the user is presented with a pen sensitive map display on which drawn gestures and written natural language statements may be combined with spoken input. As opposed to a static paper map, the location, resolution, and content presented by the map change, according to the requests of the user. Objects of interest, such as restaurants, movie theaters, hotels, tourist sites, municipal buildings, etc. are displayed as icons. The user may ask the map to perform various actions. For example :

- *distance calculation* : e.g. "How far is the hotel from Fisherman's Wharf?"
- *object location* : e.g. "Where is the nearest post office?"
- *filtering* : e.g. "Display the French restaurants within 1 mile of this hotel."
- *information retrieval* : e.g. "Show me all available information about Alcatraz."

The application also makes use of multimodal (multimedia) output as well as input: video, text, sound and voice can all be combined when presenting an answer to a query.

During input, requests can be entered using gestures (see Fig. 2 for sample gestures), handwriting, voice, or a combination of pen and voice. For instance, in order to calculate the distance between two points on the map, a command may be issued using the following:

- *gesture*, by simply drawing a line between the two points of interest.
- *voice*, by speaking "What is the distance from the post office to the hotel?".
- *handwriting*, by writing "dist p.o. to hotel?"
- *synergistic combination of pen and voice*, by speaking "What is the distance from here to this hotel?" while simultaneously indicating the specified locations by pointing or circling.

Notice that in our example of synergistic combination of pen and voice, the arguments to the verb "distance" can be specified before, at the same time, or shortly after the vocalization of the request to calculate the distance. If a user's request is ambiguous or underspecified, the system will wait several seconds and then issue a prompt requesting additional information.

The user interface runs on pen-equipped PC's or a Dauphin handheld PDA (Dauphin, DTR-1 User's Manual) using either a microphone or a telephone for voice input. The interface is connected either by modem or ethernet to a server machine which will manage database access, natural language processing and speech recognition for the application. The result is a mobile system that provides a synergistic pen/voice interface to remote databases.

In general, the speed of the system is quite acceptable. For gestural commands, which are handled locally on the user interface machine, a response is produced in less than one second. For handwritten commands, the time to recognize the handwriting, process the English query, access a database and begin to display the results on the user interface is less than three seconds (assuming an ethernet connection, and good network and database response). Solutions to verbal commands are displayed in three to five seconds after the end of speech has been detected; partial feedback indicating the current status of the speech recognition is provided earlier.

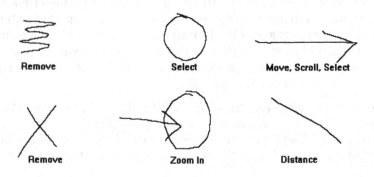

Fig. 2. Sample gestures

4   Approach

In order to implement the application described in the previous section, we chose to augment a proven agent- based architecture with functionalities developed for a synergistically multimodal application. The result is a flexible methodology for designing and implementing distributed multimodal applications.

4.1   Building Blocks

Open Agent Architecture. The Open Agent Architecture (OAA) (Cohen et al., 1994) provides a framework for coordinating a society of agents which interact to solve problems for the user. Through the use of agents, the OAA provides distributed access to commercial applications, such as mail systems, calendar programs, databases, etc.

The Open Agent Architecture possesses several properties which make it a good candidate for our needs:

- An Interagent Communication Language (ICL) and Query Protocol have been developed, allowing agents to communicate among themselves. Agents can run on different platforms and be implemented in a variety of programming languages.
- Several natural language systems have been integrated into the OAA which convert English into the Interagent Communication Language. In addition, a speech recognition agent has been developed to provide transparent access to the Corona speech recognition system.
- The agent architecture has been used to provide natural language and agent access to various heterogeneous data and knowledge sources.
- Agent interaction is very fine-grained. The architecture was designed so that a number of agents can work together, when appropriate in parallel, to produce fast responses to queries.

The architecture for the OAA, based loosely on Schwartz's FLiPSiDE system (Schwartz, 1993), uses a hierarchical configuration where client agents connect to a "facilitator" server. Facilitators provide content-based message routing, global data management, and process coordination for their set of connected agents. Facilitators can, in turn, be connected as clients of other facilitators. Each facilitator records the published functionality of their sub-agents, and when queries arrive in Interagent Communication Language form, they are responsible for breaking apart any complex queries and for distributing goals to the appropriate agents. An agent solving a goal may require supporting information and the agent architecture provides numerous means of requesting data from other agents or from the user.

Among the assortment of agent architectures, the Open Agent Architecture can be most closely compared to work by the ARPA knowledge sharing community (Genesereth and Singh, 1994). The OAA's query protocol, Interagent Communication Language and Facilitator mechanisms have similar instantiations in the SHADE project, in the form of KQML, KIF and various independent capability matchmakers. Other agent architectures, such as General Magic's Telescript (General Magic, 1995), MASCOS (Park et al, submitted), or the CORBA distributed object approach (Object Management Group, 1991) do not provide as fully developed mechanisms for interagent communication and delegation.

The Open Agent Architecture provides capability for accessing distributed knowledge sources through natural language and voice, but it is lacking integration with a synergistic multimodal interface.

TAPAGE. TAPAGE (edition de Tableaux par la Parole et la Geste) is a synergistic pen/voice system for designing and correcting tables.

To capture signals emitted during a user's interaction, TAPAGE integrates a set of modality agents, each responsible for a very specialized kind of signal (Faure and Julia, 1994). The modality agents are connected to an 'interpret agent' which is responsible for combining the inputs across all modalities to form a valid command for the application. The interpret agent receives filtered results from the modality agents, sorts the information into the correct fields, performs type-checking on the arguments, and prompts the user for any missing information, according to the model of the interaction. The interpret agent is also responsible for merging the data streams sent by the modality agents, and for resolving ambiguities among them, based on its knowledge of the application's internal state. Another function of the interpret agent is to produce reflexes: reflexes are actions output at the interface level without involving the functional core of the application.

The TAPAGE system can accept multimodal input, but it is not a distributed system; its functional core is fixed. In TAPAGE, the set of linguistic input is limited to a *verb object argument* format.

4.2   Synthesis

In the Open Agent Architecture, agents are distributed entities that can run on different machines, and communicate together to solve a task for the user. In TAPAGE, agents are used to provide streams of input to a central interpret process, responsible for merging incoming data. A generalization of these two types of agents could be:

Macro Agents: contain some knowledge and ability to reason about a domain, and can answer or make queries to other macro agents using the Interagent Communication Language.

Micro Agents: are responsible for handling a single input or output data stream, either filtering the signal to or from a hierarchically superior 'interpret' agent.

The network architecture that we used was hierarchical at two resolutions: micro agents are connected to a superior macro agent, and macro agents are connected in turn to a facilitator agent. In both cases, a server is responsible for the supervision of its client sub-agents.

In order to describe our implementation, we will first give a description of each agent used in our application and then illustrate the flow of communication among agents produced by a user's request.

Speech Recognition (SR) Agent: The SR agent provides a mapping from the Interagent Communication Language to the API for the Decipher (Corona) speech recognition system (Cohen et al., 1990), a continuous speech speaker independent recognizer based on Hidden Markov Model technology. This macro agent is also responsible for supervising a child micro agent whose task is to control the speech data stream. The SR agent can provide feedback to an interface agent about the current status and progress of the micro agent (e.g. "listening", "end of speech detected", etc.) This agent is written in C.

Natural Language (NL) Parser Agent: translates English expressions into the Interagent Communication Language (ICL). For a more complete description of the ICL, see Cohen et al. (Cohen et al., 1994). The NL agent we selected for our application is the simplest of those integrated into the OAA. It is written in Prolog using Definite Clause Grammars, and supports a distributed vocabulary; each agent dynamically adds word definitions as it connects to the network. A current project is underway to integrate the Gemini natural language system (Cohen et al., 1990), a robust bottom up parser and semantic interpreter specifically designed for use in Spoken Language Understanding projects.

Database Agents: Database agents can reside at local or remote locations and can be grouped hierarchically according to content. Micro agents can be connected to database agents to monitor relevant positions or events in real time. In our travel planning application, database agents provide maps for each city, as well as icons, vocabulary and information about available hotels, restaurants, movies, theaters, municipal buildings and tourist attractions. Three types of databases were used: Prolog databases, X.500 hierarchical databases, and data loaded automatically by scanning HTML pages from the World Wide Web (WWW). In one instance, a local newspaper provides weekly updates to its Mosaic-accessible list of current movie times and reviews, as well as adding several new restaurant reviews to a growing collection; this information is extracted by an HTML reading database agent and made accessible to the agent architecture. Descriptions and addresses of new restaurants are presented to the user on request, and the user can choose to add them to the permanent database by specifying positional coordinates on the map (e.g. "add this new restaurant here"), information lacking in the WWW database.

Reference Resolution Agent: This agent is responsible for merging requests arriving in parallel from different modalities, and for controlling interactions between the user interface agent, database agents and modality agents. In this implementation, the reference resolution agent is domain specific: knowledge is encoded as to what actions must be performed to resolve each possible type of ICL request in its particular domain. For a given ICL logical form, the agent can verify argument types, supply default values, and resolve argument references. Some argument references are descriptive ("How far is it to the hotel on Emerson Street?"); in this case, a domain agent will try to resolve the definite reference by sending database agent requests. Other references, particularly when contextual or deictic, are resolved by the user interface agent ("What are the rates for this hotel?"). Once arguments to a query have been resolved, this agent coordinates the actions and calculations necessary to produce the result of the request.

Interface Agent: This macro agent is responsible for managing what is currently being displayed to the user, and for accepting the user's multimodal input. The Interface Agent also coordinates client modality agents and resolves ambiguities among them : handwriting and gestures are interpreted locally by micro agents and combined with results from the speech recognition agent, running on a remote speech server. The handwriting micro-agent interfaces with the Microsoft PenWindows API and accesses a handwriting recognizer by CIC Corporation. The gesture micro- agent accesses recognition algorithms developed for TAPAGE.

An important task for the interface agent is to record which objects of each type are currently salient, in order to resolve contextual references such as "the hotel" or "where I was before." Deictic references are resolved by gestural or direct manipulation commands. If no such indication is currently specified, the user interface agent waits long enough to give the user an opportunity to supply the value, and then prompts the user for it.

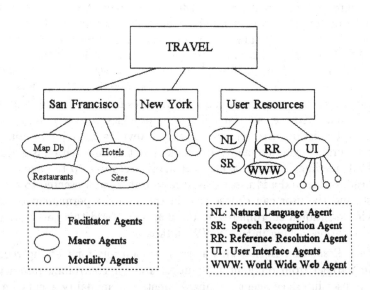

Fig. 3. Agent Architecture for Map Application

We shall now give an example of the distributed interaction of agents for a specific query. In the following example, all communication among agents passes transparently through a facilitator agent in an undirected fashion; this process is left out of the description for brevity.

1. A user speaks: "How far is the restaurant from this hotel?"
2. The speech recognition agent monitors the status and results from its micro agent, sending feedback received by the user interface agent. When the string is recognized, a translation is requested.
3. The English request is received by the NL agent and translated into ICL form.
4. The reference resolution agent (RR) receives the ICL distance request containing one definite and one deictic reference and asks for resolution of these references.
5. The interface agent uses contextual structures to find what "the restaurant" refers to, and waits for the user to make a gesture indicating "the hotel", issuing prompts if necessary.
6. When the references have been resolved, the domain agent (RR) sends database requests asking for the coordinates of the items in question. It then calculates the distance according to the scale of the currently displayed map, and requests the user interface to produce output displaying the result of the calculation.

5   Conclusions

By augmenting an existing agent-based architecture with concepts necessary for synergistic multimodal input, we were able to rapidly develop a map-based application for a travel planning task. The resulting application has met our initial requirements: a mobile, synergistic pen/voice interface providing good natural language access to heterogeneous distributed knowledge sources. The approach used was general and should provide a for developing synergistic multimodal applications for other domains.

The system described here is one of the first that accepts commands made of synergistic combinations of spoken language, handwriting and gestural input. This fusion of modalities can produce more complex interactions than in many systems and the prototype application will serve as a testbed for acquiring a better understanding of multimodal input.

In the near future, we will continue to verify and extend our approach by building other multimodal applications. We are interested in generalizing the methodology even further; work has already begun on an agent-building tool which will simplify and automate many of the details of developing new agents and domains.

References

Allegayer, J., Jansen-Winkeln, R., Reddig, C. and Reithinger, N. (1989) Bidirectional use of knowledge in the multi-modal NL access system XTRA. In *Proceedings of IJCAI-89*, Detroit, pp. 1492-1497.

Bolt, R. (1980) Put that there: Voice and Gesture at the Graphic Interface, *Computer Graphics, 14(3)*, pp. 262-270.

Cohen, M., Murveit, H., Bernstein, J., Price, P., and Weintraub, M. (1990) The DE-CIPHER Speech Recognition System. In *1990 IEEE ICASSP*, pp. 77-80.

Cohen, P. (1992) The role of natural language in a multimodal interface. In *Proceedings of UIST'92*, pp. 143-149.

Cohen, P.R., Cheyer, A., Wang, M. and Baeg, S.C. (1994) An Open Agent Architecture. In *Proceedings AAAI'94 - SA*, Stanford, pp. 1-8.

Dauphin DTR-1 User's Manual, Dauphin Technology, Inc., Lombard, Ill 60148.

Faure, C. and Julia, L. (1994) An Agent-Based Architecture for a Multimodal Interface. In *Proceedings AAAI'94 - IM4S*, Stanford, pp. 82-86.

Genesereth, M. and Singh, N.P. (1994) *A knowledge sharing approach to software interoperation*, unpublished manuscript, Computer Science Department, Stanford University.

Telescript Product Documentation (1995), General Magic Inc.

Koons, D.B., Sparrell, C.J., and Thorisson, K.R. (1993) Integrating Simultaneous Input from Speech, Gaze and Hand Gestures. In *Intelligent Multimedia Interfaces*, Maybury, M.T. (ed.), Menlo Park: AAAI Press/MIT Press.

Maybury, M.T. (ed.) (1993) *Intelligent Multimedia Interfaces*, Menlo Park: AAAI Press/MIT Press.

Neal, J.G., and Shapiro, S.C. (1991) Intelligent Multi-media Interface Technology. In *Intelligent User Interfaces*, Sullivan, J.W. and Tyler, S.W. (eds.), Reading: Addison-Wesley Pub. Co., pp. 11-43.

Nigay, L. and Coutaz, J. (1993) A Design Space for Multimodal Systems: Concurrent Processing and Data Fusion. In *Proceedings InterCHI'93*, Amsterdam, ACM Press, pp. 172-178.

Object Management Group (1991) *The Common Object Request Broker: Architecture and Specification*, OMG Document Number 91.12.1.

Oviatt, S. (1994) Toward Empirically-Based Design of Multimodal Dialogue Systems. In *Proceedings of AAAI'94 - IM4S*, Stanford, pp. 30-36.

Oviatt, S. and Olsen, E. (1994) Integration Themes in Multimodal Human-Computer Interaction. In *Proceedings of ICSLP'94*, Yokohama, pp. 551-554.

Park, S.K., Choi J.M., Myeong-Wuk J., Lee G.L., and Lim Y.H. (submitted for publication), *MASCOS : A Multi-Agent System as the Computer Secretary*.

Rhyne J. (1987) Dialogue Management for Gestural Interfaces, *Computer Graphics, 21(2)*, pp. 137-142.

Schwartz, D.G. (1993) *Cooperating heterogeneous systems: A blackboard-based meta approach*, Technical Report 93-112, Center for Automation and Intelligent Systems Research, Case Western Reserve University, Cleveland Ohio, (unpublished PhD. thesis).

Sullivan, J. and Tyler, S. (eds.) (1991) *Intelligent User Interfaces*, Reading: Addison-Wesley Pub. Co.

Warren, D. and Pereira, F. (1982) An Efficient Easily Adaptable System for Interpreting Natural Language Queries, *American Journal of Computational Linguistics, 8(3)*, pp. 110-123.

Using Cooperative Agents to Plan Multimodal Presentations

Yi Han and Ingrid Zukerman

Department of Computer Science, Monash University
Clayton, Victoria 3168, AUSTRALIA
{hanyi,ingrid}@cs.monash.edu.au

Abstract. A multimodal presentation planning mechanism must take into consideration the structure of the discourse and the restrictions imposed by partial plans generated in the early stages of the planning process. The latter requirement demands that the planning mechanism be able to transfer plan constraints from one level of planning to the next and to modify partial plans locally at each level. In this paper, we introduce a multi-agent planning mechanism based on the blackboard architecture that satisfies these requirements, and describe the facilities used by agents to communicate with each other in this architecture. In addition, we discuss the planning processes used by the agents in our prototype system.

1 Introduction

Techniques developed in recent years enable users to communicate with computer systems using a combination of several modalities, such as natural language, graphics and animation. The processes used for modality-specific presentation planning are independent of each other in the sense that individual functions and algorithms are applied to generate modality-specific presentations. These processes may need to be executed simultaneously in order to present information cooperatively, e.g., showing the direction in which to turn a knob in a picture and telling the user the result of this action.

Since different portions of a piece of discourse play different roles such as supporting or contrasting with other portions, a key concern of multimodal presentation planning is the satisfaction of constraints imposed by the discourse structure. These constraints restrict modalities and resources, e.g., time or space, to be used for presenting different portions of the discourse. For example, if two discourse components are contrasted with each other, they should be presented in the same modality and should fit on the same screen. The second requirement restricts the space consumption of the presentations generated for these items. Thus, alternatives may be rejected by the presentation planner owing to limited screen space. In addition, time is often restricted when generating presentations in human-computer interactions. Hence, a modality is not eligible to present a discourse component if it requires too much time to generate a presentation.

To satisfy the constraints imposed by the discourse structure, processes in charge of different presentation modalities need to communicate with each other when presenting related components of a discourse structure, and may need to be dynamically activated or de-activated. For example, if the modality selected for presenting the elements of a column in a table is icon, the process generating the table needs to know whether an icon can be generated for each of these elements, since these elements must be presented by means of the same modality. If the generation of one of the icons fails, all the icon-generating processes must be de-activated, and processes for a different modality (e.g., text) must be activated instead.

In order to satisfy these requirements, we cast the generation of multimodal presentations as a multi-agent planning process, where an agent is created for the generation of each modality-specific component, and a presentation planning agent is responsible for the integration of these components (Han and Zukerman, 1995, 1996b; Han, 1996). This agent takes as input a discourse structure determined by a discourse planner, such as that described by Zukerman (1993). The activated agents are then dynamically organized into hierarchical groups on the basis of the task decomposition (Section 3). Using dynamic agents for each modality supported in the system enables (1) the selection of modalities that satisfy the modality constraints through the activation and de-activation of modality-specific agents; and (2) the simultaneous generation of different components which present information cooperatively using the same modality, e.g., using two tables to present the statistics for exports produced last year and in the current year. This mechanism is scalable and portable, since additional modalities or different hardware can be adopted by defining new agents.

Our multi-agent planning mechanism is based on a hierarchical blackboard architecture which supports communication and resource sharing between agents. This mechanism provides communication primitives for agents to send requests and responses to requests, and to send urgent messages to other agents via different protocols (Section 4.2). In order to satisfy the constraints placed on the presentation components generated by different agents, a constraint satisfaction mechanism is incorporated into the mechanisms for communication and cooperation between agents. This constraint satisfaction mechanism enables agents to propagate restrictions imposed on the modalities used for presenting their components and on the space occupied by these components (Sections 7.1 and 7.2). In addition, our multi-agent architecture supports the competition for resources, such as time and space, between generators presenting components by means of alternative modalities. This is performed by activating an agent for each alternative modality, and evaluating the space and time required by each modality-specific presentation. As a result, the modality selection process can take into account the resources available in the system, which is a dynamic factor in our application domain.

Our multi-agent framework has been implemented in a prototype system called MAGPIE (Multi-Agent Generation of Presentations In Physics Education), which generates multimodal presentations for conveying concepts in high-school Physics. In this paper, we describe the multi-agent architecture used in MAGPIE, and the facilities used by agents to communicate with each other. We then discuss the generic planning process applied by the agents in MAGPIE, followed by a discussion of the considerations taken into account by several modality-specific agents.

2 Related Work

Two main planning strategies have been used in several systems which design multimodal presentations to convey composite information, namely hierarchical planning and cooperative planning.

A hierarchical content planner is used by COMET (Feiner and McKeown, 1990) to refine a hierarchy of *Logical Forms*, which are used to represent a presentation plan. Based on the characteristics of the intended information, during the plan refinement process, the media coordinator annotates the Logical Forms with instructions regarding which portions of the discourse are to be presented by the text generator and which by the graphics generator. Due to this top-down method, all the means of modality integration are pre-defined, and usually are not altered during the realization process. Communicative acts are used to represent a presentation plan in the Map Display system (Maybury, 1993) and in WIP (André et al., 1993). Since a complex act can be decomposed into a set of sub-acts, a hierarchical planning mechanism is applied in these systems to refine the communicative acts of a presentation plan. However, there may be several acts that are suitable for achieving a goal. To cope with the selection problem, WIP considers features such as effectiveness, side-effects and cost of execution, while Maybury's system considers the kind of communication being conducted and the visual properties of the intended information (e.g., size, color and shading).

The cooperative planning approach is used in the DenK system (Bunt et al., 1995) and the systems described in (Arens and Hovy, 1994; Bourdot, Krus and Gherbi 1995; Cheyer and Julia, 1995). The DenK system (Bunt et al., 1995) has a triangular architecture which consists of an electronic cooperator, a natural language processor and a visual display processor. The electronic cooperator communicates with the natural language processor and the visual display processor in order to convey the intended information, as well as to understand the user's questions. In the system described by Arens (1994), discourse planning and presentation planning are implemented as two reactive planning processes. These processes perform reasoning on a set of semantic models representing the features of the communication task required by the application domain, the features of the intended information, and the functionality of the media supported by the system. The systems described in (Bourdot et al., 1995; Bunt et al., 1995) are based on the *client-server* concept. In these systems, multimedia input is interpreted via the cooperation of multiple agents, where each agent may require supporting information from other distributed agents or from the user. The cooperation between medium-specific processes enables the simultaneous combination of direct manipulation, gestural drawing, handwriting, and typed and spoken natural language for human-computer interactions. For example, a user can ask for information by circling an item on the screen and speaking to a microphone. Our approach is similar to that used in (Cheyer, 1995). However, MAGPIE selects agents not only based upon their capabilities, which is a static factor, but also upon resource restrictions, which is a dynamic factor.

The modality selection problem has been addressed in several systems. Mackinlay (1986) and Roth and Mattis (1991) perform syntactic and semantic analysis in order to map information features into different presentation formats. They define a set of graphical techniques to describe a data set in a database. In addition, Mackinlay (1986) ranks the graphical techniques according to their relative effectiveness for presenting certain types of information, based on the tenet that people interpret different types of graphical presentations with varying degrees of accuracy.

Arens, Hovy and their colleagues investigated different ways in which a presenter can exploit modalities to convey intended information (Arens, Hovy and van Mulken, 1993; Arens, Hovy and Vossers, 1993). They classified the intended information using features regarding the role that the information plays in the communication process, e.g., conveying urgency. In addition, they used semantic models to represent features of the different modalities, e.g., number of dimensions and whether the information varies over time. The interdependencies between communicative goals, information characteristics and modality features are described by a dependency network, which is used to evaluate the suitability of candidate modalities for presenting the intended information and achieving the communicative goals. The selection of a modality is then performed by applying modality allocation rules (Arens and Hovy, 1994). The presentations produced by this approach are generally appropriate. However, this approach does not take into consideration the preferences and abilities of particular perceivers, and does not consider resource restrictions which arise during the presentation planning process (the first of these factors is considered by the PPP system (André et al., 1996).

As suggested in (Arens, Hovy and van Mulken, 1993), MAGPIE separates presentation planning from discourse planning, and views layout management as part of the presentation planning process. Constraint satisfaction has been used for layout management in several multimodal presentation systems. In COMET (Feiner et al., 1993), temporal relations between actions are described by means of temporal constraints, which are realized by the text generator using linguistic devices and by the graphics generator using editing effects. Allen's temporal logic (Allen, 1983) is employed to solve these temporal constraints. In WIP (André et al., 1993; Wahlster et al., 1993), the layout manager LayLab (Graf, 1992) considers constraints due to local relations between objects that are semantically connected, and due to global relations in the whole document. An incremental constraint hierarchy solver based on the DeltaBlue algorithm (Borning, Freeman-Benson and Wilson, 1992) is used to solve the semantic and spatial constraints associated with layout formats. WIP is more flexible than COMET, since the constraint satisfaction process during layout management can influence the presentation planning process.

MAGPIE uses unification to solve constraint satisfaction problems pertaining to modality selection, and local constraint propagation algorithms to solve constraint satisfaction problems pertaining to the allocation of space. Our approach is similar to the multi-agent simulated annealing approach described in (Ghedira, 1994) and the heuristic repair method described in (Minton et al., 1990). These approaches start with a configuration containing constraint violations and incrementally repair the violations until a consistent assignment is achieved. The multi-agent simulated annealing approach and our approach take advantage of multi-agent systems to deal with the dynamic constraint satisfaction problem, where constraints can be added or deleted during the reasoning process. However, in Ghedira's approach, variables and constraints are agents that interact with each other with respect to constraint satisfaction. For example, a constraint agent asks one of its variables to change its value, and the variable agent chooses a value that satisfies as many constraints as possible. In contrast, an agent in MAGPIE is in charge of a set of variables and a set of constraints on these variables and on other agents' variables. Thus, an agent may request the modification of variables that belong to one or more agents. However, due to MAGPIE's hierarchical architecture, the communication between agents is restricted to an agent and its children, hence it is rather simple. This ability of agents to communicate with each other with respect to the values assigned to their variables increases the likelihood that MAGPIE will obtain a 'good' solution to the space allocation problem. In addition, the ability of an agent to manage the satisfaction of a set of constraints enables individual agents to repair independently the violation of constraints that pertain to its variables (Han and Zukerman, 1996a).

3   The Multi-agent Architecture

Our multi-agent architecture consists of two types of components: *agents* and *blackboards*. An agent is an independent process which can be created or removed dynamically on demand. The use of an agent-based architecture in MAGPIE supports the dynamic activation and de-activation of modality-specific generators, and enables these processes to communicate with each other with respect to resource restrictions imposed on presentations. A blackboard is a set of facilities for agents to share information and to communicate with each other (Engelmore, 1988). It manages the registration of a group of agents, and the presentation plans and blackboard events generated by these agents. It provides communication primitives for agents in a group to send/receive blackboard events via different protocols (Section 4.2). In addition, it maintains propagation paths for constraints which are imposed on the components generated by these agents. These propagation paths are updated dynamically by the blackboard each time a constraint is added or removed (Section 7.2).

Assert [weight(object) isa force]
Assert [magnitude(weight(object)) ∝ mass(object) & gravity-acceleration]

Compare [gravity-acceleration(Earth) ≠ gravity-acceleration(moon)]
Compare [weight(object, Earth) ≠ weight(object, moon)]

Instantiate
      $Inst_1$ [weight(box, location)] (Earth moon)
      $Inst_2$ [weight(computer, location)] (Earth moon)

Fig. 1. Discourse structure that conveys the weight of objects

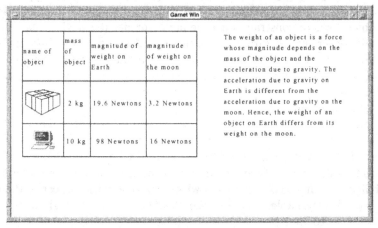

Fig. 2. Sample multimodal presentation: table and text

The presentation planning process in MAGPIE converts a given discourse structure into a multimodal presentation plan which consists of specifications for the generation of modality-specific components contained in the final presentation (Han, 1996; Han and Zukerman, 1996b). Figures 2 and 3 illustrate two presentations generated by MAGPIE from a discourse structure which conveys the weight of objects on Earth and on the moon (Fig. 1). The text in these presentations contains two Assertions: (1) the weight of an object is a force, and (2) it depends on the mass of the object and the acceleration due to gravity; and two Comparisons: (1) the acceleration due to gravity is different on Earth and on the moon, and (2) the weight of an object on Earth differs from its weight on the moon. The second Comparison is illustrated by means of Instantiations with respect to two objects: a box and a computer. These Instantiations are presented by means of a table in Fig. 2 and a bar chart in Fig. 3[1].

To generate the presentations in Figs.2 and 3, the presentation planning agent invokes a text agent to present the Assertions and Comparisons, and a table agent and a chart agent to convey the Instantiations (Fig. 4) (Han, 1996). The table agent and the text agent collaborate on the presentation of the intended information, while the table agent and the chart agent compete for the

---

[1] The dark bars in this chart appear in red on the screen and the light bars in green.

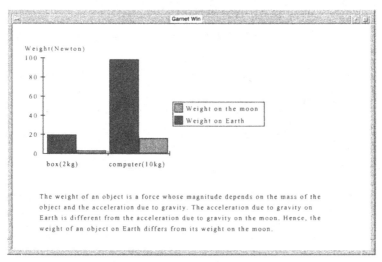

Fig. 3. Sample multimodal presentation: chart and text

presentation of the Instantiations. There are four attributes to be conveyed for the object in each Instantiation, namely (1) name, (2) mass, (3) weight on Earth, and (4) weight on the moon (Fig. 5). For each object, the table agent invokes an icon agent to present its name, three number agents (to present its mass, its weight on Earth and its weight on the moon), and three text agents (to present the units of magnitude of mass and weight). In addition, four text agents are activated to present the four table headings. Thus, the icon agent, number agent and text agent collaborate on the presentation of the table. The chart agent displays the weight of the objects on Earth and on the moon by means of bars, their name and unit of mass and weight by means of text, and their mass by means of numbers. In addition, it uses text to present the headings in the legend. The selection of an agent for conveying the Instantiations depends on the space available on the screen and the amount of time required by each agent to generate its presentation. The table in Fig. 2 occupies less screen space than the chart in Fig. 3, but takes a longer time to generate. Hence, if the system has restricted screen space for conveying the intended information, Fig. 2 is displayed, and if the system is restricted on time, Fig. 3 is displayed.

A hierarchical blackboard architecture is used in MAGPIE, where agents are dynamically organized into hierarchical groups during the presentation planning process on the basis of the task decomposition. That is, an agent may employ other autonomous agents to do the required subtasks. The agent who hires other agents is called the *master* agent, while agents who work for the master agent are called *server* agents. The master agent and its server agents form a group. A blackboard is bound to each group of agents to handle the information sharing and communication between them. This blackboard is called a *local blackboard* and is owned by the master agent.

A hierarchical blackboard architecture was selected since it represents explicitly the discourse structure. In addition, a modality-specific presentation in

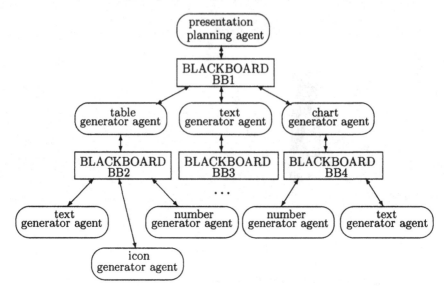

Fig. 4. Agent construction in a multi-agent planning mechanism

MAGPIE may consist of several modality-specific components. For example, a table may contain icons as its entries. Thus, the modification of modality-specific components, e.g., the icons in a table, must be agreed upon by the agent who integrates these components, e.g., the agent generating the table. In terms of the communication between agents, this means that an agent may receive requests to perform modifications to its presentation both from the agent who activated it and from the agents it activates. Such a mode of operation is catered for by a hierarchical architecture, where an agent communicates with its master and its servers. Finally, constraints in MAGPIE are imposed by each agent who is responsible for integrating components generated by other agents. The hierarchical blackboard architecture divides these constraints into groups, so that the effect of constraint propagation remains localized inside each group of constraints. The propagation of the constraints in each group is supported by a local blackboard, which stores and manages the propagation paths between variables controlled by the agents in a group.

4   Blackboard Events and Communication Primitives

Agents share partial presentation plans on a blackboard and communicate with each other through blackboard events. Each agent has a set of event handlers that determine its reaction to different blackboard events. As stated above, a local blackboard is bound to each agent group formed during the task decomposition process. Agents within a group read from the local blackboard plan requirements propagated from the previous level in the plan hierarchy and partial plans generated by other agents in the same group, and then generate their own partial plans which satisfy these requirements.

dimension:	2D
dimensional-focus:	((*object name mass*) (*weight magnitude*))
discourse-relation:	(Compare *weight*(*object*, Earth) *weight*(*object*, moon))

Instantiation₁:	**Instantiation₂:**
object:	*object:*
name: box	*name:* computer
mass:	*mass:*
value: 2	*value:* 10
unit: kilogram	*unit:* kilogram
weight:	*weight:*
location: Earth	*location:* Earth
magnitude: 19.6	*magnitude:* 98
unit: Newton	*unit:* Newton
weight:	*weight:*
location: moon	*location:* moon
magnitude: 3.2	*magnitude:* 16
unit: Newton	*unit:* Newton
importance: t	*importance:* t

Fig. 5. Refinement of the sample instantiations

Agents communicate with each other in different ways under different circumstances. For example, an agent may talk to a single agent or a group of agents. In addition, if an agent has an urgent message, it may want to interrupt another agent's process. Finin *et al.* (1994) describe an agent communication language containing a set of performatives for agents to use in the communication process. Each of these performatives identifies the protocol to be used to deliver a message and a speech act to be used by the sender to describe the content of a message. In contrast, MAGPIE organizes the communication between agents by defining several types of events, where each type of event follows a particular protocol. Due to the hierarchical architecture used in MAGPIE, the communication needs between agents are restricted. Therefore, a powerful communication language such as that described by Finin *et al.* is not necessary in MAGPIE.

Section 4.1 describes the three types of blackboard events defined in MAGPIE. Section 4.2 discusses the communication primitives provided by MAGPIE for these event types. Finally, Section 4.3 discusses problems that arise due to the need to support agent concurrency.

4.1   Blackboard Events

All blackboard events have one sender agent and either one receiver agent or a group of receiver agents. We identify three types of events: *normal event*, *urgent event* and *announcement*. Normal events are messages sent from one agent to another. They are collected in the event queue maintained by the local blackboard. In contrast, urgent events are forwarded immediately to the receiver (without staying in the event queue). Announcements are messages broadcast by a master agent to all the agents in its group. The broadcasting mechanism is the same as that used for forwarding urgent messages.

A message carried by a normal event may be either a request or a response to a request. A request from one agent demands a modification of the plan generated by another agent and specifies the type of this modification, e.g., enlargement or reduction of a display. A response from this other agent indicates whether it is able to comply with the request. MAGPIE uses constraints to describe how the variables of one agent's plan are related to the variables of another agent's plan. Hence, after receiving a request, MAGPIE's agents use constraint propagation to obtain the requirements on their variables from the values of other agents' variables.

When an agent picks up a normal event from an event queue, its event handlers determine its reaction to the event, e.g., whether constraint propagation is necessary. An agent is able to send different requests to different agents and check their response with respect to each request. For instance, if the table agent who generated the table in Fig. 2 wishes to ask an icon agent to reduce the width of the icon it generated, the table agent will generate an *asking-event* which contains this request (Fig. 6). When the icon agent picks up this event, its event handler will obtain the expectation on the icon's width by propagating the constraints pertaining to the width of the icon. The handler will then try to reduce the icon to fit the expectation. If this modification fails due to the absence of smaller icons, the icon agent will send a *rejection-event* to the table agent on the same request. Otherwise, it will send an *OK-event*. The table agent's event handler for the *OK-event* returns the process name of the icon agent, while its event handler for the *rejection-event* returns *nil*. These returned values are used in subsequent actions performed by the table agent during the presentation planning process (Section 4.2).

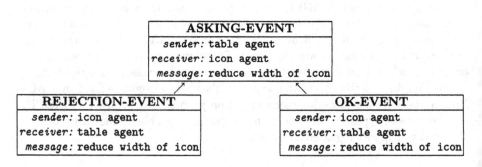

Fig. 6. Events related to a request

Announcements and urgent events carry messages which require an agent's immediate attention. They interrupt the process being carried out by an agent, and force the agent to handle these events. An example of an announcement is *time-up*, which indicates that a period of real time has elapsed. A *time-up-*

announcement is generated by an alarm process which is set up by the system for a particular amount of time at the beginning of the presentation planning process. When a *time-up-announcement* is sent, all agents stop planning to handle this announcement, which requires them to display the best presentation plan generated so far.

MAGPIE has two types of urgent events: *remove-agent-event* and *cancel-request-event*. A *remove-agent-event* indicates that a master agent is no longer interested in the display being generated by a server agent, and that the server agent should abort its presentation planning process together with that of its own server agents (if any). A *cancel-request-event* is a message sent from a master agent to a server agent in order to withdraw a previous request and reinstate the result of the previous planning process. These two types of events are described in more detail in Section 4.3.

Each agent must have an event handler for each type of event it may receive. An event handler for a particular type of event may be defined for the *agent-base*, which is the super-class of all agent classes. In this case, all agents inherit the same event handler from their super-class, and they all react to this type of event in the same way. If an agent is to react to an event in a particular way, an event handler is defined for this agent. This event handler overrides the event handler defined for the agent-base. For example, the event handler for the *time-up-announcement* defined for the agent-base causes an agent to stop planning when it receives a *time-up-announcement*, and kills this agent. However, a different event handler is defined for the presentation planning agent, so that it starts displaying the presentation plan upon receiving a *time-up-announcement*. All agents share the same event handler for the *OK-event*, the *rejection-event* and the *remove-agent-event*, but they have their own handlers for the *asking-event* and the *cancel-request-event* in order to implement individual functions in reaction to these two types of events.

4.2 Communication Primitives

The system provides communication primitives for each type of event. Agents call these primitives to communicate with each other via different protocols. Normal events are created for sending requests and receiving responses to requests. Thus, the communication between a pair of agents via normal events is two-way; both the sender agent and the receiver agent must be specified in a normal event. A pair of communication primitives, *make-normal-event* and *get-normal-event*, are provided for an agent to create a normal event and retrieve a response event respectively.

– **Make-normal-event** stores a normal event in the event queue of a particular blackboard according to the master-server relationship between the sender and the receiver. If the sender is the master agent of the receiver, this event is stored in the local blackboard owned by the sender agent, otherwise it is stored in the local blackboard owned by the receiver agent. For example, if the table agent in Fig. 4 wants to send a message to the icon agent in its group, the normal event that carries this message is kept in BB2. In contrast, if the table agent wants to send a message to the presentation planning agent, the event is kept in BB1. Direct message exchanges between two server agents are not allowed in MAGPIE so that the master agent can retain control of the integration of presentations generated by different server agents.

– **Get-normal-event** returns a normal event sent to an agent. An agent may receive messages from both its master agent and its server agents. The *get-normal-event* primitive implements a policy whereby messages from an agent's master agent have a higher priority than messages from its server agents. This is performed by checking the blackboard owned by the master agent before checking the blackboard owned by the agent itself. If no normal event is detected while an agent is waiting for responses in order to proceed with its process, the agent continues to wait without running its process.

Two planning strategies are implemented on top of these primitives, *wait-all-responses* and *wait-any-response*.

– **Wait-all-responses** – This strategy is used by an agent if its planning process cannot proceed unless all the requests sent out by this agent are satisfied. This strategy is implemented by calling *get-normal-event* and activating an event handler to process an event detected by *get-normal-event*. When this event has been processed, the agent waits for the next normal event. This process terminates when the agent receives a *rejection-event* response to one of its requests or an *OK-event* response to all of its requests. In the first case this strategy returns *nil*, and in the second case *t*.
  The chart agent in Fig. 4 applies this strategy with respect to a list of requests where it asks text agents to generate the headings in the legend, the unit of weight and the textual part of the labels, and number agents to generate numbers[2]. A failure of any request in this list results in *nil* being returned by this strategy. In this case, a *rejection-event* is sent to the presentation planning agent to report a failure. Otherwise, the chart agent proceeds with its planning process.
– **Wait-any-response** – This strategy is used if an agent requires one of its requests to be satisfied in order to carry on with its planning process. The implementation of this strategy is similar to that of *wait-all-responses*. However, this process terminates when the agent receives an *OK-event* response to any of its requests or a *rejection-event* response to all of its requests. The process name of the sender of the *OK-event* is returned in the former case, and *nil* is returned in the latter case.
  The presentation planning agent applies this strategy with respect to a request for the presentation of the Instantiations in Fig. 5. An *OK-event* from either the table agent or the chart agent results in the termination of this strategy. The returned value identifies the successful agent.

---

[2] The displays presenting the magnitude and unit of mass/weight of an object are integrated into a single entry in the final presentation (Han, 1996).

Urgent events and announcements have a higher priority than normal events. Communication via urgent events and announcements is one-way, since an agent sends an urgent event or an announcement to another agent or a group of agents without waiting for feedback. A primitive called *make-urgent-event* is provided for an agent to create an urgent event. This primitive forwards the urgent event to its receiver, selects an event handler for the receiver according to the event type (e.g., *remove-agent-event*), and activates this event handler prior to the receiving agent's normal activation when this agent is scheduled to be run. As a result, the receiving agent is forced to interrupt its normal process and handle the received event. Similarly, a primitive called *make-announcement* is provided for a master agent to make an announcement to its server agents. An urgent event must specify a receiver, but an announcement does not, as it is forwarded to all the server agents in the master agent's group.

4.3   System Concurrency

Agents work concurrently in our system. They may work on one partial plan, like the table agent and its server agents, or on competing plans, like the table agent and the chart agent (Fig. 4). As a result of concurrency the system must handle blackboard access by different agents, unexpected termination of an agent, and cancellation of requests.

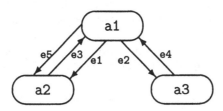

Fig. 7. Example of message passing

- **Blackboard Access** – Since a group of agents share the information on a local blackboard, more than one agent may try to write on the blackboard at the same time. To solve this problem, the system provides a lock for each blackboard. An agent must acquire the lock before it writes on a blackboard, and it releases the lock when it has finished writing. If a blackboard is locked when an agent is trying to write on it, the agent must wait until the lock is released.
- **Unexpected Termination** – An agent may be terminated by its master agent before it has completed its planning process. For example, this happens when another agent completes a competing presentation plan before the agent in question. When an agent is terminated, the system recursively terminates all the server agents created by this agent, and clears any messages from this agent to its master agent. Figure 7 illustrates the message

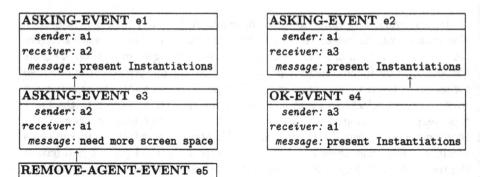

Fig. 8. Events causing termination

passing sequence in such a situation, where a1 is the presentation planning agent, a2 is the chart agent, and a3 is the table agent. The events appear in Fig. 8. The presentation planning agent uses the *wait-any-response* planning strategy when asking the chart agent and the table agent to present two Instantiations (events e1 and e2 respectively). The table agent replies with an *OK-event* (e4), while the chart agent sends a request for more screen space (event e3). However, because the *OK-event* from the table agent brings *wait-any-response* to an end, a1 decides to display the information by means of a table (Fig. 2), and to terminate the chart agent. The termination of the chart agent is performed by means of a *remove-agent-event* (e5), which is an urgent event with an empty message. This event interrupts the planning process of the chart agent. The event handler of the *remove-agent-event* for the chart agent then clears the messages sent from the chart agent to its master agent, and sends a *remove-agent-event* to each server agent before it terminates itself.

- **Request Cancellation** – A request sent to an agent may be canceled before the agent completes the process that addresses this request. In order to handle a cancellation, the agent needs to recover the plan that was current before this request, and clean up all the messages it sent out while processing this request. For instance, consider a situation where the table agent needs to enlarge a table of two rows and two columns which contains an icon in each entry of the first column and text in the entries of the second column. In order to continue satisfying the space constraints, the enlargement of the table requires that the icons in the first column be enlarged and that the font of the text in the second column be enlarged. The message passing sequence for the first requirement is illustrated in Fig. 7, where a1 is the table agent, and a2 and a3 are icon agents presenting the two icons in the first column. The events appear in Fig. 9. The table agent asks the two icon agents to enlarge their presentations (event e1 and event e2). This request is accepted by a2 (event e3), but rejected by a3 (event e4). Because of the rejection from a3, this requirement is dropped even though a2 has no objection to it. The table agent then creates a *cancel-request-event* (e5) and proceeds to consider the second of the above requirements. Event e5 interrupts a2, and causes a2 to abort its plan, clear the messages it sent to a1, and recover its previous presentation. This event differs from the *remove-agent-event* in that no recovery takes place in the *remove-agent-event*.

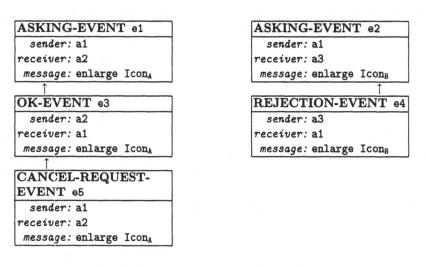

Fig. 9. Events causing a request cancellation

5   The Presentation Planning Process

Agents in MAGPIE have three basic functions: (1) task decomposition, (2) constraint satisfaction, and (3) event handling. A master agent capable of presenting composite information performs task decomposition in order to divide the task into sub-tasks. It then creates a server agent to perform each sub-task. All agents are able to evaluate the satisfaction of constraints pertaining to their presentations and to communicate with other agents by means of events.

In MAGPIE, the structure of a multimodal presentation plan consists of *segments* and *segment containers*. A segment defines a modality-specific display which presents atomic information, i.e., information which is not decomposable (Section 6). A segment container is generated to convey composite information. It includes a list of elements which in turn can be either segments or segment containers. A segment container describes the integration format of its elements on the basis of the semantic relations between the discourse components that yield these elements (Sections 7 and 8). This integration format is represented by means of constraints over the different elements, where the constraints may have different strengths (required and preferred). All the components of a modality-specific presentation are generated simultaneously and integrated into a display format determined by the agent in charge of the presentation.

When a master agent generates a segment container, it posts constraints which restrict the modality and space consumption of the components of the segment container. It then hires server agents to generate these components. These server agents generate partial plans, where each plan specifies a component of the whole multimodal presentation. In this manner, when the master agent assigns values to its segment container, the server agents in its agent group will know the requirements placed on their partial plans. A server agent can then add its own constraints if it is the master agent of another group of agents. Hence, during the planning process, requirements of an existing plan are transferred to server agents by means of constraint propagation. These constraints ensure that each component segment satisfies the requirements of the overall discourse. For instance, if the presentation planning agent in Fig. 4 wants the text to be displayed to the right of the table in the same window, it will create constraints on the width and height of the table and the text in relation to the window size (Han and Zukerman, 1995). These constraints are then propagated to the table agent, and hence restrict the expansion of the table. In this case, the space left for the text must be wide enough for the longest word in the text and must exceed a certain proportion of the window. Otherwise, the text is displayed below the table, and a different set of constraints is created.

A variable is defined as a parameter or an element of a parameter in a partial plan, e.g., the width of a column in a table. Each agent in the system is in charge of a subset of the variables and instantiates these variables while designing its partial plan for a modality-specific component. Constraints may exist between variables of different agents, and the instantiations of the variables must satisfy these inter-agent constraints. Consequently, the constraint satisfaction problem in multimodal presentation planning is a Distributed Constraint Satisfaction Problem (DCSP). Further, due to the hierarchical task decomposition process performed in MAGPIE, the constraints pertaining to the presentation plans of the different agents are distributed in the plan hierarchy formed during this process (Section 3). For instance, the presentation planning agent poses constraints on the width and height of the table and the text in Fig. 2, so that they can fit in the window. Similarly, the table agent restricts the space occupied by the entry components generated by the icon, number and text agents.

5.1 The Generic Planning Process

In order to cope with the DCSP, each agent in MAGPIE maintains the local consistency of a subset of the constraints, and cooperates with other agents with respect to the global consistency of all the constraints. In addition, an agent attempts the satisfaction of required constraints first, and then the satisfaction of additional preferred constraints if possible. The presentation planning procedure receives as input an agent to be activated, which initially is the presentation planning agent, and a discourse structure annotated with the features of the

---

Procedure *Agent-planning* (*agent, discourse-struct*)

<u>Task Decomposition</u>

1If the information in *discourse-struct* is composite then
2. Determine the format of integration and the content of each component.
3. Post constraints to restrict the modalities to be used for each component.
4. Propagate modality constraints to obtain candidate modalities for presenting each component.
5. For each component do
6.   Use heuristics to select modalities from the candidates and activate *Agent-planning* with the selected agents.
7. Post space constraints to restrict the size of each component.

<u>Initial Planning</u>

8Instantiate plan variables to satisfy the required space constraints pertaining to the variables.
9Inform the parent agent of the completion of the variable instantiation process.

<u>Reactive Planning</u>

10Wait until a normal event is received
11. If *agent* is required to modify a variable then
12.   Review the local consistency of the constraints, modify the relevant variables accordingly, and update the presentation if necessary.
13.   Report to the agent which demanded the modification.
14. If time permits and *agent* is a master agent then
15.   Modify variables to satisfy additional preferred constraints if possible.
16.   Ask relevant server agents to modify their plan variables accordingly.

Fig. 10. Presentation planning procedure

information to be conveyed. It generates a presentation by recursively activating modality-specific agents. When multiple agents are created, several processes run simultaneously, one for each agent. The generic version of this procedure, which is called *Agent-planning*, appears in Fig. 10. Refinements of this procedure for icon agents, table agents and chart agents are described in Sections 6, 7 and 8 respectively.

The presentation planning procedure is divided into three stages: (1) *task decomposition*, (2) *initial planning*, and (3) *reactive planning*.

- **Task Decomposition** (Steps 1-7) – In this stage a master agent, such as a table agent or a chart agent, distributes its task to several server agents. This task consists of the presentation of composite information. Since different integration formats are adopted by different master agents, individual methods are used by each type of agent to decompose the information (Step 2). Furthermore, specific modality constraints are imposed on the components by each integration format (Step 3).

  Modalities are selected during Steps 4-6 of *Agent-planning*, where modality constraint propagation is invoked to obtain alternative modalities for presenting each component (Section 7.1). Following this process, a master agent is able to activate server agents (Steps 5-6). Finally, space constraints pertaining to a specific integration format are created to restrict the components generated by each server agent (Step 7). These constraints are imposed after the agent activation process so that parameters of a segment or segment container can be referred to in the constraints.

- **Initial Planning** (Steps 8-9) – In this stage an agent seeks the satisfaction of required constraints. In Step 8, a master agent propagates the variables instantiated by the server agents that are activated in Step 6 in order to instantiate its own variables which pertain to the format of the integration, e.g., the width of each column in a table (Section 7). If the task of an agent is to convey atomic information, its procedure starts to run from Step 8. In this case, the variables of its plan are instantiated based on the current space constraints. If no constraints have been posted, default settings are used (Section 6).

- **Reactive Planning** (Steps 10-16) – In this stage an agent modifies plan variables to repair a constraint. To this effect, an agent waits until it receives a normal event, and performs the actions defined in the handler of this event. The agent stays in this stage after the event has been processed until a *remove-agent-event* or a *time-up-announcement* terminates its process (Section 4.1). Steps 11-13 handle a request from a parent agent to modify a variable, e.g., reduce the width of an icon. Since the satisfaction of a request for the modification of a variable (e.g., the width of an icon) may cause modifications with respect to other variables (e.g., the height of this icon), constraint propagation is used to evaluate the local consistency of the constraints pertaining to this modification. Steps 14-16 activate agents with requests pertaining to the satisfaction of additional preferred constraints in order to improve a presentation plan if time permits. Only the presentation planning agent can generate the normal event which carries such a request, and only agents which present composite information, i.e., the table agent and the chart agent, can be activated by such a request. Further, each of these agents has individual methods and heuristics for repairing violations of preferred constraints (Han, 1996). For instance, a table agent attempts to repair violations of preferred constraints pertaining to the width of columns (if any) prior to those pertaining to the height of rows, since the elements in columns tend to be of more uniform size than the elements in rows. This is because the table agent demands that the same modality be used to present the elements in a column (Section 7).

Communication between agents is necessary at different stages of this process. Firstly, since the modality which is suitable for presenting a component may be relevant to other components, the modality selected in Step 6 must be agreed on by the agents presenting related components. For instance, all the agents presenting the entries in a table column must agree on a presentation modality, since, as stated above, the table agent demands that the same modality be used to present the elements in a column. In addition, if a modality is dropped from consideration due to the violation of a modality constraint, the agents in charge of it must be removed. Space constraints restrict the size of a presentation component in relation to the size of others. Hence, communication between agents is also required for agents to satisfy space constraints cooperatively. In addition, if these components are generated by different agents, each agent must ensure the local consistency of constraints pertaining to its variables (Steps 8, 12 and 15). Finally, upon completion of the plan generation process, an agent reports back to the agent in charge of the presentation (Steps 9 and 13): an *OK-event* reports the success of the plan generation process, and a *rejection-event* reports its failure. In the former case, the effect of the modified variables on the presentation plan is determined by means of constraint propagation. Consequently, the agents in charge can evaluate their constraints and modify their variables accordingly.

Each time an agent produces a presentation component either during the initial planning stage or during the reactive planning stage, it saves the component in the blackboard owned by its master agent. Thus, a master agent can gather from the blackboard the components generated by its server agents, and integrate them into a particular format. For instance, the initial presentation of the text paragraph in Fig. 2 is generated at the same time as the table in a format that fits the width of the window, and allows the text to be presented either above or below the table. However, MAGPIE prefers to present the text next to the table because our eyes naturally move from left to right (Holmes, 1984). Hence, upon completion of the generation of the table, the presentation planning agent asks the text agent to re-format the text and place it next to the table (Fig. 2). If time is restricted or there is not enough room next to the table, the text is displayed below the table (Han and Zukerman, 1995).

As indicated in Section 4.1, the presentation planning procedure may be interrupted at any stage by an urgent event or an announcement. A *remove-agent-event* or a *time-up-announcement* brings this procedure to an end. In addition, an agent may receive a *cancel-request-event* while it is handling a request, e.g., while it is modifying a plan variable during the reactive planning stage. When this urgent event interrupts the planning process, the handler of this event aborts any action that is being carried out, reinstates the previous presentation on the blackboard, and restarts the process from Step 10 to wait for another event.

6   Presenting Atomic Information: Icon Agent

Agents presenting atomic information generate segments which specify parameters such as the font, color and size of a modality-specific display. In this section, we describe the planning process of the icon agents in MAGPIE.

An icon agent in MAGPIE generates an icon segment which specifies the width and the height of an icon (in pixels), and the entry of its bitmap in the icon library. At present, icons of different sizes are pre-stored in the icon library and retrieved using an entry code (Han, 1996). For instance, the computer icon in Fig. 2 is specified in the segment in Fig. 11, where **name** specifies the object to be conveyed, i.e., the name of the icon to be retrieved from the icon library, and computer32x32 is the entry code. The width and height of this icon are both 32 pixels, and the display position is set to (0,0) at this stage.

If the intended information is atomic, the *Agent-planning* procedure starts to run from the initial planning stage (Section 5.1). That is, the *Agent-planning* procedure of icon agents starts at Step 8. Steps 14-16 are not performed by icon agents, since these agents are not master agents.

```
modality: icon
position: (0,0)
   width: 32
  height: 32
    name: "computer"
  bitmap: computer32x32
```

Fig. 11. Sample icon segment

The size of the icon is determined in Step 8 of *Agent-Planning* using the following rules:

Rule₁ If width and height are not specified, an icon of the default size, viz 48x48, is generated. If an icon of this size is not available in the icon library, an icon of the closest size that is larger than the default size is retrieved. For example, in the current implementation, a box icon of size 64x64 is generated in Fig. 2 since the icon agent is unable to find a box icon of size 48x48. If an icon of size 64x64 is not available, an icon of size 32x32 is generated.

Rule₂ If width and height are specified, and the agent is able to find an icon of the specified size or smaller, the display is generated. These parameters are set to the icon's actual size after the icon is generated.

When an icon agent is first activated during the initial planning stage, the width and height in its segment are unspecified. Hence, *Rule₁* is used to produce an initial icon to convey the intended object. This icon is stored in the master agent's blackboard (e.g., BB2 in Fig. 4). The icon agent then sends an *OK-event* to its master agent (Step 9 of *Agent-planning*).

During the reactive planning stage (which starts at Step 10 of *Agent-planning*), the icon agent may be activated by an *asking-event* to modify the width or height of its icon (Step 11 of *Agent-planning*). The handler for the *asking-event* makes a backup of the generated icon. It propagates the constraints pertaining to the variable specified in the event, e.g., the width of the icon, in order to determine the required value, modifies the variable accordingly, and activates *Rule₂* to generate a new icon from the width specifications if possible (Step 12). The icon agent then informs its master agent whether a satisfactory icon was generated (Step 13).

If the planning procedure is interrupted by a *cancel-request-event* during the reactive planning stage, the handler of this event is triggered. This handler recovers the previously generated icon from the backup which was made by the handler of the *asking-event*. As discussed in Section 4.3, the handler locks the blackboard while deleting any events that were sent out to the master agent by the icon agent. Finally, the handler forces the icon agent to restart its reactive planning stage from Step 10 of *Agent-planning*. Consequently, any unperformed actions with respect to the previous *asking-event* are skipped.

7   Presenting Composite Information: Table Agent

A segment container is generated by agents for presenting composite information. As stated in Section 5.1, an agent decomposes a presentation task into sub-tasks based upon its discourse structure, and hires server agents to perform these sub-tasks. Each agent uses its own format to convey the intended information. Thus, specific methods are used by different agents to decompose their task. Each segment container has a segment-list which contains the components to be generated by the server agents. The segment container specifies the format for the integration of these components. Modality constraints and space constraints are imposed by the agent which creates the segment container to ensure the integration of the components. Propagation of modality constraints is performed during the task decomposition stage in order to obtain modalities capable of presenting each component (Step 4 of *Agent-Planning*). In contrast, an agent performs propagation of space constraints during the initial planning stage in order to obtain requirements from its server agents (Step 8 of *Agent-planning*), and during the reactive planning stage in order to obtain requirements from its master agent or its server agents (Steps 12 and 15 of *Agent-planning*).

A table agent generates a table container to present composite information in the format of columns and rows. Figure 12 illustrates a segment container which specifies the parameters defined by a table agent for presenting the table in Fig. 2. These parameters are: (1) the width and height of the table (in pixels), (2) the number of columns and rows, (3) the width of the different columns and height of the different rows, (4) the type of column and row separator (solid-line, which is the default, double-line, nil), (5) the alignment of each entry in each column (left, which is the default, center or right) and row (top, which is default, center or bottom), (6) the headings for columns and rows, and (7) the content to be conveyed in each entry (stored in segment-list).

A table agent determines the integration format of a table and the content of each component on the basis of (1) the dimensions of the information to be conveyed, (2) the dimensional focus of each dimension, and (3) the discourse relations to be conveyed. For the Instantiations that illustrate the Comparison between the weight of an object on Earth and its weight on the moon (Fig. 5), the information to be conveyed has two dimensions, namely *object* and *weight*. The dimensional focus of *object* is *name* and *mass*, and the dimensional focus of *weight* is *magnitude*. This information can be conveyed either by (a) putting each Instantiation in a row, or (b) putting each Instantiation in a column. The table agent in MAGPIE prefers to use format (a), where the attributes to be compared are displayed in columns, to suit our natural eye movement (Holmes, 1984). For

```
       modality: table
       position: (0,0)
          width: 316
         height: 136
        columns: 4
           rows: 2
   column-width: (76 44 102 94)
     row-height: (76 60)
column-separator: solid-line
  row-separator: solid-line
column-alignment: (center center center center)
  row-alignment: (center center)
    row-heading: nil
 column-heading: ((object name)
                  (object mass)
                  (weight(Earth) magnitude)
                  (weight(moon) magnitude))
   segment-list: ((name (object Inst1))
                  (mass (object Inst1))
                  (magnitude (weight((object Inst1) Earth)))
                  (magnitude (weight((object Inst1) moon)))
                  (name (object Inst2))
                  (mass (object Inst2))
                  (magnitude (weight((object Inst2) Earth))))
                  (magnitude (weight((object Inst2) moon))))
```

Fig. 12. Sample table container: weight of objects

the discourse plan in Fig. 5, the table agent sets up two rows since there are two Instantiations in the discourse, and four columns since four elements are generated from filtering the intended information with the dimensional focus for each dimension. These elements are: (1) the *name* of an object, (2) its *mass*, (3) the *magnitude* of its weight on Earth, and (4) the *magnitude* of its weight on the moon. The resulting table is shown in Fig. 2. The table in Fig. 13 presents the same information using format (b), where the four elements generated from filtering each Instantiation are arranged in a column. Thus, this table contains two columns (one for the box, and the other for the computer), and four rows (one for each element obtained from the dimensional focus). If there are many attributes in focus for a few Instantiations (e.g., the weight of each object on Jupiter, Mars, etc.), format (b) is used owing to the relatively small number of columns that can be displayed horizontally.

A table with many columns/rows illustrates a situation where the presentation violates the quality requirements of the discourse. Such a presentation is not acceptable due to the high density of the information being presented (Holmes,

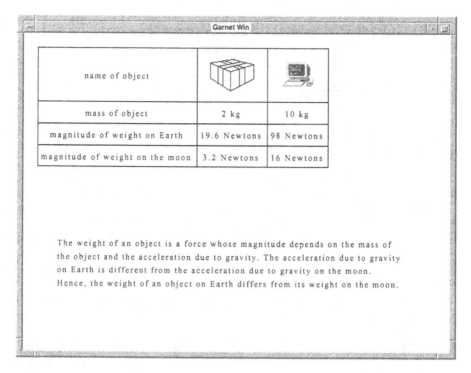

name of object		
mass of object	2 kg	10 kg
magnitude of weight on Earth	19.6 Newtons	98 Newtons
magnitude of weight on the moon	3.2 Newtons	16 Newtons

The weight of an object is a force whose magnitude depends on the mass of the object and the acceleration due to gravity. The acceleration due to gravity on Earth is different from the acceleration due to gravity on the moon. Hence, the weight of an object on Earth differs from its weight on the moon.

Fig. 13. Sample multimodal presentation: table in a different format

1984)[3]. In this case, the table agent may (1) remove rows (in format (a)) or columns (in format (b)) which contain non-essential information so long as the communicative goal is still achieved (Han, 1996; Zukerman and McConachy, 1995); or (2) merge the information presented in several columns (in format (a)) or rows (in format (b)) and select a modality capable of presenting the resulting composite information. For example, a vector may be used to convey the magnitude and direction of a force.

After the table agent decides how to break down the intended information into columns and rows, it determines the content of each entry and the headings for columns and rows (Step 2 of *Agent-planning*). For each column of the table in Fig. 2, the table agent fills in the column heading with the name of the attribute in focus and the class name of each item. For example, ⟨*object name*⟩ is used in the first column, and ⟨*weight*(Earth) *magnitude*⟩ is used in the third column (Fig. 12). Row headings are filled with the name of each Instantiation, which is *nil* in this example. Next, the table agent extracts the content of each entry from the values of the attributes in focus for each Instantiation. Finally, the alignment of each column and each row is set to center, and **column-separator** and **row-separator** are set to solid-line, which is the default value.

---

[3] At this stage, the maximum number of columns and rows in a table in MAGPIE is a constant. In future, this parameter should be determined from the user's abilities represented in a user model and the type and complexity of the information.

Name	Constraint	Strength
$tmcn_1$	(*unify* modality($entry_1$) modality($entry_2$))	required
$tmcn_2$	(*unify* modality($column\text{-}heading_1$) (`text`))	required
$tmcn_3$	(*unify* modality($entry_1$) (`icon number text`))	required
$tmcn_4$	(*unify* modality($entry_2$) (`icon number text`))	required

Table 1. Modality constraints for a column in a table

Name	Constraint	Strength
$tscn_1$	width($column_1$) = width($entry_1$)	required
$tscn_2$	width($column_1$) = width($entry_2$)	required
$tscn_3$	width($entry_1$) $\geq$ width($segment_1$) + $margin\_minimum$	required
$tscn_4$	width($entry_2$) $\geq$ width($segment_2$) + $margin\_minimum$	required
$tscn_5$	width($entry_1$) $\leq$ width($segment_1$) + $margin\_maximum$	preferred
$tscn_6$	width($entry_2$) $\leq$ width($segment_2$) + $margin\_maximum$	preferred

Table 2. Space constraints for a column in a table

A table agent uses the following rules to impose modality constraints on each entry (Step 3 of *Agent-Planning*):

Rule$_{m1}$ If format (a) is selected to compare a list of attributes (i.e., putting each Instantiation in a row), the same modality is used for all the entries in a column.

Rule$_{m2}$ If format (b) is selected to compare a list of attributes (i.e., putting each Instantiation in a column), the same modality is used for all the entries in a row.

Rule$_{m3}$ Column headings and row headings must be textual.

Rule$_{m4}$ Only `icon`, `number` and `text` may be used (at present) for presenting the content of each entry.

Rule$_{m1}$ and *Rule$_{m2}$* are based on the consideration that objects that are compared with each other should be presented in the same modality. *Rule$_{m3}$* and *Rule$_{m4}$* represent restrictions resulting from the implementation of MAGPIE. Table 1 lists the modality constraints pertaining to the first column of the table in Fig. 2. We refer to the column heading of this column as $column\text{-}heading_1$, and to the entries in this column as $entry_1$ and $entry_2$. The segments in these entries are called $segment_1$ and $segment_2$ respectively. The modality constraints are specified in terms of a unification operator whose semantics are the same as the semantics of the unification operator in Unification Grammars (see e.g. Allen, 1994). In Table 1, $tmcn_1$ is generated by *Rule$_{m1}$* since format (a) is used; $tmcn_2$ is derived from *Rule$_{m3}$*; and $tmcn_3$ and $tmcn_4$ are derived from *Rule$_{m4}$*. Additional constraints are created by the same rules for the other columns of the table in Fig. 2.

The mechanism discussed in Section 7.1 is then invoked to return suitable modalities for the content of each entry and to activate server agents (Steps 4-6 of *Agent-planning*). After server agents are created, the table agent poses space constraints on the modality-specific presentations generated by these server agents (Step 7 of *Agent-planning*). Four rules are used to create space constraints:

$Rule_{s1}$ Entries in a column must have the same width.

$Rule_{s2}$ Entries in a row must have the same height.

$Rule_{s3}$ The minimum margin surrounding a segment in an entry must be at least of a certain size (e.g., 12 pixels), so that the segment is not too big for its entry.

$Rule_{s4}$ The maximum margin surrounding a segment in an entry should not exceed a certain threshold (e.g., 42 pixels), so that the segment is not too small for its entry.

$Rule_{s1}$ and $Rule_{s2}$ restrict the width and height of each entry, while $Rule_{s3}$ and $Rule_{s4}$ restrict the size of the entry segments. Constraints derived from $Rule_{s1}$–$Rule_{s3}$ are required, while constraints derived from $Rule_{s4}$ are preferred. Table 2 shows the space constraints derived from these rules for the width of the first column of the table in Fig. 2. Additional constraints similar to $tscn_1$-$tscn_6$ in Table 2 are created for the other columns of the table in Fig. 2.

7.1   Modality Constraint Satisfaction

The modality constraints in Table 1 must be satisfied when the agent generating the table in Fig. 2 selects modalities for presenting each component of the table (Steps 4-6 of *Agent-planning*). To this effect, for each modality constraint the table agent must (1) calculate the alternative values for each variable in the constraint that satisfy the constraint (Step 4); and (2) select a value from these alternatives (Steps 5 and 6).

To calculate the alternative values for each variable in a modality constraint, MAGPIE first obtains the possible domain values for each variable, and then eliminates the values that do not satisfy the modality constraint. The domain values of a variable in a modality constraint represent all the modalities capable of presenting the information in this variable. For example, the domain values of $entry_1$ are the modalities capable of presenting a box, viz `icon` or `text`. These candidate modalities are currently attached to the input. However, in future they will be determined from the characteristics of the information being conveyed and the capabilities of each modality (Arens, Hovy and van Mulken, 1993).

Modality constraints are non-numerical, and an instantiation of the variables in modality constraints is a list of alternative modalities (Table 1). A unification algorithm is used to propagate modality constraints (Allen, 1994). It is applied to the modality constraints and a substitution of their variables, where the initial substitution of a variable is its domain values. It returns a new substitution of the variables so that the modality constraints are satisfied. For example, $tmcn_3$ is satisfied if `icon` is used in $entry_1$. If `icon` and `text` are available for $entry_2$, the result of the unification of the constraints for these entries is `icon`.

When we apply the modality selection process to $tmcn_2$ in Table 1 for each column heading, `text` is selected in Step 4 of *Agent-Planning* as the modality

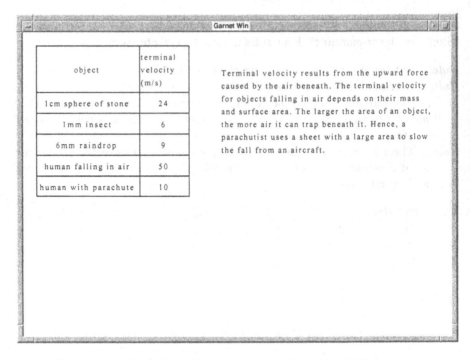

object	terminal velocity (m/s)
1cm sphere of stone	24
1mm insect	6
6mm raindrop	9
human falling in air	50
human with parachute	10

Terminal velocity results from the upward force caused by the air beneath. The terminal velocity for objects falling in air depends on their mass and surface area. The larger the area of an object, the more air it can trap beneath it. Hence, a parachutist uses a sheet with a large area to slow the fall from an aircraft.

Fig. 14. Sample multimodal presentation: table for free-fall example

for presenting the column headings, even though there may be other modalities capable of presenting the information in the headings. The candidate modalities for presenting the name of an object in the first column of Fig. 2 are `icon` and `text`. Both of these modalities remain as possible candidates after applying Step 4 of the *Agent-planning* procedure, since they unify with $tmcn_3$ and $tmcn_4$. At present MAGPIE uses numbers only to convey numerical information, and text to convey units of mass/weight. Hence, `number` and `text` remain as the modalities for presenting the magnitude of mass/weight and its unit respectively after unification with modality constraints such as those in Table 1.

MAGPIE uses heuristics to select modalities from the alternatives generated by the modality constraint propagation process (Step 6 in *Agent-planning*). These heuristics are based on a perceiver's preferences or on resource restrictions. Currently MAGPIE has a very simple user profile which contains a perceiver's age and literacy level. MAGPIE uses non-textual modalities, such as icons, to present objects to perceivers with a low level of literacy. Hence, in this example `icon` is selected for the entries in the first column.

Communication between agents is required to apply these selection heuristics. For instance, if there is no icon to present an object in the first column of the table in Fig. 2, an icon cannot be used to present the other object in this column, since $tmcn_1$ requires that the same modality be used for $entry_1$ and $entry_2$ (Table 1). In this case the second alternative, i.e., `text`, is selected. Such a situation takes place during the generation of the table in Fig. 14 for conveying the terminal velocity

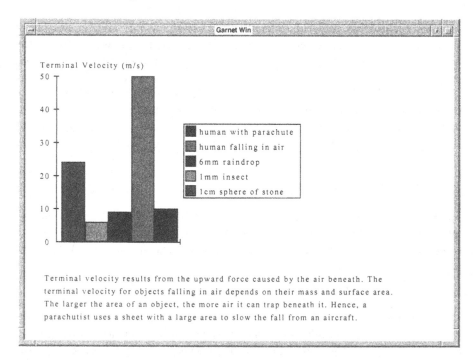

Fig. 15. Sample multimodal presentation: chart for free-fall example

of objects in free fall. The text paragraph in Fig. 14 states that (1) terminal velocity results from the upward force caused by the air beneath; (2) it depends on the mass and surface area of falling objects; (3) the larger the area of an object, the more air it can trap beneath it; and (4) a parachutist uses a sheet with a large area to slow the fall from an aircraft. The third statement is illustrated by means of five Instantiations, each describing an object and its terminal velocity reached in free fall. These Instantiations are presented in a table which presents different objects in the first column, and their terminal velocity in the second column. As discussed above, icon is selected first to present the objects in the first column, and the *wait-all-responses* strategy is applied to ensure that the same modality is used for all the segments in this column. MAGPIE does not have an icon for a stone, an insect or a raindrop, hence the icon agents send a *rejection-event* to the table agent, which brings the *wait-all-responses* strategy to an end. As a result, the table agent drops icon, and sends a *remove-agent-event* to each of the icon agents. It then selects the second alternative, viz text, and creates a text agent for each entry in the first column. This time, all the agents succeed, and the objects in the first column are conveyed by means of text (Fig. 14). The chart that conveys the same information appears in Fig. 15[4].

If the perceiver has no preferences with respect to presentation modalities, an agent is created for each alternative modality obtained from the constraint

---

[4] The actual colours of the bars in this chart are (from left to right): red, green, blue, grey and black.

propagation process, and the different agents compete for the presentation of the information. Presentations that violate the space restrictions imposed by the discourse structure are eliminated, and a heuristic based on time consumption is applied to select the modality of the final presentation among the remaining alternatives. For example, since the presentations in Figs. 14 and 15 satisfy the space restrictions, the presentation that is completed first, i.e., the chart, is displayed. If, however, none of the presentations can satisfy these restrictions, the last alternative, viz text, will be used to present the Instantiations.

7.2 Space Constraint Satisfaction

Space constraints are numerical and the values which satisfy them are nondeterministic (Table 2). For instance, when width($segment_1$) is assigned a value (as a result of a presentation generated by the icon agent for $segment_1$), two new constraints result from propagating this value:

width($column_1$) $\geq$ width($segment_1$) + $margin\_min$, and
width($column_1$) $\leq$ width($segment_1$) + $margin\_max$.

In this manner, the icon agent presenting $segment_1$ can convey to the table agent its expectation of width($column_1$). The table agent in turn can determine whether its assignment of width($column_1$) or the value of width($segment_1$) assigned by the icon agent are satisfactory.

As discussed in Section 3, constraints are distributed in the plan hierarchy. MAGPIE uses *channels* for the propagation of space constraints from one level in the plan hierarchy to the next. A channel consists of a set of constraints (usually one or two). It is a path for propagating the values of variables in an agent's plan to the variables of another agent's plan. Among the constraints in Table 2, $tscn_1$ and $tscn_3$ form a channel since the right-hand side of $tscn_1$ contains the variable on the left-hand side of $tscn_3$. Other channels can be formed from $tscn_1$ and $tscn_5$, $tscn_2$ and $tscn_4$, and $tscn_2$ and $tscn_6$. Hence, four value ranges for width($column_1$) can be obtained from the propagation of constraints through these channels (Han and Zukerman, 1996b). A value from the intersection of these four ranges satisfies $tscn_1$ to $tscn_6$ and therefore can be assigned to width($column_1$) by the table agent (Step 8 of *Agent-planning*). Since the agents presenting $segment_1$ and $segment_2$ are independent processes, they generate constraints which affect simultaneously width($column_1$). MAGPIE does not allow these agents to write directly to width($column_1$) when they advise the table agent of the value of width($column_1$) in order to prevent this value from being overwritten in unpredictable ways. Value binding is used when propagating space constraints through channels. Consequently, the two icon agents can advise the table agent of width($column_1$) independently.

As stated above, agents satisfy required space constraints during the initial planning stage (Step 8 of *Agent-Planning*) and when they receive a request for the modification of a variable during the reactive planning stage (Steps 11-13). If time permits, they repair the violation of preferred constraints while maintaining the satisfaction of the required constraints (Steps 14-16). The satisfaction of required constraints and preferred constraints is achieved through cooperation between agents. To illustrate the agent cooperation process for satisfying required constraints, consider a situation where the table in Fig. 2 has additional columns, and the two icons generated initially for $column_1$ are such that $segment_1$ is much bigger than $segment_2$. In addition, the presentation planning agent has posted constraints which ensure that the table can fit into the display window (Han, 1996). These constraints are propagated through channels formed between the table agent and the presentation planning agent. The constraint that restricts the table width to be less than the window width prevents the expansion of $column_1$, yielding an empty intersection of the ranges which specify the width of $column_1$. Since this constraint is posted by the master of the table agent, it is given priority over constraints posted by its server agents. To satisfy this constraint, the table agent sets width($column_1$) to a value that fits $segment_2$ (Step 8 of *Agent-planning*). However, this causes the violation of $tscn_3$, therefore the table agent asks the icon agent to reduce the width of $segment_1$ to fit in the column. When the icon agent receives this message in its own process (Step 11 of *Agent-Planning*), it propagates width($column_1$) through the channels formed by $tscn_1$–$tscn_3$ and $tscn_1$–$tscn_5$ (Table 2), and calculates the new value of width($segment_1$) that satisfies the constraints resulting from the propagation (Step 12). If the icon agent can retrieve a smaller icon that fits the column width, then the constraints pertaining to width($segment_1$) are satisfied (Step 12), and the icon agent reports this fact to the table agent (Step 13). In contrast, if the current icon size is the only available size for $segment_1$, failure is reported to the table agent, and the table agent tries to reduce the width of other columns. The process of asking server agents to modify their presentations is repeated until the space constraints pertaining to the table are satisfied, or until the table agent determines that these constraints cannot be satisfied. When the width and height of the table satisfy these constraints, the table agent sends an *OK-event* to the presentation planning agent to report the completion of the table (Step 9 of *Agent-planning*). Otherwise, it sends a *rejection-event*.

If time permits, during the reactive planning stage the table agent tries to repair preferred constraints which were violated during the initial planning stage (Steps 14-16 of *Agent-planning*). To this effect, it asks its server agents to modify their presentations so that a non-empty intersection is produced from propagating the constraints pertaining to their presentations. For example, if one of the generated icons is too small for its entry, the table agent sends an *asking-event* to the agent which generated this icon, requesting this agent to enlarge the icon. If the icon agent can comply without violating any of the required constraints, then the improved presentation is retained. The above discussed procedure for the satisfaction of required constraints is applied to implement this process.

In general, arranging an unordered set of objects into a layout format that occupies a minimum space is strongly NP-complete. Even with constraints such as those described in Table 2, it is expensive to find all the means of modifying entry segments for the satisfaction of preferred constraints. Thus, time restrictions are used to guide the constraint satisfaction process in MAGPIE. If time is running out, the best presentation generated so far (which satisfies all the required constraints and the highest number of preferred constraints) is displayed. If a presentation that satisfies all the required constraints cannot be generated in time, an alternative modality is selected (Section 7.1). Text presentations can normally be generated faster than visual presentations. Hence, in the worst case, the intended information is presented in text.

8   Presenting Composite Information: Chart Agent

A chart agent determines the integration format of a chart and the content of each component based upon the same factors as those considered by a table agent (Step 2 of *Agent-planning*). For the two dimensions of the Instantiations that illustrate the weight of objects, namely *object* and *weight* (Fig. 5), the discourse compares the difference between the weight of an object on Earth and its weight on the moon. The relevant information is extracted by filtering the Instantiations with the dimensional focus. The communicative goal may then be achieved by presenting the same attribute of different Instantiations, e.g., the weight of each instantiated object on Earth, either (a) in one type of bar (Fig. 3), or (b) in different types of bars (Fig. 16). The considerations applied for selecting a particular presentation format are described in (Han, 1996).

The chart container for generating the chart in Fig. 3 appears in Fig. 17. The chart agent sets **groups** to 2 since there are two Instantiations, one for the box and another for the computer. For the two attributes in focus for the dimension *object*, viz *name* and *mass*, the **labels** parameter is filled with the values of these attributes obtained from each Instantiation. There are two elements in each group, hence two types of bars are required. The weight of each object on Earth is presented in red bars, and the weight of each object on the moon is presented in green bars. This is indicated in the legend of the chart in Fig. effig:cht-tx2eg. The legend of a chart is treated as a small table without column headings, row headings or separators. Hence, the chart agent creates a table container of two columns and two rows. The first column contains a sample of each type of bar, and the second column contains the headings.

To extract the data for the bars in the chart, the chart agent filters the Instantiations with the dimensional focus of *weight*, viz the magnitude of weight. Hence, the first Instantiation produces the values 19.6 and 3.2, and the second Instantiation produces the values 98 and 16. These values are stored in **segment-list** in the order in which they were extracted. The **unit** is set to the unit of weight, viz *Weight(Newton)*. Two constants are specified in the chart container, namely diff and mini: diff represents the smallest visible difference between bars, and mini specifies the minimum width of each bar so that bars will not be reduced to thick lines. The **height** and **width** specify the size of a chart, which is calculated from the values being compared and the size of each component.

Once a chart agent determines the content of each component, it poses constraints on the modalities to be used for presenting the components (Step 3 of *Agent-planning*). Units of measurement must be presented in textual modalities,

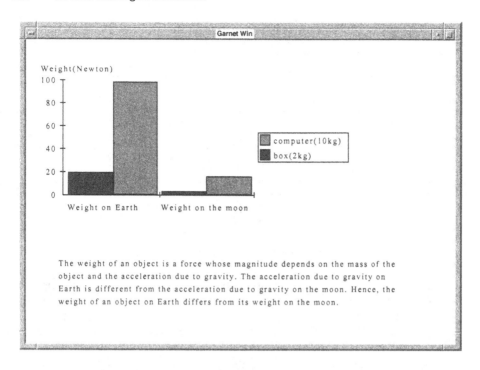

Fig. 16. Sample multimodal presentation: chart in a different format

and at this stage, labels and legend headings are restricted to textual modalities. In future, chart agents will be extended to allow icons for legend headings and labels.

Next, in Steps 4-6 of the *Agent-planning* procedure, two text agents and two number agents are activated to present the labels ("box(2kg)" and "computer(10kg)"), two additional text agents are activated to present the legend headings ("weight on Earth" and "weight on the moon"), and another text agent is activated to convey the unit of weight. The *wait-all-responses* strategy is used to process the responses from these agents since they present necessary components of the chart.

To ensure the integration of the chart components, space constraints are imposed in Step 7 of the *Agent-planning* procedure (Table 3). MAGPIE requires a chart to be big enough to attract a perceiver's attention (Holmes, 1984), hence $cscn_1$ and $cscn_2$ are created to restrict the minimum width and height of the chart. The maximum size of the chart is restricted by the size of its components. These restrictions are reflected in constraints $cscn_3$-$cscn_7$.

For the data set v in segment-list, $\{v_1, v_2, v_3, v_4\}$ are the values of v in ascending order. Constraint $cscn_3$ is imposed on the height of the chart to ensure that the smallest difference between bars is visible on the screen. The height of the first label on the X axis is added since the same font is used by all the agents presenting the labels; and diff is added since the chart must display at least the top of the smallest bar. The minimum difference between two values of

modality:	*chart*
position:	(0,0)
width:	450
height:	250
groups:	2
mini:	15
diff:	5

unit: *Weight(Newton)*
labels: $((($name$ ($object$ Inst1))$
        $($mass$ ($object$ Inst1)))$
        $(($name$ ($object$ Inst2))$
        $($mass$ ($object$ Inst2))))$
legend: $(($weight$ (Earth)) ($weight$ (moon)))$
segment-list: (19.6 3.2 98 16)

Fig. 17. Sample chart container: weight of objects

Name	Constraint	Strength
$cscn_1$	width($chart$) $\geq$ *Threshold*	required
$cscn_2$	height($chart$) $\geq$ *Threshold*	required
$cscn_3$	height($chart$) $\geq$ diff $\times \frac{v_4 - v_1}{\min_{i=1}^{9}\{[v_{i+1} - v_i]\|v_{i+1} > v_i\}}$ + diff $\\$ + height($label_1$) + height($unit$)	required
$cscn_4$	width($chart$) $\geq$ 4 $\times$ mini + width(legend) + width(v_4) + *offset*	required
$cscn_5$	width($chart$) $\geq$ groups $\times$ max { width($label_1$), width($label_2$) } $\\$ + width($legend$) + width(v_4) + *offset*	required
$cscn_6$	width($legend$) $\geq$ mini + 2 $\times$ *margin_min* $\\$ + max { width($heading_1$), width($heading_2$) }	required
$cscn_7$	width($legend$) $\leq$ *Threshold* $\times$ width($chart$)	preferred

Table 3. Space constraints on a chart

v is considered only when this difference is greater than zero (it is possible that two bars in a chart are of the same height).

The width of a chart is restricted by either the width of the bars or the length of the labels. Constraint $cscn_4$ in Table 3 pertains to the width of the bars, where mini is the minimum width of each bar, and 4 is the number of bars in the chart. The value of width(v_4) is added to account for the space required to label the scale on the Y axis, and the *offset* is added to account for the markers on the Y axis. Constraint $cscn_5$ pertains to the length of the labels. All the groups contain the same number of bars, and hence have the same width. This width is constrained by the longest label on the X axis, since one of the groups must be able to accommodate this label. Finally, the width of the legend is constrained by $cscn_6$ and $cscn_7$, where $cscn_6$ is based on the width of the legend's components, while $cscn_7$ is based on the width of the chart. For each type of bar, a sample block is generated in the first column of the legend using the minimum width allowed for bars, hence mini is added to $cscn_6$; each type of bar is described by a heading in the second column of the legend, thus the width of the longest heading is added; *margin_min* is the minimum margin required in each column of the legend. Constraint $cscn_7$ stipulates that the width of the legend should not exceed a certain proportion (*Threshold*) of the width of the entire chart.

During the initial planning stage (Steps 8-9 of *Agent-planning*), the chart agent propagates $cscn_1$-$cscn_7$ in order to determine the width and height of the chart. If the resulting width and height satisfy the constraints imposed by the presentation planning agent, the chart agent informs the presentation planning agent of the successful completion of the chart presentation process. Otherwise, a failure is reported.

During the reactive planning stage (Steps 10-16 of *Agent-planning*), the chart agent may be activated by an event demanding a modification of its plan variables or an event demanding the satisfaction of additional preferred constraints. For example, in the second case, the chart agent determines whether the width of the legend is too wide in proportion to the size of the chart. If so, the chart agent asks the text agents presenting the headings in the legend to reduce the font of the text (Step 16).

9   Conclusion

We have described a multi-agent planning mechanism for the generation of multimodal presentations which is based on a hierarchical blackboard architecture. Our mechanism combines blackboard events with constraint propagation to support communication between agents. The hierarchical architecture enables our mechanism to take into account the overall structure of the discourse; while constraint propagation supports the transfer of plan constraints from one level of the presentation plan hierarchy to the next, and enables our mechanism to take into consideration the consumption of resources. Our approach has been used for generating multimodal presentations for several discourse plans, which require the activation of up to 32 agents. Although a large number of agents slows down the presentation generation process, particularly when additional preferred constraints are satisfied, our results still demonstrate the flexibility of our approach.

The system presented in this paper may be enhanced along several dimensions. The existing agents of MAGPIE may be extended to offer more functions and format varieties. For example, chart agents should be able to relocate the legend and labels of a chart to save screen space, or allow icons to be used for the legend and the labels. In addition, table agents should be able to use modalities such as vectors to present composite information, and thereby reduce the number of columns required for the attributes in focus. Finally, MAGPIE may be extended to provide additional modalities, such as line charts and images. This requires the development of new agents and algorithms in order to handle non-linear constraints that restrict the position of different components in an image using trigonometric relations.

Future research on the constraint satisfaction mechanism of MAGPIE pertains to two interesting issues. The first issue involves using constraints to represent time restrictions on multimodal presentations, and developing a mechanism for the propagation of time constraints. This would allow the system to manipulate the time required to generate a discourse component, e.g., the time available to the table agent or the chart agent to improve a presentation. To do this, the constraint propagation mechanism must be able to propagate time intervals, and each agent must provide estimations of the time required for the generation of a component. Thus, on one hand, these estimations could be propagated from the lower level to the higher level of the presentation plan hierarchy, so that a master agent knows the minimum time required for generating each component. On the other hand, time restrictions could be propagated from the higher level to the lower level, so that an agent can ensure the generation of a component in the required time.

The second issue concerns the satisfaction of distributed constraints. In MAGPIE, these constraints are divided into several groups, and the satisfaction of each group of constraints is handled by a group of agents. Thus, MAGPIE attempts to achieve the global satisfaction of all constraints through the local satisfaction of each group of constraints. However, the latter does not always lead to the former, since agents may get stuck in a local optimum. Although the communication between agents increases the likelihood of reaching the global satisfaction of all the constraints, more efficient algorithms for the satisfaction of distributed constraints are required.

Acknowledgments

This research was supported in part by a research grant from the Faculty of Computing and Information Technology and by a Small ARC grant. The authors would like to thank Tun Heng Chiang for his work on the implementation of the display modules, and Damian Conway for his advice regarding the improvement of several tables and figures.

References

Allen, J.F. (1983) Maintaining Knowledge About Temporal Intervals. *Communication of the ACM*, 26(11), 832-843.

Allen, J.F. (1994) *Natural Language Understanding* Redwood City, CA: Benjamin-Cummings.

André, E., Finkler, W., Graf, W., Rist, T., Schauder, A., and Wahlster, W. (1993) WIP: The Automatic Synthesis of Multimodal Presentations. *Intelligent Multimedia Interfaces*, Maybury, M.T., (ed.) AAAI Press, 75-93.

André, E., Müller, J., and Rist, T. (1996) The PPP Persona: A Multipurpose Animated Presentation Agent. To appear in *Proc. of Advanced Visual Interfaces*, ACM Press.

Arens, Y. and Hovy, E. (1994) The Design of a Model-Based Multimedia Interaction Manager. *Artificial Intelligence Review*, 8(3), 95-188.

Arens, Y., Hovy, E., and van Mulken, S. (1993) Structure and Rules in Automated Multimedia Presentation Planning. *Proc. IJCAI-93*, 1253-1259.

Arens, Y., Hovy, E., and Vossers, M. (1993) On the Knowledge Underlying Multimedia Presentations. *Intelligent Multimedia Interfaces*, Maybury, M.T., (ed.), AAAI Press, 280-305.

Borning, A., Freeman-Benson, B., and Wilson, M. (1992) Constraint Hierarchies. *Lisp and Symbolic Computation* 5(3), p. 223-270.

Bourdot, P., Krus, M., and Gherbi, R. (1995) Management of Non-Standard Devices for Multimodal User Interfaces under UNIX/X11. In: H. Bunt, R.J. Beun and T. Borghuis (eds.) *Proc. CMC/95, Intern. Conf. on Cooperative Multimodal Communication,* Eindhoven, The Netherlands, 49-61.

Bunt, H., Ahn, R., Beun, R.J., Borghuis, T., and van Overveld, K. (1995) Cooperative Multimodal Communication in the DenK Project. In: H. Bunt, R.J. Beun and T. Borghuis (eds.) *Proc. CMC/95, Intern. Conf. on Cooperative Multimodal Communication,* Eindhoven, The Netherlands, 79-102.

Cheyer, A. and Julia, L. (1995) Multimodal Maps: An Agent-based Approach. In: H. Bunt, R.J. Beun and T. Borghuis (eds.) *Proc. CMC/95, Intern. Conf. on Cooperative Multimodal Communication,* Eindhoven, The Netherlands, 103-113.

Engelmore, R.S. and Morgan, A.J. (1988) *Blackboard Systems* New York: Addison-Wesley.

Feiner, S.K. and McKeown, K.R. (1990) Coordinating Text and Graphics in Explanation Generation. *Proc. AAAI-90*, Boston, MA, 442-449.

Feiner, S.K., Litman, D.J., McKeown, K.R., and Passonneau, R.J. (1993) Towards Coordinated Temporal Multimedia Presentations. *Intelligent Multimedia Interfaces*, Maybury, M.T., (ed.), AAAI Press, 139-147.

Finin, T., Fritzson, R., McKay, D., and McEntire, R. (1994) KQML as an Agent Communication Language. *Proc. CIKM'94, Third Intern. Conf. on Information and Knowledge Management*, New York, ACM Press.

Ghedira, K. (1994) Dynamic Partial Constraint Satisfaction by a Multi-Agent-Simulated Annealing Approach. *ECAI-94 Workshop on Constraint Satisfaction Issues Raised by Practical Applications*, Thomas Schiex (ed.), Amsterdam.

Graf, W. (1992) Constraint-based Graphical Layout of Multimodal Presentations. *Proc. AVI'92, Intern. Workshop on Advanced Visual Interfaces*, Rome, 365-385.

Han, Y. (1996) Cooperative Agents for Multimodal Presentation Planning. Doctoral Dissertation, Dept. of Computer Science, Monash University, Victoria, Australia (in prep.).

Han, Y. and Zukerman, I. (1995) A Cooperative Approach for Multimodal Presentation Planning. In: H. Bunt, R.J. Beun and T. Borghuis (eds.) *Proc. CMC/95, Intern. Conf. on Cooperative Multimodal Communication,* Eindhoven, The Netherlands, 145-159.

Han, Y. and Zukerman, I. (1996a) Constraint Propagation in a Cooperative Approach for Multimodal Presentation Planning. In W. Wahlster (ed.) *Proc. ECAI-96, Twelfth European Conference on Artificial Intelligence* Budapest, New York: John Wiley, 256-260.

Han, Y. and Zukerman, I. (1996b) A Mechanism for Multimodal Presentation Planning Based on Agent Cooperation and Negotiation. Technical Report No. 96/257, Dept. of Computer Science, Monash University, revised July 1996.

Holmes, N. (1984) *Designer's Guide to Creating Charts & Diagrams* New York: Watson-Guptill.

Maybury, M. (1993) Planning Multimedia Explanations Using Communicative Acts. In M. Maybury (ed.) *Intelligent Multimedia Interfaces*, AAAI Press, 59-74.

Mackinlay, J. (1986) Automating the Design of Graphical Presentation of Relational Information. *ACM Transaction on Graphics*, 5(2), 110-141.

Minton, S. Johnston, M., Philips, A., and Laird, P. (1990) Solving Large-Scale Constraint Satisfaction and Scheduling Problems Using a Heuristic Repair Method.

Proc. AAAI-90, Eighth National Conference on Artificial Intelligence, Boston, MA, 17-24.

Roth, S. and Mattis, J. (1991) Automating the Presentation of Information. *Proc. IEEE Conference on AI Applications*, Miami Beach, FL, 90-97.

Wahlster, W., André, E., Finkler, W., Profitlich, H., and Rist, T. (1993) Plan-based Integration of Natural Language and Graphics Generation. *Artificial Intelligence* 63(1-2), 387-427.

Zukerman, I. and McConachy, R. (1993) Generating Concise Discourse that Addresses a User's Inferences. *Proc. IJCAI-93, Thirteenth Intern. Joint Conf. on Artificial Intelligence*, Chambery, France, 1202-1207.

Zukerman, I. and McConachy, R. (1995) Generating Discourse across Several User Models: Maximizing Belief while Avoiding Boredom and Overload. *Proc. IJCAI-95 Fifteenth Intern. Joint Conf. on Artificial Intelligence*, Montreal, Canada, 1251-1257.

Developing Multimodal Interfaces: A Theoretical Framework and Guided Propagation Networks

J. C. Martin, R. Veldman, and D. Béroule

LIMSI-CNRS, B. P. 133, 9143 Orsay Cedex, France
martin@limsi.fr

Abstract. In this paper we propose an approach for the design of related theoretical and software tools for developing multimodal interfaces. A theoretical framework is described based on the notion of *types of cooperation* between modalities It forms the basis of a specification language that we used for developing multimodal interfaces to three test applications. This specification language is interpreted by a multimodal module made of Guided Propagation Networks.

1 Introduction

Human-computer interfaces face several requirements such as the need to be fast and robust to recognition errors, unexpected events and mistakes made by the user. The goal of our work is to study how multimodality can bring solutions to these problems and to provide tools for the development of multimodal interfaces.

As a matter of fact, the development of a multimodal interface addresses several issues (see Maybury, 1991): content selection ('what to say'), modality allocation ('in which modality to say it'), modality realization ('how to say it in that modality') and modality combination. Our work deals with the 'modality combination' issue. A multimodal interface developer has to know how to combine modalities and why this combination may improve the interaction. Although several multimodal interfaces have already been developed (see Bunt et al. (1995), Lee, 1995), there is still a lack of coherent theoretical and software tools.

In the first part of this paper, we propose a theoretical framework for analyzing modality combinations. We discuss existing frameworks in Human-Computer Interaction (HCI) and explain why our framework might be useful. The second part details two software tools based on the framework: a specification language and a multimodal module using Guided Propagation Networks. Illustrative examples are taken from a test application that we have developed.

2 A Framework for Analyzing Modality Combinations

The space of interfaces can be viewed from different standpoints, and several frameworks have already been proposed (see Bos, 1993 for a review). Such frameworks can be used for categorizing a particular interface, comparing different interfaces, inspiring designers in creating new interfaces or tools, arriving at a consensus about HCI terminology or finally for evaluating interfaces. In this section, we present some of these frameworks and explain why we believe that a framework devoted to multimodality is needed. After this, we describe a new framework and show how several multimodal interfaces and experimental results are represented within this framework.

2.1   Existing Frameworks

The framework described by Hutchins et al. (1986) considers whether the user has the feeling to converse with an intermediary performing the task. Two dimensions are proposed: 'engagement' and 'distance'. The 'engagement' dimension can take two values: 'conversation' (the user has the feeling that there is an intermediary performing the task) and 'model world' (the user has the feeling that he can manipulate artifacts directly). The 'distance' dimension can take two values ('small' or 'large') depending on the amount of cognitive effort it takes to manipulate and evaluate the system. The combination of these two dimensions produces four types of systems (see Table 1).

Table 1. Types of interactive systems

Engagement	Distance	Type of system
conversation	small	high-level language
conversation	large	low-level language
model world	small	direct manipulation
model world	large	low-level world

This space does not take into account the possible use of several devices or media of interaction. According to the semantic analysis of the design space of input devices given by Mackinlay et al. (1990), input devices are 'transducers of any combination of linear and rotary, absolute or relative, position and force, in any of the six spatial degrees of freedom'. Such input devices can be formalized and composed to describe more complex devices. The description of a mouse in such a framework is given in Fig. 1.

Instead of focusing on devices, the classification of Frohlich (1991) links *modes* (language or action), *channels* (audio, visual, haptic/kinesthetic), *media* (speech, text, gesture, sound, graphics, motion) and *styles* (programming language, command language, menu selection...). The combination of one mode, one channel and one medium enables a limited set of interaction styles. As an example, the combination of the language mode, the audio channel and the speech medium enables the following styles: *programming language, command language, natural language, field filling* and *menu selection*. Although this classification considers several media, it does not focus on the *combination* of these media.

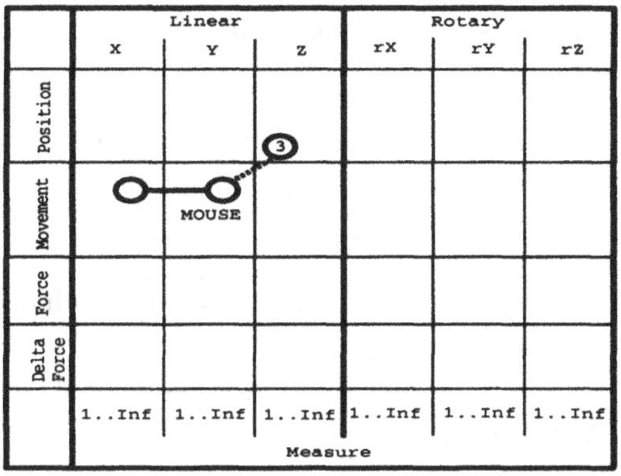

Fig. 1. Representation of a mouse with three buttons in the 'semantic analysis of input devices' proposed by Mackinlay et al. (1990). A mouse with three buttons is depicted as a circle on X movement, a circle on Y movement and a circle containing the number 3 on Z positioning. It means that a mouse is a layout combination (dotted line) of four devices: three simple buttons and one device that is itself the merge composite (bold horizontal line) of two elementary devices sensing changes in X and Y. The placement of the X and Y circles to the right of their column indicates nearly continuous resolution (Measure = Inf). The location of the '3' button circle to the left of the Z column indicates control with only two states. (Modified from Mackinlay et al. 1990.)

Nigay and Coutaz (1993) describe one of the few frameworks dedicated to multimodality. It is composed of two dimensions. The 'fusion' dimension considers whether or not the events detected on several modalities have to be merged. Thus, this dimension can take two values: 'combination' or 'independence'. The 'use of modality' dimension can also take two values: 'sequential' or 'parallel', depending on whether the modalities are active at the same time or not. Combining these dimensions, four types of multimodality appear, shown in Table 2.

Table 2. Types of multimodality

Fusion	Use of modality	Type of multimodality
combination	sequential	alternate
combination	parallel	synergistic
independence	sequential	exclusive
independence	parallel	concurrent

This framework is focusing on the use of temporal criteria (coincidence or sequence) to decide whether or not to merge multimodal pieces of information. It aims at classifying systems more than helping HCI designers to make a appropriate use of multimodality.

2.2   TYCOON: a Framework based on TYpes and goals of COOperatioN

What is an appropriate use of multimodality? We believe that a system should use multimodality only if it helps in achieving usability criteria, such as:

- enabling a fast interaction,
- adapting to different environments, users or user's behaviors,
- being intuitive or easy to learn,
- improving recognition in a noisy (audio, visual or tactile) environment,
- enabling the user to easily link presented information to more global contextual knowledge (interpretation),
- translating information from one modality to another modality, ...

These usability criteria are quite general and may depend on the application to be developed. From a multimodal point of view, they can be seen as 'goals of cooperation between modalities'. How can modalities cooperate and be combined to achieve these goals? In what follows we will define five types of cooperation between modalities. We will take illustrative examples from several multimodal interfaces using COMIT, a multimodal test application that we have developed. COMIT features twenty commands helping a user to build a MOTIF graphical interface composed of buttons, scrollbars, menus, graphics ... The user can combine a Datavox speech recognizer (the linguistic analysis limited to keyword detection), a mouse and a keyboard (see Fig. 2).

When interacting with COMIT, the user can create a reactive button by saying *"I want a button called ... here"*. She types the name of the button on the keyboard while saying *"called"* and produces a mouse click indicating the location of the button while saying *"here"* (Fig. 3).

2.3   Transfer

When several modalities cooperate by *transfer*, this means that a chunk of information produced by one modality is used by another modality.

Transfer is commonly used in hypermedia interfaces when a mouse click provokes the display of an image (Inder et al., 1995). In information retrieval applications, the user may express a request in one modality (speech) and get relevant information in another modality (video) (Foote et al., 1995). Output information may not only be retrieved but also produced from scratch. In COMIT, the user can utter *"there is a button on the left"* and the system creates a graphical representation of the button on the left-hand side of the screen. Several systems generate more complex graphical descriptions of a scene from a linguistic description (O'Nuallain and Smith, 1994; Olivier and Tsujii, 1994). For instance, natural language instructions can be used to create animated simulations of virtual human agents carrying out tasks (Webber, 1997). Similarly, the visual description of a scene can be used to generate a linguistic description (Jackendoff,

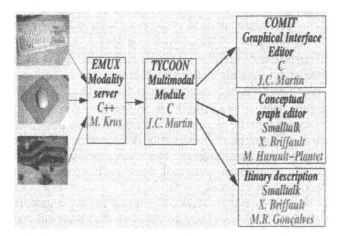

Fig. 2. Our multimodal module is connected with several modules developed in different languages by different people. Events detected on the speech, keyboard and mouse modality (left-hand side) are time-stamped coherently by EMUX, a modality server (Bourdot et al. 1995). The events are then integrated in our TYCOON multimodal module. Three multimodal interfaces have been developed for three test applications (right-hand side): a graphical interface editor (COMIT), a conceptual graph editor (Hurault-Plantet and Briffault, 1996) and itinerary description (Briffault, 1996; Gonçalves, 1996).

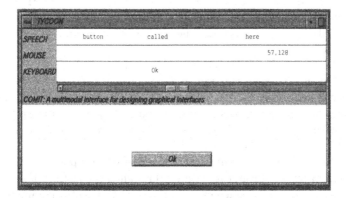

Fig. 3. Multimodal interaction in COMIT for creating a button. The events detected on the three modalities are displayed as a function of time in the upper part. The result of the multimodal command is the creation of a button labeled 'Ok' in the COMIT window.

1987; Daniel et al., 1994) or a multimodal description (André and Rist, 1995). All these examples can be said to involve transfer for a goal of translation.

Transfer may also be involved in other goals such as improving recognition: mouse click detection may be transferred to a speech modality in order to facilitate the recognition of predictable words (here, that...) as in the GERBAL system (Salisbury et al., 1990) and in COMIT.

Transfer may also be used to enable faster interaction: in the MAAR system (Cheyer and Julia, 1995), when part of an uttered sentence has been misrecognized, it can be edited with the keyboard so that the user does not have to type or utter again the all sentence. Finally, the WIP system (Wahlster et al., 1991) produces coordinated natural language and graphics output. The two modalities work concurrently to produce an output based on instructions received from a multimodal manager. If necessary, when one of the modalities cannot produce a given piece of information, on-line information can be transferred from this modality to the other. As an example, the graphical modality can be told by the manager to produce a textual label and it may turn out that it is not possible because it would hide parts of the graphics. This information is sent to the natural language modality which is able to adapt its output dynamically to insert the new textual information. This on-line transfer of information and the parallelism of processing in the two modalities enables faster human-computer interaction.

Transfer may thus intervene for different reasons either between two input modalities, between two output modalities, or between an input modality and an output modality.

2.4   Equivalence

When several modalities cooperate by *equivalence*, this means that a chunk of information may be processed as an alternative, by either of them.

In COMIT, the user can for instance either utter or type *"create a scrollbar"* to create a new scrollbar.

The EDWARD system (Huls and Bos, 1995) is applied to hierarchical file system management. It allows the user to choose at any time during the interaction the style that suits best at that moment (mouse or natural language). Experimental tests have shown that subjects tended to choose the mouse for selecting an object with a long name. Yet, when the object was difficult to locate on the screen, subjects preferred typing.

In TAPAGE (Faure and Julia, 1994), the user of a graphical editor may specify a command either through speech or through the selection of a button with a pen. In this case, equivalence enables the user to select a command with the pen when the speech recognizer is not working accurately because of noise, and hence to improve recognition of the commands.

Equivalence also enables adaptation to the user by customization: the user may be allowed to select the modalities he prefers (Hare et al., 1995). The development of accurate mental models of a multimodal system seems dependent upon the implementation of such options over which the user has control (Sims and Hedberg, 1995). Finally, equivalence also enables faster interaction, since it allows the system or the user to select the fastest modality. Equivalence thus means alternative. It is clear that differences between each modality, either cognitive or technical, have to be considered.

2.5   Specialization

When modalities cooperate by *specialization*, this means that a specific kind of information is always processed by the same modality.

Specialization is not always absolute and may be defined more precisely: one should distinguish *data-relative* specialization and *modality-relative* specialization. In several systems, sounds are specialized in error notification (forbidden commands are signaled with a beep). In a *modality-relative* specialization sounds are not used to convey any other type of information. A specialization is *data-relative* if errors only produce sounds, no graphics or text. When there is a one-to-one relation between a set of information and a modality, we will speak of an *absolute* specialization.

Specialization may help the user to interpret the events produced by the computer (to link them to global contextual knowledge). This means that the choice of a given modality adds semantic information and hence helps the interpretation process. Specialization may also improve recognition. In the example of a tourist information system, the user may always provide the name of towns using the keyboard (or only the first letters). This specialization enables an easier processing (and hence a better recognition) in other modalities. It improves the accuracy of the speech recognizer since the search space is smaller (Baekgaard, 1995). In COMIT, for the same reason the user cannot specify the name of a button by using speech or the mouse; he has to use the keyboard. This specialization may also enable faster interaction since it decreases the duration of the integration and modality selection process.

When a modality is specialized, it should respect the specificity of this modality including the information it is good at representing. For instance, in reference interpretation, the designation gesture aims at selecting a specific area and the verbal channel provides a frame for the interpretation of the reference: categorical information, constraints on the number of objects selected (Bellalem and Romary, 1995). In an experimental study (Bressolle et al., 1997) aiming at the understanding of cooperative cognitive strategies used by air traffic controllers, non-verbal resources are revealed to form a specific dimension of communication for some types of information which are not verbally expressed, such as the emergency of a situation. Intuitive specialization of a modality may go against its technical specificities. In the Wizard of Oz experiment dealing with a tourist application described in (Siroux et al., 1997), despite the low recognition rate of town names, users did not use the tactile screen to select a town but used speech instead.

2.6   Redundancy

If modalities cooperate by *redundancy*, this means that the same information is processed by these modalities.

In COMIT, if the user types *"quit"* on the keyboard or utters *"quit"*, the system asks for a confirmation. But if the user both types and utters *"quit"*, the systems interpret this redundancy to avoid a confirmation dialogue, thus enabling faster interaction by reducing the number of actions the user has to perform (see Fig. 4).

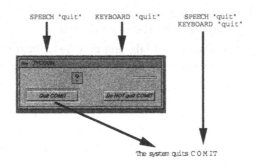

Fig. 4. Redundancy enables fast interaction in COMIT. When the command *"quit* is detected only on speech or keyboard, the system asks for confirmation. When it is detected in both speech and keyboard modalities within the same temporal window, the system does not ask for confirmation and directly quits (right-hand side).

Regarding intuitiveness, redundancy has been observed in the Wizard of Oz study described in (Siroux et al., 1997): sometimes the user selected a town both by speech and a touch on the tactile screen. Regarding learnability of interfaces, it has been observed that a redundant multimodal output involving both visual display of a text and speech restitution of the same text enabled faster learning of the interface (Wang et al., 1993).

An important issue here is to know if the visual channel should carry exactly the same message as the auditory channel (verbatim reinforcement) or a shorter one (priming reinforcement). The type of reinforcement chosen by the system and the information to be transmitted seems to have consequences for the cognitive compatibility of spoken and manual responses from the user (Dowell et al., 1995). Redundancy between visual and vocal text with verbatim reinforcement was also tested in (Huls and Bos, 1995) with natural language descriptions of the objects the user manipulates and the action he performs. Although speech coerced the subjects into reading the typed descriptions, the subjects made more errors and were slower than with the visual text output only.

2.7   Complementarity

Finally, when modalities cooperate by *complementarity*, different chunks of information are processed by each modality and have to be merged.

Systems enabling the *'put that there'* command for the manipulation of graphical objects are described in (Carbonnel, 1970; Bolt, 1980). In COMIT, if the user wants to create a radio button, he may type its name and select its position with the mouse. These two chunks of information are merged to create the button with the right name at the right position. Complementarity may enable faster interaction, since the two modalities can be used simultaneously and with shorter messages, which are moreover better recognized than long messages.

In Multimodal Maps (Cheyer and Julia, 1995), pen and voice modalities cooperate by complementarity and synergy: the user may ask *"what is the distance from here to this hotel?"* while simultaneously indicating the specified locations by pointing or circling. Other examples of complementarity can be found in this volume: multimodal presentation planning with tables combining text and icons (Han and Zukerman, 3D modeling (Bourdot et al.), and experiments showing that the use of complementarity input such as *"Is this a report?"* while pointing on a file, increases with the user's experience (Huls and Bos, 1995),

Complementarity may also improve interpretation, as in (Santana and Pineda, 1995) where graphical output is sufficient for an expert but need to be completed by textual output for novice users. An important issue concerning complementarity is the criterion used to merge chunks of information in different modalities. Classical approaches merge these because they are temporally coincident, temporally sequential, or spatially linked. Regarding intuitiveness, complementarity behavior was observed in (Siroux et al., 1995). Two types of behavior showed feature complementarity. In 'sequential' behavior, which was rare, the user would for example utter *"What are the campsites at"* and then select a town with the tactile screen. In the 'synergistic' behavior, the user would utter *"Are there any campsites here?"* and select a town with the tactile screen while pronouncing *"here"*. Regarding the output from the computer, it was observed in the experiment described in (Hare et al., 1995) that spatial linking of related information encourages the user's awareness of causal and cognitive links. Yet, when having to retrieve complementary chunks of information from different media, user behavior tended to be biased towards sequential search, avoiding synergistic use of several modalities.

Modalities cooperating by complementarity may be specialized in different types of information. In the example of a graphical editor, the name of an object may be always specified with speech while its position is specified with the mouse. But modalities cooperating by complementarity may be also be equivalent for different types of information. As a matter of fact, the user could also select an object with the mouse and its new position with speech (*"in the upper right corner"*). Nevertheless, the complementary use of specialized modalities gives the advantages of specialization: speech recognition is improved since the vocabulary and syntax is simpler than a complete linguistic description. Finally, the use of the natural complementarity of speech audio and images of lip movements improves speech recognition (Vo and Waibel, 1993).

The difference between redundancy and complementarity is not always clear. The information processed by two modalities may be the same and yet be used differently. For instance, in the MIX 3D system (Bourdot et al., 1997), some vocal outputs are associated with a textual message in a standard output window. The vocal output avoids the user having to stop watching the 3D object being designed. The textual output serves as tracing and may be used for control later in the work session. Although redundant regarding the information they transmit, the two modalities are used in a complementary fashion.

2.8   Formal Notations

To define these types of cooperation more precisely, we propose formal logical notations. They aim at stating explicitly the parameters of each type of cooperation and the relation between these parameters which is inherent to the type of cooperation. We consider the case of input modalities (human towards computer); definitions for output modalities are similar (Martin, 1996).

Modality
We define a *modality* as a process receiving and producing chunks of information. A modality M is formally defined by two sets:

$E(M)$: the set of chunks of information received by M;
$S(M)$: the set of chunks of information produced by M.

Transfer
Two modalities M_1 and M_2 cooperate by *transfer* when a chunk of information produced by M_1 can be used by M_2 after translation by a transfer operator tr which is a parameter of the cooperation. Formally:

$$transfer(M_1, M_2, tr): \ tr(S(M_1)) \subset E(M_2)$$

Specialization
An input modality M cooperates by specialization with a set of input modalities M_i in the production of a set I of chunks of information if M produces I (and only I) and no modality in M_i produces I. Formally:

$$specialization(M, I, \{M_i\}): \ I = S(M) \ \wedge \ \forall M_i, I \not\subset S(M_i)$$

Equivalence
Two input modalities M_1 and M_2 cooperate by *equivalence* for the production of a set I of chunks of information when each element i of I can be produced either by M_1 or by M_2. An operator eq controls the choice of modality. It may take into account user's preferences, environmental features, information to be transmitted... Formally:

$$equivalence(M_1, M_2, I, eq): \ \forall i \in I, \ \exists e_1 \in E(M_1), \ \exists e_2 \in E(M_2),$$
$$i = eq((M_1, e_1), (M_2, e_2))$$

Redundancy
Two input modalities M_1 and M_2 cooperate by *redundancy* for the production

of a set I of chunks of information when each element i of I can be produced by an operator re merging a pair (s_1, s_2) produced by M_1 and M_2, respectively. re will merge (s_1, s_2) if their *redundant attribute* has the same value and a criterion $crit$ is true. A chunk of information has several attributes. For instance, a chunk of information sent by a speech recognizer has the following attributes: time of detection, label of recognized word, recognition score. The 'redundant' attribute of two modalities plays a role in deciding whether two chunks of information produced by these modalities is redundant or complementary. Formally:

$$redundancy(M_1, M_2, I, redundant\_attribute, crit): \ \forall i \in I, \exists s_1 \in S(M_1),$$
$$\exists s_2 \in S(M_2), \ redundant\_attribute(s_1) = redundant\_attribute(s_2)$$
$$\wedge \ i = re(s_1, s_2, crit)$$

Complementarity

Two input modalities M_1 and M_2 cooperate by *complementarity* for the production of a set I of chunks of information when each element i of I can be produced by an operator co merging a pair (s_1, s_2) produced by M_1 and M_2, respectively. co will merge (s_1, s_2) if their 'redundant' attribute does not have the same value and a criterion $crit$ is true. Formally:

$$complementarity(M_1, M_2, crit): \ \forall i \in I, \exists s_1 \in S(M_1), \exists s_2 \in S(M_2),$$
$$redundant\_attribute(s_1) \neq redundant\_attribute(s_2) \ \wedge \ i = co(s_1, s_2, crit)$$

2.9   Discussion

A graphical representation of TYCOON is given in Fig. 5. Part of our framework has already been used by other researchers. Our 'types of cooperation' dimension, initially introduced in (Martin and Béroule, 1993), has been renamed 'the CARE properties' (Coutaz and Nigay, 1994; Nigay and Coutaz, 1995) with slight differences: the 'transfer' type, the 'goals of cooperation' dimension and the distinction between data-relative and modality-relative specialization are not considered. Our dimension of types of cooperation has also been used for the description of the multimodal behavior of a user by Catinis and Caelen (1995) and Coutaz et al. (1996).

As a matter of fact, as shown in our examples, TYCOON can be used to describe multimodal systems, as well as experimental results in HCI or human-human interaction. It should be clear that a multimodal system often offers several types of cooperation between modalities and is thus represented by several boxes in TYCOON. However, since multimodal interfaces have a shorter history than classical interfaces, it is difficult to ensure that TYCOON is complete and can cover any kind of multimodal interaction.

The lack of multimodal and multimedia theory is obvious in existing multimedia authoring tools which often enable only the multimedia developer to combine modalities along temporal and spatial dimensions. A common deficiency of these tools is the lack of support mechanisms for design and implementation tasks (Vaananen, 1995). We have developed two software tools to facilitate the development of multimodal interfaces: a command language for specifying cooperations between modalities, and a multimodal module based on Guided Propagation Networks. The framework provides theoretical foundations for the multimodal aspects of both of these tools. COMIT, the multimodal interface that we introduced previously, has been developed with these tools and is described in more detail in the next section.

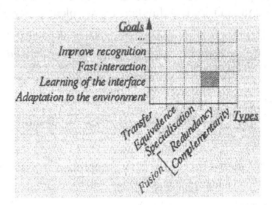

Fig. 5. Graphical representation of TYCOON, the proposed framework. Several *types of cooperation* between modalities (horizontal axis) may be involved in several *goals* of cooperation, which are general usability criteria (vertical axis). TYCOON can be used to represent examples of multimodal interaction and experimental results. For instance (dark box), it has been shown that with redundant displayed text and vocal output, a user learned faster how to use a graphical interface (Wang et al., 1993).

3   COMIT: a Multimodal Interface

In this section, we give illustrative examples of the multimodal types and goals of cooperation between modalities in COMIT. We also describe how they are specified. COMIT has so far only been tested by its developer, yet and experimental tests remain to be done to evaluate its intuitiveness and appropriateness.

The specification language is based on *keywords* and *variables*. There is at least one keyword for each type of cooperation. The variables defined in a declaration can be used as shown in the following examples. In Fig. 3 we already gave an example of multimodal interaction in COMIT for the creation of a button. The specification of this multimodal command involves three variables V1, V2, and V3 in the following way.

- **specialization V1   SPEECH button**
  Creates a variable V1 which will be activated if the word *"button"* is recognized by the speech modality.

- **complementarity_coincidence V2   SPEECH called   KEY-BOARD** *

  Creates a variable V2 involving cooperation by complementarity with a temporal coincidence criterion which enables the word *"called"* on the speech modality to be merged with any word typed on the keyboard (which is the meaning of the *) in the same temporal window.

- **complementarity_coincidence V3   SPEECH here   MOUSE click** *

  Creates a variable V3 which involves cooperation by complementarity and enables the word *"here"* to be merged with a mouse click at any location in the same temporal window.

- **complementarity_sequence   V1 V2 V3**

  The three variables are linked sequentially.

- **coincidence_duration   300**

  The length of the temporal window is specified; the given value (300) is interpreted as a number of processing cycles of the multimodal module.

In COMIT, the user can also create a list of words from which a selection is to be made. Since the number of words is a priori unknown to the system, it is not possible to use a temporal coincidence criterion to merge them. Instead, the user can specify the end of the list by uttering *"end of list"* (Fig. 6). The

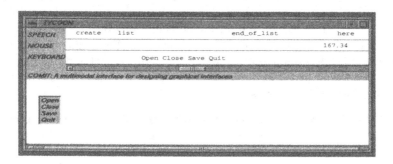

Fig. 6. Multimodal interaction (top) for creating a list containing several words (lower left-hand side).

specification of this command involves what we call a 'structure completion' criterion enabling the fusion of all the words typed before the utterance of *"end of list"*:

- **complementarity_structural V5   KEYBOARD *   SPEECH end_of_list**

Two theoretically-inspired features of COMIT enable fast interaction: parallelism and redundancy. Simultaneous or overlapping independent commands can be recognized in parallel in COMIT. For instance, the user may ask for the date with the speech modality while editing an object with two other modalities (keyboard and mouse). The temporal coincidence between these two independent commands is not enough for the system to integrate them. As already mentioned before, redundancy also enables faster interaction in COMIT (cf. the 'quit' example in Fig. 4).

In COMIT, modalities may also cooperate to improve recognition. Although speech recognition systems have become much more robust in recent years with respect to both speaker and acoustical variability, the performance of even the best state-of-the art systems tends to deteriorate when:

- the user speaks before the system is ready,
- speech is transmitted over telephone lines,
- the signal-to-noise ratio is extremely low,
- the speaker's native language is not the one with which the system was trained,
- the speaker has a cold,
- the speaker has performed an out-of-vocabulary utterance.

(see Stern, 1995; Yankelovich et al., 1995). Thus, any chance of improving speech recognition by taking into account events detected in other modalities is of interest. COMIT is only a test application yet, with a small speech vocabulary (30 words). The speech recognition system is a VECSYS-datavox. The branching factor is also small (between 1 and 3) except for the first word which has 10 possible values. Yet, recognition errors happen. Moreover, we are also building multimodal interfaces to more complex applications (Fig. 2) like itinary description (Briffault, 1996) where the vocabulary (including street and building names) and the branching factor are greater. Multimodal interfaces thus have to cope with speech recognition errors.

In COMIT, transfer and complementarity are used to improve recognition through predictions. The activation of a variable leads to a transfer of information by lowering the threshold of predicted events (Fig. 7).

Most speech recognition systems provide recognition scores. Words provided by the recognizer without having been uttered often have a low score. Recognition thresholds make it possible to filter such words. These scores can also be used to compare several candidates.

Unexpected events also occur in multimodal interfaces: one or several words may be misrecognized (or even not uttered by the user), the user may make mistakes while typing on the keyboard, the user switches very slowly between modalities ... Considering all the possibilities in the specifications would be very complex. Instead, we have chosen to specify only one prototype per command, and to provide a *multimodal recognition score* which is proportional to: the temporal matching between the sequence of detected events and the prototype (Fig. 8), the number of detected events which were expected in the prototype (Fig. 9), and the recognition scores provided by the speech recognizer. When several prototypes are activated, the prototype with the higher multimodal recognition score

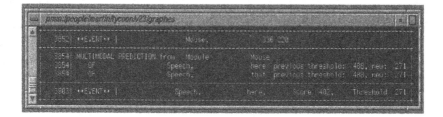

Fig. 7. Improving recognition thanks to multimodal predictions (comments printed during a COMIT execution). At time t=3852 (first line, left-hand side), a mouse click is detected at the location 336, 220. At time t=3854, the recognition threshold of all the words which may occur within the same temporal window (here, that) is temporarily lowered. At time t=3903, the word *"here"* is recognized. The score given by the speech recognizer is 402, which is higher than the new threshold (271). Hence, this word is considered by the multimodal module (the comment EVENT is printed).

Fig. 8. Multimodal recognition scores as a function of the temporal mismatch between a sequences of events and command prototypes. *Top:* the sequence of events is very close to the prototype of the command *"CreateButton"*. This command has been recognized with a maximal recognition score: 1000. Another command has been activated (ChangeColor) but with a lower score: 583. *Middle:* in this sequence, some events (*"here"* and *"Ok"*) appear a bit sooner. The recognition score is lower: 962. *Bottom:* the weaker the expected temporal coincidence between events, the lower the recognition score: 836.

is selected. This is useful when one or several words are missing (even more if they are at the beginning of the sentence).

This recognition score may also be used to regulate the width of the temporal window used for coincidence detection. The width of this window changes from one user to the other, and also during a single-user interaction. Thus, it is very difficult to fix. If the recognition scores get lower and lower, the system should enlarge the window.

4 A Multimodal Module Based on Guided Propagation Networks

The multimodal module used in COMIT is founded on a computational memory model called Guided Propagation Networks (GPN) (Béroule, 1985; 1990), together with an architecture which implements synchrony coding (Martin, 1995).

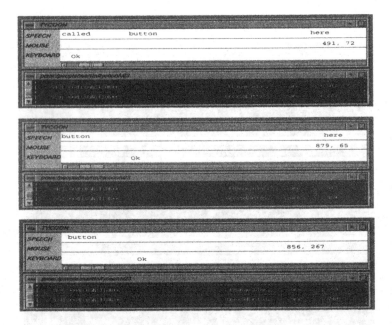

Fig. 9. Multimodal recognition score with inverse or missing events. *Top:* When the groups (button) and (called, Ok) are in inverted order, the score is 775. *Middle:* When the word *"called"* is missing, the command is recognized but with a score of 889. *Bottom:* When the words *"called"* and *"here"* are missing, the command is recognized but with a score of 740.

Learning mechanisms may facilitate the specification of multimodal interfaces and the adaptation of the interface to users' multimodal preferences. In COMIT, a multimodal prototype can be created from a sequence of events such as *"line ... here* (click) *... here (click)"*. Initially, the system has to know the size of the temporal window used for temporal coincidence detection and the fact that some events, such as mouse click position, are 'variable events' which change from one instance of the command to the other. When events coming from several modalities are detected, COMIT builds a multimodal complementary prototype which can then be used to recognize a similar sequence of events (the events may appear a bit sooner or later, the mouse click locations may be different). This prototype is also used to produce corresponding specification commands (see Fig. 10) which may facilitate the process of multimodal specification. The association between the prototype built and the application still has to be specified.

Fig. 10. Building a multimodal prototype in COMIT. *Top:* The initial specification file describes the modalities, the coincidence duration (300) and the events to be detected (*"line, "here"*). Variable events (mouse click position) are not described. The goal of cooperation 'building prototypes' is selected by the user. *Middle:* The sequence of detected events. *Bottom:* The specification file has been extended with commands corresponding to the detected events.

In the next section, we explain how the multimodal module enables these properties of COMIT.

4.1   Guided Propagation of Internal Signals

A GPN comprises elementary processing units which selectively respond to events at the moment they occur in the environment. These 'event detectors' can all be fed by spontaneous internal flows of activity. As shown in Fig. 11, the network internal activity may be guided in the course of time towards one specific event detector under the influence of environmental stimuli (keyboard keys, speech features...). This guiding process is carried out through the detection of coincidence between stimuli and the internal flows. It may be noticed that the usual digital *comparison* between input sets of vectors and internal numerical references is replaced here by the *detection of space-time coincidence* between input stimuli and internal contextual signals. This 'comparison' is performed by chains of processing units which form memory *pathways* driving the internal flow to event detectors. Since each of these units responds to specific stimuli in a certain context (given by the preceding unit in the pathway), they are termed 'Context-Dependent' (CD). A CD unit corresponds to a variable in the multimodal specifications.

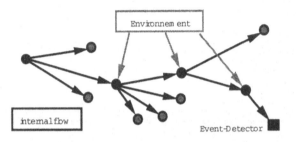

Fig. 11. Principle of guided propagation. The internal flow, which in this figure originates from the left-most cell (root unit), is guided by a series of environmental stimuli towards one of the output event detectors.

A central feature of GPNs is their hierarchical and parallel organization, thanks to which several knowledge levels and several simultaneous analyses can participate together in a multimodal task. A module with this architecture receives space-time patterns of activity delivered by several peripheral modules, and facilitation flows issued from either deeper modules or parallel ones. This facilitation mechanism, which lowers the unit's response thresholds, can facilitate (or even force) the propagation of activity along a selection of memory pathways. Another important feature of a GPN is its ability to grow in the course of processing for learning purposes, allowing the complete set of pathways to sprout from root units. Current monomodal applications of GPNs include speech recognition (Escande et al., 1991), strategies of syntactic learning (Roques, 1994), robust parsing (Westerlund et al., 1994), a model of reading (Béroule et al., 1994), and pattern generation.

4.2   Synchrony Coding and Multiplexing Units

Thanks to unsupervised learning mechanisms, a new pathway can be built whenever a new combination of events occurs in the environment. Although this possibility can be used along with a kind of 'garbage collector' process to free useless units (Blanchet, 1992), another method has been proposed which does not require many elementary processing units. This solution brings into play a coding dimension which is quite compatible with the space-time coding used in GPN: the *synchrony* between periodic pulse-like internal signals (Martin, 1995). An architecture has been developed for the management of this temporal coding, which involves *multiplexing units* (mpx) and which allows several variables to be simultaneously supported by prototypical representations. Figure 12 gives an example of the recognition of a multimodal command in COMIT. In the following sections we explain how these techniques enable the results observed in COMIT.

4.3   Fast Interaction

In a GPN, any word detector is connected to as many CD units as different contexts (multi-modal commands) in which the word may occur. When activated, the detector feeds in parallel into several CD units, among which one may simultaneously receive the contribution of the internal flow, together with possible stimuli from other modalities. Most of the activity delivered by the word detector appears to be unprofitable, but the appropriate memory location (CD) can thus be retrieved in one shot, independent of the amount of CDs associated with the detector. In sum, the modalities possibly represented in a GPN work in synchrony with the environmental stimuli. Due to this parallel processing, independent commands which overlap in time can be recognized without cross-talk (Fig. 13).

Time delays constitute a basic parameter of GPNs, since they are responsible for the time coincidence of stimuli originating from several modalities, at the level of every CD unit. In order to favour the fast interpretation of redundant information, these time delays can be regulated so that CD units receiving monomodal information be activated later than CDs fed by several redundant modalities with the same information.

4.4   Predictions

While proceeding along memory pathways, the front of a GPN internal flow anticipates the next events to come. If the anticipation of a given command component is strong enough due to several factors (activity level of the current stimuli, familiarity of the command, strong background context), then the identification of expected components is facilitated through the lowering of their associated thresholds. Recognition carried out within a given modality can thus take advantage of the expectations made at the multimodal level, using the information delivered by other modalities. In this case, according to the framework described in section 2, modalities cooperate by complementarity and transfer of information (the predictions) to improve recognition.

4.5   Multimodal Recognition Scores

In a GPN, the activity level of a detector at the end of a multimodal command pathway corresponds to the way an occurrence of this command matches its in-

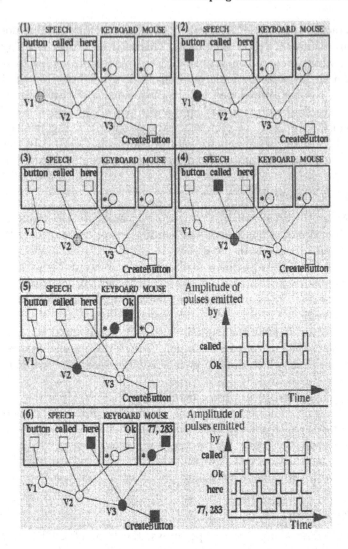

Fig. 12. Representation and recognition of a multimodal command in the multimodal module. **(1)** The command for creating a button is represented by a pathway linking event detectors (squares), three CD units (V1, V2, V3) and two mpx units (labelled '*') in charge of binding variables and values. Initially, V1 is activated below its threshold (light grey circle). **(2)** The word *"button"* is detected and its associated detector is activated above its threshold (dark square). Hence, it sends a signal to V1 which in turn becomes activated and sends a signal to V2. **(3)** V2 is activated below its threshold. **(4)** The word *"called"* is uttered, its detector is activated and a signal is sent to V2. V2 becomes more activated but still below its threshold (dark grey). **(5)** The word *"Ok"* is typed on the keyboard in the same temporal window. V2 is fully activated by the rough time coincidence of the signal emitted by V1, the *"called"* detector and the mpx unit of the mouse modality. This gates a dynamic binding process which results in the emission of synchronized periodic pulses by the event detectors which participated in the activation of V2 (histograms on the right-hand side). **(6)** Since a distinct phase originates from each variable, when the command is fully recognized, the bindings are readable without cross-talks.

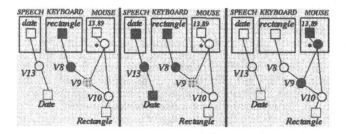

Fig. 13. Parallel recognition of two independent commands overlapping in time. *Left:* The user has started a command drawing a rectangle by typing *"rectangle"*. *Middle:* The user switches to another command by asking for the date (or any request of information he needs to complete the drawing). The activities dealing with the two commands propagate in different pathways and do not overlap. *Right:* The user continues the rectangle drawing by pointing at a corner with the mouse.

ternal representation. This 'matching score' accounts for the degree of distortion undergone by the reference multimodal command, including noisy, missing or inverse components. Initially applied to robust parsing (Westerlund et al., 1994), this feature has been adapted to multimodality in COMIT (Veldman, 1995). This quantified matching score results from three properties of GPNs, described in Fig. 14. Appendix 1 describes the computation of the corresponding parameters of the network.

4.6   Learning

The learning mechanisms of guided propagation enable the construction of multimodal representations. Depending on a time coincidence criterion, newly detected events are linked to existing units (*generalization*) or lead to the creation of a new pathway (*differentiation*). An example of pathway sprouting is shown in Fig. 15.

4.7   Towards Syntactic and Semantic Interpretation of Multimodal Commands

In the current multimodal module, the parsing of multimodal commands is limited to keyword detection. As a perspective, two possibilities of improvement are investigated in parallel, yet not implemented. The first possibility is to connect the multimodal module with syntactic and semantic modules developed with another approach than GPN: syntactic charts and conceptual graphs (Hurault-Plantet and Briffault, 1996). This is currently under way in the application of itinary description. The second possibility is to exploit the capabilities of GPNs for syntactic and semantic analysis. As already mentioned, GPNs have already been applied to syntactic parsing (Westerlund et al., 1994). We describe here the possibilities of semantic processing using a GPN.

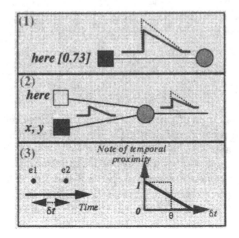

Fig. 14. The multimodal module provides multimodal recognition scores thanks to three properties of Guided Propagation Networks: **(1)** The amplitude of the signal emitted by a speech detector is proportional to the recognition score provided by the speech recognizer (0.73). **(2)** A variable unit can be activated even if some expected events are missing (in this case, the amplitude of the signal emitted by this variable unit is lower than the maximum). **(3)** The greater the temporal distortion between two events e1 and e2, the weaker their summation (or note of temporal proximity), because of the decreasing shape of the signals.

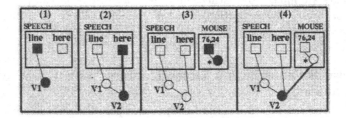

Fig. 15. Building a multimodal prototype with a GPN. **(1)**: A first variable unit is created and activated when the word *"line"* is detected (differentiation). **(2)**: The word *"here"* is detected in another temporal window, which results in the creation and activation of a second variable unit (differentiation). **(3)**: Within the same temporal window, a mouse click and its position have been detected. **(4)**: V2 is the last activated unit in the same temporal window as the mouse mpx unit. The two units are thus connected (generalization). And so on until the end of the events sequence...

Given the general definition of a symbol, *a figurative sign which stands for certain values*, the question of its computational implementation can be considered beyond the von Neumann architecture framework. In von Neumann computers, a symbol can be represented by a given memory register filled with one of several possible values. For binding symbols, this content-based coding requires an extra dimension, aimed at allowing their mutual addressing. Initially restricted to the management of data by the processor, pointers have been included in the data on which symbolic programming languages work, so as to temporarily bind memory registers. The spatial relations, or virtual connectivity of these registers in working memory, constitute a topological coding which has been added to the content-based one. Accordingly, an architecture, already based on the topological relations of its memory units, such as a GPN, can be completed by the content of these units for the same symbolic programming purpose. The use of these two coding dimensions is inverse: whereas a symbol is represented in (von Neumann-) computers by a given memory location receiving a variable content, the same symbol is represented in GPNs by a given signal having a particular content, and being propagated towards variable memory locations (Beroule, 1990). The main advantage of this alternative representation lies in the possible simultaneous assignment of several values it allows for a given symbol, since a signal can be propagated in parallel towards several locations. The adequacy of every symbol in the current context can thus be evaluated in one shot, provided an appropriate architecture. Besides, a register cannot receive more than one value at a time in the sequential computer. Another advantage of the proposed representation is that it does not require any change of the data structure, whereas a new combination of symbols to be memorized must be stored in the knowledge base of (von Neumann-) computers. Compared with classical AI approaches such as conceptual graphs (Sowa, 1983), symbols are bound through the propagation of the same signal content instead of building specific graphs. But then a new signal content must be dynamically allocated whenever a new combination of symbols occurs. There should also be inferential mechanisms inherent to the architecture for retrieving specific symbol combinations in working memory. This manifestation of semantic compositionality is addressed now, together with the type of 'content' an internal signal could convey.

Although GPN internal signals can be specified in several ways for representing symbols, the precise location in time of a pulse has been demonstrated to be the most convenient format (Martin, 1995). First, with regard to the management of symbols, this temporal coding can be processed through the basic computational mechanism of GPNs: coincidence detection. Second, this solution allows several symbols (pulses) to share the same value (memory location) without interfering, since each symbol occupies a specific time slice. Third, it is compatible with the GPN management of noisy and partial data, as shown in the previous section. Because of coincidence detection, a pulse signal propagating through a frame structure for data-retrieval purposes will activate all the previously assigned slot values with which this pulse is synchronized (synchrony coding). As shown in Fig. 16, a semantic frame could be represented by a tree-like structure where each branch codes for a frame slot. Instantiating a branch of this structure brings mechanisms into play which make the memory units involved temporarily and together sensitive to a new precise time location. This is the way variables participating in the same relation can be bound. Thanks to the absence of interaction between pulse signals tuned to different time slices (so-called 'phases'), several searches can be carried out in parallel when the system deals with an utterance to be analyzed. Given that interpretation depends on the simultaneous activation of several instantiated frames, and that word representations can share the same frame, synchrony coding binds items participating in a frame instance without interferences with other instances of the same frame.

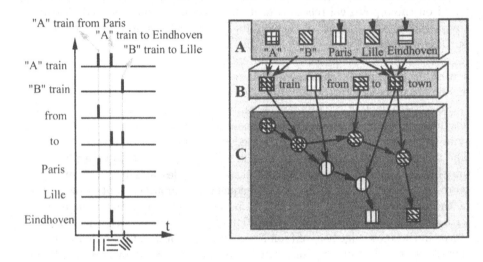

Fig. 16. Internal representation of frame instances in 3 GPN modules : A, whose output are word detectors; B, made of class detectors, and C which contains the frame pathways. The long-term storage of a frame is performed through the creation of a new pathway, whereas the short-term storage of frame instances makes use of the time coding shown at the left. Three frame instances have been temporarily memorized using three pulses, respectively tuned to phase **1**, **2** and **3**. The question *"Is there a train to Eindhoven?"* partly activates all the frame pathways. The pathway activated the most is facilitated at phase **3** of *"Eindhoven"*, which results in the sole activation of the *"A train"* instance of the *"train"* class.

The third point, that is the possibility of using synchrony coding while dealing with partial data, is crucial for implementing semantic inferences if we assimilate an input utterance with a partial version of the frames it refers to. The interpretation process can be viewed as the shift of the internal activity towards other items than the ones that are directly under the influence of the input, thanks to 'semantic' pathways. These pathways are aimed at conveying activation towards the internal representations of relevant symbols that are not actually present in the input, although related to the input. The actual direction taken by the activation depends on the way the current combination of words in the input sentence will be able to feed into frame-like representations. The most active frame propagates its activation towards missing input items, thus carrying out inferences by shifting the internal activation. The principle of phase coding has already been used in (Shastri and Ajjanagadde, 1993) to make several inferences in parallel. In this view, compositionality relies on the partial coincidence of input items with internal references (frames), leading to the activation of other concerned internal items as a manifestation of the interpretation process.

5   Conclusion and Future Research

In this paper, we have presented three parts of our work concerning the development of multimodal interfaces. First, we have described a theoretical framework built around types and goals of cooperation between modalities, and we considered examples of multimodal interaction and experimental results with this framework. Second, we have described a command language for specifying cooperation between modalities and illustrated it with COMIT, a multimodal interface developed for graphical interface design. Third, we have explained the functioning of a multimodal module made of Guided Propagation Networks.

Future research will include the evaluation of COMIT with several users, the development of an interface for the itinary description application (Martin 97), and the empowering of the multimodal module with linguistic and semantic capabilities using well-established approaches. Guided Propagation Networks and synchrony coding are also planned to be used for reasoning purposes, a possibility addressed in the last part of this paper. A multimodal application would then take advantage of the simultaneous, adaptive and robust management of variables within a multi-level homogeneous system.

Acknowledgments The research by Jean-Claude Martin was financed by a DRET-CNRS grant.

References

André, E. and Rist, T. (1995) Generating coherent presentations employing textual and visual material. *Artificial Intelligence Review 9 (2-3)*, 147–165.

Baekgaard, A. (1995) Constraining of input media in a spoken dialog system. In *Proc. 4ᵗⁿ European Conference on Speech Communication and Technology* (EUROSPEECH '95), 1181–1184.

Bellalem, N. and Romary, L. (1995) Reference interpretation in a multimodal environment combining speech and gesture. In: Lee, J. (1995) *Pre-Proceedings First Int. Worskhcp on Intelligence and Multimodality in Multimedia Interfaces: Research and Applications*, University of Edinburgh.

Béroule, D. (1985) *Un modelè de mémoire adaptative, dynamique et associative pour le traitement automatique de la parole.* Thesis, University of Paris XI, Orsay.

Béroule, D. (1988) The never-ending learning. In R. Eckmiller and C. v. d. Malsburg (eds.), *Neural Computers.* NATO ASI Series F, vol 41. Berlin: Springer, 219–230.

Béroule, D. (1990) Guided propagation: current state of theory and application. In F. Fogelman Soulié and J. Hérault (eds.) *Neurocomputing*, NATO ASI Series, Vol. F 68, 241–260. Berlin: Springer.

Béroule, D., Von Hoe, R. and Ruellan, H. (1994) A Guided Propagation Model of Reading. *Annual Progress Report 28*, Instituut voor Perceptie Onderzoek IPO, Eindhoven, 21–29.

Blanchet, P. (1992) *Une architecture connexionniste pour l'apprentissage par l'expérience et la représentation des connaissances*. Thesis, University of Paris XI, Orsay.

Bolt, R.A. (1980) 'Put - That - There': Voice and Gesture at The Graphics Interface. *Computer Graphics 14 (3)*, 262–270.

Bos, E. (1993) Easier said or done? Studies in multimodal human-computer interaction. *NICI technical report 93-02*, University of Nijmegen.

Bourdot, P., Krus, M., Gherbi, R. (1995) Management of non-standard devices for multimodal user interfaces under UNIX/X11. *This volume*.

Bressolle, M.C, Pavard, B., Leroux, M. (1997) The role of multimodal communication in cooperation and intention recognition: the case of air traffic control. *This volume*.

Briffault, X. (1996) Une interface multimodale pour l'aide a la navigation. Working paper, LIMSI, Orsay. http://www.limsi.fr/Individu/xavier/index.html

Bunt, H., Beun, R. J., and Borghuis, T. (eds.) *Proceedings of the International Conference on Cooperative Multimodal Communication CMC/95*. Eindhoven, May 24–26.

Carbonnel, J.R. (1970) Mixed-Initiative Man-Computer Dialogues. Bolt, Beranek and Newman (BBN) Report N 1971, Cambridge, MA.

Catinis, L., Caelen, J. (1995) Analyse du comportement multimodal de l'usager humain dans une tache de dessin. *Actes des 7. Journées sur l'Ingéniérie de l'Interaction Homme-Machine (IHM'95)*, 123–129.

Cheyer, A. and Julia, L. (1995) Multimodal maps: an agent- based approach. *This volume*.

Coutaz, J., Salber, D., Carraux, E. and Portolan, N. (1996) NEIMO, a multiworkstation usability lab for observing and analyzing multimodal interaction. To appear in *CHI'96 Conference Proceedings Companion*. Video.

Coutaz, J. and Nigay, L. (1994) Les propriétés CARE dans les interfaces multimodales. *Actes des 6èmes Journées sur l'Ingéniérie de l'Interaction Homme-Machine (IHM'94)*, Lille, p. 7–14.

Escande, P., Béroule, D. and Blanchet, P. (1991) Speech recognition experiments with Guided Propagation. *Proc. of IJCNN'91*.

Daniel, M.P., Carite, L. and Denis, M. (1994) Modes of linearization in the description of spatial configurations. In Portugali, J. (ed.), *The construction of cognitive maps*. Dordrecht: Kluwer, 297–318.

Dowell, J., Shmueli, Y., and Salter, I. (1995) Applying a cognitive model of the user to the design of a multimodal speech interface. In: Lee, J. (1995) *Pre-Proceedings First Int. Worskhop on Intelligence and Multimodality in Multimedia Interfaces: Research and Applications*, University of Edinburgh.

Faure, C. and Julia, L. (1994) An agent-based architecture for a multimodal interface. *Working notes of the AAAI symposium on Intelligent Multi-Media Multi-Modal Systems*. March 21-23, Stanford.

Foote, J.T., Brown, M.G., Jones, G.J.F., Sparck Jones, K., and Young, S.J. (1995) Video mail retrieval by voice: towards intelligent retrieval and browsing of multimedia documents. In: Lee, J. (1995) *Pre-Proceedings First Int. Worskhop on Intelligence and Multimodality in Multimedia Interfaces: Research and Applications*, University of Edinburgh,

Frohlich, D.M. (1991) The design space of interfaces. In L. Kjelldahl (ed.) *Multimedia: principles, systems and applications.* Berlin: Springer.

Gonçalves, M.R. (1996) Working notes on itinerary descriptions. LIMSI, Orsay. http://www.limsi.fr/Individu/goncalve/index.html

Hare, M., Doubleday, A., Bennett, I., and Ryan, M. (1995) Intelligent presentation of information retrieved from heterogeneous multimedia databases. In: Lee, J. (1995) *Pre-Proceedings First Int. Worskhop on Intelligence and Multimodality in Multimedia Interfaces: Research and Applications,* University of Edinburgh,

Han, Y. and Zukerman, I. (1997) A cooperative approach for multimodal presentation planning. *This volume.*

Huls, C. and Bos, E. (1997) Studies into full integration of language and action. *This volume.*

Hurault-Plantet and Briffault (1996) Atelier de génie linguistique et visualisation graphique. http://www.limsi.fr/Individu/gs/GroupeLC/Outils.html

Hutchins, E. L., Holland, J. D. and Norman, D. A. (1986) Direct manipulation interfaces. In Norman, D. A. and Draper, S. W. (eds.), *User centred system design: new perspectives on human computer design.* Hillsdale, NJ: Lawrence Erlbaum.

Inder, R., Oberlander, J., and Tobin, R. (1995) Intelligent support for navigation in hypermedia: discourse structure and the Web. In: Lee, J. (1995) *Pre-Proceedings First Int. Worskhop on Intelligence and Multimodality in Multimedia Interface: Research and Applications,* University of Edinburgh.

Jackendoff, R. (1987) On beyond zebra: the relation between linguistic and visual information. *Cognition 26 (2),* 89–114.

Lee, J. (ed.) (1995) *Pre-Proceedings First International Workshop on Intelligence and Multimodality in Multimedia Interfaces: Research and Applications.* University of Edinburgh.

Mackinlay, J., Card, S.K. & Robertson, G.G. (1990) A Semantic Analysis of the Design Space of Input Devices. *Human-Computer Interaction.* vol. 5, no 2-3, pp. 145–190.

Martin, J.C. (1995) *Coopérations entre modalités et liage par synchronie dans les interfaces multimodales.* Ph.D. Thesis, TELECOM Paris. http://www.limsi.fr/Individu.martin

Martin, J.C. (1996) Types et buts de coopération entre modalités dans les interfaces multimodales. *Techniques et Science Informatiques* 15, 10/1996, 1367–1397.

Martin, J.C. (1997) Towards intelligent cooperation between modalities. The example of a system enabling multimodal interaction with a map. *Proc. IJCAI'97 International Workshop on Intelligent Multimodal Systems,* 63-69. http://www.limsi.fr:80/Individu/martin/ijcai/article.html

Martin, J.C. and Béroule, D. (1993) Types et buts de coopérations entre modalités. In *Proc. 5th Conf. on Human-Computer Interaction IHM'93,* 17–22.

Martin, J.C. and Béroule, D. (1995) Temporal codes within a typology of cooperation between modalities. *Artificial Intelligence Review 9,* 1–8.

Maybury, M. (1991) Introduction. *Intelligent multimedia interfaces.* Cambridge, MA: AAAI Press.

Nigay, L. and Coutaz, J. (1993) A design space for multimodal systems: concurrent processing and data fusion. *Proc. of Interchi'93,* 172–178.

Nigay, L. and Coutaz, J. (1995) Multifeature systems: from HCI properties to software design. In: Lee, J. (1995) *Pre-Proceedings First Int. Worskhop on Intelligence and Multimodality in Multimedia Interfaces: Research and Applications,* University of Edinburgh.

O'Nuallain, S. and Smith, A.G. (1994) An investigation into the common semantics of language and vision. *Artificial Intelligence Review 8 (2-3),* 113–122.

Olivier, P. and Tsujii, J.I. (1994) Quantitative perceptual representation of preposi- tional semantics. *Artificial Intelligence Review 8 (2-3)*.

Roques, M. (1994) Dynamic Grammatical Representations in Guided Propagation Net- works. In R. C. Carrasco and J. Oncina (eds.) *Grammatical Inference and Applica- tions*, Lecture Notes in Artificial Intelligence 862, 189–202. Berlin: Springer.

Salisbury, M. W., Hendrickson, J. H., Lammers, T. L., Fu, C., and Moody, S. A. (1990) *Talk and draw: bundling speech and graphics*. IEEE Computer 23 (8), 59–65.

Santana, S. and Pineda, L.A. (1995) Producing coordinated natural language and graphical explanations in the context of a geometric problem-solving task. In: Lee, J. (1995) *Pre-Proceedings First Int. Worskhop on Intelligence and Multimodality in Multimedia Interfaces: Research and Applications*, University of Edinburgh.

Shastri, L. and Ajjanagadde, V. (1993) From simple associations to systematic reason- ing: a connectionist representation of rules, variables and dynamic bindings using temporal synchrony. *Behavioural and Brain Sciences, 16*, 417–494.

Sims, R. and Hedberg, J. (1995) Dimensions of learner control: a reappraisal of interac- tive multimedia instruction. In: Lee, J. (1995) *Pre-Proceedings First Int. Worskhop on Intelligence and Multimodality in Multimedia Interfaces: Research and Applica- tions*, University of Edinburgh.

Siroux, J., Guyomard, M., Multon, F., and Remondeau, C. (1997) Modeling and pro- cessing of the oral and tactile activities in the Georal tactile system. *This volume.*

Sowa, J. (1983) *Conceptual Structures: Information Processing in Mind and Machine*. Reading, MA: Addison-Wesley.

Stern, R.M. (1995) Robust speech recognition. Section 14 in electronic book: *Survey of the State of the Art in Human Language Technology*. http://www.cse.ogi.edu/CSLU/HLTsurvey/ch1node6.html/

Vaananen, K. (1995) Four pillars for improving the quality of multimedia applications. In *Proc. First Int. Workshop on Evaluation Methods and Quality Criteria for Mul- timedia Applications*, San Francisco.

Vo, M. T. and Waibel, A. (1993) Multimodal Human-Computer Interaction. In *Proc. International Symposium on Spoken Dialogue: New Directions in Human and Man- Machine Communication*, Tokyo, 95– 101.

Veldman, R. (1995) Experiments on robust parsing in a multimodal Guided Propaga- tion Network. LIMSI (ERASMUS) Report 95-11, Orsay,

Wahlster, W., André, E., Finkler, W., Profitlich, H.J., and Rist, T. (1991) Plan-based integration of natural language and graphics generation. *AI Journal 63*, 387–427.

Wang, E., Shahnvaz, H., Hedman, L., Papadopoulos, K., and Watkinson, N. (1993) A usability evaluation of text and speech redundant help messages on a reader inter- face. In G. Salvendy & M. Smith (eds.), *Human-Computer Interaction: Software and Hardware Interfaces*, 724–729.

Westerlund, P., Béroule, D. and Roques, M. (1994) Experiments of robust parsing using a Guided Propagation Network. In *Proc. International Conference on New Methods in Language Processing (NEMLAP'94)* Manchester.

Webber, B. (1997) Instructing Animated Agents: Viewing Language in Behavioural Terms. *This volume.*

Yankelovich, N., Levow, G., Marx, M. (1995) Designing Speech Acts: Issues in Speech User Interfaces. *Proc. of CHI '95, Conference on Human Factors in Computing Systems.*

Appendix: Computation of Guided Propagation Network Parameters to Obtain a Multimodal Recognition Score

The following parameters of a CD unit participate in multimodal recognition scores:

- the Ratio (R_i) between context and stimuli contributions (R_i is the contextual weight if the Stimulation weight is equal to 1),
- the Excitability (E_i), which defines the cell threshold in the following way:

$$\theta_i = \frac{A_{max} * (1 + R_{i-1})}{E_i}$$

where A_{max} is the maximum value of the signal delivered by a cell (Fig. 17).

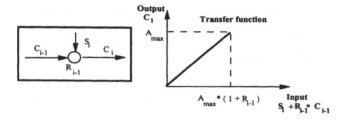

Fig. 17. Parameters of a CD unit. Each CD unit computes an output value C_i as a function of its incoming contextual signal C_{i-1} and stimuli S_i (to the left). To obtain a recognition score which is a function of the differences between the detected sequence of events and the prototype of a command, the transfer function has to be linear (to the right-hand side).

The output value should be equal to the maximum A_{max} for the maximum input:

$$(S_i + C_{i-1})_{max} = A_{max} * (1 + R_{i-1})$$

In the simplified case, $\theta_i = 0$ and the cell output is given by:

$$C_i = \frac{S_i + R_{i-1} * C_{i-1}}{1 + R_{i-1}}$$

By replacing C_{i-1} by its value in the above recursive formula, we obtain the following expression, in term of a sum of weighted stimuli.

$$
\begin{aligned}
C_n =\ & \frac{1}{1 + R_{n-1}} * S_n \\
& + \frac{R_{n-1}}{(1 + R_{n-1})(1 + R_{n-2})} * S_{n-1} \\
& + \frac{R_{n-1} * R_{n-2}}{(1 + R_{n-1})(1 + R_{n-2})(1 + R_{n-3})} * S_{n-2} \\
& + \ldots \\
& + \frac{R_{n-1} * R_{n-2} \ldots * R_1}{(1 + R_{n-1})(1 + R_{n-2}) \ldots (1 + R_0)} * S_1
\end{aligned}
\tag{1}
$$

If C_n is the output of a pathway comprising n cells and which is therefore fed by n stimuli, it should follow the conditions below :

$$\forall i \in [1, n], S_i = A_{max} \quad \Rightarrow \quad C_n = A_{max}$$

in other words, if the pathway is fed by all its stimuli with a maximum value, its output should be maximum. This can be verified by replacing every S_i by A_{max} in (1), provided that $R_0 = 0$.

$C_n = A_{max}/p$ if $1/p$ of the stimuli is actually participating to the pathway activation. This should be true for the limit case: when only one stimulus activates the pathway, whatever its location in time and along the path.

$$
\begin{aligned}
C_n =\ & \frac{A_{max}}{n} \\
= & \frac{1}{1 + R_{n-1}} * A_{max} \tag{2} \\
= & \frac{R_{n-1}}{(1 + R_{n-1})(1 + R_{n-2})} * A_{max} \tag{3} \\
= & \frac{R_{n-1} * R_{n-2}}{(1 + R_{n-1})(1 + R_{n-2})(1 + R_{n-3})} * A_{max}
\end{aligned}
$$

$$\ldots$$

$$= \frac{R_{n-1} * R_{n-2} * \ldots * R_1}{(1 + R_{n-1})(1 + R_{n-2}) \ldots (1 + R_0)} * A_{max}$$

The first equality (2) gives $R_{n-1} = n - 1$, from which (3) gives $R_{n-2} = n - 2$, and so one until $R_0 = 0$.

Cooperation between Reactive 3D Objects and a Multimodal X Window Kernel for CAD

Patrick Bourdot, Mike Krus, Rachid Gherbi

LIMSI-CNRS UPR 3251, University Paris XI, BP 133, 91403 Orsay cedex, France
mix3d@limsi.fr.

Abstract. From the early steps of sketching to final engineering, a frequent and very important activity in designing objects is to perform graphical and spatial simulations to solve the constraints on the objects which are being designed. But when we analyse work situations involving the use of CAD systems, it is today an acknowledged fact that these tools are not helpful to perform these types of simulations. While knowledge modeling based on *form feature* concepts already offers some possibilities for attaching behaviour to objects, the simulation activity requires in addition a 'real time' and 'intelligent' management of the interactions between the 3D virtual objects and the CAD user.

Our general purpose is to study how future CAD systems could be improved to achieve the simulation steps of object design. In this context we present some issues concerning the cooperation between a model of reactive 3D objects and a multimodal X Window kernel. We have developed a prototype of a system where objects with reactive behaviour can be built, and with which the user can interact with a combination of graphical actions and vocal commands. This prototype is used to evaluate the feasability and the usefulness of the integration of such techniques in futur applications that would be used by object designers in a real working context. We describe the current state of this system and the planned improvements.

1 Introduction

One of the most promising results of the research on multimodal user interfaces is their capacity to transform industrial applications which manipulate 2D or 3D virtual spaces. For example, it has been shown that a user can be more 'productive' using a CAD program when keyboard interactions are replaced by vocal ones (Martin, 1989). Hence some researchers propose to rethink these tools in terms of multimodal interaction (Gaildrat et al., 1993).

More than with simple substitutions of modalities added to the traditional user interface of CAD systems, our interest is to study how multimodal interaction could make these systems contribute better to object design. In fact, object design is not only an engineering activity, for which CAD systems are already useful. A frequent and very important activity is to perform graphical and spatial simulations to solve the constraints on the objects which are being designed. Unfortunately, these simulations are not easily performed with current CAD systems, and the use of such tools for this activity requires complicated work organisations (Lebahar, 1992). We will hereafter refer to such simulations as 'object simulations' or '3D simulations'.

In this context, our general purpose is to study how future CAD systems could be really helpful for object simulation. Indeed, this activity requires a 'real time' and 'intelligent' management of the interactions between the 3D virtual objects and/or between these objects and the CAD user. An object (already built by the user or under construction) must have short-delay reactive behaviour in relation to the other objects of the virtual space it has dependencies with. Additionally, the user's interactions with these virtual objects must be efficient, requiring advanced combinations of modalities both for input and output, syntactic and semantic dialogue analysis, and so on.

But reactive behaviour as well as multimodal interaction with 3D virtual objects presuppose knowledge modeling for these objects. During the last ten years, knowledge modeling for CAD/CAM is one of the main purposes of the *form feature* approach. According to Shah (1990), "a *form feature* is a physical constituent of a part with a generic shape realisable or abstract, it has significance in design, analysis, manufacturing, or some other engineering domain and has predictable behaviour or properties". From this perspective, parametrical and variational modeling concepts of 'form feature' are very close to the requirements of a CAD system when used for 2D or 3D object simulations. On the other hand, we have to take into account that the simulation activity for object design can start from the first steps of sketching in the design process. In other words, during some simulation steps the objects might not have sufficient properties to be attached to form feature classes but only to geometrical semantics. Considering that 'good' knowledge modeling generally requires a hierarchical strategy, we chose to focus our work on the simulation activity with geometrical and topological objects. Indeed, our objective is to construct a 3D modeling kernel for object simulation that future CAD systems dedicated to particular object design domains could share.

However, manipulating virtual spaces requires a powerful graphical environment. Today, many of these applications are developed on UNIX workstations using X Window as a standard windowing environment, sometimes with additional graphical hardware. In spite of the various functions it can realise, the X server only manages, in terms of input modalities, mouse and keyboard events. In order to support the kind of interactions we require, we have created an architecture which seamlessly integrates new advanced modalities.

In the remainder of this chapter, we first define some basic concepts of multimodality and we show the importance of semantic representations for multimodal user interfaces. We subsequently present the geometrical and topological model of MIX 3D *(Multimodal Interactions under X environment with a 3D virtual space)* and we explain how knowledge modeling in MIX 3D is used to manage objects simulation. We then present examples of cooperation between reactive 3D objects and multimodal interactions. Finally, we discuss the design of our multimodal interface architecture in the X Window environment and consider some general requirements for future enhancements.

2   Multimodal Interactions: Main Concepts

2.1   Definitions of Multimodality

Multimodal user interfaces are frequently opposed to multimedia applications (Bellik et al., 1995a; Schomaker et al., 1995). The task of a multimedia application is to allow users to manage large volumes of information represented by means of several different media (images, texts, sounds, etc.). The task of a multimodal user interface is at the input side to analyse, recognise and merge information coming from several devices, and on the output side to determine an appropriate combination of media to deliver a message.

Using distinctions of this kind, a three dimensional classification of multimedia and multimodal systems was introduced by Nigay and Coutaz (1993). One dimension describes the *levels of abstraction* of a system, while the two others represent respectively the *fusion levels* and the *use of modalities* that a system is able to support. For instance, a multimedia application uses low levels of abstraction because it does not take into account any semantics of the data to determine meaning. At the opposite end, a multimodal user interface has several levels of abstraction from raw data to symbolic representations. These representations allow the system to perform artificial reasoning and to improve the human-machine interaction. The 'fusion levels' dimension introduces a distinction between *independent* and *combined* user interfaces. The former are able to use one modality to receive or produce an expression, while the latter allow to build expressions from (resp. with) several input (resp. output) modalities. In the same way, the 'use of modalities' dimension has two possible values. A user interface is *sequential* or *parallel* if a single modality or several modalities are managed at the same time.

The possibility of combining several modalities which are chronologically or synchronously processed is thus an important characteristic of multimodal systems. In the following we study the fusion of input modalities. An input modality produces monomodal events. By hypothesis, a monomodal event can be the result of a recognition system associated with the modality's input device. Furthermore, we will see that the state of some devices and the state of their associated recognition systems are also useful for the fusion of modalities.

2.2   Temporal Proximity as a Fusion Criterion

The main concept of multimodal systems is the combination of monomodal events. It is necessary to define some criteria allowing us to decide how and when it is possible to achieve this combination. For instance, temporally close events in one or several modalities may have to be merged into the same multimodal expression. But the detection of this temporal closeness might not be sufficient to perform a semantic interpretation. Below we will discuss some other criteria that can be used to supplement this *temporal proximity* criterion. Nevertheless, it is important to take this proximity in account. Indeed, in conjunction with a precise time stamping (or *'dating'*), this criterion allows us to overcome the problem of parallelism in monoprocessor systems in order to simulate *parallel* and *combined* multimodal interaction. More importantly, temporal proximity management seems well-adapted to the physiological behaviour of the human operator when he interacts with a multimodal system. Indeed, when a human uses more than one modality, the temporal synchronisation of his actions does not have the exactness of dating by the machine.

Temporal proximity is the main criterion for combining different modalities. For instance, the fusion of input events proposed by Bellik and Teil (1993) first determines the events which are produced within a short time range, and then combines some of them with respect to other criteria. With this fusion process, the classical multimodal expression *"put this here"* associated with two graphical selections becomes possible. The temporal proximity filter allows the determination of the co-references between the *"this"* and *"here"* vocal events, and the first and the second selection, respectively.

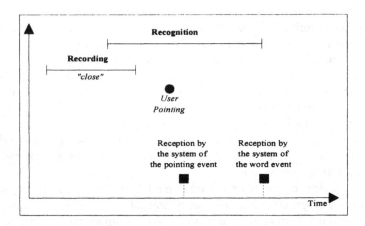

Fig. 1. The problem of device response times with speech recognition (taken from Bellik et al., 1995a).

A sequence of monomodal events can also produce different multimodal expressions, however, because the semantic interpretation can depend on the chronology of events. As explained by Bellik et al. (1995a), misinterpretations are possible at the fusion decision step (Fig. 1), since the devices associated with recognition processes (speech, gesture, ...) need much more time to analyse an expression than any standard input devices (mouse, keyboard, ...) or than any non-standard devices without recognition process (tactile screen, eye-tracker, ...). Hence, the only solution to avoid undesirable actions on the objects of the multimodal application is to know exactly the starting date and the duration of the recognition process of each monomodal expression.

A precise time stamping is a difficult problem, because our management of non-standard devices has to be done within a UNIX / X Window environment (and the same probably holds for other environments). Section 5 of this chapter will show how we manage the temporal proximity criterion for the fusion of input modalities in such an environment.

2.3   Other Fusion Criteria and Semantic Information

We described above the concept of the temporal proximity fusion criterion. In order to achieve a complete and valid fusion, it is necessary to use additional criteria which provide more semantic information. We present here four fusion criteria introduced by Coutaz et al. (1992).

1. *logical complementarity*:
   This criterion allows the merging of temporally distant events within the same command. Still, the fusion's validity depends mainly on a value of this temporal distance. Indeed, when the user interacts with an object, the 'shorter' this distance, the more the fusion can be done at interface level. When it gets longer, it becomes very difficult to perform the fusion without the control of the application. So if we do not want to restrict the user's actions, it is necessary to implement a reactive object mechanism allowing the application to overcome such restrictions.
2. *data structure completeness*:
   Generally, this constitutes a condition to move within the *abstraction levels*. Usually, the generic levels concern the interface while the semantically complex levels are managed by the application. This completeness is also useful to stop waiting for other eventual events. Indeed, this criterion allows the system to decide if all the arguments of a command match with the data.
3. *dialogue context*:
   This criterion uses the historical log of the interactions. With this criterion it is possible on one hand, to determine the co-references between modalities (when a modality cannot be correctly understood without events or states from other modalities), and on the other hand, to handle anaphora, ellipsis and deictic expressions.
4. *incompatibility of modalities*:
   This criterion forbids the integration of modalities that cannot be used together. In particular, it detects contradictory monomodal expressions. While the interface can in most cases detect lexical, syntactic and semantical incompatibilities, some of these cannot be handled without knowledge of the application domain.

For most criteria it seems that some part depends on the user interface process while another requires interaction with the application:

$$Criteria(interaction) = Criteria(interface) \cup Criteria(application)$$

For the application, the validation of these criteria generally requires an analysis of complex semantic representations. Furthermore, for the 3D simulations required by object design, the access to these representations must be immediate to guarantee natural user actions and realistic object reactions. The next two sections present how the MIX 3D application controls and validates some of these criteria with the help of reactive objects.

3   A Semantic 3D Model for Object Simulations

CAD systems generally use a B-REP model (Boundary REPresentation) to describe solid objects. Historically, the first one was the Winged-Edge structure for polyhedron entities (Baumgardt, 1972), but now other data structures are existing which authorise quadric (Levin, 1980) or bicubic patches (Carlson, 1982; Casale, 1987). Although a B-REP accepting free-form surfaces is very interesting for design activities of complex objects, the resulting curves of intersecting surfaces have often must be computed by approximation methods. Consequently, this type of B-REP depends on the precision of the representation needed. As this precision is liable to change during the design process, a complementary data structure must save the modeling steps.

A solution is to use CSG trees (Constructive Solid Geometry), where the leaves are volumetric primitives, while the nodes are regular operators (Tilove and Requicha, 1980) combined with a geometric transformation or a shape deformation (Barr, 1984). But CSG trees are not well adapted to manage curves, surfaces or any free-form objects, because they were initially created to manage internal composition laws defined on a set of solid objects. On the other hand, though a CSG tree can be used to re-play the 3D modeling steps, it is clear that something else is necessary to give reactive behaviour to objects in order to make simulation activities possible during the design process.

For MIX 3D we have defined a model which combines knowledge modeling of geometry and topology with a generalisation of CSG trees. In the rest of this section we present these two aspects of our approach, followed by an example of the reactive behaviour of MIX 3D objects.

3.1   Knowledge Modeling for Geometrical and Topological Properties

Figure 2 presents an overview of the three typologies used in MIX 3D: the *geometrical* typology which represents the shape and the metric of 3D objects; the *fitting* typology which describes metric relationship properties between objects; and the *topological* typology which defines non-metric properties.

MIX 3D objects are identified primarily according to one of the generic semantic types of the geometrical typology: `Point`, `Curve`, `Surface`, `Volume`, `Structure` and `System`. By definition, a MIX 3D object is described as a set of data representations. Each representation is an instantiation of one structural specialisation of its generic semantic type. We explain later how we manage these sets of data representations (section 3.2).

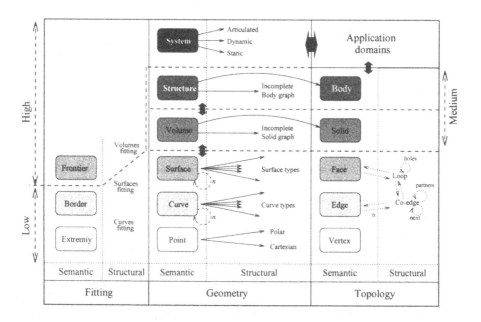

Fig. 2. The three typologies of MIX 3D.

Examples of geometrical knowledge According to Fig. 3 and the previous definition of MIX 3D objects, a Curve whose semantic aspects are free and cubic has two possible basic data representations: a SplineCurve object and a Composite object defined by BézierCurve objects. But it is also possible to give it more complex representations, by using the (possibly recursive) definition of the Composite type with SplineCurve elements, or BézierCurve elements, or both. In the same way, the data representation of a Curve which is semantically free but now mixed is a Composite object defined (recursively or not) by any Parametric object.

Besides the planar and closed aspects, a polygon has the same possible representations as a linear free Curve: a PolyLine or a Composite object defined (recursively or not) by LineSegment and/or PolyLine objects. But the default data representation of the polygon is a non-recursive Composite object defined by LineSegment components only, simply because this decomposition is useful to describe the fitting properties of a polygon. On the other hand, the default data representation of a segment is a LineSegment, but it may also have a PolyLine or a SplineCurve representation when this is useful for some 3D modeling operations. Additionally, the representation of a conic Curve can be

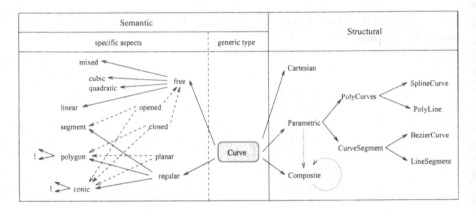

Fig. 3. Curve specialisations of the geometrical typology.

its Cartesian equation or a specific SplineCurve (a quadratic Non-Uniform Rational B-Spline).

These examples of the Curve specification clearly show that a similar semantic and structural classification must exist for the Surface type. Concerning the Volume and Structure generic geometrical types, no specific semantic aspects were identified. In fact, these two types of object are very important for the construction of the topological graphs, using some of the properties of the lower levels of the fitting and the geometrical typologies.

Fitting and topological knowledge   An instantiation of a generic semantic class of the geometrical typology can be specialised with the help of the semantic class of the same level within topological or fitting typologies (Fig. 2). For instance, a Curve can describe the Border (fitting type) of a Surface. Moreover, if another Border of another Surface is described by exactly the same Curve and if these two Surface objects have a C^0 continuity, then this Curve is the metric of an Edge (topological type). In fact, this Curve is a kind of 'pivot' of the relationship which exists between the two Surface objects to make them fit with this specific property of continuity.

The fitting typology covers more general cases than simple C^0 continuity between two Surface objects. Figure 4 shows an example of all the structural relations that a SurfaceFitting object describes. Some properties (and constraints) that a SurfaceFitting object is presently supposed to support are for instance: α properties (angular relationship), β properties (i.e. the *shape parameters* introduced by De Rose and Barsky (1985) for *geometric continuity*), δ properties (linear or arc lengths), π properties (parallel relationship) and so on. Additionally, combinations of these properties define some macro-properties. For instance, an α property specifies a β property as a *continuity* if $\alpha = 180°$, as a *coincidence* if $\alpha = 0°$, or as an *incidence* for other values of α. On the other hand, a SurfaceFitting object can describe the fitting of $i \times j$ Surface objects

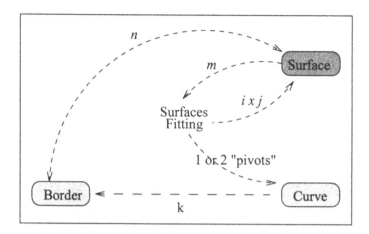

Fig. 4. Some classes of the fitting typology and their relations with the geometrical typology.

which is useful to build surfaces with a patchwork structure (Macé and Bourdot, 1991).

3.2   The Generalised Constructive Graph

One of the main principles which appeared in our previous discussion about knowledge modeling for MIX 3D objects is that the semantic aspects of a generic type of a typology is related to one or more primitives of its structural specialisation. Our goal is to allow the user to ignore the low-level data structures of a CAD application to let him manipulate the semantic aspects of geometry, fitting and topology only (a Curve, a Surface, their degrees, closures, fitting properties, their topological aspects and so on). So far we have only presented which knowledge we describe and how, but not how this knowledge is used during a 3D modeling tasks and spatial simulations. In MIX 3D, knowledge is managed by means of the Generalised Constructive Graph (GCG).

Definition of GCG nodes Two types of nodes of our GCG are structures called Form (F) and Instantiated-Form (IF) (see Fig.5). A node of the type Instantiated-Form is a MIX 3D object. Its spatial position is given by a localisation matrix. The modeling description of an Instantiated-Form is a set of data representations that a MIX 3D object may have according to the semantic aspects it has with respect to its generic geometrical type (see section 3.1 and Fig. 2). A Form node is a user class of MIX 3D objects. Any data representation of an Instantiated-Form is inherited from its Form. This is done according to the localisation matrix and the 3D modeling context in which this Instantiated-Form is used.

On the other hand, a Form results of the application of an *operator* to an ordered list of components. An operator is any 3D modeling method that MIX 3D

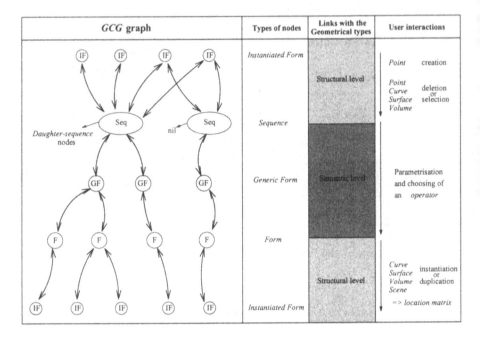

Fig. 5. The Generalised Constructive Graph used by MIX 3D.

objects can support, while each component of this ordered list is an existing Instantiated-Form. Because the Instantiated-Form nodes can be shared by several lists of components, we manage these lists with a third type of node called Sequence (S). According to the knowledge carried by the GCG nodes, a Sequence under construction dynamically determines the list of *possible operators* which can be applied to its list of Instantiated-Form components.

Finally, a fourth type of node is the Generic Form (GF) structure, which represents a set of Form nodes sharing the same Sequence and having the same generic type according to the geometrical typology. It is through Generic Form nodes that the semantic aspects of a Form are managed. For instance, this node is used to determine, for an Instantiated-Form within a given Sequence, which data representation is useful to support the application of one of the possible operators this Sequence authorises.

Properties of the GCG Instantiated-Form nodes also have components, but the components of such nodes sharing the same Sequence generally don't have the same geometric localisation as the components of this Sequence. If the Sequence attached to its Instantiated-Form node has no component that matches the node, then it is not used to define Form nodes. The GCG must manage these components to help the graphical interactions with the Instantiated-Form they describe. The components shared by several Instantiated-Form nodes which depend of the same Sequence are therefore within this Sequence or inside Daughter-sequences associated with this Sequence (see Fig. 5).

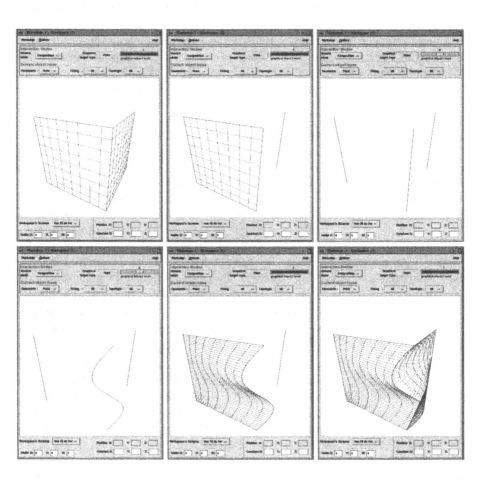

Fig. 6. Interactive steps required in a conventional modeler for transforming two **planar Surface** objects sharing a **segment** into two **free Surface** objects sharing a **free Curve** (left to right, top to bottom).

Additionally, each GCG is associated with one 'database project'. Following the idea that the GCG must help the object design activity, the graphical deletion or the moving of any **Instantiated-Form** never implies the destruction of this GCG node. In fact, these actions on MIX 3D objects are managed through state modifications of some GCG nodes. If an **Instantiated-Form** is not recovered after a given time delay, some data representations are transferred from the current GCG to its database. This approach allows the combinatory control of the GCG, while giving the user the possibility of recovering any previous step of his work.

We also need to consider the role of the GCG with respect to the multimodal user interface. The GCG has an important contribution to apply the criteria of *logical complementary* and *data structure completeness* of the multimodal user interface manager (see section 2.3). It is the only place where the user's interactions on 3D virtual objects are decided to be valid or not. It manages the semantic aspects of the applications, but its work is 'amodal'. It can thus be considered as the 'melting-pot' of the multimodal user interaction.

3.3   Reactive Behaviour of MIX 3D Objects

All MIX 3D user interactions are defined with respect to several interactive modes. Some of them identify the *current object* type which is managed by the user interface, while a *generic mode* makes a distinction between three main contexts of interaction: *simulation*, *composition* and *instantiation* (see Fig. 10 and section 4.2). The *simulation* context is a direct interactive mode to study the evolution of the geometrical, fitting and topological properties of any 3D object, with real-time feedback. We present here a simple example of reactive behaviour that the GCG allows on MIX 3D objects within this simulation mode.

Suppose we have two `planar Surface` objects defined by three `segment` objects (first picture of Fig. 6). With a classical CAD system data structure, several interactions are required to modify the `segment` shared by the two `Surface` objects and to transform them into the two `free Surface` objects of the last picture of Fig. 6. For instance, it is necessary to delete the initial `planar Surface` objects and their shared `segment`, to build a `free Curve` from this `segment` and some input `Point` objects, to finally construct the two `free Surface` objects.

These transformations are made in several interactive steps (Fig. 6). In contrast, the reactive behavior of 3D objects in MIX 3D allows these transformations to be performed in one single step (Fig. 7).

The management of such behavior within the GCG is shown in Fig. 8. The shared `segment` ($c0$ node) being defined from a `Sequence` of two `Point` objects ($Seq0$ node), any input `Point` on this `Sequence` creates a new `Sequence` ($Seq0'$ node) to which 'dynamic inheritance' is applied until the `Instantiated-Form` level ($c0'$ node). According to the knowledge carried by the GCG nodes, semantic and data type conversions are managed for `Form` and `Instantiated-Form` nodes. For instance, since $c0$ is a `segment` (i.e. an `opened Curve`) and there is at least one input `Point` within the $Seq0'$ `Sequence`, the default semantic aspect of the resulting $c0'$ `Curve` is supposed to be `opened`, `free` and `cubic`. Additionally, the semantic specialisation of the `Curve` type allows $c0'$ to know that its default data representation is a `SplineCurve`. Recursive propagation of this management in the GCG is sufficient to obtain directly $S1'$ and $S2'$, the two `free Surface` objects sharing $c0'$.

More complex situations of reactive 3D objects suppose that the propagation which takes place within the GCG uses a 'width first' strategy and must respect

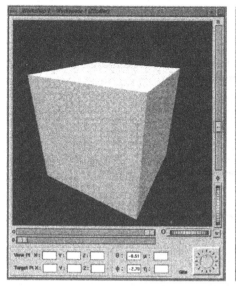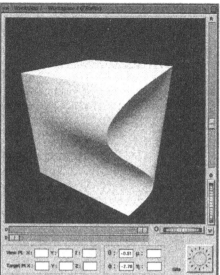

Fig. 7. Immediate transformation allowed by the GCG for the example of Fig.6.

in 'depth' the 'longest paths' of GCG compositions which depend of the current user interaction.

4   Cooperation Between Reactive 3D Objects and Multimodal Events

Using the concept of reactive objects, we study here the contribution of multimodality for interacting with a CAD system in the design process of 3D objects.

4.1   Vocal Inputs as Shortcuts for Menu Command Selection

One of the simplest ways of using multimodality is to exploit the equivalence of certain modalities, where either of two or more modalities can be used for the same interaction. We use this form of cooperation so that a user may issue commands which are normally menu-based by using a vocal equivalent. MIX 3D uses many commands which are laid in menus and cards (see Fig. 9). No matter how much care is put into conceiving these menus and cards, the user will, at least initially, waste time looking for the right command. Furthermore, this requires the user to shift his attention from the 3D working area to the menu and card boxes.

In order to limit the amount of attention shifting, we have provided the user with a set of vocal commands which can be substituted for menu and button actions. Interaction can then take place entirely in the working area and the

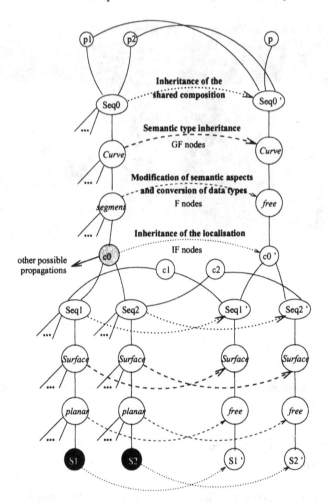

Fig. 8. Management of reactive behaviour in the GCG.

user can apply commands whose corresponding button or menu item are not actually visible. Of course, the user still has to learn the appropriate vocabulary but by using synonyms and abbreviations this can be made easier. The only problem then is the limitation in the size of vocabulary that current real-time voice recognition systems can handle. We estimate that the vocabulary for a full-fledged CAD system would contain over a thousand words, a lot more than our Datavox[1] system can handle.

---

[1] Datavox is a speech recognition system created at the LIMSI-CNRS laboratory and distributed by VECSYS.

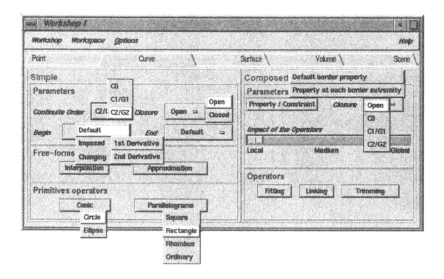

Fig. 9. Commands card and some of its sub-menus for the **Curve** type.

4.2   Just Name It: Vocal Modality for Deictic Interaction

The use of a variety of modalities can help the application to remove ambiguity from the user's actions. Figure 10 shows the control board of MIX 3D for managing the direct interaction of the user within the working area. In section 3.3, we already discussed the *simulation* context of interaction. But the *generic mode* menu gives the user two other contexts of interaction: the *composition* mode to manage the creation of new user classes (i.e. **Form** nodes) and the *instantiation* mode to build new MIX 3D objects (i.e. **Instantiated-Form** nodes) from any of these user classes. On the other hand, a deictic interaction is also defined according to the types of the *graphical target* and the *current object*. The former is automatically determined from the event selections and gives the interaction manager information about the precision of the object selections,[2] while the latter is fixed by the user to specify which geometrical, fitting or topological type of MIX 3D objects he wants at a given moment during the deictic interaction.[3] Furthermore, the difference between the *current object* and *graphical target* types defines the *graphical impact* level of a selection (in Fig. 10, the feedback at this level is the current value of the horizontal scale).

These menus and widgets are only here to help the user to remove the deictic ambiguities that the high level of knowledge modeling implies for MIX 3D objects. When the number of combinations of the possible ambiguities increases,

---

[2] At the present time, the event selections which find the closest **Point** or the closest **Curve** are the only two *graphical target* types implemented in MIX 3D.

[3] *Current object* types have logical dependencies; for instance, the **Edge** and **Border** types are attached to the **Curve** level, but conversely a **Curve** (resp. **Border**) type does not imply a link with a **Border** (resp. **Edge**) type (see section 3.1).

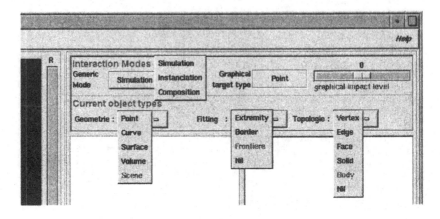

Fig. 10. Menus and widgets for controlling interactive modes.

the classical solution, which requires the human operator to use keyboard modifiers when selecting objects, becomes awkward for simple ergonomical reasons. In fact, the only powerful alternative is the use of the vocal modality. For instance, by making deictic references the user would be able to say *"check this border"* when clicking near a Curve which describes a Border of a Surface, and the application would activate a set of interactive cards according to the fitting properties of this Border. Taking this approach even further, the user would be able to give names to objects and refer to them later using these names. This should prove useful for managing complex virtual scenes.

As we saw before, the GCG is already able of managing the reactive behaviour of MIX 3D objects. The use of the vocal modality makes it possible to avoid latencies in interacting with reactive virtual objects. In other words, the vocal input associated with reactive objects is convenient to support 3D simulation activities in object design.

4.3   Just Draw It: Sketch Recognition as a Non-Standard Modality

Another way of using multimodality is to combine modalities to perform a complex task. Within MIX 3D, we are introducing a multimodal sketching interface called PADEM, which tries to simulate the familiar working context of a draftsman (paper and pen) with a tactile screen and an electronic pen. But as hand drawn sketches may have several semantic interpretations, we choose to assist the sketch recognition process by means of vocal interaction. This research is presently focused on 2D drawing recognition.

The principle of this sketch recognition lies in two sub-processes. The first one manages a 'signal analysis' and a recognition of 'single' sketches (Fig. 11). By 'signal analysis' we mean that the set of pixels of a 'single' sketch is segmented according to geometrical features (C^0 continuity, alignment of pixels, curvature, and so on) from which semantic aspects of the Curve geometrical type are identified as well as fitting properties (see section 3.1). The second process makes a 'contextual analysis' of the resulting objects to improve recognition scores. Some ergonomical strategies are also used; for instance, the `polygon` recognition cases of Fig. 11 take in account the fact that the first pixels of a sketch are more important than the others, because the precision of a drawing gesture is generally better at its beginning. Additionally, the fitting properties are also used to perform the drawing recognition within both sub-processes; for instance, specific graphs of `CurveFitting` objects identify the semantic aspects of any `polygon`.

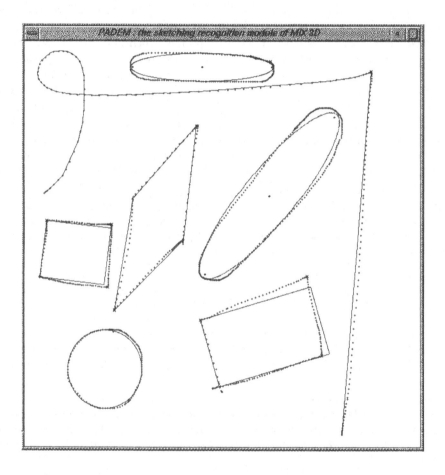

Fig. 11. Examples of 2D drawing recognition for 'single' sketches.

In many cases, several semantic interpretations are possible, simply because nothing is more different than two similar hand drawn sketches! When the drawing recognition process fails, PADEM will allow the user to correct this with vocal inputs, specifying the semantic aspects the shape must have. This extra modality will give the human operator the opportunity of supervising the sketch recognition process.

4.4 About Vocal and Textual Output

Just as multimodality takes input interaction a step further, it can also enhance output interaction to provide the user with more accurate information, by making use of the properties of the various modalities and by combining some of them to produce output messages (Krus, 1995).

For example, a message can be presented using text and vocal output. This presentation may have redundancy and/or complementarity effects. Text can be used to confirm information in the vocal message, while voice allows the user to remain focused on his job (which is very useful for simulation activities). Indeed, these modalities have different properties which influence the way they are perceived by the operator. Textual output is persistent and may contain detailed information which can be accessed at a later time. Vocal output, by contrast, is short-lived and can convey less information than text, but it will get the user's attention more easily, especially if he is already busy looking at some part of his work. Thus, use of the characteristics of the modalities and of cooperation between these modalities can produce efficient presentations.

At this time, MIX 3D uses these considerations in a simple way: feedback messages from most user commands are in textual form. For some commands which do not produce visual results a prerecorded vocal message is also sent. We are currently considering the value of adding more vocal outputs, in particular as an option for menu commands. Carefully chosen messages could in effect help the user learn the correct vocabulary for the vocal commands that he can use for input. This kind of loopback should prove very valuable.

5 A Real-Time Multimodal User Interface Architecture

In order to implement the kind of interaction required by multimodal applications, we have developed a software architecture which was designed to be efficient, portable and extendable. This is a distributed architecture where use of load-sharing ensures near-real-time performance. Figure 12 describes this architecture, which is based on the X Window library and the widget toolkit (Nye, 1989; Nye and O'Reilly, 1989). It extends these low-level components with new modalities and accurate dating and ordering of events, so that high-level multimodal fusion modules can be implemented (Bellik et al., 1995b; Martin et al. 1995).

The architecture is divided into two parts. The *modality server* is responsible, along with the standard X server, for the dating and the delivering of events to the application. The *modality toolkit* is used by the applications to add multimodal event to widgets and can filter events based on their type. The toolkit guarantees that the handlers will receive events in the order in which they are produced.

For the remainder of this chapter, we will refer to modalities other than those provided by X Window (such as mouse and keyboard) as *non-standard* modalities and to the events they produce as *non-standard* events. We will first describe the nature of non-standard modalities, then present both parts of the architecture.

5.1   Non-Standard Modalities and Events

Non-standard modalities usually require a recognition process before events can be produced. For example, voice events (words) need to be recognised from the speech signal. Such recognition processes are typically heavy tasks which require a lot of machine power. As such, it seems unfeasible for them to reside in a system which requires near-real-time response for other tasks such as managing the interaction between user and application. We have therefore decided to implement these processes on slave machines which only send the results of their recognition to the modality server. Communication between slave processes and the server can be done via a serial link or a network connection. Recognition results are sent to the modality server along with additional status information.

The events produced by non-standard modalities have the interesting feature of having a length in time; events like words have distinct beginning and ending dates. We treat standard events as having a zero length in time, i.e. their beginning and ending dates are the same.

Our architecture is currently validated for one non-standard modality: the Datavox voice recognition system, installed on a PC. It transmits the words it has recognised, along with a score and a time frame number for the beginning and the ending of each word. Additionally, we support a tactile screen by using the *X Window Input Extension protocol* (Nye, 1989) for sketch recognition.

5.2   The Modality Server

The modality server is responsible for dating the events it receives from the recognition modules. It sends these events to the application that currently has the input focus (as defined by the X Window system) using the X server.

The modality server is organised in modules. As described in Fig. 12, a *modality module* is defined for each modality. These modules have the appropriate know-how to compute the date for the events. The entire process of computing the date and sending the events takes several steps.

First, the transport module receives events from the serial or network ports, and sends them to the appropriate modules based on a type identifier attached to the messages. This module then computes the beginning and ending dates for each event. This process is modality dependent (and even recognition system dependent). The module should take into account the time that it took for the recognition system to recognise the events and for these to travel to the server. A recognition system can produce several events for one signal (like several words in one sentence). These events are sent together to the modality server in one message, and the modality modules are responsible for producing individual events out of that message.

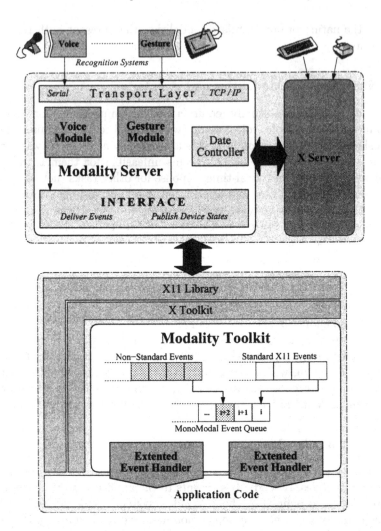

Fig. 12. Architecture for 'Real-Time' Multimodal User Interface based on X Window.

An important part of the server is the *dating module*. This a responsible for maintaining an accurate equivalence between the Unix idea of date (which is used to know when an event arrived to the transport module) and the X Window idea of date (which we use for dating the events, standard or non-standard). Since these two representations are not the same, the dating module constructs an equivalence at start up, adjusts it continuously while it is running, and can make conversions either way at any time. Once the events are dated, they are passed to the *interface module*. This module uses the X server to send them to the appropriate application.

As we saw in the previous section, recognition systems can also send messages indicating what state they are in. These messages are treated in much the same way. The modality modules receive them, but they then instruct the interface module to *publish* that information for clients to read it at any time. This publishing is done using X properties for the modality server's window (Nye, 1989).

5.3   The Modality Toolkit

This toolkit extends the standard X toolkit (Xt) to support an extended event handler. This handler can request events (standard or non-standard) based on their type and is guaranteed to receive them in the order that the signal for the events was produced, *not* the order in which the signal was processed. This is crucial to ensure an accurate fusion of monomodal events.

The toolkit contains a main controller which keeps track of which widget currently has the input focus and dispatches the events. The dispatching differs from the normal Xt mechanism only for non-standard events.

The toolkit also builds a controller for each widget that requires an extended event handler. Each controller contains an event queue where standard and non-standard events are stored as they arrive. They are ordered in this queue based on their beginning date.

Since events produced by the keyboard or the mouse are produced very rapidly by the hardware, they arrive sooner than voice events even though the signal for these might have been produced earlier. The controller for each widget ensures that no event is delivered while a non-standard modality is analysing a signal to produce new events. Every time the controller receives an event, it stores it at the appropriate position in the queue. It then scans all devices, using the modality server, to know if any of them are currently analysing a signal.[4] If none of them is building a new event, then the event at the head of queue is popped and delivered to the extended event handlers that have requested that type of events. On the other hand, if an event is being produced by a modality, then the controller holds the events in the queue until user-specified delay expires.[5]

5.4   Other Requirements for a Multimodal User Interface System

The architecture we have developed can be used as a basis for a complete multimodal user interface system. It contains most features required by multimodal fusion systems, for which various architectures have been proposed (Bellik et al. 1995b; Martin et al, 1995). There is one additional issue that needs to be addressed by these systems. Applications typically have several widgets, even sometimes several windows (such as in our case). While the modality toolkit can

---

[4] Standard devices are never considered to be producing an event, since they do this in one single unit of time.

[5] Setting this delay to zero makes the controller deliver events in the order they arrive.

handle event queues for each widget so that chronological sorting and fusion can take place, what happens if interactions require events from different widgets to be merged? A simple example would be the copying of a 3D object from one window to another, using the *"put this here"* vocal command and two designations to identify the object and the new destination. Such high-level interaction require events to be propagated to the parents in the hierarchy of widgets. However, in most cases, this need not be done for all events and through all widgets in the path to the root widget. But identifying the appropriate events and widgets seems too application-dependent to be integrated within our architecture, as it requires contextual knowledge of the interaction and the application. Thus, multimodal fusion systems and/or application developers should be aware of this when designing the interface.

As mentioned before, our architecture needs to be extended in several ways. First, it should probably also manage the input signals for non-standard modalities, delivering them to the appropriate slave processes. For example, the signal from the microphone could delivered to the recognition process. This would be the first step toward a multimodal terminal.

Fig. 13. MIX 3D's multimodal environment with the input and output voice devices.

But the most important extension would be to support multimodal output. As specified in (Krus, 1995), multimodal presentations are more efficient for displaying complex or critical information. Furthermore, they should be adapted to take into account the characteristics of the message, of the task that is being performed, of the user, and of the environment where the interaction is taking place. Such multimodal presentations systems also have requirements for the selection, the combination, the layout and the synchronisation of modalities which should be integrated in our system.

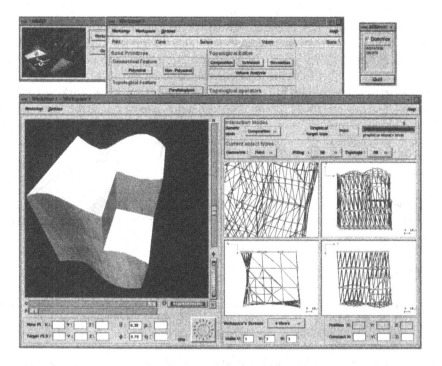

Fig. 14. X Window user interface of MIX 3D and **Modality Server** for vocal input recognition (top-right corner), with a Solid Volume described by free Surface objects and resulting of a topological cut operation between two previous Solid Volume objects.

6   Conclusion

We have analysed and presented the requirements for a next generation of CAD software, an advanced 3D system which allows graphical and spatial simulations for virtual objects. Using powerful multimodal interfaces, MIX 3D, our working prototype (see Fig. 13), gives life to objects with behaviour. Based on the characteristics of these objects and the tasks that designers perform, simulations and manipulations can now easily be applied to objects while they are being designed. We have shown that these objects must have fast reactive behaviour and an appropriate knowledge representation in order to allow the user to perform these simulations in real time with multimodal interaction combining graphical actions and vocal commands. To manage object simulations, we have elaborated a powerful 3D object representation model combining geometrical and topological knowledge modeling with the Generalised Constructive Graph (a generalisation of CSG trees). In order to support high level interaction, we have created a distributed architecture based on the X Window system. It provides most services required by multimodal fusion systems.

As Fig. 14 shows, the working MIX 3D prototype is now turning into a full-fledged CAD package which can handle solid modeling with objects described by free-form surfaces. Consequently, a short-term objective is to perform ergonomical experiments in order to evaluate the contribution of cooperative tools, reactive 3D virtual objects, and multimodal user interfaces in a real working context. In parallel, more advanced interaction techniques are being introduced. Sketch recognition is improved, and 3D gesture recognition (using a numerical data glove) is considered. A complete multimodal fusion system will integrate all these modalities.

Acknowledgements We wish to thank L. Arnal, J.P. Di Lelle, and F. Ledain for their work on MIX 3D and their help in producing the images for this chapter.

References

Barr, A. H. (1984) Global and local deformations of solid primitives. *Computer Graphics*, 18(3), 21–30.

Baumgardt, B. (1972) Winged-edge polyhedron representation. Technical Report CS 320, Dept. of Computer Science, Stanford University.

Bellik, Y. and Teil, D. (1993) A Multimodal Dialogue Controller for Multimodal User Interface Management Systems. Application: a Multimodal Window Manager. In *Proc. INTERCHI'93*, New York: ACM Press, 24–29.

Bellik, Y., Ferrari, S., Néel, F. and Teil, D. (1995) Requirements for multimodal dialogue including vocal interaction. In *ESCA Tutorial and Research Workshop on Spoken Dialogue Systems*, Hanstholm (Denmark), May 1995, 161–164.

Bellik, Y., Ferrari, S., Néel, F., Teil, D., Pierre, E. and Tachoires, V. (1995) Interaction Multimodale : Concepts et Architecture. In *4èmes Journées Internationales sur l'Interface des Mondes Réels et Virtuels*, Montpellier (France), June 1995, 37–45.

Carlson, W.E. (1982) An algorithm and data structure for 3d object synthesis using surface patch intersections. *Computer Graphics*, 16(3), 255–263.

Casale, M.S. (1987) Free-form solid modelling with trimmed surface patches. *IEEE Computer Graphics and Applications*, January 1987, 33–43.

Coutaz, J. et al. (1992) Interfaces multimodales et architecture logicielle. In *Workshop Report of IHM'92, 4èmes Journées sur l'Ingénierie des Interfaces Homme - Machine*, Paris (France), December 1992, 9–44.

Gaildrat, V., Vigouroux, N., Caubet, R. and Pérennou, G. (1993) Conception d'une interface multimodale pour un modeleur déclaratif de scènes tridimensionnelles pour la synthèse d'images. In *2èmes Journées Internationales sur l'Interface des Mondes Réels et Virtuels*, Montpellier (France), March 1993, 415–424.

Krus, M. (1995) Présentation multimodale d'information. Master's thesis, Université Paris XI, Orsay (France).

Lebahar, J. C. (1992) Quelques formes de planification de l'activité de conception en design industriel. *Le Travail Humain, Presse Universitaire de France*, 55(4), 329–351.

Levin, J.Z. (1980) Quadril: a computer language for the description of quadric surface bodies. *Computer Graphics*, 14(3), 86–92.

Macé, P. and Bourdot, P. (1991) A method to control continuity: Application to easy patches fitting. In *International EUROGRAPHICS Workshop on Computer Graphics and Mathematics*, Genova (Italy), October 1991, 150–169.

Martin, G. L. (1989) The utility of speech input in user-computer interfaces. *International Journal of Man-Machine Studies*, 30, 355–375.

Martin, J. C. Veldman, R. and Béroule, D. (1995) Towards Adequate Representation Technologies for Multimodal Interfaces. In *CMC/95, International Conference on Cooperative Multimodal Communication*, Eindhoven (The Netherlands), May 1995, pages 207–224. *Reprinted in revised form as Martin et al. (1997) in this volume.*

Martin, J. C. Veldman, R. and Béroule, D. (1997) Towards Multimodal Interfaces: a Theoretical Framework and Guided Propagation Networks. *This volume.*

Nigay, L. and Coutaz, J. (1993) A design space for multimodal systems: Concurrent processing and data fusion. In *Proc. INTERCHI'93*, New York: ACM Press, 172–178.

Nye, A. (1989) *Xlib Programming Manual (Vol. One of The X Window System Series).* Sebastopol, CA: O'Reilly and Associates.

Nye, A. and O'Reilly, T. (1990) *X Toolkit Intrinsics Programming Manual (Vol. Four of The X Window System Series).* Sebastopol, CA: O'Reilly and Associates.

DeRose, T. D. and Barsky, B. A. (1985) *An intuitive approach to geometric continuity for parametric curves and surfaces.* In *Computer-Generated Images - The state of the art,* edited by N. Magnenat-Thalmann and D.Thalmann, Heidelberg: Springer, 159–175

Shah, J. J. (1990) Philosophical development of form feature concept. In *Proc. of the Features Symposium, Computer Aided Manufacturing - International, CAM-I 90,* Boston (USA), August 1990, 113–128

Schomaker, L. et al. (1995) A taxonomy of multimodal interaction in the human information processing system. Technical report, ESPRIT PROJECT 8579 MIAMI, February 1995.

Tilove, R. B. and Requicha, A. A. (1980) Closure of boolean operations on geometric entities. *Computer Aided Design*, 12(5), September 1980, 219–220.

A Multimedia Interface for Circuit Board Assembly

Fergal McCaffery, Michael McTear and Maureen Murphy

Faculty of Informatics, University of Ulster,
Newtownabbey, N.Ireland. BT37 0QB
f.mcaffery@ulst.ac.uk, mf.mctear@ulst.ac.uk, m.murphy@ulst.ac.uk

Abstract. Interfaces combining natural language, speech and graphics take advantage of both the individual strengths of each communication mode and the fact that these modes can be employed in parallel. It is important to co-ordinate these media so that they improve communication capabilities. This paper describes the MICASSEM (Multimedia Interface for Circuit board ASSEMbly) system that applies user modelling to solve the problems associated with the selection and integration of multimedia output for both engineers and operators within NorTel. The paper also details how the system incorporates co-ordinated graphics, text, verbal and audio input and composes multimedia output for use by both engineers and operators.

1 Introduction

The MICASSEM system is a multimedia extension to an existing application that incorporates voice, graphics and text in such a way that it adds to the user friendliness of the package, and enables production line operators and engineers to use the package both efficiently and comfortably. This interface enables operators to gain instructions on how to assemble circuit boards on the NorTel shop floor, as well as allowing engineers to change the content of the circuit board layout diagrams. The objective of the MICASSEM system is to simplify the interaction of the shop-floor operators by developing an interface that accepts co-ordinated graphical and textual input and composes multimedia output which best conveys the information to the operator or engineer.

2 MICASSEM's Environment and Problem Definition

The MICASSEM system is currently being developed for the NorTel plant, which is based at Monkstown, outside Belfast, Northern Ireland. Within this plant the production process has been largely automated, but there is a stage of manual assembly which is completed by operators on the shop floor. Manual assembly is supported by a set of manual assembly sheets which are displayed on a terminal in front of the operator and which do not make allowances for different skill levels and different types of users. The manual assembly process information is provided by NorTel's ASSET (ASsembly SETup) system. The ASSET system, which runs on a variety of UNIX workstations, uses a design data file for a particular design along with a manufacturing process plan to create a set of shop-aids (circuit board drawings and assembly instructions) automatically. The shop-aids may be viewed and/or manipulated interactively, or may be plotted or printed.

The aim of the MICASSEM project was to enhance the manual assembly process provided by NorTel's ASSET system by creating an interface that enables the assembly sheets to be displayed automatically on a terminal by either pressing the keys on a keyboard or by clicking on a mouse button. The MICASSEM system also removes any ambiguities or misconceptions that previously existed for inexperienced assembly line operators when they used the ASSET system. This is achieved by the system providing easy to follow screens for inexperienced users and less informative screens for the more experienced users. Also users of the MICASSEM system may choose how they wish to interact with the system. For example, a user may choose to interact by pointing (clicking on a mouse button), using written natural language, or a combination of these interaction types. Another problem with the manual system currently in use at NorTel is that it is impossible for the engineers to take a circuit layout diagram and amend it so that each operator or engineer automatically receives an updated copy of the circuit board layout diagram as well as the new assembly instructions, and for the new details to be automatically added to the database. The introduction of the MICASSEM system also overcomes these problems and ensures that each operator has an on-line copy of the current circuit board diagram layout as opposed to a paper copy which may be out of date.

3   MICASSEM's Requirements

The main requirements for the system are that:

1. Users should be able to communicate with the system by use of a variety of media, including natural language and graphics.
2. The dialogue should be adapted to the user's tasks, preferences and level of technical expertise both in terms of the content and the medium of presentation.

4   MICASSEM's Development Environment

A software development environment known as Hipworks (developed by Integral Solutions Ltd.) was used to develop the MICASSEM system. Hipworks runs on a UNIX platform and incorporates hypertext, multimedia and expert system facilities, with POP-11 being used as the underlying development language. However it should be noted that while Hipworks enabled attractive multimedia presentations to be displayed, the selection and allocation of media as well as the user modelling aspects of the system were created using POP-11 code. Figure 1 illustrates the high-level architecture of the system.

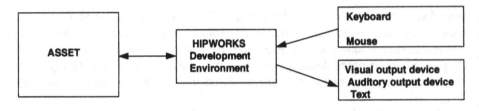

Fig. 1. High-level system architecture

5   Task Analysis of the ASSET System

Figure 2 shows a Task Hierarchy Diagram (THD) (Browne, 1994) for the ASSET system.

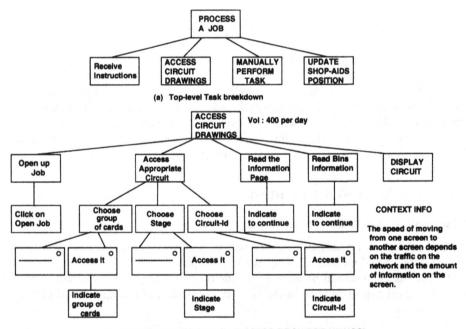

Fig. 2. Task hierarchy diagram (THD)

The diagram (shown in Fig. 2) represents the manual assembly process in terms of the sub-tasks and events that begin and end the task as well as the sub-tasks that progress the task towards completion. This information was obtained through observation of the shop-floor assembly unit and interviews with the parties involved. An overview of the task performed is that initially the operators receive their assembly instructions in hardcopy format, then the operators access the appropriate circuit diagram (using the ASSET system) and manually perform the corresponding task (assemble a component into the desired location on a circuit board). Finally, the ASSET system is updated to reflect the task that has recently been performed. Figure 2a illustrates that the processing of a job (task) is broken down into four events, three of which are sub-tasks which can be further broken down. In Fig. 2b, the ACCESS CIRCUIT DRAWINGS sub-task is broken down as illustrated, indicating the sequence and selection of events. THD's are an abstract representation of user tasks and do not include mention of such things as input devices, which are amenable to change and therefore constrain the design. Figure 2 also contains contextual information which was gathered during the user analysis of the ASSET system. This contextual information reflected that the response time of the system depends on both the number of users currently using the system and the amount of information they wish to access.

The information obtained from the user analysis of the system reflected that inexperienced users found it difficult initially to access assembly instructions from the ASSET system and then after managing to access the instructions they experienced problems understanding these instructions. The operators also felt that inexperienced users required the assistance of more experienced operators in order to complete their assembly tasks and this lowered throughput figures on the production line. Hence experienced and inexperienced users of the ASSET system agreed that the shop-aids information should be displayed differently for operators of differing experience levels.

6   MICASSEM's Facilities

The MICASSEM system helps to overcome difficulties such as ambiguities and misconceptions encountered on the shop floor by combining media to accomplish certain tasks. For example, illustrating assembly instructions on a circuit board screen layout by pointing at them with a mouse, and then eliciting a textual explanation along with a voice output. The selection of output media is based on:

(i) the technical aspects of the task and context (the type of information that has to be displayed),

(ii) the user's preferences (the media the user wishes to use in order to interact with the system, and the media they wish the output from the system to be presented in) and

(iii) the type of user (novice, expert, viewer or updater).

The MICASSEM system caters for four different types of users: novices, experts, viewers and updaters. A novice user is a new assembly line operator who has previously never used this interface to access instructions for assembling a circuit board, or has only recently started using the MICASSEM system and is not yet completely familiar with how to use the application. The novice user thus requires information consisting of:

(1) a description of the circuit board to be assembled,
(2) the assembly instructions for each component,
(3) details concerning the location of each component before it is assembled into
     the circuit board (the Bin number containing the desired component), and
(4) help information on how to use the interface.

The expert user also requires the above information, however this type of user is an operator who is familiar with using the MICASSEM system and therefore requires less help information, fewer detailed instructions and descriptions and a more concise interaction. Such users also expressed a desire to be able to perform a large number of tasks on a single screen, whereas the novice users requested more screens, but with less content on each screen so that they could easily understand each specific task before progressing to the next screen, which would contain the next task.

The viewer user category is reserved for NorTel engineers as opposed to assembly line operators. A viewer user may query details concerning a previously created circuit board layout. The details the viewer user requires access to are as follows:

(1) component name,
(2) organisational layout of the component,
(3) access time of the component,
(4) supply voltage,
(5) supply current, and
(6) standby current.

The updater user category is also reserved for NorTel engineers. An updater user is required to have the same level of knowledge of technical terms as the viewer, and in addition, this user must be knowledgeable in updating the shop-aids database.

7   System Components

The MICASSEM system includes an input coordinator to cater for the compound input streams, a database, and knowledge sources to permit a basis for decision making. Due to the use of different media the interface offers the user the option of choosing which medium or combination of mediums they would prefer to use in order to interact with the system. The system also automatically composes and generates relevant output to the user in the form of co-ordinated multi-media using both canned text and templates as generation techniques. The components for the MICASSEM system are shown below in Fig. 3.

The Input Component contains a keyboard and a mouse. The Input Coordinator accepts input from the two input devices. The Parser then accepts the input stream produced by the input coordinator and produces an interpretation of this stream. Then the Execute Task component carries out the appropriate action. This could be for example to obtain

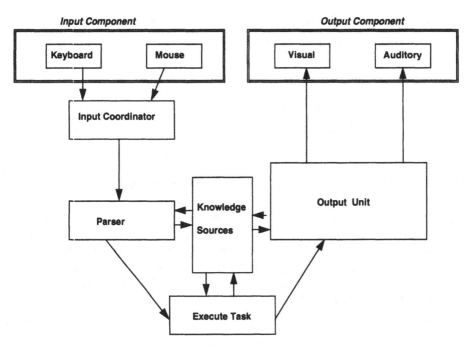

Fig. 3. MICASSEM's system components

(1) the assembly instructions for a selected component,
(2) the location (bin number) of a selected component,
(3) a description of the circuit diagram.

The Output Unit then analyses the results of the Execute Task component and decides how these results should be communicated to the user. The Output Unit then produces visual/auditory output. This module is responsible for ensuring that the corresponding output is carried out in the correct sequence. The Output Component contains both a visual component (text and graphics output) and an auditory component (speech output).

The system also uses Knowledge Sources for understanding the input to the system and generating the output from the system. These are:

(1) a focus pointer that is used to avoid ambiguous reference by highlighting the object most relevant to the user's task,
(2) a user model that takes into consideration the user's level of expertise in performing the current task as well as preferences concerning the mode of communication,
(3) a database of shop-aids components which includes all the information concerning a particular component that may be assembled on a circuit board.

This is a simulated database which contains both operator information and technical information. This database contains the shop-aids information that is generated by the ASSET system, as MICASSEM is concerned with converting this information into a format that is understandable for all the users of the system. The database contains the following fields:

(1) Common Product Code Number,
(2) Stage/Cell information,
(3) Description of component,
(4) Bin information,
(5) Assembly instructions.[1]

8   A Sample Interaction Using the Interface

This sample interaction illustrates how by using the interface a novice user may obtain assembly instructions for one or all of the components displayed in the diagram. Initially the screen shown below in Fig. 4 is displayed along with a spoken message 'Please click on one of the components in the diagram' to attract the novice user's attention and reinforce both the textual and graphical information that is displayed on the screen.

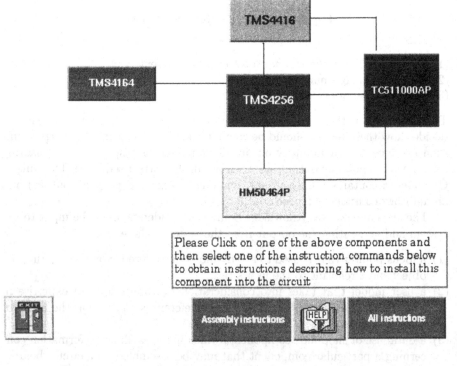

Fig. 4. Novice user screen for requesting assembly instructions

---

[1] A help module is linked to the user model and it ensures that the user gets the appropriate help (at the right technical level) and not pages of irrelevant information.

Then once the novice user has clicked on a component, the screen display shown in Fig. 5 is displayed and the spoken message of 'Please click on one of the assembly instruction buttons' is used to enhance the screen display. The screen display eliminates any ambiguities and misconceptions by highlighting the selected component (the MICASSEM system then focuses on this component until another component is selected). If the novice user then clicks on one of the instruction buttons the result is retrieved from the database and displayed as a textual message along with a spoken message stating that 'this is the answer to your query'. The system then prompts the novice user by asking them if they have finished reading the output and if the user states 'Yes' then the output disappears.

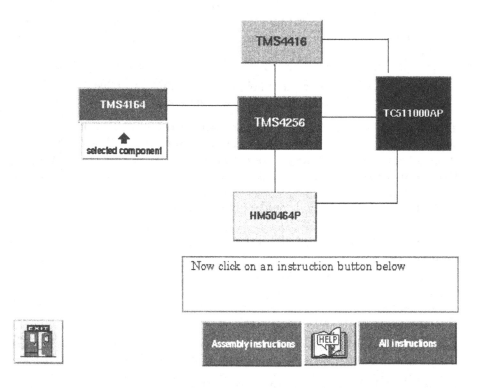

Fig. 5. Novice user screen after having selected a component

9 Media Selection and Allocation

The Output Unit is responsible for the message content and mode selection of the MICASSEM system. The task of the output unit is to divide a communicative goal into subgoals which can be satisfied by specific mode generators so that they complement each other. Within the system the user can specify if they want to have output in the form of speech, text, graphics or any combination of these three presentations (provided that it is viable for the type of query and the category of user that is involved). The output media may be chosen by the user or may be set automatically by the system depending on the type of user. For example, speech output, text and graphics pointers are all provided together as a default for novice users. This is to ensure that possible ambiguities that may arise from presenting the information using a single media are removed. However novice users may turn any of these media displays off if they wish. For example, if the novice users wish to turn the voice output off they may simply click on the sound off icon.

The relation governing the allocation of media is:

- Display (Type of Media, Content, Flag)
- Type of Media - this attribute may take the value of either Speech, Text or a Graphics pointer, as these are the types of media that the system may generate.
- Content - this attribute may contain either the filename of an audio file, a textual message or a graphics pointer with an attached label.
- Flag - this attribute may contain either the values true or false.

The Flag attribute indicates whether or not the Content section of the relation should be displayed using the media type stored in the Type of Media attribute. If the value of the Flag attribute is set to true, then the information is displayed. Otherwise the value of the Flag attribute is set to false, then the information is not displayed. For example, the attribute values of this relation for allocating media to a novice user (by default) would be as follows:

Display(Speech, Recorded speech filename, true);
Display(Text, text-message, true);
Display (Graphics pointer, label, true).

If the value of the attribute Flag is true, then the Display task is performed. If however the user clicks on a Text off icon on the screen, the value of the Flag attribute for Text is then reset to 'false'. The display relations would then become equal to:

Display(Speech, Recorded speech filename, true);
Display(Text, text-message, false);
Display (Graphics pointer, label, true).

If the user then clicks on an "Assembly instruction" button (see Fig. 5) a PERFORM relation is used in conjunction with the interaction modes to produce the desired output. The structure of the PERFORM relation is: PERFORM(database, focus pointer, information type). The database attribute will contain the information retrieved from the database. The focus pointer attribute contains the Common Product Code Number of the component which is currently in focus. The information type attribute contains either the words "Assembly instructions", "Bin information", "Component description information", "Circuit board description information", "Help information" or a "Graphical pointer" as these are the different types of information that may be requested by the operators of the system.

The database is then searched for the assembly instructions (as assembly instructions have previously been requested by the operator) of the component whose value is equal to that of the current focus pointer attribute of the PERFORM relation. For example, if "TMS4164" is the Common Product Code Number of the component in focus this yields the following: PERFORM(database, TMS4164, assembly instructions). The PERFORM relation is in effect the <Content> attribute of the Display relation, and therefore in this example the Display relation would become: Display(Type of Information, PERFORM(database, TMS4164, assembly instructions), Flag). Here the value of Type of Information is decided by the user's preferences for a particular type of interaction. In this example the system displays the assembly instructions of component "TMS4164" in the form of a voice output and a graphics pointer highlighting the component which is currently in focus. This is due to the fact that the Flag attribute corresponding to the Type of Media attribute with a value of Speech is set true, and that the Flag attribute corresponding to the Type of Media attribute with a value of Graphics Pointer is also set to true. The resulting relations are as follows:

Display(Speech, PERFORM(file1.au, TMS4164, assembly instructions), true);
Display(Text, PERFORM(Connect Pin 4 to Pin 6 of TMS4256, TMS4164, assembly instructions), false);
Display(Graphics Pointer, PERFORM(selected component, TMS4164, assembly instructions), true).

Therefore the output generated from this example is an audio file (file1.au) which describes the assembly instructions for TMS4164 and a graphics pointer which contains the label "selected component".

As well as the selection of a particular medium being determined through the use of the media allocation rules, it may also be determined either in terms of the task involved or in terms of a preferred user style of communication. Speech output is particularly useful when presenting messages to attract the operators attention, and other information when the operator is unable to attend to the screen. Graphics are a useful medium for showing the circuit board chip and highlighting areas of the circuit board, while natural language is appropriate for textual messages, as well as an accompaniment to graphical displays. The integration of these different modes of interaction brings several advantages, as potential ambiguities and misconceptions may be eliminated if two or more media are used together, for example, having a picture combined with a textual explanation.

The particular media chosen for output allocation is based on rules by Arens, Hovy, and Vossers (1993). These rules were used prior to designing the MICAS-

SEM system as a means of deciding which media should be chosen for a particular instance. An example is now shown of how these rules were applied to produce sample displays. We present three simple tasks in parallel given the following:

1. Task: the task of presenting a RAM chip (as a chip to be used on circuit board).
2. Available information (three separate examples): the coordinates of the chip, the name of the chip, and a photographic image of a chip with a code name TM54416-15NL.
3. Available media: board layout diagram, spoken and written natural language, photographic pictures, tables, graphs, ordered list, and unordered lists.

Table 1 shows the characteristics of the information to be presented, for information concerning this refer to Arens, Hovy and Vossers (1993).

Table 1. Characteristics of the information to be presented

	Coordinates	Name	Photograph
Information	40,20	TMS4416-15NL	Ram chip
Dimensionality	double	single	complex
Volume	little	singular	singular
Density	dense	discrete	dense
Transience	dead	dead	dead
Urgency	routine	routine	routine

The allocation rules classify information characteristics with respect to characteristics of media. The medium with the most suitable characteristics is then selected to perform the task.

Handling the coordinates

The rules specify that information with double dimensionality are best presented in a background with a two dimensional value (i.e., board layout diagrams, pictures, tables and graphs). Since there is little volume, transient media are not ruled out, however the value dense for the characteristic density rules out tables and the values for transience and urgency do not effect the outcome. Taking into account the rules dealing with the internal semantics of media, everything except the board layout diagram is immediately ruled out.

Handling the name

The code name TMS4416-15NL has single dimensionality and the rules specify that the background should be natural language, and since the volume is singular, a transient medium is not ruled out. Also none of the other characteristics have any effect on the possible medium to be selected, leaving the possibility of communicating the single name TMS4416-15NL or of speaking or writing a sentence such as "this is RAM chip TMS4416-15NL".

Handling the photograph
The photograph has a complex dimensionality, for which the rules specify that the only possible solution is to simply represent the photograph itself.

10   The Provision of System Adaptivity through User Modelling

Most user modelling systems are concerned with generating output to the user which has a content that is both relevant to the current user and matches the user's level of expertise. The MICASSEM system extends this idea by also considering the user's interaction preferences. Benyon (1992) noted that whenever there are different types of users, with different levels of experience that information should be expressed in a manner that best suits each type of user. Hence it was important that the MICASSEM system catered for the different skill levels and the different types of users. This was possible through the use of user modelling, which enabled the MICASSEM system to overcome the problems that previously arose for inexperienced operators (who used the ASSET system) by providing easy-to-follow screens and allowing users to interact with the system using their preferred type of interaction media. For example, a user may choose to interact by pointing, using written or spoken natural language, or a combination of some or all these interaction types. The MICASSEM system is also able to present help messages, circuit descriptions and instructions in formats that are suited to the different levels of users.

10.1   Acquiring the User Model

User modelling involves acquiring and storing information about users and then utilising this information to guide the behaviour of the system (Kobsa and Wahlster, 1989; McTear, 1993). The user model used within the system has the following characteristics:

(1) it is based on stereotypes, as it groups the users into different categories,
(2) it is a mixture of both static and dynamic models, in that the user's stereotype, which is determined initially, may change over the course of an interaction, however it only changes from one stereotype classification to another, i.e. there is no finer distinction among different levels within a stereotype which would be necessary for precise adaptation to the individual needs of each user,
(3) it involves both explicit and implicit acquisition.

Initially rules infer both explicitly and implicitly from the user's primary interaction with the system and the appropriate trigger is fired. The user is thus assigned to a particular stereotype on the basis of this trigger (this is similar to stereotype triggers that were used in GRUNDY (Rich, 1979)).

The MICASSEM system adopts a double-stereotyping formalism for grouping users which is similar to that used in the KNOME system (Chin, 1989), and creates classes of users, and classes of knowledge (see Table 2, below).

Table 2. Use of stereotypes

	Knowledge Classes			Media Preferences	
	Technical Assembly Terms	Engineering Terms	Database Updating	Output Media	Input Media
Novice (operator)	NEVER	NEVER	NEVER	T,G,S	T,G v G,S v G v T v S
Expert (operator)	ALWAYS	NEVER	NEVER	T	T,G v G,S v G v T v S
Viewer (engineer)	SOMETIMES	ALWAYS	NEVER	T,G,S	T,G v G,S v T v S
Updater (engineer)	SOMETIMES	ALWAYS	ALWAYS	T,G,S	T,G v G,S v T v S

Each stereotype category indicates the level of knowledge which a user requires in order to belong to that particular user group. For example, it is assumed that a novice operator will never understand technical assembly terms, and will never understand engineering terms, and will also never have knowledge of how to update the database. Also included in Table 2, is the output media that may be used to display the desired information, as well as the types of input media that may be used for each user stereotype. For example, the novice user may receive their output in a combination of text (T), graphics based pointing (G), or speech (S), so that any ambiguities that may arise through the use of one media will be removed. Also a novice user may input a query using either: text (T) and pointing (G), pointing (G) and speech (S), text only (T), or speech only (S). The system supports the presentation preferences of users, by displaying the information in the media which best meets the user's requirements from the range of media that is available within that particular user's stereotype. Thus the output that users receive is differentiated according to their level of expertise, which determines the nature of the information provided. Novice users receive detailed information. Expert users receive brief descriptions with more technical details included. Technical users receive technical details concerning the circuit boards and are also permitted to add new components to the circuit board, and this automatically updates the shop-aids database.

Information inherited from stereotypes is treated as default information which may be overwritten if more specific or conflicting information is provided about a particular user (McTear, 1993). The MICASSEM system creates separate stereotypes for novice and expert assembly line operators, as well as for technical users (engineers: viewers, updaters) as shown below in Fig. 6.

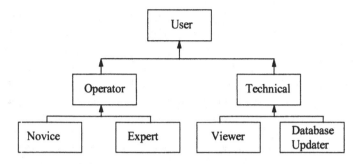

Fig. 6. Stereotypes within the MICASSEM user model

10.2   Moving between Different Stereotype Categories

Although similar classifications of user type and level have been widely used
(Chin, 1989; Murphy and McTear, 1993), it is recognised that this basic method
of user classification is not without its problems. A false classification of users
may arise if users over-estimate, or under-estimate their abilities. Furthermore,
users may be an expert in some parts of the system, but a complete novice
in other areas. One possible solution is given within the system by providing a
more dynamic user model which is amended according to inferences based on the
ongoing dialogue, such as the time the user takes to respond to a prompt, the type
of error messages displayed, the detail of help provided (Murphy and McTear,
1993), or the type of query entered. The interaction model of the adaptive system
monitors the interaction of users with the system to ensure that users have not
classified themselves in the wrong expertise category. For example, novice users
tend to become very confused if they are interacting within the expert category,
because little help and assistance is provided for entering queries within this
category. Therefore, the user is likely to make many mistakes, thus invoking the
system to ask the user if they actually are an expert user. The interaction model
contains details concerning: the invoking of errors made, the use of different
media for interactions, the extent to which help was required, the ability to
initially have the capability to navigate to the correct screen, the use of colour
to reference a component on the screen as opposed to using a component name,
and the exceeding of interaction time limits. For example, if the user is classified
as a novice and then proceeds to request very little help during the interaction,
or invokes very few error messages, then the user is asked if they really are
a novice. Another example of how the user model monitors the interaction of
the user with the system is that expert users should make few errors, request
very little help, and prefer not to receive speech output (expert users tend to
find speech output annoying after only a few interactions), and complete their
interaction within the allocated time. If a user is classified as an expert but the
user's behaviour does not correspond to these criteria, then the system suggests
that the classification could be changed.

The mechanism for modifying a user's stereotype were based on an analysis of the typical characteristics of each user stereotype in terms of behaviours and preferences, as well as on a set of score adjustments that are activated on the basis of the user's interaction with the system. After the user has been allocated to a particular stereotype, the system can then decide how appropriate this stereotype is for this user by analysing the interaction model. Linear stereotype parameters are set up separately for operators (novices and experts) and engineers (viewers and updaters). Due to the use of the two separate parameters (operator and engineer) the case will never arise were an operator will become an engineer and were an engineer will become a novice. The initial value of the parameters are as follows:

- a novice user initially has an operator parameter value of 0;
- an expert user initially has an operator parameter value of 20;
- a viewer initially has an engineer parameter a value of 0;
- updater initially has an engineer parameter a value of 20.

Table 3 (shown below) summarises the effect that invoking a certain feature of the system has on the value of the parameter concerning a particular stereotype.

Table 3. The values that different features of the system have within the interaction model

Feature	Stereotype			
	Novice	Expert	Viewer	Updater
1. Use of help facility	0	−1	0	0
2. Help facility not used	+2	0	0	0
3. Invoking error messages	0	-2	0	0
4. Using component codes to query the system	+2	+1	0	0
5. Using colour to query as opposed to using component codes	0	-1	0	0
6. Unable initially to navigate to the correct screen	0	-1	0	0
7. Use of voice input	0	-3	0	0
8. Interaction complete within time limit	+1	+1	0	0
9. Interaction exceeds time limit	0	-1	0	0
10. Familiar with how to update the database	0	0	+5	0
11. Unfamiliar with how to update the database	0	0	0	-5

If the interaction characteristics of the user are not compatible with those of the stereotype characteristics which this user has inherited, then this results in a series of conflicts. If after a series of these conflicts the value of the parameter becomes equal to a value that is within a different stereotype zone, then the user

is asked if they wish to inherit the characteristics of this new stereotype zone.
The stereotype zone values for the system are shown below in Table 4.

For example, if an expert user initially requests voice output, the initial
stereotype parameter value of 20 is then reduced by 3 (see feature 7 of Table 3),
thus giving a new parameter value of 17. If this user then causes an error message
to be displayed, his parameter value is then further reduced by 2 (see feature
3 of Table 3), thus giving a new parameter value of 15. This series of conflicts
may eventually result in a parameter value being obtained that is equal to 0, and
MICASSEM system will then ask the user if they wish their user classification to
be changed to that of a novice. If however, the user does not wish to be classified
as a novice, then the user may continue to interact as an expert and will have
a new stereotype parameter value of 20 (the initial stereotype parameter value
for an expert).

Table 4. Stereotype zone values

Zone values for operator parameters	Zone values for engineer parameters
$0 \leq$ novice < 20	$0 \leq$ viewer < 20
$20 \leq$ expert $<$ infinity	$20 \leq$ updater $<$ infinity

10.3   Summary of MICASSEM's Adaptation

The MICASSEM system has a user-centred, user modelling component that
combines the use of explicit methods, stereotyping, and implicit methods which
enables instructions to be generated that fulfil the requirements of each type
of user. At first, users explicitly enter information into the system concerning
their level of expertise, the type of information they require, and any interaction
preferences they may have. Then this information triggers the appropriate user
stereotype, and sets the appropriate default value for this user's stereotype parameter. The system then collects implicit information, by monitoring the user's
interaction, and altering the value of the user's stereotype parameter to reflect
the user's interaction. If a user's interaction is inappropriate for the current user
stereotype to which this user has been assigned, then this will be reflected by
the value of the user's stereotype parameter exceeding either the upper or lower
range of the stereotype parameter values that are permitted for a user within
this class. The system then asks the user if they wish to change from one stereotype class to another. The user may then choose to either remain a member of
the current stereotype class, or become a member of the stereotype class whose
permitted range of stereotype parameter values includes the current value of
this user's stereotype parameter value. The user modelling component of the
MICASSEM system enables it to both generate information that is tailored to
the requirements of the user type (operator or technical), and the knowledge

level (novice, expert, updater, viewer), as well as presenting the output in the user's preferred choice of media.

11 Future Enhancements

At present the system alters the value of the user's stereotype as a direct result of the implicit information collected from the user's interaction. However in order for the MICASSEM system to truly be both powerful enough for expert users, but yet simple enough for novice users the system would need to concentrate more on the user's cognitive style and personality factors. Therefore some additional models will be required to capture and store this information. Benyon and Murray (1993) devised a conceptual structure for adaptive systems, which consists of a user model, a domain model and an interaction model. The user model may be fed with either knowledge that is inferred from the user's interaction, or previously stored cognitive knowledge of the user. The domain model represents the aspects of the system that are essential for the operation of the adaptive interface and the aspects of the application that may be adapted. The domain model captures descriptions of the application at three levels. These levels are the task level (describes the user goals in the domain), the logical level (what the system believes the user understands about the logical concepts of the domain) and the physical level (system infers how the user should interact with the system). The interaction model is concerned with inferring knowledge about users as a result of users interacting with the system. From the inferred knowledge the system can make inferences concerning such concepts as the user's previous experience, the user's beliefs, the user's goals, and the user's cognitive factors. Thus in order to improve the usability of the MICASSEM system it would be necessary to follow Benyon's architecture and hence redesign the user modelling component of the MICASSEM system. Also empirical investigations will be required to validate the usability of the system for the relevant groups of users and to determine user preferences for different media as well as the effectiveness of the interface.

References

Arens, Y., Hovy, E., and Vossers, M. (1993), On the Knowledge Underlying Multimedia Presentations. In *Intelligent Multimedia Interfaces.*, Maybury, M. (ed.), Cambridge (MA): MIT Press, pp. 280-306.

Benyon, D. (1992), *Adaptive Systems: from Intelligent Tutoring to Autonomous Agents*, Open University Technical Report 92/04.

Benyon, D. and Murray, D. (1993), Applying User Modelling to Human-Computer Interaction Design, *The Artificial Intelligence Review, 6*, pp. 43-69.

Browne, D. (1994), *STUDIO: Structured User-interface Design for Interaction Optimisation*, Prentice Hall International (UK).

Chin, D. (1989), KNOME: Modelling what the user knows in UC. In *User Models in Dialog Systems*, Kobsa, A. and Wahlster, W. (eds.), Heidelberg: Springer Verlag.

Kobsa, A. and Wahlster, W. (eds.) (1989), *User Models in Dialog Systems*, Heidelberg: Springer Verlag.

McTear, M. (1993), User Modelling for Adaptive Computer Systems: a Survey of Recent Developments, *Artificial Intelligence Review, 6*, pp. 1-28.

Murphy, M. and McTear, M. (1993), Intelligent Technology and Open Learning. In *Proceedings of the First European Congress on Fuzzy and Intelligent Technologies*, Aachen, Germany, pp. 975-981.

Rich, E. (1979), User Modeling via Stereotypes, *Cognitive Science, 4*, pp. 329-354.

Visual Language Parsing:
If I Had a Hammer...

Kent Wittenburg[*]

GTE Laboratories, 40 Sylvan Rd., Waltham, MA 02254, USA
kentw@gte.com

Abstract. Since the 1960s, grammatical formalisms and parsing methods developed originally for natural language strings have been extended to represent and process two-dimensional visual expressions such as mathematics notation and various kinds of diagrams. But despite all of the effort, there has been negligible impact on human-computer interfaces to support visual modes of communication. Why? As with all tech transfer issues, some of the reasons may be beyond a researcher's control. However, I believe that two of the contributing factors in the case of visual language (VL) parsing can and should be addressed by the research field. First, the field needs to consolidate and communicate its results. This is in fact not trivial for higher-dimensional visual language representation and parsing, and I will try to illustrate why. Second, researchers have to look harder for the right application domains. One of the obvious applications is the interpretation of visual language expressions constructed with GUIs. While grammatical representation and parsing may bring something to the table, the problem of interpretation may be solvable with simpler techniques. I will discuss some other application areas and my experience with them: design support, smart screen layout for electronic publishing, and visual focusing for attributed graphs.

1   Introduction

It is natural that researchers in the field of multimodal communication look to theories and practice in computational linguistics for directions and techniques in supporting communication more generally. One hypothesis is that language models appropriate for verbal modes might extend to nonverbal ones. As it turns out, there is a large, though fragmented literature on the subject of generalizing syntax representation and analysis techniques to visual languages (VLs). Examples of such languages are mathematical notation, finite-state diagrams, flowcharts, chemistry diagrams, and electronics schematics. These examples all have the property that the syntax seems to be relatively well-behaved and 'generative'. We can envision, at least naively, that methods for string-based languages could be extended to account for representations of these visual expressions. It seems reasonable to suppose one could enumerate a finite vocabulary of symbols

---

[*] The original version of this paper was written while the author was with Bellcore, Morristown, NJ, USA.

and a set of relations among symbols that might be used to compose higher level expressions for the syntax. The semantics, in turn, stands a chance of bearing a close relationship to a syntactic structure that is associated with a derivation, or parse tree.

What is meant by visual languages here is then a class of notations that might reasonably be construed as languages in the classical sense. That is, we can first characterize an infinite set of expressions using a finite discrete vocabulary together with a set of combinatory operations. We then characterize languages with grammars that can generate (or perhaps just recognize) subsets of the freely composable expressions. While such a definition certainly does not preclude languages that might incorporate temporal or 3-dimensional spatial relations, I will focus here on the two-dimensional graphical domain.

Not all sorts of visual, nonverbal expressions that we might want to include in multimodal communication will pass the test of visual-language-hood. For instance, simple pointing and hand-gesturing behaviors are not always usefully decomposable into a collection of discrete events with certain relations between them. It has been argued by Weimer and Ganapathy (1992), for instance, that three-dimensional hand-tracking as an input modality is best suited for continuous physical manipulations rather than for discrete symbolic expressions as we find in languages in the classical sense. Wahlster (1991) provides an interesting discussion of coordinated pointing as input to multimodal communication systems, but the specification and syntactic analysis of the pointing gestures themselves are not an issue.

The focus here will be on the mode of visual communication only, and our main question is whether grammatical approaches to visual language representation can bring value to human-computer communication. We should distinguish visual language interfaces from Graphical User Interfaces (GUIs) and also from the use of visualization more generally. A visual language interface implies that composition operators used in the language to instruct the computer are two (or more)-dimensional and that the program semantics in some way depends on these geometric or topological relationships. There is the implication that users must be able to interactively construct and/or manipulate expressions in the visual language. Visualization systems do not necessarily support this sort of interactivity; the main emphasis is on the generation side. Graphical user interfaces, while not necessarily visual language interfaces themselves, may be used to construct visual language expressions. For instance, a standard graphical editor might be used to construct a graph consisting of geometric shapes for nodes and lines for arcs. The test of a visual language interface is whether that graph lends semantics to the application through its structure or visual properties. Besides mouse pointing and clicking of GUIs, other input devices and media may be utilized for forming visual language expressions. For example, keyboard input in the form of 'shortcuts' can and does in many applications form visual language expressions that have a significant semantics for the application. Pen-based systems provide another means for input.

As it turns out, there are some very challenging technical problems in representing visual languages directly as well as in producing tractable recognition and parsing algorithms. But the first impression on a newcomer to this area has to be the amazing proliferation of approaches to specifying visual languages. While I can't hope to chart all this work in this short chapter, I can at least provide mention of some of the more visible landmarks. See Marriott et al. (1997) for a comprehensive survey that covers logical and algebraic approaches as well as the grammatical approaches that I touch on here.

2 Higher Dimensional Grammars

Natural generalizations of strings from a formal standpoint include the following classes of expressions:

    two-(or n-) dimensional arrays

    trees

    graphs

Any of these basic formal constructs may be further enhanced through the addition of attributes. There are numerous proposals for rewriting systems for all these forms. Rosenfeld (1990) provides a synthesis of results with an emphasis on array grammars. From the engineering pattern-matching perspective, Fu (1974) is the classic reference. Although interest in array grammars seems to have largely died out, there was a lot of formal work in the 60s and 70s. Tree grammars have received less attention, with the notable exception of tree-adjoining grammars in computational linguistics (Joshi, 1985), than the more general subject of graph grammars.

The formal properties of graph grammars have been exhaustively studied. See, for example, the proceedings of a series of workshops on graph grammars (Cuny, 1995). A now long-outdated bibliography on graph grammars, Nagl (1983), is no less than 33 pages long. Many members of the graph grammar community recognize the need to synthesize results, but it is not easy to do. There are many kinds of graphs, and even more definitions for rewrite rules for graphs. There are, however, signs of convergence on a Chomsky-style hierarchy for graph language classes. Brandenburg (1989) has shown there to be a general class of polynomial-time recognizable graph grammars characterized by having the finite Church Rosser property (confluence) and by generating connected graphs of bounded degree. This general class has come to be known as *context-free graph grammars*. In practice, parsing of even this restricted class of graphs may in fact not be feasible since the degree of the polynomial may be high. An approach to achieving efficient parsing in practice has been to use so-called 'programmed grammars', a technique for adding procedural control methods to the parser (Bunke, 1982).

The basic idea at the core of higher-dimensional approaches is to extend the classical definition of string grammars by substituting other mathematical constructs for the expression class that comprises the input and output of each replacement step in a derivation. A generic context-free template for higher dimensional grammars follows.

Context-free Higher Dimensional Grammars A *Context-free Higher Dimensional Grammar* is a 4-tuple $G = \; < N, T, S, P >$, where

N is a set of nonterminals
T is a set of terminals disjoint from N
S, a member of N, is the start nonterminal
P is a set of productions of the form $A \rightarrow a$
where a, a replacement for A, is a composite mathematical construct such as an n-dimensional array, a tree, a graph, a set of relations...

The languages generated by higher-dimensional grammars are defined in the usual way as a set of expressions determined by derivations beginning with the start nonterminal where each step in a derivation is defined through a replacement operation using a production rule.

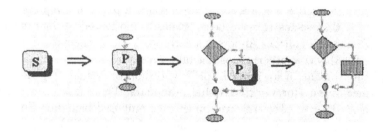

Fig. 1. An example of a derivation in a node-replacing graph grammar

Figure 1 shows an example of a higher-dimensional derivation yielding a flow-graph. Each step here involves the replacement of an attributed node in the emerging diagram with a graph. The definitions of the productions determine how the replacing graph is connected to the graph in which the original node was a member.

For array grammars, a cell in an array might be replaced in a derivation step by another array, but something has to be said about how the surrounding context will be affected by such a replacement. One can't replace a single cell in the middle of a two-dimensional array with another two-dimensional array and still have a coherent array as a result unless there is some shuffling. Definitions for replacement operations for trees or graphs also are, unfortunately, not so obvious as they are for strings. Tree-adjoining grammars, well-known in the computational linguistics community, define replacement through the operation of tree adjunction. Node-replacing graph grammars must specify how incoming and outgoing arcs of a nonterminal node will be rerouted to nodes of the replacement graph on the right-hand-side of the production. There are many variants of such replacement operations in the literature of array and graph grammars. Each definitional variant of a replacement operation is typically accompanied by a unique definition of grammar productions.

The main reasons for the proliferation of approaches for higher dimensional grammar representations are two:

(1) there is no standard class of expressions generated by these grammars;
(2) there is no standard notion of replacement in derivations analogous to concatenation for strings.

3   Visual Languages

Paralleling the formal language and engineering literature, there has been since the 60s an independent body of work that has focused on specifying visual languages in the context of graphical interfaces, pen-based input, and even architectural designs. Applications in handwriting, mathematics, and character recognition provided one thread. Another was parsing of hand-drawn diagrams. Shaw's work on Picture Description Languages (Shaw, 1969) is often cited. The basic idea there was to rewrite pictures to pictures, where a particular representation was developed that seems to have been primarily motivated by line drawings and handwriting recognition. Anderson's early work on mathematical notation (Anderson, 1968) was another important milestone.

The establishment of an annual IEEE workshop on visual languages provided another avenue for work on visual grammars. There has been a somewhat fragmented series of alternative frameworks proposed including Positional Grammars (Chang, 1988; Costagliola, Tomita, and Chang, 1991), Picture Layout Grammars (Golin and Reiss, 1989), Constraint Set Grammars (Helm and Mariott, 1991), Relation Grammars (Crimi et al., 1991), and extensions to unification grammars (Wittenburg , Keitzmann, and Talley, 1991; Wittenburg, 1992; 1996). One influence on some recent work in this area has come from constraint logic programming, which is evident in Helm and Marriott's work among others. Very recently there has been an effort to define a unifying framework for visual language grammars under a Chomsky-like hierarchy (Mariott and Meyer, 1997).

Many of the visual language frameworks do not fall into the context-free arena. In fact, Marriott and Meyer (1997) argue that some forms of context-sensitivity are intrinsic to visual languages. Examples of context-sensitive approaches include Rekers (1994) and Minas and Viehstaedt (1995), who have incorporated general graph-rewriting, and Meyer (1992) and Pineda (1992), who have incorporated general inferencing from logic programming paradigms. Golin and Reiss (1989), working in the attribute grammar paradigm, have proposed a mechanism that allows for some limited node sharing in derivation trees. The computational complexity of most of these approaches is known to be intractable in the general case, although Golin (1991) has reported a polynomial bound on recognition for Picture Layout Grammars.

Figure 2, adapted from Rekers (1994), is an example of a non context-free graph-rewriting system used in visual language interpretation. Figure 2a shows an example of the input, a finite state diagram. Finite state diagrams are an interesting case since they seem to be one of the more basic examples of visual languages and yet they are not context-free. Figure 2b is the lexical representation used as input to the syntactic processor. Figure 2c is the result of a syntax analysis. All of these representations are graphs and graph rewriting systems are used to move from one level of representation to the next.

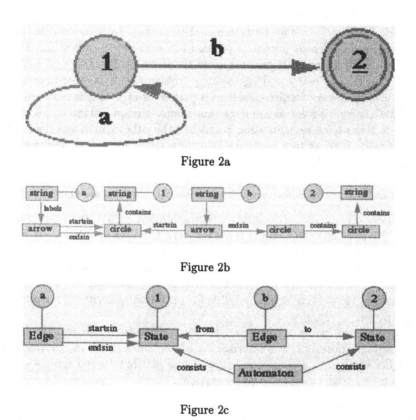

Figure 2a

Figure 2b

Figure 2c

Fig. 2. An example of a non context-free approach to language interpretation

4   Visual Language Interpretation

What sort of impact on the visual language interpretation problem has been achieved by this work in visual grammars? Particularly when compared with the influence of string-based grammars on computing, it is startling to note that high-dimensional grammars in general have had such little impact.

In the domain of image processing, Henry Baird (1990) in a survey of industrial applications of syntactic and structural pattern recognition (SSPR) writes that "Outside of ... OCR, very few applications of SSPR have surfaced." He attributes the relatively low acceptance to a number of factors, some of which have to do with problems particular to image recognition. For example, the complexity of image segmentation and other low-level processes tend to take center stage in real world imaging applications. Practicioners are then reluctant to turn to other technologies that may be perceived as complex and unproven. Further, many image recognition problems are less like a formal language problem in which idealized models may be articulated than they are akin to general real-world perception, which formal grammars are probably unsuited for. He also mentions the problem of fragmentation in the technical literature, along with a lack of attention to real world engineering problems such as error management and clear statements of which problems a particular approach is best suited for.

While interpreting visual language expressions in graphical interfaces may not share the lower-level segmentation problems, the other comments hold. There are also some barriers to acceptance in using parsing for visual language interpretation in particular. One is the lack of articulation of exactly what benefits declarative specifications will bring to visual language interfaces.

The main arguments for using declarative specification are the following:

(1) By providing a layer of declarative representation, visual language grammars can obviate the need to build complex event handling systems anew for each variant of a visual language.
(2) Since visual language grammars may be decoupled from parsing and generation algorithms, they may offer flexibility in processing the order of user input expressions as well as provide for optimized algorithms for particular purposes.
(3) The abstract structure associated with a derivation tree can be used for various purposes such as information hiding through visual encapsulation, higher-level editing operations, layout, and attribute-based semantic evaluation (for translation or code generation).

Ad hoc approaches that interpret visual language expressions through procedures attached to events often have a difficult time coping with confluent and nonmonotonic events. The confluence issue arises since visual language expressions acquire their semantics from their pictorial properties and not from the order in which they are created. If interfaces allow users the ability to construct the same expression in more than one order then naturally they should get the same interpretation, but this may be made more difficult with procedural code. Nonmonotonic events such as deletion also require updates to intermediate interpretations. Handling these complexities may be easier when a representation based on the visual properties of the expressions are the basis for their interpretation (Mariott, Meyer, and Wittenburg, 1997).

On the other hand, most grammatical approaches to visual language specification so far have offered little in the way of guidance for interfaces. It is not sufficient merely to define a representation and off-line parsing algorithm for a class of visual languages. There need to be deterministic predictive algorithms if syntax-directed editing methods are used, or error correcting methods if compile/edit models of interfaces are used. There are no known LL- or LR-style parsing algorithms (Aho, Seti, and Ullman, 1986) for visual languages of any complexity, and therefore syntax-directed approaches to visual language editing using formal grammars have not borne fruit. However, some researchers have begun to investigate error-correcting models. Chok and Marriott (1995) suggest how incremental error-correcting methods can be incorporated with Constraint Multiset Grammar representations. Minas and Viehstaedt (1995) have made preliminary suggestions that error-correcting methods could be added to a modified Cocke-Younger-Kasami parsing algorithm (Aho, Seti, and Ullman 1986) for diagrammatic interfaces specified with graph grammars. Wittenburg and Weitzman (1997b) suggest that rewrite rules might be utilized for correcting user editing actions in a VL interface for flowgraphs, but these rules must be composed manually.

Other researchers have prototyped toolkits in which a representation of the visual language is used as the basis for generating the interface without using that VL specification itself for parsing user input (e.g., Backland, Hagsand, and Pherson, 1990; Üsküdarli and Dinesh, 1995). Commercial visual language systems, e.g., Prograph (Cox, Giles, and Pietrzykowsky, 1989), LabView (Jagadeesh and Wang, 1993), SDT (Telelogic, 1997), even if they use formal methods in the backend, normally do not use formal methods for interpretation of expressions based on their visual properties. The view is that one does not need to specify visual languages in terms of their visual properties in order to create interpreters since the application has control over user events. In fact, sequences of keyboard commands can generate visual language expressions just as easily as drag and drop actions typical of generic graphical editors. Soiffer (1991), for instance, has developed an extendible specification language that includes keyboard sequences to construct mathematical notation, and his work has been incorporated into the product Mathematica (Wolfram, 1996). But this grammar-based specification language is not higher-dimensional since it describes linear sequences of user events such as keyboard presses or drag and drop actions. Note, however, that there are potentially interesting ordering issues lurking in user event specifications for creating visual expressions. Unlike text, there is no intrinsic ordering for creating diagrams. Specification languages for user events may be able to make use of work in (partially) free word order models for natural languages.

A last point concerns interoperability. When compared to text-based parsing tools such as YACC (Aho and Johnson, 1974), interoperability will be more difficult to achieve with visual language parsing tools. The first problem is the lack of a standard representation comparable to ASCII. Kahn and Sawarasat (1990) suggest that postscript might serve that role for visual language toolkits. They experimented with pen-based drawings created with independent tools as input to their visual language interpeter. Any tool could be used to create the drawings as long as it could export postscript. But there are specific problems with postscript as a VL lingua franca:

(1) it is not the right level of description – a visual specification would like to use explicit relations like *touching* or *above* that are not apparent in postscript output;

(2) postscript is a procedural language in which the output is affected by the order of drawing commands. It would be difficult to factor out the effect of different orderings.

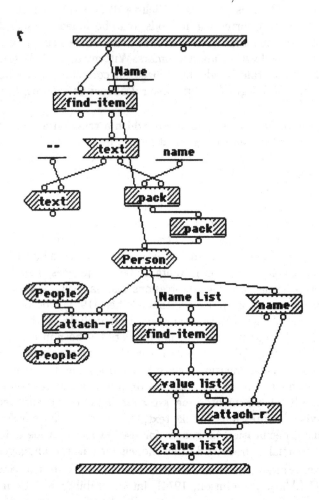

Fig. 3. A visual programming language expression

A second interoperability problem is that visual language editing requires customization to a greater extent than does text. Consider the visual languge expression from ProGraph (Cox, Giles, and Pietrzykowsky, 1989) in Fig. 3. It is unrealistic to expect that users would use a generic graphical editor to create the expression in Fig. 3. The user interface requires a customized palette of graphical objects and relationships. Users should not be required to place each of the objects individually in exactly the correct position. Rather, as a user adds an arc between two nodes, for instance, the small circles should be added automatically. The design and implementation of such editors is more of an issue to applications developers than the interpretation of visual language expressions considered independently.

5   Other Applications of Visual Language Parsing

A different slant on human-computer communication may be helpful when considering other applications of visual language parsing. Unlike keyboard input, speech utterances, or hand gestures, graphical representations may represent an artifact whose creation is the object of the communication between the human user and the computer. Instead of being a means of communication, the graphical expression may be the goal of a creative or engineering enterprise. In this light, it may be useful to consider how higher-dimensional parsing methods can aid in the enterprise independently from the problem of 'interpreting' the expression.

Three areas that my collaborator and I have looked into are design assistance (Weitzmann and Wittenburg, 1993), generation-as-parsing for multimedia documents (Weitzmann and Wittenburg, 1996), and visual focusing for diagrams (Wittenburg and Weitzmann, 1997a; 1997b).

5.1   Design assistance

Weitzman and Wittenburg (1993) have suggested how higher-dimensional rules together with a bottom-up parser can recognize fragments in the visual language of the design application. Fragments being recognized can result in various actions to provide assistance.

In an example page layout design senario shown in Fig. 4, the grammar rules capture a particular graphic style and embody various layout conventions such as graphic rule bars above chapter titles and section headings; default font sizes and styles; and spacings for margins.

The interaction sequence begins with the user selecting primitive elements from a palette and adding them to the working space. In this example, there are four basic categories of input of type text, number, image, and graphic rule. As events proceed, the system interactively parses the input and makes suggestions to automatically form new composite structures and install various constraints. Typically, multiple graphical constraints are used to enforce the position and size relations between elements. Constraints may also make individual changes to elements (e.g., changing their color or font specification). Relationships can be defined so that the elements involved only roughly match the desired requirements. In this way, input can be loosely sketched and the application of the rules will clean up the input.

At the beginning of the sequence in Fig. 4, the user has added three basic elements: a text object, a number object, and an image object. On the right hand side of Fig. 4a-c is an agenda, which is a visual indication of design assistance actions that can be exercised. These are the result of the parser recognizing

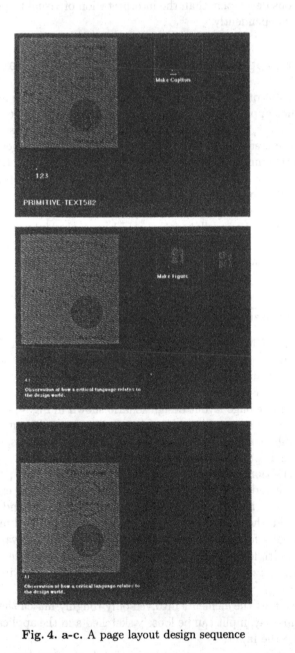

Fig. 4. a-c. A page layout design sequence

expressions in the input. In Fig. 4a, it can be noted that the number item is roughly above and left aligned to the text item. A pattern has been recognized that can lead to the automatic creation of a caption object. In Fig. 4b, this action has been excercised, and, in the process, the basic elements are left-aligned exactly and certain font styles are selected. Then this newly created caption object is added to the input and another fragment is recognized whose constituents are an image and a caption. The action to create a figure composite object is exercised, which results in constraints for left-alignment and certain marginal spacing arrangements.

The architecture for such design assistance parallels visual language interpretation. Obviously there is a different 'semantics'. Other than that, the primary difference has to do with the fact that a full interpretation, and thus a full parse, is not required, so there is a different interaction loop. This loop allows more flexibility to the user, which is appropriate in applications where suggestions and help are welcome but deviations from the norm are to be tolerated. In such an application, bottom-up parsing rather than syntax-directed editing is a requirement.

Similar functionality in the context of sketching with pen-based input has been suggested by Gross (1994), Landay and Myers (1995), and Kramer (1994), although none of them make use of grammar-based specification or parsing methods. Earlier work by Wittenburg et al. (1991) used a grammar-based framework to interpret pen-based input, but did not consider design support as an application.

5.2   Multimedia Document Generation

Another application area involves multimedia document generation. Weitzman and Wittenburg (1996) propose grammar-based methods for what they refer to as 'articulation' of electronic documents in heterogeneous environments. In the generation-as-parsing model, the input is abstract representations of content, and the output is forms for creating multimedia objects and their layout. Figures 5 and 6 illustrate one of the primary motivations for a system such as this. They are examples of realized output of the system.

The information is the same in the two figures but its presentation is not, motivated by differences in presentation resources available in the end-delivery environments. The design in Fig. 5 is appropriate for a large, high-resolution display; the one in Fig. 6 is appropriate for a small screen device, such as a hand-held digital assistant. Figure 6 displays just the first step of a complete repair procedure. As part of the presentation, the horizontal bar at the top of the page becomes an active object which controls the presentation of remaining elements. As the user interacts with the bar, information is presented temporally that is all laid out spatially in Fig. 5.

While designers could create each of these alternative designs individually by hand, the complexity of accommodating myriad variations in today's networked environments is enormous. The Weitzman/Wittenburg proposal is that the designers might be able to author a set of general realization rules using design

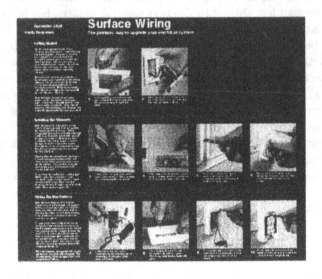

Fig. 5. A presentation for a large display

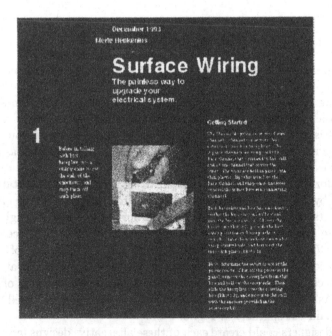

Fig. 6. A presentation for a small display

assistance technology such as was discussed in the last section. The architecture is shown in Fig. 7. Abstract content takes the form of objects and relations,

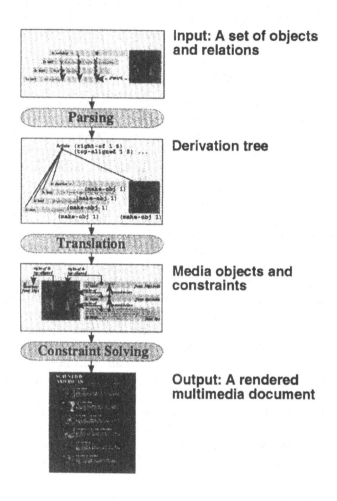

Fig. 7. System architecture

and could be held in a database. Rules include a syntax, i.e., a specification for matching against abstract content, and a semantics, i.e., a set of forms to define multimedia objects and layout constraints. Given the content as input together with parameters that define different environment conditions, higher-dimensional parsing is used to map to different abstract structures and different realization rules. Decompositions evident in the parse trees determine, for instance, different screens of information. A translation step employing attribute evaluation then produces forms for creation of media objects and temporal and spatial constraints that need to be satisfied. Constraint solving is then utilized to produce the final layout.

Brandenburg (1994) has a similar architecture for layout of hierarchically structured graphs in which he uses dynamic programming methods to control the search through alternative design solutions at each node of the derivation tree. He assumes classical attribution techniques, rather than general contraint solving, for the actual computation of values necessary for full layout specifications.

5.3 Hierarchical Aggregation

The last application area I will mention is one involving visualization of attributed graphs. As in the previous examples, a derivation tree is the starting point for providing useful services to the underlying application. Wittenburg and Weitzman (1997a; 1997b) have authored an application to support documentation and redesign of work process flows. Workflow models can be large and complex, and, just as with computer programming, good design entails decomposition into manageable chunks. For workflows, repeatable processes should be encapsulated so as to be reuseable in other parts of the models. Existing commercial flowgraph drawing tools standardly support the feature of hierarchically structured flowgraphs, where a single node in a graph can be expanded into another window, in which more detail is shown. However, these hierarchical structures must be assembled by hand and, once created, they are permanent. A feature offered in this tool is for users to be able to dynamically aggregate subgraphs in a larger graph through interactive parsing. The subgraphs can then be collapsed or expanded to suit visualization and modeling needs. This allows the creation of views of workflow processes that can span a large part of the relevant business domain but that nonethless contain a manageable level of detail. Figure 8a shows a subgraph that has been selected through interactive parsing. In Fig. 8b, the user has chosen to collapse that subgraph.

It is possible that higher-dimensional parsing techniques can be used in other information domains that can benefit from hierarchical aggregation. Sablowski and Frick (1997), for example, used a technique similar to graph grammar parsing to form hierarchical structures over World Wide Web link graphs.

6   Conclusion

This chapter has considered how higher-level grammars and parsing might contribute to visual modes of human-computer communication. The results so far have been mixed. It is not clear that visual parsing is actually necessary to interpret visual language expressions under the control of a Graphical User Interface. Nevertheless, there are potential benefits when/if more progress can be made on error-correction and incremental editing. The field really must agree on standard formalisms (Constraint Multiset Grammars is one candidate) as well as standard representations for input. The continuing proliferation of ill-understood variations on visual language formalisms is not helpful.

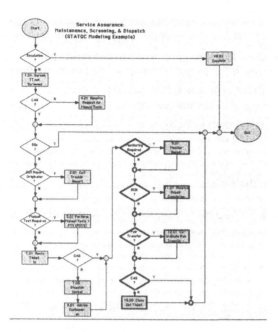

Fig. 8a

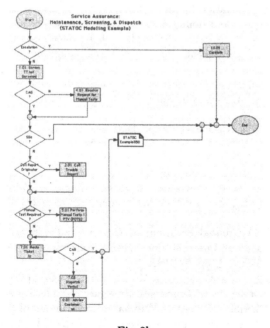

Fig. 8b

Fig. 8. Interactive parsing in support of visualization

I am more sanguine about the immediate prospects of higher-dimensional parsing for solving problems in other areas of visual communication. I mentioned the examples of design support, generation-as-parsing, and hierarchical composition in support of visual focusing and modeling. These techniques are one level removed from the basic interpretation processes. They are applicable once visual objects and relations are formed, which makes it possible for them to be used with GUIs as well as with pen-based systems or perhaps with other input devices such as data gloves or eye-tracking.

Acknowledgements

I am grateful to Kim Marriott, Bernd Meyer, and Franz Brandenburg for conversations on topics related to this paper.

References

Aho, A., and Johnson, S.C. (1974), Programming Utilities and Libraries – LR Parsing, *Computing Surveys, June 1994.*

Aho, A., Sethi, R., and Ullman, J. (1986), *Compilers: Principles, Techniques, and Tools*, Addison-Wesley.

Anderson, R.H. (1968), Syntax-Directed Recognition of Hand-Printed Two-Dimensional Mathematics. In *Interactive Systems for Experimental Applied Mathematics*, Klerer, M., and Reinfelds, J. (eds.), Academic Press.

Backlund, B., Hagsand, O., and Pehrson, B. (1990), Generation of Visual Language-oriented Design Environments, *Journal of Visual Languages and Computing 1*, pp. 333-354.

Baird, H. (1990), Industrial Applications. In *Syntactic and Structural Pattern Recognition: Theory and Applications*, Bunke, H. and Sanfeliu, A. (eds.), World Scientific, pp. 369-380.

Brandenburg, F. 1994. Designing Graph Drawings by Layout Graph Grammars. In *Graph Drawing: DIMACS International Workshop*, R. Tamassia and I.G. Tollis (eds.), Lecture Notes in Computer Science 894, Springer-Verlag, pp. 416-427.

Brandenburg, F. (1989), On Polynomial Time Graph Grammars. In *STACS 88: 5th Annual Symposium on Theoretical Aspects of Computer Science*, Goos, G., and Hartmanis, J. (eds.), Lecture Notes in Computer Science 294, Springer-Verlag, pp. 227-236.

Bunke, H. (1982), Attributed Programmed Graph Grammars and their Application to Schematic Diagram Interpretation, *IEEE Transactions on Pattern Analysis and Machine Intelligence 4*, pp. 574-582.

Chang, S.-K. (1988), The Design of a Visual Language Compiler. In *Proceedings of IEEE Workshop on Visual Languages*, Pittsburgh, Pennsylvania, USA, pp. 84-91.

Chok, S.S., and Marriott, K. (1995), Automatic Construction of User Interfaces from Constraint Multiset Grammars. In *Proceedings of IEEE Workshop on Visual Languages*, Darmstadt, Germany, pp. 90-98.

Costagliola, G., Tomita, M., and Chang, S.K. (1991), A Generalized Parser for 2-D Languages. In *Proceedings of IEEE Workshop on Visual Languages*, Kobe, Japan, pp. 98-104.

Cox, P.T., Giles, F.R., and Pietrzykowsky, T. (1989), Prograph: a step towards liberating programming from textual conditioning. In *Proceedings of IEEE Workshop on Visual Languages*, Rome, Italy.

Crimi, A., Guercio, A., Nota, G., Pacini, G., Tortora, G., and Tucci, M. (1991), Relation Grammars and their Application to Multi-dimensional Languages, *Journal of Visual Languages and Computing 2*, pp. 333-346.

Cuny, J. (1995), *Graph Grammars and Their Application to Computer Science: 5th International Workshop*, Williamsburg, Va, Usa, Springer-Verlag.

Fu, K.-S. (1974), *Syntactic Methods in Pattern Recognition*, Academic Press.

Golin, E., and Reiss, S. (1989), The Specification of Visual Language Syntax. In *Proceedings of IEEE Workshop on Visual Languages*, Rome, Italy, pp. 105-110.

Golin, E. (1991), Parsing Visual Languages with Picture Layout Grammars, *Journal of Visual Languages and Computing 2*, pp. 371-393.

Gross, M. (1994), Recognizing and Interpreting Diagrams in Design. In *Proceedings of Advanced Visual Interfaces (AVI)*, Catarci, T. Costabile, M., Levialdi, S., and Santucci, G. (eds).

Helm, R., and Marriott, K. (1991), A Declarative Specification and Semantics for Visual Languages, *Journal of Visual Languages and Computing 2*, pp. 311-331.

Jagadeesh, J. and Wang, Y. (1993), Labview, *Computer, February 1993*.

Joshi, A. (1985), Tree Adjoining Grammars: How Much Context-Sensitivity is Required to Provide Reasonable Structural Descriptions? In *Perspectives*, Dowty, D., Karttunen, L., and Zwicky, A. (eds.), Cambridge University Press, pp. 206-250.

Kahn, K. and Saraswat, V. (1990), Complete Visualizations of Concurrent Programs and their Executions. In *Proceedings of IEEE Workshop on Visual Languages*, Skokie, Illinois, USA, pp. 7-14.

Kramer, A. (1994), Translucent Patches–Dissolving Windows. In *Proceedings of the ACM Symposium on User Interface Software and Technology (UIST)*, pp. 121-130.

Landay, J. and Myers, B. (1995), Interactive Sketching for the Early Stages of User Interface Design. In Proceedings of ACM Conference on Human Factors in Computing (CHI), pp. 43-50.

Marriott, K. and Meyer, B. (1997), The CCMG Visual Language Hierarchy. In *Theory of Visual Languages*, Marriott, K. and Meyer, B. (eds.), Lecture Notes in Computer Science, Springer Verlag (in press).

Marriott, K., Meyer, B., and Wittenburg, K. (1997), Survey: Visual Language Specification and Recognition. In *Theory of Visual Languages*, Marriott, K. and Meyer, B. (eds.), Lecture Notes in Computer Science, Springer Verlag (in press).

Meyer, B. (1992), Pictures Depicting Pictures: On the Specification of Visual Languages by Visual Grammars. In *Proceedings of IEEE Workshop on Visual Languages*, Seattle, Washington, USA, pp. 41-47.

Minas, M. and Viehstaedt, G. (1995), DiaGen: A Generator for Diagram Editors Providing Direct Manipulation and Execution of Diagrams. In *Proceedings of IEEE Workshop on Visual Languages*, Darmstadt, Germany.

Nagl, M. (1983), Bibliography on Graph Rewriting Systems (Graph Grammars), *Bulletin of European Association of Theoretical Computer Science 20* (Austria), pp. 114-148.

Pineda, L. (1992), Reference, Synthesis and Constraint Satisfaction, *Eurographics 11*, pp. C333-C344.

Rekers, J. (1994), On the Use of Graph Grammars forDefining the Syntax of Graphical Languages. In *Proceedings of Colloquium on Graph Transformation and its Application in Computer Science*, Palma de Mallorca, Spain.

Rosenfeld, A. (1990), Array, Tree, and Graph Grammars. In *Syntactic and Structural Pattern Recognition: Theory and Applications*, Bunke, H. and Sanfeliu, A. (eds.), Singapore: World Scientific.

Sablowski, R. and Frick, A. (1997), Automatic Graph Clustering. In *Graph Drawing: Symposium on Graph Drawing GD '96*, North, S. (ed.), Berkeley, California, USA, Lecture Notes in Computer Science 1190, Springer-Verlag, pp. 4395-400.

Shaw, A.C. (1969), A Formal Picture Description Scheme as a Basis for Picture Processing Systems, *Information and Control 14*, pp. 9-52.

Soiffer, N.M. (1991), *The Design of a User Interface for Computer Algebra Systems*, Ph.D. Thesis, University of California at Berkeley.

Telelogic (1997), http://www.telelogic.se.

Üsküdarli, S. and Dinesh, T.B. (1995), Towards a visual programming environment generator for algebraic specifications. In *IEEE Symposium on Visual Languages*, Darmstadt, Germany.

Wahlster, W. (1991), User and Discourse Models for Multimodal Communication. In *Intelligent User Interfaces*, Sullivan, J.W. and Tyler, S.W. (eds.), ACM Press, pp. 45-67.

Weimer, D. and Ganapathy, S.K. (1992), Interaction Techniques Using Hand Tracking and Speech Recognition. In *Multimedia Interface Design*, Blattner, M.H. and Dannenberg, R.B. (eds.), ACM Press, pp. 109-126.

Weitzman, L. and Wittenburg, K. (1993), Relational Grammars for Interactive Design. In *Proceedings of IEEE Symposium on Visual Languages*, Bergen, Norway, pp. 4-11.

Weitzman, L., and Wittenburg, K. (1994), Automatic Generation of Multimedia Documents Using Relational Grammars. In *Proceedings of ACM Multimedia 94*, San Francisco, California, USA, pp. 443-451.

Weitzman, L. and Wittenburg, K. (1996), Grammar-based Articulation for Multimedia Document Design, *Multimedia Systems 4*, pp. 99-111.

Wittenburg, K., Weitzman, L., and Talley, J. (1991), Unification-Based Grammars and Tabular Parsing for Graphical Languages, *Journal of Visual Languages and Computing 2*, pp. 347-370.

Wittenburg, K. (1992), Earley-style Parsing for Relational Grammars. In *Proceedings of IEEE Workshop on Visual Languages*, Seattle, Wa., USA, pp. 192-199.

Wittenburg, K. (1996), Predictive Parsing for Unordered Relational Languages. In *Recent Advances in Parsing Technologies*, Bunt, H. and Tomita, M. (eds.), Kluwer, pp. 389-411.

Wittenburg, K. and Weitzman, L. (1997a), Qualitative Visualization of Processes: Attributed Graph Layout and Focusing Techniques. In *Graph Drawing: Symposium on Graph Drawing GD '96*, North, S. (ed.), Berkeley, California, USA, Lecture Notes in Computer Science 1190, Springer-Verlag, pp. 401-408.

Wittenburg, K. and Weitzman, L. (1997b), Relational Grammars: Theory and Practice in a Visual Language Interface for Process Modeling. In *Theory of Visual Languages, Lecture Notes in Computer Science*, Marriott, K. and Meyer, B. (eds.), Springer Verlag (in press).

Wolfram, S. (1996), *The Mathematica Book*, Cambridge University Press.

Anaphora in Multimodal Discourse

John Lee and Keith Stenning

Human Communication Research Centre, University of Edinburgh
2, Buccleuch Place, Edinburgh EH8 9LW, Scotland, UK
john@cogsci.ed.ac.uk

Abstract. The question is addressed whether the linguistic phenomenon of anaphora exists in multimodal dialogue. Anaphora is contrasted with deixis and ellipsis as being an essentially co-referential phenomenon; it is argued that existing discussions in the areas of HCI and presentation generation, e.g. by Singer and Wahlster, have failed to demonstrate multimodal anaphora. This is argued to be because the 'token-referential' nature of graphics (as opposed to the 'type-referential' nature of language) means that identification and predication can't be separated; hence graphics tends to be 'unfocussed', and re-identification of refeerents for further predication does not happen.

1 Introduction

This chapter seeks to clarify some of the issues concerning the phenomenon of anaphora in natural language, and its extension to multimodal discourse and dialogue. The literature on human-computer interaction (HCI), in particular, contains a number of examples where the concept of anaphora has been applied to graphical expressions, and to the relation between graphical and linguistic expressions, in ways which sometimes do not relate clearly to the issues underlying the uses of the term in linguistics.

The general question that needs to be confronted is what the use would be of speaking of cross-modal anaphora; i.e. what theoretical utility could be derived from the analogy with language implied by the term. In linguistics, it is intended to pick out a set of phenomena that support interesting generalisations. They are all coreferential cases; they often have certain constraints concerning e.g. gender and animacy of the coreferring expressions; they may relate particularly to the claims of a theory, such as Chomsky's 'government and binding' structures. Even here it can be difficult to decide whether a relationship is best accounted for by such quasi-syntactic issues, or whether it should be treated as resulting from an inference based on semantic and pragmatic information about some situation. In the final analysis, it may in fact appear that anaphora is simply a subclass of cases of reference-assignment which it is wholly artificial and ultimately pointless to single out. This conclusion would be strongly resisted in linguistics, and perhaps with good reason, but is not so clearly resistible in multimodal contexts.

Although anaphora is often discussed in the context of *discourse*, we believe that this is an important first step to understanding the issues at play in the wider context of *dialogue*; and indeed some of the examples we discuss can be seen as essentially interactive.

We begin by outlining the concept of anaphora in language, and then consider some possibilities for extending it. The emphasis is on assessing the theoretical utility of such extensions. Finally, we consider some more abstract ideas about the underlying basis of coreference in language and other modalities.

2   Anaphora in Linguistic Discourse

The phenomenon of anaphora, as traditionally described in linguistic contexts, has to do with the identification of the referents of referring expressions. Paradigmatically, it arises when two or more expressions co-refer, as when an entity first referred to by name is subsequently referred to by using a pronoun, as in the following example (1), which might relate to some scenario in a Western film.

(1)   a. Fred fired the gun.
       b. Then he turned and ran.

In this case, the referent of *he* in (b) is taken to be the same as the referent of *Fred*, which noun is for that reason said to be the antecedent of the pronoun. Anaphora may be inter-sentential, as in (1), or intra-sentential, as in (2).

(2)   Fred was his own worst enemy.

Sometimes it's possible to take advantage of ellipsis, which occurs when a referring expression is left out altogether and recovered from the context, as in (3), where there is no anaphoric element.

(3)   Fred fired the gun, then turned and ran.

(We are speaking here only of noun-phrase ellipsis: in other cases, a verb phrase or other non-referential expression may be elided instead.)

If a pronoun has a referent which is not referred to earlier in the discourse, it's not taken to be anaphoric. Typically, the reference is secured by some sort of indexical relationship with something in the non-linguistic context, in many cases indicated e.g. by an accompanying pointing action (which is known as *deixis*). Thus (1b) can have a non-anaphoric reading, where *he* refers deictically to someone other than Fred.

Even where a pronoun is taken to be anaphoric, it can easily be ambiguous, e.g. as in (4b) *he* might be either Fred or Bill, since either (4c) or (4d) might consistently follow.

(4)   a. Fred fired the gun at Bill.
       b. He turned and ran ...
       c. ... but Bill chased him.
       d. ... but Fred got him with a second shot.

But in some cases, especially reflexives, coreferentiality seems to be syntactically guaranteed, as in (5).

(5)   Fred shot himself.

Notice that not all pronouns behave the same way in similar syntactic contexts. Whereas in (1b) *he* might just be a deictic reference to someone not previously mentioned, in (6b) *it* has to be anaphoric (to *the gun*), even though we can easily imagine a situation where something else which was hit by the shot happened to fall. (Of course, we assume here that there's no discourse previous to (6) containing a possible antecedent for *it*.) *It* cannot be interpreted deictically, at least not in this case, but perhaps not ever. Contrast this with (7).

(6)   a. Fred fired the gun.
       b. It fell to the floor, smoking.
(7)   a. Fred fired the gun.
       b. He fell to the floor, gasping.

In cases such as where (8a) is followed by either (8b) or (8c), the *it* is either anaphoric to something such as the entire action or situation (at least if we take the verb as providing a reference to an action), or else it has a conventionally indeterminate reference and is not clearly either anaphoric or deictic.

(8)   a. Fred fired the gun.
       b. It seemed a good idea at the time.
       c. It was raining at the time.

In some cases the coreference relation is more difficult to describe. In cases like (9), we might want to say that the pronoun refers to one of the guns implied, taken as an arbitrary example to show what was done with all of them.

(9)   Each man pulled out a gun, firing it wildly.

These cases are especially associated with conditionals and universally quantified sentences, where a set of similar entities is posited and the anaphor may be taken to identify as referent any particular one we may choose to consider, or alternatively the whole set, as in (10).

(10)   The men pulled out guns, firing them wildly.

Referring expressions other than pronouns may also be considered anaphoric in appropriate circumstances. In (11b), we'd tend to suppose that *the fool* referred back to Fred, whereas in (11c) *the weapon* would be the gun.

(11)   a. Fred fired the gun.
        b. The fool was obviously drunk.
        c. The weapon was wreathed in smoke.

There's a subtle difference between this and (12), on which basis it is generally held that *the trigger* in (12b) is *not* to be considered anaphoric. No expression which *corefers* has occurred in the preceding discourse.

(12)   a. Fred fired the gun.
       b. The trigger was rather stiff.

Even though *the trigger* is conceptually related to *the gun*, there's no real reference relationship between the two, and so the example should not be considered anaphoric any more than should (13).

(13)   a. Fred fired the gun.
       b. The bank manager fell to the floor.

A question that arises is whether there is sufficient reason to distinguish between (11), (12) and (13) in a theoretical account, or whether all of these are based in a similar way on inferences from general knowledge about the features of situations such as the one described and its constituent objects and actions. Then coreference relations would emerge as independent of syntactic considerations.

In summary, in anaphora in a linguistic discourse, a usually 'reduced' *expression* takes its meaning (reference or sense) by being identifiably related to another fuller *expression* (or one with a clearer referent) and thereby inheriting some of the 'identification' of referent/sense achieved by that fuller expression. Generally, except in very specific syntactic circumstances (known as 'cataphora'), the fuller expression precedes the following reduced one. It can become hard to distinguish cases in which the interpretation of the whole preceding discourse, and background knowledge, provides the context in which the 'reduced' expression is interpreted (and interpretable) from cases in which there is a single preeminent antecedent *expression*; and then the notion of 'anaphora' as such becomes less clearly useful. One possible way of thinking about this is that expressions sometimes 'point' into the text, sometimes into the discourse structure, and sometimes into the world. In beginning here to examine how studying multimodal communication can contribute to understanding these issues, we seek first to establish whether the specific notion of anaphora, which seems to be usefully distinguishable in analysis of language, can bear similar weight in treating multimodality. In particular, we consider the case of graphics.

3   Can There Be 'Graphora'?

So can there be *graphical* anaphora? What's central to anaphora, on the above view, is that two (or more) different expressions in the same discourse corefer. So graphical anaphora might exist if we can make sense of the notion of a graphical discourse, and if different graphical expressions can corefer. Similarly, graphical and textual referents might stand in anaphoric relationships in multimodal discourse. One could say this of e.g. a picture showing Fred firing a gun at Bill, with (14) as caption or accompanying remark, where the coreference relations seem obvious.

(14)   The idiot nearly killed him.

But are the relations anaphoric or something else (e.g. deictic)? There's something much more odd about accompanying that picture with a sentence such as (15).

(15)   Then it fell to the ground, smoking.

This, as a piece of communicative discourse, is different from a book illustration, which one can also imagine, showing the gun in mid-air with (15) as caption, being a sentence that also occurs somewhere in the text.

The issue here is perhaps one of focus: drawings are not good in general at establishing focus; one needs artificial conventions, or the use of a sequence. The apparent possibility of a sequence of pictures which establish the gun clearly as focus, followed intelligibly by (15), may seem to show that cross-modal anaphora can occur, given that *it* cannot be deictic: one couldn't use *it* deictically in the context of a picture, any more than in the presence of the actual gun. However, even this isn't completely clear, since there is a general use of *it*, which is nether anaphoric nor in the usual sense deictic, but gets its reference somehow from a contextual focussing which seems especially common in dialogue, e.g (16).

(16)   A: What's the problem?
        B: [fiddling with his computer] It's not working.

Here the context is so clear as to make almost plausible an analysis of A's question as containing a suppressed "... *with that computer*", thus supplying an antecedent for B's *it*. Similarly, in the presence of the gun, simply to say *It's loaded* is to secure reference. All the same, we resist a deictic analysis here on the grounds that deixis inherently involves *explicit selection*, which in these kinds of cases is rendered unnecessary by the clarity of the context.[1]

The possibility of purely graphical anaphora remains still more obscure, since there are few cases in which it's clear that the interpretation of a depiction depends on some other depiction. It's a distinctive feature of anaphoric phenomena that reference is established *through* coreference, i.e. coreference doesn't simply result from two expressions being *independently* established (e.g. by deixis etc.) as referring to the same thing. It needs to be the case that a contextual relationship exists between expressions in virtue of which one as it were inherits the referent of the other. In graphics as such there are two problems with this: on the one hand we cannot find clear-cut cases where these conditions are met, and on the other it is not apparent that even if we could there would still be a strong analogy to linguistic cases. It is certain that 'graphical reference'[2] sometimes

---

[1] Speculatively, one can note that even though a pointing action may be explicitly involved in the 'computer' example, there's a clear difference from saying *This isn't working*, which is reflected in spoken stress: *it* is unstressed, whereas a normal deictic expression, even a pronoun used deictically, is stressed. This quasi-deictic *it* perhaps occurs only in speech (or directly reported speech). A similar class of cases arises with other pronouns, e.g. where a secretary arrives at work to be told by another "*He's in a foul mood today*" — meaning, of course, the boss.

[2] Even this is a fraught notion; we mean here something like the relation of *depiction*.

requires contextual linking to some other picture element with a clearer reference (Schier, 1986, has an instructive discussion of how seemingly clear pictorial elements can be completely uninterpretable out of context), but this doesn't normally appear to be any kind of *co*-reference.

An example worth considering is the use of schematic depictions of repeated components, e.g. in architectural drawings, where there is one occurrence given in full detail which acts as contextually-accessed pointer to the full reference. (It may of course be encountered later in one's viewing of the drawing, hence being possibly analogous to either cataphora or anaphora.) Even here, though, it's not clear that the bare referent of the schematic depiction (as opposed to the full description of the referent) could not be recovered without the existence of the detail — and it looks as though the 'antecedent', although it gives the *type* of the referent we are interested in, does not point to the *individual* in a way that seems characteristic in the linguistic examples.

In multimodal contexts, the idea of anaphoric relations holding between expressions in different modes has attained a certain degree of currency. Here, we examine some examples of this, to see how the phenomena in question relate to the kinds of linguistic cases of which they are being treated as analogues.

Wahlster et al. (1991, pp. 21-22) discuss some examples which they describe as involving anaphora between graphics and language. These are of two kinds. In the first, pictures (generally diagrams of a coffee machine) are accompanied by texts like those reproduced as (17) and (18).

(17)   a. The machine is running.
        b. The on/off switch was turned on.
(18)   a. Fig. 3 provides a survey.
        b. The on/off switch ...

In terms of the above discussion, these do not appear anaphoric. What happens is that reference (*not* coreference) is established by context and/or the use of background knowledge. (17) is very similar to (12) in involving no coreferring element, though having a clearring element, though having a clear conceptual link. The argument for (18), if one were given, would have to be along the lines that the picture referred to in (18a) itself forms part of the discourse, perhaps (18a*/*), and it includes an element depicting the switch that is then anaphorically coreferred to by the expression *the on/off switch* in (18b). We return later to discuss why we are unsatisfied by such an argument.

Wahlster et al. (loc. cit.) also discuss an example concerning a 'metagraphical arrow', which points from the textual annotation *"Water outlet"* to a particular item in the picture of a coffee machine (depicting the water outlet). The arrow is said to be "the equivalent of a pronoun, since it focuses attention on a specific part of the visual antecedent". However, in terms of the above discussion, the idea that such an arrow is somehow analogous to a pronoun seems strained. There's no sense in which the arrow itself is a referring expression of any kind. In fact, it seems much more persuasively to resemble simply a deictic pointer whose role is to focus attention on a specific part of the visual context (whether this is antecedent being perhaps dependent on reading strategy). The arrow combined with text is straightforwardly analogous to a finger combined with speech. (It could be redundant if the text were positioned carefully, but then I don't have to point if I say *"this is my office"* while standing in it.) However, the point about focus is critical, and we shall return to this also.

The idea that anaphora might appear in graphical *interaction*, in the absence of language, has been proposed, for example, by Singer (1990), who discusses firstly some standard Macintosh programs such as *MacDraw*, and then a system of his own design. In our view, Singer's argument fails to persuade that the concept of anaphora sheds light on his examples, though there remains room to investigate whether other kinds of examples might leave space for a more convincing argument.

According to Singer, a dialogue with *MacDraw* is making use of anaphora when, e.g. one selects an object and then applies an operation (such as *filling* it with a pattern) from a pull-down menu. The idea is that this sequence of actions parallels a natural language discourse in which one refers somehow to the object and then says, e.g.: *Fill* **it** *black*. (Similarly, one can select a set of objects, in which case the parallel is *Fill* **them** *black*.) We suggest that this 'translation' of the user's dialogue with the program is unsupportable, since there is nothing that fills the role of the anaphor (*it* or *them*). One might at least as plausibly suggest a very natural translation (if with rather un-English word order) as, e.g., *This fill black*, or even *This fill with this pattern*, or any of a number of similar possibilities which capture other aspects of the interaction such as the indexical character of graphical selection. The notion of *coreference*, for example, is doing no work at all here.

Singer goes on to discuss *MacPaint* in similar terms which, although this may represent something of a digression from the main theme of the present paper, allows us to note a point of some importance for interfaces generally. Singer characterises the 'Lasso' and 'Selection' tools in *MacPaint* as being ways of referring to existing objects, as in *MacDraw*; but this is misleading because *MacPaint* is (paradigmatically) a painting tool based on the notion of a bitmap, whereas *MacDraw* is an object-oriented drawing program. The significance of this apparently pedantic distinction arises from the fact that pure painting programs have no data types other than areas of bitmap, and consequently these are all that it makes sense to speak of a user of such a program as *referring to* in the interface dialogue. The 'Selection' tool, described by Singer as limited in referring only to rectangular objects, in fact cannot even do that: it can only define arbitrary rectangles of bitmap which at best gratuitously coincide with something the user regards as an 'object'. Even the 'Lasso' tool, which constricts itself around non-blank areas, will only identify an 'object' if the object is a discrete non-blank area (not e.g. overlapping another 'object'). These observations are a digression in as much as Singer might hold that his point is made even if the anaphoric reference is simply to an area of screen; but the discrepancy between this and his 'translation' of the discourse into natural language emphasises the problems of such translations, and in particular that what counts as a reference to what may be very unclear.

Singer goes on to describe his own system, known as *Circuit*, which provides interactions concerning an electrical circuit diagram. These interactions are said to mirror phenomena of anaphora and ellipsis in natural language. In a typical example, the diagram is displayed along with buttons labelled "amps", "volts" and "ohms" (Fig. 1).

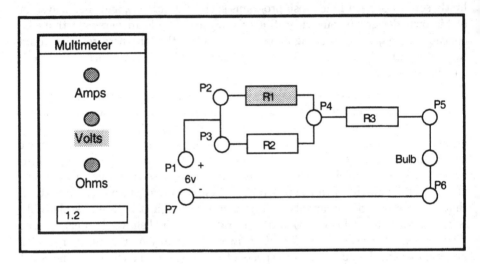

Fig. 1. A typical *Circuit* display (simplified; after Singer 1990)

Components in the circuit, e.g. resistors, can be graphically selected[3] — this equates to referring to them, so that selecting R1 and pressing the "volts" button amounts to asking (19).

(19)   What is the voltage across R1?

Then pressing the "ohms" button is held to be equivalent to saying (20); and then (21) is obtained by pressing the "amps" button.

(20)   What about *its* resistance?
(21)   And *its* current?

Although it's clear here that there is anaphora in the proposed natural language 'translation', it's completely unclear why this translation is proposed.

---

[3] When selected, they become highlighted and remain so until deselected.

Since R1 remains visible and highlighted throughout, the translation for (20) might just as well be (22)[4].

(22)   What is the resistance across R1?

The central characteristic of linguistic anaphora — the need to derive reference through context from a coreferring and typically different antecedent — is completely lacking here, and so it is not at all evident what contribution can be made to the discussion of the example by importing the linguistic concept. An analysis of the example in terms of, say, a persistent form of deixis, seems at least as compelling (cf. the *MacDraw* example). Some notion of anaphora might be more plausibly involved if R1 became unhighlighted, or the diagram disappeared altogether. But this would be gratuitously to introduce a problematic phenomenon into a situation where it is simpler to avoid it. Some of the confusion here would seem to result from emphasising too greatly the *sequence* of interaction *events* (and treating it rather as a linguistic string) while actually *ignoring* the information present in the graphics.

We conclude that Singer has shown at most that graphically-mediated dialogues can achieve communicational results that might have exploited anaphora to appear naturally in language. This is scarcely surprising, since almost any natural multisentence discourse in natural language is likely to involve anaphora and/or deixis and ellipsis. It falls far short of sustaining Singer's claims that "[g]raphical interfaces ... allow the user to express some types of discourse phenomena more easily than is possible in a NL interface" (p. 79), and that "graphical treatment of NL is feasible" (p. 94), since there is no real basis for claiming that clearly analogous discourse phenomena are actually arising or being treated. It may simply have been shown that the sort of sophisticated discourse processing which natural language depends on is just not required in these cases where graphical support is available[5].

4   Why Is There No 'Graphora'?

If our review of the phenomena is correct in concluding that there is no very persuasive case for the existence of multimodal anaphora, we may ask why this should be. Is it simply that extended multimodal discourse is uncommon enough

---

[4] Or for that matter, simply *What about resistance?*, or even just *Resistance?* — if one ignores the diagram, there is nothing to play the role of the pronoun; but in the diagram there is no 'pro-'aspect to any analogue of a referring expression.

[5] Indeed, it's *possible* in some of these cases to use a more telegraphic form of language, which involves no anaphora as such but hence does not help us greatly to understand that particular class of discourse phenomena. This is not to say that we find Singer's defence of the idea that graphics can 'handle' *ellipsis* — based on proposed translations of various manipulations of Macintosh windows — to be any more persuasive than his analyses using the concept of anaphora. There also seems to be no clear or principled difference between the types of graphical phenomena he translates in these different terms.

that conventions have not yet arisen? This hardly seems likely since, as has been argued elsewhere (Neilson and Lee 1994), discourse is probably more often and more primitively multimodal than purely linguistic. If the reason is not lack of opportunity, then what is it?

We believe that an outline answer to this question is quite revealing of fundamental characteristics of the two modalities of graphics and language. We now attempt to sketch an explanation.

One fundamental is that, in establishing reference, anaphora is involved with relating the content of a communicative expression to an existing state of knowledge. We tend to take this view even of a situation where the existing knowledge is perhaps only accepted very tentatively and perhaps has been only very recently acquired, e.g. in the previous sentence of a discourse. The view is not uncommon in linguistic treatments, being essentially that processing of discourse involves the incremental construction of a *discourse model* representing the current state of knowledge about the immediate context. (Note that this model is distinct from, though in various ways perhaps related to, 'background knowledge' about the general domain of discourse and other things.) Hence establishing coreference for an expression is typically concerned with establishing whether it refers to an entity already in the model, and if so which, or whether it introduces a new entity. If an existing entity is being referred to, this is usually for a specific purpose such as to add new information about it, or give a new instruction concerning it, etc. — and this much is common with e.g. Singer.

We can see that in practical terms the establishing of coreference depends a good deal on what kind of access can be supported to the current discourse model state. Where a dialogue, say, is being conducted entirely over the telephone, or a discourse entirely in unillustrated text, there is no way to establish the reference of an expression other than through its relations to previous expressions, or to things in the world which are directly named or described. Where, on the other hand, a system for *external representation* is available to both participants in a dialogue, it may be used to maintain persistent information about their discourse, which in turn may function as an auxiliary representation of (part of) the discourse model.

Obviously, any dynamic use of graphics is likely to play this kind of role. While a discourse model in language is a purely conceptual structure, it may have in graphical or pther physical contexts a partial physical counterpart, and hence reference can be secured by a combination of physical and linguistic means. This gives rise to the familiar use of deixis, which secures reference for language in graphical and other contexts; many phenomena which establish reference are, however, much more subtle than the paradigm cases of rather overt deixis. As observed by Neilson and Lee (1994), a complex process of inference, often bringing in background knowledge, seems to be required to account for many of the referential relations that arise in multimodal dialogue.

Given a view of this sort, it is natural to suppose that anaphora as such (i.e. the fairly precise phenomenon considered in linguistics) fails to arise in many cases where graphics is present, simply because it isn't necessary to establish coreference by the same means. And equally, where various kinds of direct-manipulation interfaces are available (as in Singer), there will be phenomena which make more or less use of the graphical context, and hence may need mechanisms respectively less or more like those found in language[6], and so may more or less closely resemble anaphora.

It needs to be noted, of course, that the mere *persistence* of an external representation is not sufficient to establish its role as being different from that of language. Written text is usually persistent, but nonetheless entirely linguistic (unless it is illustrated). The graphic serves as a representation that still needs to be related to some ongoing linearised flow of communicative expressions. Some considerations about anaphora arise from this, that relate to the distinctions between graphics and language and help to indicate at a very basic level why graphics functions differently from text.

A useful distinction between the semantic character of graphics and language is that between *type-* and *token*-referential systems[7]. In a type-referential system, such as most languages, occurrences of tokens of the same type of expression (e.g. the same word) constitute recurring references to the same entity. In a token-referential system, occurrences of multiple tokens of the same type indicate references to distinct entities (usually sharing some property denoted by their type)[8]. So distinct tokens of the pawn 'icon' on a diagram of a chess board each refer to distinct pawns, whereas in language we would have to invent distinct names (types) and call them e.g. *Pawn-1, Pawn-2* etc.

For anaphora to arise, a type-referential system is required, because multiple occurrences of *related types of expression* (such as repetitions of *he*, and even *Fred* and *he*, which must minimally be masculine singular designators) must refer to the same entity. In a token referential system a single occurrence of a token icon in a given place represents everything that is represented about that individual. A recurrence of the same type of token elsewhere (or something we conventionally recognised as a 'reduced' form of the same type) would automatically signal a self-sufficient reference to another individual.

This explains why the nearest examples of anaphora within a graphic which we have come up with (e.g., in the 'reduced detail' repeated window on an architect's drawing suggested above) are closer to 'anaphora of sense' than to anaphora of reference: *co-reference* can fundamentally not occur in a fully token-referential system, where there can be only one token for each referent.

It also explains why the nearest examples to anaphora of reference are cartoon-strips where there is at least the possibility of construing the repeated reference to a character by an icon recurring in successive frames as type-referential. But it

---

[6] Cf. the parallel between language and streams of interaction events considered e.g. by Lee and Zeevat (1990).

[7] We owe this terminology to John Etchemendy (personal communication).

[8] Note that this characterisation is somewhat approximate and strictly holds at best only within a specific context, since types such as pronouns (*he* etc.) refer to different individuals in different contexts, and of course proper names often do so as well.

also explains why such examples are better analysed as re-references by the same icon, like re-using a name — there are no conventions for establishing 'sketchy' versions of characters in later frames as pointing to fuller antecedents in earlier frames. The job of a pronoun (for instance) is simply to secure reference to something already given, so that new predications can be made; but this is in a situation, in linguistic discourse, where the emphasis is on the incremental construction of a representation rather than the extraction of information from an already existing graphic. In the case of cartoon-strips, the problem of distinguishing given from new and determining what is predicated in each succeeding picture is something very different, almost the inverse of what happens in combining the information from a sequence of sentences. Our architectural-drawing example would have much more the character of anaphora if it appeared in a cartoon-strip showing, say, a sequence of operations to be applied to a given window, where perhaps only the most relevant parts of it were detailed, than in the single picture where it is clear that different individual windows are meant.

Another way of putting the point we have made here is to note that anaphora requires a certain separation between identification and predication. The paradigm case is one in which a noun phrase (NP) successfully refers in a first occurrence (and lets something else be predicated of its referent) whilst a following pronoun, which wouldn't have succeeded without the occurrence of the NP, then 'reidentifies' the same thing (and allows yet further information to be predicated of it).

A corollary of their token-referential nature, there is no distinction between identifying properties and predicated properties in a token referential system. A diagram showing a pawn on king's bishop four may tell us where a certain piece is, or which piece is in a certain place, but there is no real distinction between these informational perspectives because the representation is not 'focussed'. In language, it is of course possible for different hearers to be in different informational positions with regard to utterances, so that *John is tall* may tell us about John's height, or about which person is called John, but the point is that the sentence is focussed from the first information perspective, not the second. (Compare *The tall one is John*, which throws the focus the other way.)

This issue returns us to consideration of the Wahlster examples. We agreed in the case of the 'metagraphical arrow' that the focussing function was critical, and the graphic creates a focus in the sense that one can easily see what part of the diagram is most relevant compared to other things that might be present in the same diagram. But this notion of focus appears rather different from the concept of 'discourse focus' that relates to informational perspective, which here remains unclear. If the water outlet were in this sense focussed, it would be natural to read the diagram as saying *"the water outlet is to be found here on the machine"*, whereas otherwise it might more naturally be read *"this part of the machine is the water outlet*. The arrow does nothing to discriminate between these. In the other Wahlster example (18), on the other hand, neither kind of focus can be established simply by the picture, and hence we do not see it as a convincing way to introduce an antecedent for *The on/off switch*.

We can also rethink Singer's *Circuit* example in this context, by relating it to a certain approach in the treatment of language. Some of the phenomena of natural languages, treated under the label 'iconicity' by linguists, can be thought of as arising when some aspects of the structure of a represented situation correspond not to the *semantic* relations, but to the *syntactic* relations in a linguistic expression. Roughly, imposing an abstract syntax that differentiates identification and attribution functions (which, as we have seen, is required in type-referential systems) means that although semantic abstraction becomes possible, it becomes impossible to avoid assuming a specific information perspective. A language allows us to leave many semantic relations unspecified, but syntactic categories are now obligatory. We must partition material into subject and predicate, and this enforces a partitioning into given and new information (see Haiman, 1985, especially the paper by Givón).

In the context of this theoretical analysis, the Singer example can be re-assessed. His control panel has to be separated into two sub-diagrams: one consisting of a circuit diagram, and one consisting of the function buttons. The presence of a box around the buttons makes the structure more salient, but is not necessary: the fact that these are not a unitary diagram is attested to by the heterogeneity of interpretation found *across* the sub-diagrams. The fact that the "ohms" button is found to the left of the resistor R1 is not interpreted to mean that R1's resistance is to the left of R1. There is no interpretation of the spatial relations between sub-diagrams, whereas spatial and topological relations within the diagram of the circuit are interpreted. Notice that the possibility of contextual determination of 'reference' in a stream of mouse clicks is the result of segregating the identifying and predicating functions into these two semantic spaces. Just as the syntax of language provides for nouns, verbs, pronouns and other syntactic categories that have distinct functions, so the framework of Singer's system provides a 'syntax' for the sequences of mouse-clicks that it supports, with the same parallelism of syntactic and semantic categories that provides for compositionality in language. A graphical interaction 'sentence' can be taken as predicating the property — resistance, current borne, etc. — of the resistor referred to in the earlier click (cf. also the sequences of mouse events considered in Lee and Zeevat, op. cit.). In linguistic terms this might be ellipsis, rather than anaphora. However, there remains the extra-linguistic factor, potentially crucial in processing terms, that reference continues to be indicated by persistent highlighting[9].

While streams of mouse clicks have a typically closer, and obviously deictically-mediated, relationship to a graphical context than does natural language, their tendency to exhibit linearity, token-referentiality and focus phenomena take them a long way towards the linguistic end of the communication spectrum, and indicate why we may expect to find in them more linguistic features resembling anaphora, ellipsis, etc. In this sense, we support some of the spirit of

---

[9] Cf. footnote 5.

Singer's examples, but we do not find the relationships between the phenomena of natural language and these examples, or the others we have found, to be at all simple or direct.

5   Concluding Note

The above theoretical sketch is related to an extended analysis of semantic differences between graphical and linguistic modalities (Stenning, Inder and Neilson, 1995). There the distinction between type and token referential systems is founded in an analysis of how graphical systems, which interpret directly and exhaustively a rich variety of representing relations, enforce the expression of information. Languages which only give interpretation to one spatial/temporal relation (concatenation) and then only mediated through an abstract syntax, cancel these information enforcements. That this analysis can motivate practical analyses of graphical interaction is an indication of the contribution that natural language semantics can make to the understanding of multimodal and multimedia communication. In arguing that anaphora is an essentially linguistic phenomenon we are arguing for a deeper application of semantic concepts, not for their irrelevance. It is also possible that the multimodal perspective could deepen the linguistic analysis of anaphora, by helping to show which cases are best seen as very general processes of discourse context, and which are due to particular mechanisms operating on the linguistic surface.

References

Haiman, J (ed.) (1990) *Iconicity in Syntax*. Amsterdam: John Benjamin.

Lee, J. and Zeevat, H. (1990) Integrating natural language and graphics in dialogue. In D. Diaper, D. Gilmore, G. Cockton and B. Shackel (eds.) *Human Computer Interaction* – INTERACT '90, Amsterdam: North-Holland Elsevier, 479–484.

Neilson, I. and Lee, J. (1994). Conversations with graphics: implications for the design of natural language/graphics interfaces. *International Journal of Human-Computer Studies*, 40, 509–541.

Schier, F. (1986) *Deeper into Pictures*, Cambridge, UK: Cambridge University Press.

Singer, R. A. (1990) Graphical treatment of anaphora and ellipsis within intelligent tutoring systems. *Journal of Artificial Intelligence in Education*, 2, 79–97.

Stenning, K., Inder, R. and Neilson, I. (1995) Applying semantic concepts to analysing media and modalities. In G. Glasgow, N. H.Narayanan, and B. Chandrasekaran (eds.) *Diagrammatic Reasoning: Computational and Cognitive Perspectives*, Cambridge, MA: AAAI/MIT Press, 303–338.

Wahlster, W., André., E, Finkler, W., Graf, W., and Rist, T. (1991) Designing illustrated text: how language production is influenced by graphic generation. Technical Memo RR-91-05. Saarbrücken: Deutsches Forschungszentrum für Künstliche Intelligenz.

Speakers' Responses to Requests for Repetition in a Multimedia Language Processing Environment

Laurel Fais, Kyung-ho Loken-Kim and Young-Duk Park*

ATR Interpreting Telecommunications Res. Labs.
2-2 Hikaridai Seika-cho Soraku-gun, Kyoto 619-02, Japan
`fais@itl.atr.co.jp`

Abstract. This paper investigates the linguistic and modal aspects of responses made by subjects in a Wizard of Oz experiment to repetition requests made by the 'Wizard.' English-speaking 'clients' participating in a task-oriented cooperative dialogue with Japanese-speaking 'agents' were asked to clarify utterances that were complex or lengthy. The discourse, syntactic, and modal structures of these clarifications are examined. While linguistic factors are characterizable as 'reducing' and 'converging,' media use in these responses does not exhibit a clear pattern. Implications are drawn for future investigations into the use of multimedia configurations and for the integration of multimedia technologies in automatic speech processing.

1 Overview

Natural language processing systems are beginning to approach the difficult goal of handling unconstrained spontaneous speech. One way to improve the performance of such systems in this context is to supplement their processing capabilities with multimedia technologies designed to lessen the burden on the processing system. But the optimal configuration of supplemental media is not yet well understood; even less clear is the nature of the speech behavior we can expect from humans using multimedia speech processing systems. One thing is clear, however, from earlier work (Zoltan-Ford, 1991): completely unconstrained spontaneous speech is likely to be too difficult to process entirely automatically for some time. Systems will have to be able to request, and receive, clarifications of users' utterances (Boitet, 1993; Blanchon et al., 1995).

This work reports on a Wizard of Oz experiment in which English-speaking and Japanese-speaking subjects took part in a cooperative, task-oriented dialogue via a supposed 'automatic machine translation system,' (i.e., the Wizard), in two communication conditions: telephone-only and multimodal (MM), using the Environment for MultiModal Interaction (EMMI) designed and built at

* Young-Duk Park is an Exchange Researcher from the Electronics and Telecommunications Research Institute, Taejeon, Korea. The authors would like to thank Tsuyoshi Morimoto and Yasuhiro Yamazaki for their continued support.

the Advanced Telecommunications Research Institute in Kyoto, Japan (ATR) (Loken-Kim et al., 1993). It examines English-speaking subjects' clarification utterances and describes the ways in which these speakers accommodated, both linguistically and modaly, to breakdowns in the understanding of the 'machine'.

There are a number of reasons why the nature of this behavior should be of interest. Most superficially, the fact that automatic processing systems dealing with spontaneous speech currently perform less than perfectly implies that requests by the machine for clarification from the human are a necessary feature of such systems. Knowledge of what strategies speakers are apt to employ in their clarification utterances can be used to enhance the ability of the processing system both to interpret the clarification itself and to situate it in the ongoing discourse. If we can specify consistent and predictable relationships among the discourse, syntactic, and lexical structures of pre- and post-clarification-request utterances, we can use even partial information from the processing of the initial utterance to process the clarification utterance, increasing our chances of characterizing the speaker's contribution correctly.

Further, an examination of pre- and post-clarification request utterances reveals what modifications speakers can be expected to make *voluntarily* to instances of communication breakdown. We conjectured that speakers might slow their speaking rate, use fewer words, repeat a high percentage of words, or speak more fluently after a request for repetition. Constraints that must be built into the communication environment so that the system can handle spontaneous speech more effectively can exploit these types of modifications either explicitly, through instruction, or implicitly, through discourse context (Zoltan-Ford, 1991). It seems likely that encouraging those strategies that come naturally to speakers will be a more effective way to modify their communication behavior than trying to exploit strategies which are unfamiliar or, worse, difficult to carry out.

The investigation of these strategies in the context of a multimedia communication environment adds one further dimension to these issues. Does the availability and use of non-speech media affect subjects' clarification strategies and lead to more easily processed spontaneous speech?

Finally, the nature of these accommodations is indicative of the aspects of speech behavior that speakers themselves feel generate 'standard,' understandable language. Studying speakers' responses to requests for clarification is similar to gaining an understanding of language by studying language pathologies such as stuttering or aphasia, or by examining disfluencies such as false starts or repairs.

While the latter is an interesting line to pursue, here we will focus on the more practical issues outlined above. That is, what is the relationship between the linguistic and modal behavior of speakers before and after repetition requests? What strategies do speakers use to modify their input in cases of communication breakdown? And finally, what are the implications of these results for automatic processing of spontaneous speech?

2   Methods

Twenty subjects, ten native speakers of American English and ten native speakers of Japanese, took part in the experiment. The English-speaking subjects, acting as 'clients,' were instructed that their task was to get directions to a specific place (the site of a conference they were supposedly attending) and to make a hotel reservation, by engaging in a cooperative dialogue with the Japanese-speaking 'conference agents.' All subjects were told that their speech would be translated by 'ASyST,' supposedly an 'Automatic System for Speech Translation' which had been developed at ATR.

The 'Wizards' for the experiment were experienced interpreters; a native American English speaker translated from Japanese to English and a native Japanese speaker translated from English to Japanese. These 'Wizards' modulated their speech to be as monotonic and syllable-timed as possible, simulating the layman's impression of computer speech. The speech of both interpreters was passed through a Technics Mic Mixing Amplifier SH-3026 in order to make it sound more 'machine-like' to the subjects. Each person taking part in the experiment, i.e., the two interpreters, the 'client,' and the 'agent,' could hear all of the speech produced by every other person. No subject indicated any doubt that his or her speech was being translated by a machine.

None of the subjects knew one another, nor were they at all familiar with EMMI. The subjects were told that they were to enact the experiment scenario twice, once via telephone and once via the multimedia interface. Five agent-client pairs participated in the telephone condition first; five used the multimedia set-up first.

In the MM condition, subjects sat in front of a NeXT computer monitor, with touch screen, keyboard, and mouse. On the screen appeared a video image of the person with whom they were talking, a field for typing in written input, and an area in which several different maps or the hotel reservation form could be displayed by the agent. Subjects could draw on the map by dragging with the mouse or by hand, could type on the keyboard (activating the field by mouse or hand), or could use speech to communicate. Subjects were encouraged to practice with the drawing and typing capabilities of EMMI until they felt comfortable, and those acting as agent were thoroughly instructed in the information they had available to impart to the client.

In the telephone condition, subjects spoke into standard telephones. In both conditions, subjects wore Sennheiser HMD 410 headsets with microphone (one ear piece was turned up to allow for the telephone handset in the telephone condition).

An experimenter monitoring the conversations instructed the Wizards to ask the subjects to repeat an utterance during the course of the experiment when it was especially long, disfluent, or complex. Since this determination had to be done in real-time, during the course of the conversation, it was impossible to apply rigid standards to the decision of whether an utterance was 'long,' 'disfluent,' or 'complex.' However, an attempt was made to be consistent across conversations. These utterances by the Wizards, called 'repetition requests' (RR), were usually of the form *"Please repeat"* for English.[1] This paper examines the clarifications that clients made in response to these requests, and compares them with the initial utterances that provoked the requests.

Acoustic speech data was recorded on digital audio tapes using a SONY DAT deck, DTC-77ES. The acoustic tapes of the experiment sessions were transcribed, including notations for false starts; filled pauses such as *"ah"* and *"uhum"*; non-speech noises such as deep breaths or lip smacks; and simultaneous speech. The ten conversations comprised more than 12,600 words in over 1900 turns. There were 161 turns flanking requests for repetition; pre-RR utterances contained 2100 words; post-RR utterances contained 1580 words.

3   Results

3.1   Linguistic Accommodations

We investigated a variety of levels at which subjects made linguistic adjustments to their post-RR utterances: discourse and syntactic structure, lexical choice and number, and disfluency and speaking rates.

Discourse strategies Pre- and post-RR utterances were analyzed by hand for discourse units. The Communicative Acts (CA's) in each utterance were labelled using the bilingual set of CA labels developed at ATR (Seligman et al., 1994). CA's are roughly equivalent to speech acts, and capture the illocutionary intent of a phrase or clause. Labels are assigned based on the surface structure of the utterance. The frequencies of the most common CA's are given in Fig. 1. (For the sake of simplicity, since results did not differ very much for telephone and MM modes, they are collapsed in Fig. 1. See below for discussion of minor differences.) CA's which appeared rarely (once or twice in the utterances of only one or two speakers, for example) are not included in this discussion.

Reductions in frequency are observable for all CA's except WH-QUESTION. The percent of decrease for INFORM, YES/NO-QUESTION, and ACT-REQUEST are roughly the same, between 27 and 29%, with that for YES slightly lower at 21%. The slight increase in the frequency of WH-QUESTION is due to a discourse strategy apparent in the data: some subjects replaced a YES/NO-QUESTION or a series of YES/NO-QUESTION's with a single WH-QUESTION, as the client (C) did in example (1):

(1) C: But that says "Keage." Is "Keage" "Keitsu?" Are they the same?
     WOZ: Please repeat
     C: [um] I don't see "Keitsu" on the window. Where is "Keitsu?"

---

[1] Occasionally, the 'Wizard' said *"please speak slowly."* These cases have been included in the analysis below when subjects in fact changed their utterances beyond merely slowing their speech. They have been excluded, however, from analyses involving speaking rate.

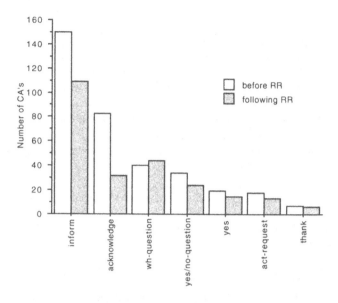

Fig. 1. Number of major Communicative Acts used before and after RR

Note the much higher rate of decrease for ACKNOWLEDGE (Fig. 1). There was a strong tendency for subjects to eliminate from their speech short acknowledging phrases such as *"OK," "great,"* and the like (see 'Structural clarification' below). However, this decrease is significant only in the telephone mode ($p < 0.05$).

Although ACKNOWLEDGE was the only CA to show significant effects of modality, there were some interesting intersubject effects for YES and YES/NO-QUESTION. While the frequency of use of these CA's varied significantly by subject in the utterances *before* a RR, that variation was not significant in the *responses* to RR's. That is, although subject behavior was significantly different (with respect to these communicative acts; $p < 0.05$) in the utterances before RR's, it was much more consistent in responses to RR's.[2]

Structural clarification Utterances occurring before and after RR's were analyzed by hand for their syntactic structure and wording. In the course of the analysis, a number of distinct strategies for structurally modifying utterances became apparent. The three major strategies (in order of frequency) involved:

– eliminating short, idiomatic acknowledging structures, such as *"OK," "all right,"* and *"I see",*

---

[2] The frequency of use of INFORM also showed a tendency to vary in this way. However, because INFORM is such an integral part of conveying information, the variation among subjects with respect to use of INFORM was not quite significant before RR's ($p = 0.11$). It was much less significant, however, after RR's ($p = 0.55$).

- eliminating clauses,
- changing lexical items (often phrasal idioms) so that their meaning was clearer.

Three secondary strategies, employed more or less equally frequently, involved:

- reducing the complexity of an utterance structure by simplifying the syntax,
- reducing the complexity of a structure by eliminating adjuncts,
- amplifying a lexical item to make it more easily understood by providing a more specific or complete reference.

Example (2) illustrates the first three, most common, strategies:

(2) C: All right. I also will need to have a hotel reservation. Can you give me a hotel reservation please?
    WOZ: Please repeat
    C: I would like to get a hotel reservation please

In this case, the client eliminates the *"all right"* (an acknowledging phrase), drops the second clause, and changes the choice of lexical items in the first clause from *"I will need to have"* to *"I would like to get"*, a slightly less indirect, slightly more transparent way to make the request for a hotel reservation. In example (3), the client eliminates a clause, and also amplifies *"it"* to *"the bus ride"*:

(3) C: [im] [ah] How many stops is that and how long does it take?
    WOZ: Please repeat
    C: [um] How long is the bus ride?

In example (4), the subject simplifies the grammatical structure by changing a conjoined yes-no question (one clause of which itself contains a conjunction) into a single WH-QUESTION; in example (5), simplification has been achieved by dropping two adjunct appositive clauses:[3]

(4) C: [ah] (is it thi) Is it a straight walk or should I take a taxi or bus?
    WOZ: Please repeat
    C: (what's the) What's the best way to get there?

(5) C: [ah] (can I s) Can I make a reservation for an economy hotel, a cheap hotel, inexpensive hotel?
    WOZ: Please repeat
    C: [ah] I want to stay in a inexpensive hotel

The strategies described above are listed to the left of the dark vertical line in Fig. 2. Subjects also employed strategies which would seem to be counter-productive to enhancing understanding. They sometimes added clauses, acknowledgment idioms, or adjuncts, made the meanings of phrases more opaque,

---

[3] *"thi"* is the transcription for *"the"* pronounced with a long *"e"* sound.

or changed simple syntactic structures into more complicated ones. However, these strategies were employed significantly less frequently than the strategies described above. The frequencies for these less productive strategies are displayed to the right of the dark vertical line in Fig. 2. There were no significant differences in usage dependent upon communication modality.

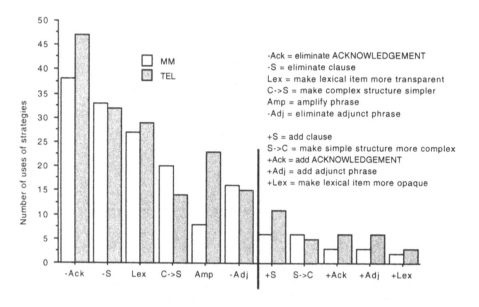

Fig. 2. Frequency of use of syntactic clarification strategies

Number of words As a natural byproduct of using simpler or fewer syntactic structures, subjects reduced the number of words they used in post-RR utterances. This reduction (Fig. 3) is not statistically significant. This is not surprising; subjects were constrained by the task to convey and request certain information and could not reduce their use of words beyond the threshold required to accomplish this task.

Although there were no significant differences across subjects, the same inter-subject trend that was observed above for CA's is evident here. While subjects did vary significantly ($p < 0.05$) in the number of words used in pre-RR utterances, they did not vary in the number of words used in post-RR utterances.

Lexical choice As we conjectured, subjects showed a strong tendency to repeat the lexical items used in pre-RR utterances when constructing clarification

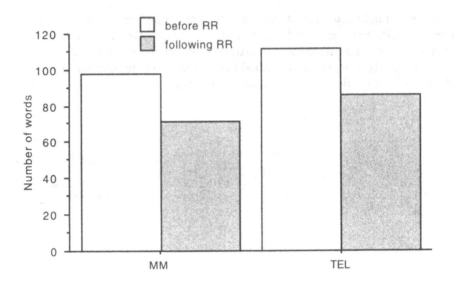

Fig. 3. Number of words used before and after RR's in telephone and multimedia conditions

utterances after RR's. Individual subjects repeated a minimum average of 23% and a maximum average of 80% of the words in their pre-RR utterances, with an average repetition rate of 50%. There were no significant differences dependent upon mode.

Disfluency Disfluencies are defined as the filled pauses and false starts uttered by a speaker. Speakers significantly decreased the number of disfluencies they uttered when making clarification (post-RR) utterances (Fig. 4). There were no modal effects.

There was the same intersubject effect for number of disfluencies as was observed above for CA's and number of words. While the differences in numbers of disfluencies were significant across subjects in the pre-RR cases $(p < 0.05)$, those differences were not significant across subjects in the post-RR cases.

Speaking rate Measurements for speaking rate were quite crude and revealed no modal differences. However, speaking rates tended to slow in the post-RR utterances, and showed the same sort of intersubject differences as those observed above; while speakers differed significantly in speaking rate before the RR, they did not in their responses to the RR.

3.2 Media Use

During the MM condition of the experiment, subjects were able to type in a text window at any time, and they could draw on a map or type in the slots of a form

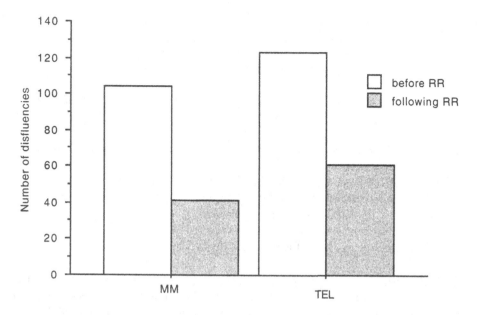

Fig. 4. Number of disfluencies before and after RR in telephone and multimedia conditions

during any time that these graphics were displayed. In previous experiments in EMMI (involving same-language and human-interpreted situations, but not Wizard of Oz), subjects rarely availed themselves of these options (Park et al., 1994; Loken-Kim et al., 1994). However, we hypothesized that the increased processing demands placed on them by the 'machine translation' environment would encourage subjects to increase their use of these options as they attempted to make themselves understood. The overall use of keyboard and touchscreen media in this experiment, was, in fact, much higher than that in previous experiments (Park et al., 1994; Loken-Kim et al., 1994; Park et al., 1995). Here we will report on the relationship between the use of these additional media and the incidence of RR's.

One of the ten subjects did not use any media other than speech. Three other subjects used non-speech media infrequently and with no apparent relation to RR's. The non-speech media use of the remaining six subjects, discussed below, seemed to bear some relationship to RR's. Our criteria for positing such a relationship is the presence of non-speech media use in either a response to a RR or in the next contribution after a response to a RR. The client's drawing in example (6) is an example of the former case; the client's typing in example (7) is an example of the latter. (In the examples below, italics mark the speech that was simultaneous with drawing.)

(6) C: /ls/ I see, and that's thi Maiyako Hotel?
WOZ: Please repeat
C: [ah] I see thi hotel circled. Is that thi Maiyako Hotel?
WOZ: Please repeat
C: [ah] I see the circle. [ah] What is the hotel that is also circled? *This hotel.* Is this the closest hotel?

(7) C: OK, can you book me a room for three nights, starting tonight?
WOZ: Please repeat
C: OK, I need a room for three nights. Can you book?
WOZ: hai, sanpaku, shitainodesuga, yoyaku dekimasuka?
A: hai, itsukara otomarini narimasuka?
WOZ: Yes, from what day will you stay?
Client then types days of arrival and departure

Use of map As in previous experiments, both client and agent drew on the map as one way to communicate location and direction. Subject drawing took a number of forms. Frequently, subjects drew a line showing direction while they described the same direction in speech. Sometimes, their line drawing followed the relevant speech. Subjects also circled their location or attempted to mark their location with a single point[4]. (For an in-depth description of media use in this experiment, see Park et al. (1995).)

Three subjects used map drawing in response to RR's. Two of these subjects had only a small number of RR's in the direction-giving portion of the conversation, but both accompanied their speech with drawing in a significant number of their responses to those RR's (one out of one; two out of three). The third subject clearly depended upon drawing to help clarify his utterances; in six out of eight RR responses, he used drawing along with speech. A typical example follows:

(8) C1:   /ls/ OK, I'm looking at the map. It looks like
WOZ: Please repeat
C2:   [ah] I see the map. [ah] It looks like Kyoto Station. Where is thi
WOZ: Please repeat
C3:   I see the map. How do I get to the Conference Center?
WOZ: chizu wo mite imasu. lokusai koryu senta madeno, annai wo
     onegaishitainodsuga
A: maaku-san wa, ima, kyooto eki nodonoatarini imasuka?
WOZ: Mr. Mark[5], where in Kyoto Station are you?
C4:   I'm at thi Kintetsu Line. *I'm putting a mark where I'm standing*
WOZ: Please repeat
C5:   I'm standing at *thi mark* near the Kintetsu Line

---

[4] Eight out of ten subjects also gestured toward the screen, usually pointing, but sometimes describing a line, even though they were making no contact with the screen and, thus, were making no visible mark. These gestures often followed RR's.

The subject deals with the first two RR's verbally; the information he wants to convey does not allow a graphic rendering. However, when he is asked a location question after those RR's, he responds by making a mark on the map as he speaks the italicized portion of utterance C4. That is, although it was not possible to respond visually to the first two RR's, he could and did respond appropriately using the graphic medium to the question following those RR's. When he was asked to repeat this utterance as well, he continued to use the graphic medium in his response by drawing a circle around his mark as he said *"thi mark."*

A fourth subject showed a very clear and quite interesting use of drawing with respect to RR's. This subject used drawing extensively from the beginning of her conversation, and kept her hand near the monitor screen for most of the direction-giving portion of the conversation. Because she drew on the map a number of times, there were three occasions on which her drawing coincided with a pre-RR utterance. In every case, she took her hand *away* from the screen and refrained from drawing during the RR response.

Use of keyboard In previous experiments in the EMMI environment, clients rarely used the keyboard (Park et al., 1994; Loken-Kim et al., 1994). However, in the WOZ experiment reported here, clients much more readily typed on the keyboard to convey information. Only three subjects did not use the keyboard at all.

Two subjects typed in all hotel reservation information once they began using the keyboard, (one subject even typed in requests and short acknowledgments like *"I understand,"* and *"thank you"*). As a result, they used speech very little and completely avoided generating utterances which 'the machine' would be unable to understand. Thus, it is difficult to assess the relationship between their use of the keyboard and RR's. Three other subjects also used the keyboard, but with no apparent relationship to RR's.

Two subjects showed behavior, which does, however, conform to our hypothesis about media use. One typed in information after RR's on three occasions. Another behaved similarly and then avoided further RR's by typing all remaining information. Example (7) above is a typical example of the use of the keyboard in response to RR's.

Use of Video Finally, recall that clients and agents could also see one another's faces in a video image in one corner of their monitors. We have noted before the total lack of use of this video image in previous experiments (Fais and Loken-Kim, 1994), perhaps because there is no eye contact (due to the position of the video cameras). In this experiment, however, three subjects did utilize the video medium. Two clients nodded to their agents to confirm cross-language information (such as the agent's spelling of the client's name). A third subject used the video in response to RR's. He was attempting to ask the agent to type some information to him, and he had been requested twice to *"please repeat."*

After the second RR, he held his hands up to the camera and made typing motions while he asked again to have the information typed. (At that point, the agent complied.)

4   Discussion

4.1   Linguistic Variables

Linguistic adjustments to RR's can be characterized as *reduction* and *convergence*. Subjects reduced the number of virtually all CA's used. Their syntactic adjustment strategies also tended toward reduction, e.g., the elimination of structural elements ranging from clauses to adjuncts to idiomatic expressions. There was also a trend to use fewer words in post-RR utterances.

Certainly the reduction in number of words and complexity of structure means less strain on an automatic language processing system. There were other trends which would also reduce the language processing burden. Lexical adjustments away from idiomatic phrases to more literal phrases could simplify language processing. Even the tendency to amplify phrases, while sometimes adding more lexical items or creating more complex structures, resolves problems of ambiguity of reference (as in example (3) above). The reduction in disfluency and in speaking rate also results in a more easily processed language input.

Speakers did not only *reduce* aspects of their utterances after RR's, they also *converged* toward more similar language use. The lack of significant variation among subjects' post-RR utterances for certain CA's, number of words, disfluency and speaking rate suggests that the language behavior after RR's can be more easily and more productively modeled. The high rate of repetition of lexical items post-RR represents a similar trend toward reduction of variability, or convergence toward a consistent, predictable behavior.

Modality effects on linguistic adjustments were minimal. This seems to imply that subjects' linguistic adjustments are independent of the availability and use of modality options.

4.2   Modal Variables

Subjects' use of non-speech options, being difficult to analyze numerically, are consequently difficult to interpret in the same way as linguistic adjustments. Note that when we discuss linguistic factors, we are discussing adjustments made to a message within a particular medium, i.e., speech[6]. Media use, on the other hand, involves replacing one modality with another (e.g., typing instead of speaking) or supplementing one modality with another (e.g., drawing concurrent with speaking). This, then, is one of the difficulties subjects experience in using the media

---

[6] Of course, it would be possible to compare messages across modalities, especially for the two subjects who used extensive typing in their conversations. We could compare their oral utterances with their (usually post-RR) typewritten utterances. This, however, has not yet been done.

available: they must either switch media or coordinate the use of one medium with another.

Speakers engage in the kind of purely oral conversation they used in the telephone condition, every day of their lives. In case of a lack of understanding on the part of an interlocutor, their linguistic options are well-known and their clarification strategies are familiar if not habitual, learned from prior verbal interaction with and observation of other speakers. Thus, it is perhaps not too surprising that we should find some general trends in the linguistic approaches used by subjects for resolving a lack of understanding.

However, in the novel MM conversational environment, not only are the options themselves new, but also speakers have had no experience observing others use different communication media in clarification. So it is to be expected that speakers should show wide variation in their approaches to utilizing non-speech options.

In general, the approaches to non-speech media use that we described above seemed to be motivated by two different assumptions. Five subjects apparently assumed that using non-speech options would only make matters worse. These are the subjects who used non-speech media infrequently if at all, and the one subject who *refrained* from using them in his post-RR utterances, even though, judging from his use of them earlier in the discourse, he seemed to think that non-speech media were generally useful.

The other five subjects attempted to use MM options to help them out of their communication difficulties. The most heavily used modality for these subjects was the typewriting modality. Notice that this is the modality closest to speaking; it involves linguistic input which is familiar to the subjects, unlike the sort of visual input used in map drawing, for which they know no 'grammar' or social conventions.

5 Conclusions and Directions

This work examines spontaneous adjustments speakers make when difficulties in communication with a 'machine' are encountered, and the role that the use of multimedia systems plays in such cases.

The results regarding linguistic adjustments are encouraging. Even assuming that pre-RR utterances are ignored by a language processing system, post-RR utterances represent an improvement in the quality of input for such a system. Speakers do tend to make linguistic reductions that would lessen the burden on automatic speech processing: reductions in illocutionary force units and syntactic structures requiring processing, in number of words used, in disfluency and speaking rates, and in lexical variability.

But speakers go beyond simple reduction. They also tend to converge to a more consistent language behavior after difficulties in communication (i.e., requests for repetition) are encountered. This means that partial parsing or recognition results from a pre-RR utterance will have a number of predictable relations to the following utterance and thus can be used to enhance the processing of the post-RR utterance. Our next step in working with this data will be to incorporate these relations in a statistical language model for speech recognition, exploiting these relationships to improve performance.

On the other hand, very few of these linguistic results were in any way affected by the media through which the conversation took place. An examination of media use suggests that, since users are largely unfamiliar with non-speech options for (real- time) communication, their use of these options is dependent upon their own, individual, judgments rather than upon any generalized social conventions. The wide variety of ways of using non-speech media observed in the course of the experiment do not reveal any particular recurring, consistent pattern that could be exploited in enhancing the performance of automatic language processing systems.

We suggested that the results reported here have implications for the nature of effective constraints for a system processing spontaneous speech. Speakers should be encouraged to reduce the linguistic aspects of their utterances in ways in which they are already inclined to do so: by eliminating unnecessary phrases from their syntactic structures, reducing lexical variability and disfluencies, and slowing down their speech. Instructions to speak simply, clearly and slowly would make explicit the strategies that speakers employ spontaneously when faced with a difficult communication situation.

The next step, then, is to provide some sort of constraint upon media use. This constraint could be imposed in one of two ways, either by providing explicit instructions or by encouraging pre-existing 'intuitive' strategies. Recall that, in this experiment, the primary phrase used by the Wizard to indicate lack of understanding was *"please repeat."* For certain types of language processing breakdown, the 'machine' might be given the option to request the client explicitly to *"please type"* or *"please draw."* Pre-conversation instructions which contain even more specific injunctions, say, to type *all* hotel reservation information or to draw a circle on the map to indicate location, could also be included.

Ultimately, however, we would hope that constraints on media use will parallel those on language use. That is, as more and more people become experienced in the use of multimedia systems, it will be possible to draw on their intuitive, *media-related* responses to communication difficulties just as we propose to draw on the intuitive *linguistic* responses of the subjects in this experiment. One very recently completed experiment in EMMI involved frequent users of multimedia systems, whose experience has supplied them with some internal model for efficient and effective use of non-speech options. Preliminary results indicate some ways in which these users differ from 'naive' users: experienced users are much more likely to repeat their utterances exactly, instead of changing them for clarification; they also appear to use typing especially as a means to clarify utterances, to a greater extent than the subjects reported above. By studying how these users respond to RR's in this way, it will be possible to design media systems that encourage 'natural' media-related responses to communication difficulties, and to build these designs into effective language processing systems employing multimedia technology.

References

Blanchon, H., Loken-Kim, K. H., Fais, L. and Morimoto, T.(1995) A pattern-based approach for interactive clarification of natural language utterances. *Proc. Information Processing Society of Japan SIG-NL Workshop, Tokyo. May 25-26.*

Boitet, C. (1993) Practical speech translation systems will integrate human expertise, multimodal communication, and interactive disambiguation. *Proc. MTS-IV, Kobe.*

Fais, L. and Loken-Kim, K. H. (1994) Effects of mode on spontaneous English speech in EMMI. *ATRTechnical Report TR-IT-0059.* Kyoto: ATR Interpreting Telecommunications Research Laboratories.

Loken-Kim, K. H., Yato, F., Fais, L. and Morimoto, T. (1994) (Linguistic and paralinguistic differences of telephone-only and multi-modal dialogues. *Proc. ICSLP, Yokohama, September.*

Loken-Kim, K. H.F. Yato, F., Kurihara, K., Fais, F. and Furukawa, R. (1993) EMMI-ATR environment for multi-modal interactions. *ATRTechnical Report TR-IT-0018.* Kyoto: ATR Interpreting Telecommunications Research Laboratories.

Park, Y. D., Loken-Kim, K. H. and Fais (1994) L, An experiment for telephone versus multimedia multimodal interpretation: Methods and subjects' behavior. *ATRTechnical Report TR-IT-0087.* Kyoto: ATR Interpreting Telecommunications Research Laboratories.

Park, Y. D., Loken-Kim, K. H., Fais, L. and Mizunashi, S. (1995) Analysis of gesture behavior in a multimedia/multimodal interpreting experiment; Human vs. Wizard of Oz interpretation method. *ATRTechnical Report TR-IT-0091.* Kyoto: ATR Interpreting Telecommunications Research Laboratories.

Seligman, M., Fais, L. and Tomokiyo, M. (1994) A bilingual set of Communicative Act labels for spontaneous dialogues. *ATRTechnical Report TR-IT-0081.* Kyoto: ATR Interpreting Telecommunications Research Laboratories.

Zoltan-Ford, E. (1991) How to get people to say and type what computers can understand. *International Journal of Man-Machine Studies 34.*

Object Reference in Task-Oriented Keyboard Dialogues

Anita Cremers

Center for Research on User-System Interaction (IPO)
P.O. Box 513, 5600 MB Eindhoven, The Netherlands
cremers@ipo.tue.nl

Abstract. In the DENK project a multimodal interface is developed where natural language is combined with graphical interaction. For the design of this interface, knowledge is collected about how humans refer to objects in a task-oriented environment, by means of natural language and gestures. In this paper we report results of an experiment concerning referring behaviour in tasd-oriented keyboard dialogues. The results are compared with those of an earlier experiment we performed with spoken dialogues. The differences were all found to be related to the so-called *principle of minimal cooperative total effort*, which says that, within the limitations of the available modalities, the participants aim at spending as little total effort as possible on referring to a certain object on the other hand, and on identifying the object on the other hand. Based on the results, we formulate recommendations for the design of multimodal interfaces which include typed natural language.

1 Introduction

The research reported here was carried out as part of the DENK project (see Bunt et al., 1997), in which a multimodal interface is developed that combines graphical interaction and communication by means of natural language.[1] The DENK interface can be represented by a triangle, as shown in Fig. 1, where the angles stand for the user, the domain and the 'cooperative assistant', the latter two being components of the interface. The domain is the collection of objects represented on the screen and the relations between them. The cooperative assistant is that part of the system that supports natural language communication with the user, and is also able to perform actions in the domain. The user is allowed to point at objects in the domain and to manipulate them directly by means of a mouse. The user can also instruct the cooperative assistant in natural language to carry out certain actions in the domain, and can ask questions about objects or events that play a role in the interaction.

---

[1] DENK stands for 'Dialoogvoering en Kennisopbouw' in Dutch, which means 'Dialogue Management and Knowledge Acquisition'. It is a joint research program of the universities of Tilburg and Eindhoven, and is partly financed by the Tilburg-Eindhoven Organisation for Inter-University Cooperation.

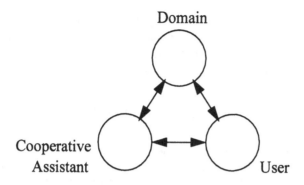

Fig. 1. The DENK triangle

When the user wants to ask questions or give instructions, it is important to make clear which objects are involved. In a multimodal interface the act of referring to objects can be performed either by using natural language expressions or by pointing, or by a combination of the two. In any case, the user should take care to provide appropriate information for the system to be able to identify the intended object (the *target object*).

To equip the system with knowledge of how humans refer to objects, research on this topic is needed. One of the most natural ways for humans to communicate is by means of speech. Owing to technological limitations, however, most natural language systems today allow only typed input. Unfortunately, results from research on natural spoken dialogues cannot be extrapolated to written dialogues. There are essential differences between the two modes of communication, in particular with respect to length and syntax (Hauptmann and Rudnicky, 1988), speed of production and planning of utterances, and types speech acts used (Oviatt and Cohen, 1991). For instance, in spoken dialogues more indirectness is found than in keyboard dialogues (Beun and Bunt, 1987). With respect to referential behaviour it was found that, when objects are referred to for the first time, in spoken (telephone) dialogues more requests for identification occur than in keyboard dialogues (Cohen, 1984). (However, this study dealt with telephone dialogues, where only linguistic interaction was possible.) The formulation of well-founded claims about referential behaviour in multimodal situations requires further research on both spoken and typed dialogues.

The referential behaviour of participants in spoken tasd-oriented dialogues in a situation designed to mimic the DENK triangle has been investigated in an earlier study (Cremers and Beun, 1995). The present paper deals with an empirical study of the way humans refer to objects in keyboard dialogues of a similar type. We will focus on the type and amount of information used in referential expressions, and on the use of gestures; the results will be compared with those results of our earlier study of spoken dialogues.

In section 2 results from the study of spoken dialogues will be presented briefly. In section 3 we will formulate a number of expectations about keyboard dialogues, based on the results from spoken dialogues and findings from the literature. In section 4 we will check these expectations for keyboard dialogues and compare the results with spoken dialogues. In conclusion, in section 5 the results will be discussed in the context of the DENK project.

2 Referential Behaviour in Spoken Dialogues

In an earlier study of spoken dialogues (Cremers and Beun, 1995), we studied the referential behaviour of ten pairs of subjects. The setup of this experiment is depicted in Fig. 2a. The study was designed to mimic the triangular DENK paradigm and can be described as follows. Two participants were seated side by side at a table, separated by a screen. To prevent communication other than by speech and gesturing, only the hands were visible to the other participant, and only when placed on top of the table. One of the participants (the instructor) was to instruct the other (the builder) to reconstruct a building of toy blocks on a toy foundation plate, placed on the table top, in accordance with an example provided to the instructor.

In this setup the role of the instructor is similar to that of the user and the role of the builder is similar to that of the cooperative assistant in the DENK interface. Both participants were allowed to observe the building domain, to talk about it and to gesticulate (in it), but only the builder was allowed to manipulate blocks. The main results of this experiment are the following.

The Principle of Minimal Cooperative Total Effort
Participants were found to adhere to the so-called *principle of minimal cooperative total effort*. This principle expresses the idea that together the participants try to say (Clark and Wilkes-Gibbs, 1986) and do (Cremers and Beun, 1995) as little as possible, but just enough to be able to reach mutual agreement that a target object has been identified. For the speaker this means that he will on the one hand transfer minimal information and information of a particular type, to allow the hearer on the other hand to easily identify the object, by having to consider as few objects as possible. Consequences of this principle in spoken dialogues relate to the choice of features in referential expressions and the use of a focus of attention.

Speakers were found to prefer to use *absolute features* over *relative features*. Absolute features such as 'red' can be understood by considering only the target object. Relative features can be understood only by also considering other objects present. Relative features may be implicit or explicit. To understand implicit relative features, such as 'large', other objects have to be considered. To understand explicit relative features, such as 'to the right of', other objects have to be identified to identify the target object. Absolute features are consequently easier to work with than relative features.

Concerning the focus of attention, it was found that speakers use less information to refer to objects located in the area of the building domain that was in the focus of attention than to those located outside this area. In the task, changes had to be made to parts of the block building under construction. When changes are made in a certain part of the building, the speaker can assume that the focus of attention of both himself and his partner is directed at this area of the domain. For instance, participants used the referential expression 'the red block' to refer to the only red block within the current focus area, although many red blocks were present in the domain as a whole. Compared with the situation where the entire domain is taken into account, this means a reduction of words in the referential expression for the speaker, and fewer objects for the addressee to consider in order to find the target object.

Furthermore, it was found that in choosing the next object participants preferred to refer to an object that was in the current focus of attention. This resulted in a larger proportion of references to objects in focus (68%) than to objects out of focus (32%). In terms of minimal effort, this can be explained as a strategy to make optimal use of the current focus area.

The Process of Object Reference
In the spoken dialogues we investigated, there were usually several turn-takings before the participants reached agreement that the target object had been identified. The number of turns needed was found to be related to the focus of attention (Cremers (1995)). To reach agreement on the identification of objects located within the current focus area fewer turns were needed than to refer to objects outside the current focus area.

3 Keyboard Dialogues

In this section we will first describe the experimental setup used in the study of multimodal keyboard dialogues, and compare this with the study of spoken dialogues discussed in Sect. 2. On the basis of findings from the literature and from the study of spoken dialogues, we will make predictions for the outcome of this experiment.

The Experiment
An experiment was carried out that was identical to the one described in Sect. 2, except that the participants communicated via keyboard and screen. In the DENK triangle this means that the mode of communication between the user and the cooperative asssistant is typed natural language. To prevent participants from talking to each other, they wore headphones where background music was played.[2] The experimental setup is shown in Fig. 2b.

The change from spoken to typed communication may be expected to have important consequences for the manner in which object reference is performed. First, the coordination of different modes of communication is expected to be different. In the spoken modality it is possible to speak and inspect the domain

---

[2] This setup served its purpose: the 10 pairs of subjects who participated never spoke to each other at any time during the experiment.

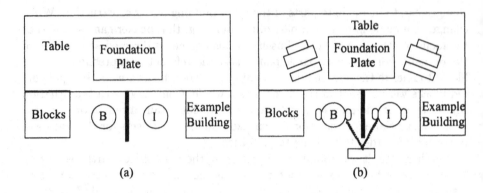

Fig. 2. Experimental setup for (a) spoken dialogues and (b) keyboard dialogues

or point at objects in the domain at the same time. This is not possible in the keyboard situation. When a participant is typing, his attention is directed at the screen and the keyboard, so he cannot see what is going on in the block-building process. Also, since his hands are busy typing, he cannot use them to point at objects in the domain. Another difference is that it is more difficult to take turns. To pass the turn to the partner, a participant had to explicitly press a certain key. Only after that the partner could type. If a participant wanted to take his turn to type, he had to ask for it explicitly by means of a special key, and the partner had to acknowledge the switch of turn by pressing another key.[3] From the differences between typed and spoken communication, we can expect to find the following phenomena in keyboard dialogues.

Expectations for Keyboard Dialogues

Minimal Effort. A general prediction with respect to keyboard dialogues is that it normally takes more effort to conduct a keyboard dialogue than a spoken dialogue, due to the characteristics of the communicative modalities. This difference will be reflected in the length of referential expressions, the features chosen in referential expressions, and the use of gestures.

It is known from the literature that written dialogues generally take longer and contain fewer words than spoken dialogues (e.g., Oviatt and Cohen, 1991). This was also expected in the present experiment, as a consequence of the principle of minimal cooperative total effort. Since it takes more effort to type than to speak, fewer words will be used when typing. Written dialogues take more time than spoken dialogues, but this increase would probably be even larger if more words were typed. However, the increase in time is due not only to the increase in effort. It can also be a consequence of the fact that participants do not feel as pressed for time as in spoken dialogues, so they take more time to formulate

---

[3] If the participants had been allowed to type at the same time, this would have caused problems for them, especially since actions in the domain had to be monitored as well. In particular, the order of the turns and actions would have been less obvious.

their utterances (Beun and Bunt, 1987). With respect to the use of referential expressions, participants in keyboard dialogues are expected to try to express the same information but use fewer words than in spoken dialogues. Also, more gestures are expected to be used, in order to compensate the reduction in words.

With respect to the choice of features, the prediction is that, just as in spoken dialogues, participants will have a preference for using absolute features. There is no reason to assume that *more* absolute features will be used in keyboard dialogues, since the process of understanding a referential expression and identifying the referent is the same in both situations. An effect is, however, expected in the coordination of language and gestures. Since it is not possible to type and gesture at the same time, pointing gestures accompanied by demonstratives are expected to occur less in keyboard dialogues.

As a result of an expected reduction in number of words and increased use of gestures, some of the features that were used in spoken dialogues will be replaced by gestures in typed dialogues. Tentative predictions are that absolute features containing information that cannot be expressed very easily by gestures (e.g. colour) will continue to be used, but that the rather verbose explicit relative features will be replaced by gestures.

The reduction in number of words as a result of using the current focus of attention is expected to occur more often in keyboard dialogues than in spoken dialogues. Fewer words means less typing, and therefore less effort. However, since the coordination of typing and inspecting the domain is difficult in keyboard dialogues, it is expected that participants will easily loose track of the current focus area. This will probably result in a relatively smaller number of references to objects in focus than in the spoken dialogues.

Expectations about Object Reference Processes

In the spoken dialogues it was easy to react immediately to something the partner said, resulting in a mean number of 2.7 turns before mutual agreement was reached about identification of the target object. For keyboard dialogues the effort to take the turn and type is much greater, hence much fewer turn-takings are expected to take place. This could mean that more information will be given in the first turn, to avoid having to use more (verbal) turns. This would contradict the expected reduction in number of words in referential expressions in keyboard dialogues. Another possible consequence is that the reduction in verbal turns will be compensated by an increase in non-verbal turns since there is no inherent difficulty in taking turns in gesturing during keyboard dialogues.

There could be a reason for an *increase* in verbal turns as well, namely the occurrence of more miscommunications in keyboard dialogues, although it is suggested in the literature (see Cohen, 1984) that this effect does not exist. A miscommunication is defined as an event where a wrong selection takes place before the right target object is identified. The expectation of an increase in miscommunications is a consequence of the expected decrease in words in keyboard dialogues. To correct the miscommunication and identify the right target object additional turns will be needed. However, if the expectation about giving more information in the first turn to avoid having to engage in tedious turn-takings is correct, an increase in miscommunications is not likely to occur.

Finally, it is not clear whether in the keyboard dialogues, as in the spoken dialogues, the number of turns to refer to objects in focus will be lower than those to refer to objects out of focus. In keyboard dialogues, where the attention has to be divided between keyboard, screen and domain, it is harder to continue focusing the attention on the current focus area. This could mean that the benefit from the focus area is less than in spoken dialogues.

4   Results

In the collected keyboard dialogues a total number of 156 referential acts occurred, which is almost the same as in the spoken dialogues we collected (viz. 145). This is not surprising, since both experiments involved exactly the same task and the same objects. Our main findings w.r.t. the principle of minimal cooperative total effort and the process of reaching mutual agreement on object identification are the following.

4.1   Minimal Effort

Length of dialogues. According to the literature, fewer words are used and more time is needed in keyboard dialogues than in spoken dialogues (Oviatt and Cohen, 1991; Beun and Bunt, 1987). This was also found in the present study (see Table 1). The participants took a mean time of 12 minutes to complete the keyboard dialogues, during which they used 189 words. It took the participants a mean time of only 4 minutes and 47 seconds to complete the spoken dialogues, but in that time they used 729 words.

However, not all the time was devoted to typing or speaking. A part of the time was used to carry out physical actions: pointing actions and manipulations of objects in the domain. In the keyboard dialogues, 7 minutes and 56 seconds were used for the typing, which means that typing rate was 0.4 words per second. In the spoken dialogues, 4 minutes and 17 seconds were used for speaking, which yields a speaking rate of 2.8 words per second.

The figures show that in keyboard dialogues a relatively large part of the time was devoted to physical actions only, namely 4 minutes and 4 seconds, which is 34% of the time. In spoken dialogues 30 seconds were used for performing physical actions only, 10% of the total time.

These results show that, indeed, it takes more time to conduct a keyboard dialogue than a spoken dialogue, under exactly the same conditions. It takes exactly seven times longer to type a word than to utter it. Also, the amount of time spent on carrying out physical actions is different for the two types of dialogue. In keyboard dialogues over three times longer is spent carrying out actions than in spoken dialogues. Since the task in the two experiments was exactly the same, this result cannot be explained by a difference in manipulating

Table 1. Mean length of dialogues

	keyboard	*spoken*
mean length	12 min.	4 min. 47 sec.
	(189 words)	(729 words)
mean length	7 min. 56 sec.	4 min. 17 sec.
of language	(0.4 words/sec.)	(2.8 words per sec.)
mean length	4 min. 4 sec.	30 sec.
of actions	(34% of total time)	(10% of total time)

objects in the domain. The dissimilarity is therefore probably due to an increase in the use of referential actions, i.e. pointing or other gestures to indicate an object in the domain.

Length of referential expressions. A more specific hypothesis concerns the length of referential acts in keyboard and spoken dialogues. Since fewer words are used in keyboard dialogues, the length of referential acts is expected to be shorter. This was not quite confirmed. Although the mean number of content words (i.e. all words except determiners) used in keyboard dialogues was 1.8 (s.d. = 2.53), compared to 2.2 (s.d. = 2.69) in spoken dialogues, this does not mean that most references in keyboard dialogues were shorter than in spoken dialogues. First, the standard deviations are too large to show a significant difference in length. Second, similar percentages of all lengths of referential expressions occurred in both types of dialogue, except for the referential expressions of length 0 or 1 (see Table 2). More content-less referential acts, i.e. gestures or demonstratives or combinations of these, occurred in keyboard than in spoken dialogues (46% vs. 15%). In contrast, fewer referential acts containing only one content word occurred (12% vs. 46%).

Table 2. Number of content words in referential acts

length	*keyboard*	*spoken*
0	46%	15%
1	12%	46%
2	15%	16%
3	9%	2%
4	3%	6%
5	3%	6%
> 5	12%	9%

These figures seem to indicate that at times when typists use gestures only, or gestures accompanied by a demonstrative expression, speakers use one feature, possibly accompanied by a gesture, and vice versa. Since no significant reduction of words in referential expressions could be demonstrated, the total reduction of words in keyboard dialogues must be due to a reduction of words in the remaining parts of the utterances, i.e. where the action to be carried out is expressed.

However, if we do not count the number of words in the referential expressions but the referential expressions in which features are used, a clear difference can be found. In keyboard dialogues fewer features (either absolute or relative or both) were used than in spoken dialogues, namely in 56% and 85%, respectively, of the referential expressions (see Table 3). This result is mainly due to the fact that in keyboard dialogues far more gestures without any language were used than in spoken dialogues, namely in 44% and 4%, respectively, of the references. Contrary to expectations, no difference could be found with respect to the total number of gestures used in keyboard and spoken dialogues. In both types of dialogue the percentage was exactly the same, viz. 53%.

Preference for absolute features. One of the findings relating to the principle of minimal cooperative total effort in keyboard dialogues is, not surprisingly, that participants have a preference for using absolute rather than relative features, as is shown in Table 3. Absolute features only were used in 47 cases (30%). In spoken dialogues absolute features only were used in 88 (61%) of the referential acts. The use of relative features was more or less the same in both types of dialogue (1% in keyboard dialogues, 2% in spoken dialogues). Also, combinations of absolute and relative features occurred equally often in keyboard and spoken dialogues (25% and 22%, respectively).

Table 3. Features and gestures used in keyboard and spoken dialogues

| | keyboard (156) | | spoken (145) | |
	+gesture	−gesture	+gesture	−gesture
absolute	9 (6%)	38 (24%)	45 (31%)	43 (30%)
relative	− −	2 (1%)	2 (1%)	2 (1%)
abs. & rel.	4 (3%)	35 (22%)	7 (5%)	24 (17%)
demonstr.	− −	− −	17 (12%)	− −
gesture only	68 (44%)	− −	5 (4%)	− −
Total	81 (53%)	75 (47%)	76 (53%)	69 (47%)

At first sight it may seem surprising that fewer absolute features were used in keyboard dialogues than in spoken dialogues. This seems to weaken the principle of minimal cooperative total effort. The solution lies in the use of gestures. When we assume that the use of gestures only or of gestures combined with demonstratives is a means to reduce effort, then the figures for the choice of features in keyboard and spoken dialogues become very similar. For keyboard dialogues this would mean that the referential acts which involve the least effort are those in which gestures only are used plus those in which only absolute feature are used. These two percentages add up to 74%. In spoken dialogues, summation of the numbers of referential acts by means of gestures only, gestures plus demonstratives, and absolute features only, amounts to 77%.

To summarize, both in keyboard and in spoken dialogues participants try to reduce effort by choosing particular features. However, the choice of features is different in the two types of dialogue. In keyboard dialogues relatively more gestures only are used, and in spoken dialogues relatively more absolute features only.

Coordination of typing and gesturing. With respect to the coordination of typing and gesturing, it was expected that in keyboard dialogues fewer demonstratives accompanied by gestures would occur. This was confirmed. In keyboard dialogues no such cases occurred at all, whereas in spoken dialogues this occurred in 17% of the cases. This difference could even be extended to the use of absolute features accompanied by gestures. In keyboard dialogues they were used in 6% of cases, whereas in spoken dialogues they occurred in 31% of cases. Relative features and combinations of absolute and relative features accompanied by gestures occurred equally often in keyboard and in spoken dialogues.

Types of features and gestures. Concerning continuation of the use of features that cannot be expressed by means of gestures, it was found, according to expectations, that nearly the same percentage of absolute colour features was used in both types of dialogue (keyboard: 100%, spoken: 97% of the absolute features used). However, there was a difference in the use of absolute shape features (e.g. 'square'). In keyboard dialogues 46% of the absolute features contained shape information, whereas in spoken dialogues this was the case in only 17%. A possible explanation of this difference is that in spoken dialogues absolute features were about 4 times more often accompanied by gestures than in keyboard dialogues (keyboard: +gesture 9%, −gesture 46%; spoken: +gesture 36%, −gesture 47%). Since the use of pointing gestures makes the use of shape information superfluous, this type of information may be used less in keyboard dialogues. (The feature 'colour' is probably so salient that participants tend to keep using it, even though the use of a pointing gesture makes that superfluous.)

The use of relative features in both types of dialogue was almost the same (keyboard: 1%, spoken: 2%). Although the number of explicit relative features in keyboard dialogues was lower than in spoken dialogues (keyboard: 23%, spoken: 39%) no clear difference was found. However, there is a difference in relative features that were used to refer to locations within the domain. If a location in the domain is indicated, this generally takes more words than if only physical features of objects are mentioned. It could be shown that in spoken dialogues more relative features were used to refer to locations (91% of the relative features used) than in keyboard dialogues (68%). This suggests that participants in keyboard dialogues tend to avoid these relatively long expressions, and probably point instead.

Focus of Attention. In keyboard dialogues 86 out of 156 referential acts were used to refer to objects in the current focus of attention (55%). The 70 remaining referential acts (45%) were used to refer to objects outside of the current focus area (see Cremers and Beun (1995) for the criteria used to make this distinction). Hence, no clear preference for choosing the next object in or out of the current focus area could be detected, as was the case in the spoken dialogues (68% in focus, 32% out of focus). This result confirms the expectation and is probably due to a coordination problem between typing and inspecting the domain.

Among the 86 references used in the keyboard dialogues to refer to objects in the current focus of attention, focus reduction was applied in 20 cases (23% of 86). This percentage is very close to that found in spoken dialogues, where focus reduction was applied in 27% of the cases. Our prediction was, however, that in keyboard dialogues more cases of focus reduction would occur owing to a general reduction of words. The result seems to suggest that this was not the case. However, when we again consider the use of gestures as a means to reduce effort, some evidence in support of the hypothesis can be found.

Participants in keyboard dialogues used gestures without any language to refer to objects in 35 (41%) of the in-focus cases. In spoken dialogues this was done in 13 cases (13%), where the gesture was accompanied by just a demonstrative. When we add the cases of gesture-related focus reduction to those where only a verbal reduction took place, the total number of cases of focus reduction in keyboard dialogues becomes 55 (64% of the in-focus cases). In spoken dialogues the total number of focus reduction then becomes 40 (40% of the in-focus cases). This suggests that, in the latter interpretation of focus reduction, participants in keyboard dialogues indeed use more reduced information when referring to objects within the focus area than participants in spoken dialogues. However, this reduction is due more to the use of gestures than to the use of reduced verbal information. An overview of the findings is given in Table 4.

Table 4. Focus reduction in keyboard and spoken dialogues

	keyboard (86)	spoken (99)
verbal	23% (20)	27% (27)
gestures	41% (35)	13% (13)
Total	64% (55)	40% (40)

4.2 The Object Reference Process

Number of Turns. The mean number of both verbal and non-verbal turns needed to arrive at mutual agreement that the target object has been identified is exactly the same in keyboard and spoken dialogues, namely 2.7 (s.d. 1.04 and 1.38, respectively). However, this does not mean that the process is exactly the same for both types of dialogue. The difference lies in the relative use of verbal turns and (referential) actions in this process. In keyboard dialogues 98 (63%) of the turns were non-verbal, whereas in spoken dialogues gestures or actions were used only in 23 (16%) of the turns. No indication was found that more information was given in the first turn to avoid turn-takings, since the mean lengths of first referential acts in keyboard and spoken dialogues were very similar (keyboard: 1.8, spoken: 2.2) and even shorter in keyboard dialogues.

With respect to the number of turns necessary to refer to objects in or out of focus, a difference was found between spoken dialogues and keyboard dialogues. In spoken dialogues more turns were needed to refer to an object out of focus (3.2) than to one in focus (2.4), whereas no difference was found in keyboard dialogues (both 2.7). This confirms our expectation that participants in keyboard dialogues do not benefit very much from the focus area, probably due to coordination problems between typing and inspecting the domain.

Miscommunications. One of the expectations about object reference processes, mentioned above, was that in keyboard dialogues more turns due to miscommunications would occur, since participants use fewer words to refer to objects. In the preceding section it was shown that no difference was found in mean number of turns between keyboard and spoken dialogues. This means that, if more miscommunications occurred, they did not increase the mean number of turns significantly. The results of analysing the occurring miscommunications are given in Table 5.

Table 5. Miscommunications in keyboard and spoken dialogues

	keyboard	spoken
Total	25 (16%)	6 (4%)
focus	13 (65%)	5 (83%)
mistake	4 (16%)	1 (17%)
determiner	8 (19%)	–
focus-det.	13 (77%)	5 (83%)

In keyboard dialogues miscommunications occurred in 25 (16%) of the cases before identification took place. In spoken dialogues only six (4%) of the first references were initially misunderstood. These miscommunications were found to be due mainly to misunderstandings related to focus (in five cases, 83%). The one remaining case was due to a mistake made by the speaker.

In keyboard dialogues 13 (65%) of the misunderstandings were in some way related to focus. In four cases (16%) mistakes were made by either one of the participants. In the remaining eight cases (19%) the misunderstanding was a result of confusion as to whether a new object should be introduced or the referential act was meant to refer to an object in the domain. These confusions were directly related to the fact that the typists did not add any determiner to the referential expression. This is a clear consequence of the modality of communication that was used. In order to type as few words as possible, typists omitted determiners.

Since the latter group of misunderstandings was a direct result of the available modalities of communication, they can be omitted from the comparison between keyboard and spoken dialogues. The percentage of misunderstandings due to focus then becomes 77% (13 out of 17 cases), which is close to the 83% found in spoken dialogues.

To summarize, more or less the same percentage of focus-related misunderstandings occurred in keyboard dialogues as in spoken dialogues. However, the total percentage of misunderstandings in keyboard dialogues was greater since more misunderstandings occurred due to mistakes and, most importantly, due to omitting determiners in descriptions. This result stresses the importance of determiners as providing information about the accessibility of a referent (see Piwek, Beun and Cremers, 1995).

5   Discussion and Conclusions

The differences between the uses of referential expressions and gestures in keyboard and spoken dialogues can be explained to a large extent by the differences in the respective experimental paradigms as illustrated by the DENK triangle.

A direct consequence of typing rather than speaking is the length of the referential expressions used. Since it takes more effort to type than to speak, fewer words were used in referential expressions in keyboard dialogues. However, since the difference not very great, the largest reduction of words occurred in the non-referential parts of the utterances. Furthermore, participants in keyboard dialogues were not found to use fewer gestures than those in spoken dialogues. The total number of gestures was the same, although the distribution over accompanying features was different. These results may be domain-dependent, since objects that are more difficult to describe are expected to be pointed at more often.

The difference found in the distribution of gestures is a direct consequence of the difficulty to coordinate verbal and non-verbal information in keyboard dialogues. Since it is not possible to gesture and type at the same time, hardly any occurrences of short referential expressions were found, such as demonstratives or absolute features only. In spoken dialogues the demonstratives and absolute features that accompanied gestures can be said to have the function of either attracting the attention of the partner to an area in the domain or of keeping the conversation flowing by avoiding silences. In keyboard dialogues the latter function is not prevalent, since there is less time pressure (Beun and Bunt, 1987). Participants in keyboard dialogues do not have the possibility to apply the former function, i.e. to attract attention. However, these participants were observed to point with more emphasis, i.e. repeatedly or for a longer period than participants in spoken dialogues did. The emphasis can be interpreted as a means to make sure that the partner has observed the gesture.

A second consequence related to the coordination of modalities is the fact that typing and simultaneously inspecting the domain was difficult. This resulted in difficulty in keeping track of the current focus area. This difficulty was reflected in the same number of references to objects in focus and to objects out of focus (in spoken dialogues far more references to objects in focus occurred).

As a consequence of the difficulty to change turns in keyboard dialogues, fewer verbal turns took place. However, the loss of verbal turns was compensated by more non-verbal turns. There was no indication that more information was given in the first utterance to try to avoid having to use more turns. However, this could be a consequence of the relatively simple objects used in the experiment. It was probably not necessary to use more words to indicate a certain object unambiguously. Although more miscommunications occurred in an absolute sense, they did not affect the mean number of turns used to reach agreement that the target object had been identified.

The differences between keyboard and spoken dialogues were all found to relate to the principle of minimal cooperative total effort. In a situation where different modalities of communication are available which have different characteristics and possibilities, other means have to be found to minimize effort. The main difference with respect to spoken dialogues was in the use of gestures to refer to objects. the same numbers of gestures were used in spoken dialogues and keyboard dialogues, but they were used at different moments. At moments where participants in spoken dialogues used limited information, participants in keyboard dialogues tended to use more pointing gestures.

From these findings some implications can be drawn for the design of a multimodal interface, such as the DENK interface. First, in our domain we did not find a great reduction of words in referential expressions, but we did find a great reduction in the rest of the utterances, i.e. in the part were the action that has to be carried out is formulated. Further research should be conducted to figure out whether this reduction causes more or other types of miscommunication.

In the design of a multimodal interface special attention should be devoted to the coordination of verbal and non-verbal information. Procedures should be developed to make links between verbal expressions, especially longer ones, and gestures that are meant to refer to the same objects but do not occur at the same time. This is necessary in order to avoid confusions about whether in these cases only one object or two separate objects are referred to.

In keyboard dialogues participants apparently did not make use of the current focus area as often as participants in the spoken dialogues, but reduced expressions referring to objects in the current focus area still occurred regularly. This means that the interface should adopt a notion of focus area in order to enable these expressions to be understood.

Finally, the interface should allow users to change turns quickly since almost the only type of feedback that was provided in keyboard dialogues consisted of gestures or actions in the domain. It is probably easier for the interface to understand verbal feedback than to analyse the meaning of gestures and actions. However, provisions should be made for listing the verbal and non-verbal turns in a convenient way so that no confusions will arise, because the correct order of turns is not clear.

References

Ahn, R.M.C., Beun, R.J., Borghuis, T., Bunt, H.C. & Overveld, C.W.A.M. van (1995) The DENK-architecture: a Fundamental Approach to User-Interfaces. *Artificial Intelligence Review, 8*, 431-445.

Beun, R.J. and Bunt, H.C. (1987) Investigating Linguistic Behaviour in Information Dialogues with a Computer. *IPO Annual Progress Report, 22*, 77-86.

Bunt, H.C. (1997) Issues in Multimodal Human-Computer Communication. *This volume.*

Bunt, H.C., Ahn, R.M.C., Beun, R.J., Borghuis, T., & Overveld, C.W.A.M. van (1997) Cooperative Multimodal Communication in the DENK System. *This volume.*

Clark, H.H. and Wilkes-Gibbs, D. (1986) Referring as a collaborative process. *Cognition, 22*, 1-39.

Cohen, P.R. (1984) The Pragmatics of Referring and the Modality of Communication. *Computational Linguistics, 10(2)*, 97-125.

Cremers, A.H.M. (1995) The Process of Cooperative Object Reference in a Shared Domain. In: E. Fava (ed.) *Speech acts and linguistic research: proceedings of the workshop, July 15-17, 1994.* First International Summer Institute in Cognitive Science, Center for Cognitive Science, State University of New York at Buffalo, NY. Padova: edizione nemo, 139-153.

Cremers, A.H.M. and Beun, R.J. (1985) *Object Reference in a Shared Domain of Conversation.* Eindhoven, Institute for Perception Research, manuscript no. 1089.

Hauptmann, A.G. and Rudnicky, A.I. (1988) Talking to Computers: an Empirical Investigation. *International Journal of Man-Machine Studies, 28*, 583-604.

Oviatt, S.L. and Cohen, P.R. (1991) Discourse Structure and Performance Efficiency in Interactive and Non-interactive Spoken Modalities. *Computer Speech and Language, 5*, 297-326.

Piwek, P., Beun, R.J. and Cremers, A.H.M. (1995) Deictic Use of Dutch Demonstratives. *IPO Annual Progress Report, 30*, 99-108.

Referent Identification Requests in Multi-Modal Dialogs

Tsuneaki Kato and Yukiko I. Nakano

NTT Information and Communication Systems Labs.
1-2356 Take, Yokosuka-shi, Kanagawa 238-03 JAPAN
kato@nttnly.ntt.jp

Abstract. This paper describes an empirical study on what kinds of information are appropriate for referent identification requests in multi-modal dialogs, and how that information should be communicated in order to achieve the request desired. We conduct experiments in which experts explain the installation of a telephone in four situations: spoken-mode monolog; spoken-mode dialog; multi-modal monolog; and multi-modal dialog. Referent identification requests could be well analyzed from two perspectives: information communicated and the style of goal achievement. We find that there is a close relationship between the information conveyed via different communicative modes, and sketch a model that explains these results. In the model, information cannot be divided into the semantic content conveyed and the communicative modes employed, and is treated as the primitive unit for consideration. Pointing is considered as information in this sense. We also find that in dialogs, especially in spoken-mode dialogs, the speakers realize identification requests as series of fine-grained steps, and try to achieve them step by step.

1 Introduction

Two kinds of actions are ubiquitous in every dialog: referent identification, by which the hearer identifies the object described linguistically by a noun phrase or pointed to through a physical action, and referent identification request, by which the speaker makes the hearer identify the referent. Especially in instruction-giving dialogs on physical objects, these actions appear frequently and play a central role. As a consequence, all multi-modal dialog systems have to have a framework to realize referent identification requests.

An interesting point is that there is no agreement between researchers on how referent identification requests should be realized. According to the relationship between communicative modes, COMET's media coordinator decides which portion of a given semantic content should be realized in which mode (Feiner and McKeown, 1990). The relationship of communicative modes is limited to only the aspect of how to communicate a given content. By contrast, in the framework proposed by Maybury, during planning for achieving a mode-independent rhetorical goal, mode allocation and content selection are achieved simultaneously, and can co-constrain (Maybury, 1993). In the examples shown in Maybury (1993), however, he used the same schema for linguistic identification requests, independently of whether visual actions could be used. Based on this example only, he looks to treat visual identification requests such as pointing actions as just supplemental; they have no effect on linguistic requests. On the other hand, WIP uses cross-modal references, the references between modes that are possible only when the system can utilize more than one mode (André and Rist, 1994; Wahlster et al., 1991).

Several systems have different criteria on what reference expression should be preferred. For example, Neal and Shapiro (1991) claim that graphic/pictorial presentation is always desirable, and that natural language can always be used as a last resort. In Claassen (1992), contextual factors such as salience play an important role, while whether the object is currently visible or not is taken into account towards the bottom of the decision tree. Although it is obvious that these criteria depend on the domains that the systems are concerned with and do not need to be identical, some criteria based on empirical studies is needed.

The objective of our research is to empirically determine what kinds of information are appropriate for referent identification requests in multi-modal dialogs, and how that information should be communicated. The long term goal of this study is to provide useful suggestions for designing more sophisticated multi-modal dialog systems. Cohen also picked up referent identification requests and compared the kinds of speech acts used to achieve them for two dialog situations: keyboard dialog and telephone dialog (Cohen, 1984). Our research not only extends the situations considered to the multi-modal one in which conversants have audio and visual channels, but also considers the kinds and amounts of information used for referent identification and clarifies how they are influenced by the communicative modes and contextual factors. Moreover, elaboration related phenomena and the roles of the addressee are also examined.

2   The Experiments and the Corpus

Experiments were conducted to obtain the corpus needed to design multi-modal dialog systems. The task is the installation of a telephone with an answering machine feature. In this task, the telephone set is unpacked, then eight settings, such as checking the volume, adjusting the clock and recording a response message, are accomplished. Finally, some function buttons are explained.

In order to consider the effect of communicative modes and level of interactivity, we recorded explanations in four situations: SD (Spoken-mode Dialog), MD (Multi-modal Dialog), SM (Spoken-mode Monolog) and MM (Multi-modal Monolog). In all situations, the experts were able to handle the telephones in front of them freely. In the dialog situations, SD and MD, each expert conversed with a remote apprentice to lead him/her through installation. In the monolog situations, SM and MM, the experts verbalized the instructions with no audience in the setting that an apprentice will follow his/her instruction afterwards by listening to an audiotape in SM or watching a videotape in MM.

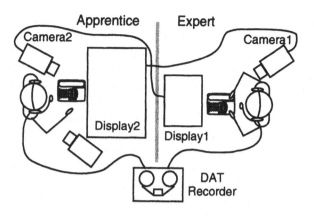

Fig. 1. Experiment setting for multi-modal dialogs

In SD and SM, explanations were given using just voice; head sets were used for voice transfer or collection. In the multi-modal situations, both voice and visual information could be communicated. MM had a video camera record the telephone in front of the expert and his/her pointing actions. In MD, a deliberately designed combination of video cameras and displays allowed the conversants to communicate and share the view of the expert-side telephone and both conversants' pointing actions. Figure 1 shows the setting in MD. The picture of the expert-side telephone and the expert's pointing actions to it is taken by Camera 1, and is displayed on Display 2. The apprentice watches the picture on Display 2, and can point to it. This action is captured by Camera 2 and is displayed on Display 1. As the result, as shown in Fig. 2 schematically, the expert can see his/her own telephone and his/her pointing actions and also the apprentice's pointing. This is similar to face-to-face dialog situations except for the absence of eye contact and various body movements. It is worth noting that this situation accurately simulates a user working with a multi-modal dialog system with speech output and video display, that accepts user's voice input and pointing actions to items on the display.

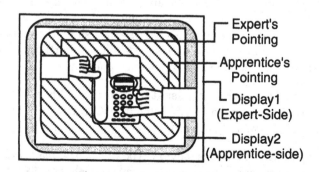

Fig. 2. Schematic view of the expert-side display

Five experts participated in the experiments. Each expert made eighteen explanations: six each for SD and MD, and three each for SM and MM. 90 explanations were obtained in total. 60 apprentices received one explanation apiece. Miscellaneous constraints compelled the experiment to be divided into two parts. First, SD dialogs were recorded. Four months later, MD dialogs and both SM and MM monologs were recorded. In both sets of experiments, the experts and experiment controllers gathered on the day prior to the recording. Experts received an explanation about the items to teach and their rough order, read out the manual together, and conducted simulated explanations a few times. Thus the outlines of the explanations were almost same, i.e. independent of the experts. There was no instruction or suggestion on the explanation details and expressions they were to use, however. Moreover, various situations took place initiated by failures of settings and apprentices' responses. The average explanation lengths were 27' 57" for SD, 25' 59" for MD, 22' 27" for SM and 21' 13" for MM. All explanations were done in Japanese, and this paper provides their direct English translations.

3   Referent Identification Requests Recorded and Coding

As a preliminary step, for each expert we selected three SD and MD explanations and two SM and MM explanations, 50 explanations in total. First, we picked out referent identification requests made for setting some thing, such as checking the volume, adjusting the clock or recording a response message. The referent identifications so extracted contained descriptions of the object to be identified and the subsequent explanation or request of the appropriate physical action to be performed upon it. For example, an apprentice may be requested to identify the SET button and be instructed to push it. S/he may also be instructed to find the volume switch and set it loud. These situations are similar to the one described in Cohen (1984) and Oviatt and Cohen (1991), so we can compare results. The portion extracted is from the beginning of the explanation of an action to the point when the mutual understanding of the action seems to be established. It includes the additional utterances initiated by apprentices' implicit or explicit feedback. The extraction was done based on both the transcript and audio/video tapes. In addition, explanations in multi-modal situations were annotated with accompanying actions like pointing. The following are examples of extracted identification requests. Double slashes show the existence of the apprentice's back channel response or acknowledgment. Portions surrounded by square brackets are accompanied by actions like pointing.

> Then, first, um, open the cassette cover. // Then, I think
> buttons are lined in rows. // Push the SET button, the second
> one from the left. (situation SD)

> [First, open the cassette cover. {*points to the main body then
> the cassette cover; opens the cassette cover*}] Push the SET button.
> (situation MD)

The extracted and annotated referent identification requests were scored and analyzed from the following two perspectives.

3.1   Information Communicated

What kind of and what amount of information was communicated in each identification process? In this study, information was captured in its widest sense. First, a linguistic description of the proposition that concerns the features of the object is regarded as the piece of information communicated. Such type of information includes descriptions of its shape, size, position, and so on. In addition, usage of a pronominal, description of contextual information, and description of landmark objects are all regarded as communicating some piece of information. As a pointing action conveys some visual information, it is also regarded as information in itself. Information was divided into the following categories.

pronominals pronominals including pronouns e.g. "this", "it".

context reference an indication that the object was already identified in the current discourse. e.g. "that we used before"

general name an object category name that identifies the type of thing but does not clearly identify which thing is being referred to. e.g. "button", "switch"

proper name a name that distinguishes the object from others. e.g. "the SET button", "the telephone circuit selector"

shape/size a description of the color, size and shape of the object. e.g. "red", "big"

position a description about where the object is. e.g. "on upper right of the main body"

characters/marks a description of the characters or marks attached on/by the object. e.g. "with the characters, OUT"

functions a description about the function(s) the object has. e.g. "for controlling the volume"

related objects a description about a set that contains the object or a landmark around the object. e.g. "a group of buttons"

others other linguistic information such as features of the set containing the object. e.g. "lined in two rows"

pointing a pointing action to the object.

All information except pointing were communicated through the audio channel, and were captured in the transcript. The appropriate portions were picked from the extracted referent identification requests, and were classified. In this study, we define the amount of information as the number of such portions and the existence of accompanying pointing. In the case of pronominals, general name and proper name, the number of tokens is used. In other cases, number of types is used. That is, in the latter case, a literal repetition that conveys the same content is counted just once. Obviously, it is considered as two pieces of information communicated in the case that two types of information of the same category, such as "on upper left of the body" and "above the dial buttons", appear in a referent identification request. In the case of pointing, only its usage was checked so that its amount is always zero or one regardless of its continuation time.

This examination and enumeration also revealed that almost all usages of "this" in MD and MM were accompanied with pointing, and could be regarded as cross-modal references.

3.2 Goal Achievement

What type of surface speech act form was used in a referent identification request, and through what process was the identification request expressed and achieved?

The first characteristic examined in this perspective is what type of surface speech act form was used in a referent identification request. This characteristic was also examined in Cohen (1984). We examined whether a referent identification request is subsumed in the following action request as its case element without any clue, or is to be regarded as an explicit goal and realized as a sentence. In the latter case, what kind of sentence is used was also examined. Utterance forms were divided into the following categories. Referent identification is considered an explicit goal when NP fragment, Existential Prop., or Perception-base is used. This is not the case when Case is used.

Case an unmarked noun phrase describing the object appearing in another request, e.g. *"Push the SET button"*.

NP fragment an utterance consisting of an isolated noun phrase describing the object, e.g. *"The SET button, this is it, push it"*.

Existential Prop. an utterance that asserts object existence, e.g. *"There is the SET button on upper right of the main body"*.

Perception-base an utterance that requests the addressee perform an action to make him/her aware of the object, such as looking and opening, e.g. *"Look at the upper right of the dial buttons. Push the SET button there"*.

Others other types of utterances.

The second characteristic examined is whether confirmation such as use of a tag question and an interrogative sentence, was made to check the accomplishment of the request

The third characteristic is how often the expert used expressions closely related to elaboration. The style and amount of elaboration relate the processes in order to achieve the referent identification requests, and were also examined in Clark and Wilkes-Gibbs (1990) and Oviatt and Cohen (1991). In our study, elaboration related expression were divided into the following categories.

Apposition an appositive expression, that is a noun phrase explaining the object expanded by a subsequent parenthetical noun phrase.

Supplement a supplementary copula or a noun phrase fragment that explains the object and follows a sentence or clause that contains a noun phrase explaining that object. In Japanese, as a main verb follows its case element, appositions and supplements can be distinguished easily. The following two Japanese expressions, for an example, both have the almost same meaning as the English expression, "Push the OUT button, the red button.", one contains an apposition and the other contains a supplement.

Apposition
rusu   botan,   akai botan,   wo   oshite-kudasai.
OUT button, red button, Obj push please.
Supplement
rusu   botan wo   oshite-kudasai, akai botan.
OUT button Obj push please,   red button.

Replacement expressions that have the same syntactic structure as appositions or supplements but whose semantic content contradicts that of the one uttered immediately before and replaces it. For example, "push the leftmost button, rightmost one". Articulation level errors, phonetic repair in Levelt (1983), are not included.

The above definition does not take it into account whether there is an utterance boundary somewhere in those expressions, though, as Clark and Wilkes-Gibbs (1990) pointed out, the existence of utterance boundary and the apprentice's implicit request of refashioning can be a clue for determining whether an elaboration is reactive or previously designed. Experts' intonation was also not taken into consideration.

The fourth and last characteristic examined is the apprentices' contributions in dialog situations. The number and categories of apprentices' utterances were examined. The utterances were categorized into five categories: acknowledgments, which include back channel responses; repetitions with down intonation; follow-up questions including repetitions with rising intonation; spontaneous elaboration; and replacements.

4   Results

This section shows the results on how the characteristics of referent identification requests described in the previous section are influenced by the available modes of communication and the level of interactivity. It is obvious that identification requests depend on the contextual factor of the referent. That is, initial identification, which is used to make the first effective reference to an object must show different characteristics from other identifications, which are used to refer to objects already introduced. Accordingly, we first analyzed how objects were first introduced in order to examine, independently of the contextual factors, the communicative modes available and interactivity dependency. Second, how referent identification requests depend on position in the discourse was examined.

4.1   Initial Identification

How objects were first introduced was analyzed in order to examine, independently of the contextual factors, the communicative modes available and interactivity dependency. We examined the introduction of twelve objects.

Table 1. Information communicated in initial identification

Sit	Pros	General Proper Shape Name Name Size			Pos	Chars Marks	Funcs	Rel Obj	Others	Pointing
SD	1.01	1.45	0.68	0.34	1.08	0.70	0.11	0.29	0.18	–
MD	0.99	1.24	0.78	0.12	1.06	0.44	0.12	0.12	0.10	0.98
SM	0.75	1.32	0.88	0.19	1.13	0.52	0.09	0.19	0.16	–
MM	0.95	1.21	0.91	0.14	0.90	0.34	0.13	0.13	0.11	0.86

Table 1 shows the results in terms of the amount and kind of information communicated. Each cell shows the average amount of information of a given type used in one reference. That is, information communicated in extracted referent identification requests were enumerated and classified according to the criterion described. The average number per identification request were calculated in each situation and each information type. Obviously, context references are not used and so do not appear in the table. Fig. 3 shows the histogram of the total amount of information, the number of pieces of information, communicated in one request for each situation. Fig. 4 and Fig. 5 show the ratio of usage of a given type of information in referent identification requests, as related to their total amount of information. For example, we can see that shape/size information was used in 44% of references that communicated five or six pieces of information in situation MD. For all types of information, if no identification request was observed to communicating a given amount of information, its ratio was scored as 0%. The reliability of the ratios depends on the total number of identification requests made. These are the reasons why Fig. 3 is shown.

These results are summarized as follows.

- Pointing actions accompanied by cross-modal references are used frequently in the multi-modal situations, MD and MM. [from Table 1]
- The amount of linguistic information used is smaller in the multi-modal situations, MD and MM, than in the spoken-mode situations, SD and SM. This effect is especially significant with shape/size, characters/marks and related objects ($F(1,55) = 15.91$, $p < 0.001$, $F(1,55) = 28.96$, $p < 0.001$, and $F(1,55) = 10.17$, $p = 0.002$ respectively). It is also the case, but not so significant, for position ($F(1,55) = 5.19$, $p = 0.027$). [from Table 1]
  These types of information, the usage of which is reduced in multi-modal situations, are used in spoken-mode situations only when references have a relatively large total amount of information. [from Fig. 4 and Fig. 5]

Table 2, 3 and 4 show the results in terms of the style of goal achievement. Table 2 shows the percentage of those cases in which a given utterance form was used for identification requests. Table 3 shows the percentage of those cases in which confirmation was made in each situation. Table 4 shows the number of elaboration-related expression usages per reference in each situation. The result

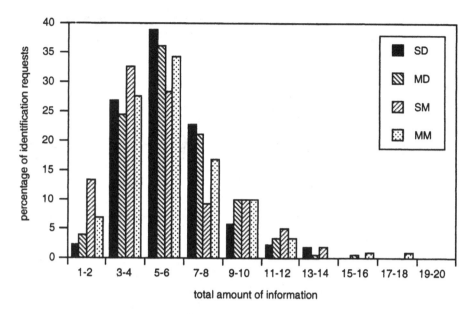

Fig. 3. Histogram of the total amount of information in initial identification

of the contributions of apprentices in dialog situations shows that, in situation SD, the average number of apprentices' utterances per identification is 4.97, and 92% of those are acknowledgments. In situation MD, the number of utterances is 3.36, and acknowledgments amount to 96%. In both situations, more than half the utterances, excluding acknowledgments, are follow-up questions including repetitions with rising intonation. These results are summarized as follows.

- The utterance form used differs with the situation ($\chi^2(12) = 55.90$, $p < 0.001$). Identification requests as an explicit goal (i.e., NP fragments, Existential props. and Perception-base) appear most frequently in SD, next in MD and rarely in SM and MM. [from Table 2]
- The frequency of using confirmation differs significantly with the situation ($\chi^2(12) = 65.43$, $p < 0.001$). Confirmation appears most frequently in SD, next in MD and seldom in either monolog situation. [from Table 3]
- Appositions are used frequently in monolog situations ($F(1,55) = 5.53$, $p = 0.022$), especially in MM. Supplements are used frequently in dialog situations ($F(1,55) = 12.11$, $p = 0.001$), especially in SD. [from Table 4]
- Apprentices utter more frequently in SD than in MD ($t(59) = 6.21$, $p < 0.001$). Non-acknowledgment utterances also appear more frequently in SD ($z = 3.38$, $p < 0.01$).

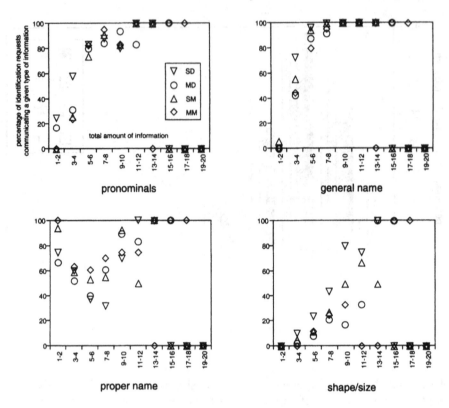

Fig. 4. Percentage of usage of a given type of information

4.2   Contextual Effect

In order to identify how referent identification requests depend on position in the discourse, we examined the data in which four objects were identified at least three times: the first two times in the same setting task and the third time in another task. For example, the SET button is used twice for clock adjustment, and once for one-touch dial setting. As utterances made for different setting tasks can be regarded as constituting different discourse segments, the third identification belongs to a discourse segment different from that of the first and second.

Table 5 shows the kind and amount of information communicated as related to the first, second and third identification. Types of information not shown in the table was not used in any situation. We can see the following characteristics.

- The amount of linguistic information radically decreases after the first identification. The usage of pointing actions does not significantly decrease.
- The amount of linguistic information used recovers slightly in a new discourse segment (the third identification). Context references appear to be more

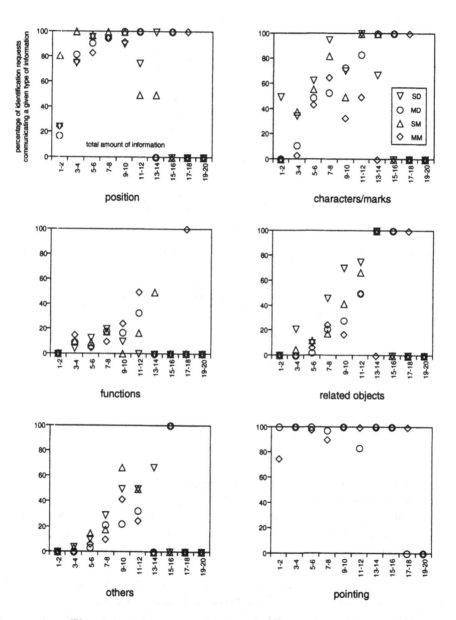

Fig. 5. Percentage of usage of a given type of information

frequent in SD and MD, $(F(1, 15) = 4.29, p = 0.06)$, while position references seems to be more frequent in SD and SM $(F(1, 15) = 6.82, p = 0.02)$.

Table 2. Percentage of utterance forms used in initial identification

Sit	Case NP Fragment	Existential	Perception	Others
SD	18	3	47	23	9
MD	29	11	33	12	16
SM	42	7	32	8	13
MM	38	20	20	5	17

Table 3. Percentage of confirmation made in initial identification

Sit	SD	MD	SM	MM
with Confirmation	38	19	3	2

Table 4. Average number of elaboration-related expressions in initial identification

Sit	Apposition	Supplement	Replacement
SD	0.28	0.43	0.28
MD	0.32	0.29	0.27
SM	0.42	0.21	0.33
MM	0.53	0.23	0.31

Although the raw data regarding the style of goal achievements is omitted for brevity, we found the following characteristics.

- Identification requests were realized rarely, 10% or less, as an explicit goal in the second and third times in all situations.
- Confirmations were not made at all in the second time references in all situations. In the third time identification, only 2% of references contain confirmation in dialog situations, and no reference contained confirmation in monolog situations.
- Appositions and supplements were used less than 0.2 times per reference in the second and third time identifications in all situations.
- The number of cases in which identification requests were realized as the explicit goal, confirmation, and the usage of appositions and supplements decrease dramatically in the second time identification, and very slightly recover in the third time.

Table 5. Information communicated in the first, second and third identification

First identification

Sit	Pros	General Name	Proper Name	Shape Size	Pos	Chars Marks	Funcs	Rel Obj	Others	Pointing
SD	0.72	1.55	1.12	0.30	1.02	0.60	0.03	0.42	0.25	–
MD	0.83	1.13	1.08	0.03	1.03	0.43	0.05	0.08	0.12	1.00
SM	0.48	1.00	1.15	0.05	1.15	0.53	0.00	0.18	0.20	–
MM	0.83	0.83	1.20	0.00	0.83	0.25	0.05	0.08	0.10	0.95

Second identification

Sit	Pros	General Name	Proper Name	Pos	Pointing
SD	0.06	0.17	0.89	0.02	–
MD	0.25	0.15	0.81	0.08	0.81
SM	0.03	0.08	1.00	0.18	–
MM	0.31	0.19	0.88	0.09	0.81

Third identification

Sit	Pros	Context Refs	General Name	Proper Name	Pos	Chars Marks	Pointing
SD	0.05	0.10	0.17	1.03	0.23	0.05	–
MD	0.27	0.12	0.10	1.03	0.07	0.03	0.82
SM	0.03	0.03	0.00	1.15	0.25	0.03	–
MM	0.18	0.03	0.03	1.05	0.08	0.03	0.83

5   Discussion

5.1   Information Communicated

One of the findings in terms of the kind and amount of information communicated is that the availability of pointing, information communicated through a visual channel, reduces the amount of information conveyed through the speech or linguistic channel. There must be some relationship between these two types of information, which are conveyed via different communicative modes. In initial identification, the usage of linguistic information of shape/size, characters/marks and related objects decrease in multi-modal situations, in which experts can use pointing. In third time identification, the usage of position information decreases slightly. It is also interesting that these types of information, the usage of which is reduced in multi-modal situations, are used in spoken-mode situations only when the references have a relatively large total amount of information. Other findings include that pointing is used very frequently in multi-modal situations, and it is almost always accompanies linguistic information. Proper names are used sometimes accompanied with other information such as position in third time identification, even though the proper name would seem to be enough by itself for identifying objects already introduced.

According to the theoretical framework of reference proposed by Appelt (1985), a referent identification request, or just a reference, is intended to activate the concept in the addressee's mental space. In order to achieve that, the speaker has to provide sufficient description for the addressee to distinguish the object from others. Moreover, the amount of description used is minimized because the speaker does not want to generate extraneous information. The appropriateness of the description provided depends on mutual beliefs and the center of discourse.

There are some problems in his theories, however. First, his claim that pointing is enough to activate the object is not consistent with our findings. It is difficult to consider that all linguistic information is conveyed opportunistically, and only pointing is used for identification, though it might be the case for descriptions of the functions and labeling of proper names. One support for the idea that information of those plays different roles is shown in Fig. 4 and Fig 5; the pattern of usage as related to the total amount of information looks different from other information. Second, minimization of descriptions must be reconsidered from the perspective of reference as a collaborative process of the conversants. The total effort of the speaker and the addressee should be minimized rather just that of the speaker (Clark and Wilkes-Gibbs, 1990). In spite of these problems, his framework, which claims that sufficient and necessary amount of information is communicated for activating the concept well explains our results.

The results described in this paper suggest a model for referent identification requests made using different communicative modes. As such, it can be seen as an extension of Appelt's model. Descriptions are extended to pieces of information that cover the widest possible extent, and include not only linguistic description about colors and shapes, but also pointing actions and contextual references. Information in this sense can be considered as the pairing of the semantic content conveyed and the communicative mode employed. Our claim is that those two constituents of information are inherently associated with each other and cannot be divided. In the model, each piece of information, either linguistic or other, is assigned two measures: its effectiveness in activating a given concept and its cost, the amount of effort required to make it. In any situation, the speaker chooses and combines the pieces of information that achieve concept activation with provably minimal cost.

It is natural to consider that the amount of information needed for activation is influenced by several contextual factors such as saliency (Alshawi, 1987) and attention stack position (Grosz and Sidner, 1986). That is, initial identification of an object needs a large amount of information to introduce and activate its concept. A smaller amount of information is needed to reactivate an object introduced recently. With time or the introduction of different discourse segments, more information is needed to reactivate the original concept. Related to this idea, the observed result that proper names do not suffice to reactivate an object already introduced suggests the validity of context models as was discussed in Walker (1992).

The communicative mode dependency reported here is derived naturally from our model because each identification request was expressed using a combination of information pieces. If the speaker can use visual information, such as pointing, and activates the concept up to some extent, his/her usage of linguistic information decreases as it is used only for the remainder of the activation. This means that pointing is not just supplemental. Therefore, there must be some relationship among pieces of information, which are conveyed via different communicative modes. The next question is what kind of relationship it is. As COMET (Feiner and McKeown, 1990) decides which portion of a given semantic content should be realized in which communicative mode, just how contents are communicated depends on the modes available, while the contents communicated don't. According to the framework of COMET, pointing is regarded as an alternative way of communication, and it must convey some of the contents that would be conveyed linguistically in the situation that pointing could not be used. According to our results, in initial identification, such contents included those conveyed by information of shape/size, characters/marks and related objects. It was related to position information in third time identification. That is, according to the COMET framework, we have to attribute several roles to pointing actions depending on contextual factors. This is complicated and unnatural.

On the other hand, our model claims that semantic content conveyed also depends on the available modes, as information cannot be divided into its semantic content conveyed and its communicative mode(s) employed. Our model interprets the role of pointing as follows. Let us consider an object, for example. In a spoken-mode situation, the combination of three pieces of information, say description of its general name, position, and shape, is enough to activate this object with the least expense. We assume also the cost required for shape information is most expensive. In the case of identifying this object in a multimodal situation, our model predicts that the speaker will first choose to use pointing, as it is very cost-effective information to activate the concept up to some extent. Next s/he uses linguistic description for the remainder of the activation. In this case, for example, the combination of two pieces of information is enough, so s/he doesn't need to communicate shape information. Comparison of these two situations shows that the usage of shape information decreases in multi-modal situations. It is important that this model does not consider the contents conveyed and mode employed separately, but considers information as a primitive. We cannot ascribed a fixed semantic content to pointing. Pointing is a piece of information in itself, and cannot be divided into its content and its communicative mode.

Reactivating an object is easily achieved. Its proper name also can be used with low cost, if it was labeled before in initial identification. In a spoken-mode situation, the combination of two pieces of information, proper name and position, is enough for reactivation. In a multi-modal situation, the combination of pointing and the proper name is enough. In this case, the comparison of these two situations shows the usage of position information decreases in multi-modal situations. That is, according to our model, it naturally depends on contextual factors as to what types of information decrease in multi-modal situations. Moreover, the information, the usage of which is reduced in multi-modal situations, is expensive, and used in spoken-mode situations only when the references need relatively large amounts of information. We claim that information, the pairing of the semantic content conveyed and the communicative modes employed, is a primitive unit of consideration, and those two constituents of information are inherently associated with each other and cannot be divided. This implies pointing is not a complete alternative way to linguistic communication, and does not convey the contents that must be conveyed linguistically.

5.2   Goal Achievement

Is has been reported that referent identification requests in spoken-mode dialog tend to be realized in an explicit goal more than in spoken-mode monolog (Oviatt and Cohen, 1991). It has been asserted that the speaker attempts to achieve finer-grained goals in spoken-mode dialog compared to keyboard dialog (Cohen, 1984). Our study also showed that referent identification requests in dialogs tend to be realized as an explicit goal more often than in monologs. This tendency is very obvious in spoken-mode dialogs. In addition, in spoken-mode dialog, confirmation is made more frequently; supplemental noun phrase fragments are used more frequently for elaboration than appositions, which constructs a large noun phrase; and, the apprentices utter more frequently and their utterances contain more non-acknowledgments. That is, in spoken-mode dialog, the experts realize an identification request as a series of fine-grained steps, and try to achieve it step by step, in various aspects of communication.

Comparing this characteristic between keyboard-dialog, spoken-mode dialogs and multi-modal dialogs, we can see that multi-modal dialogs resemble keyboard dialogs more than spoken-mode dialogs. On the other hand, we can consider that conversants can communicate the largest amount of information through multi-modal dialog, and smallest in the keyboard-dialog. Multi-modal dialogs and keyboard dialogs are two extremes. If we consider that communication modes are distinguished only by communication capacity, we cannot explain the resemblance of multi-modal dialogs and keyboard dialogs. Similar results were obtained in a study on the degree of recipient's contribution in information providing dialogs (Ishikawa, 1994). The model proposed there and the study on communication strategies and their efficiency (Walker, 1994) do help to understand this issue.

As for the second and third time identification, it is unclear how the method of goal achievement is influenced by communication modes available. In all situations, identification requests are rarely realized as an explicit goal, and the number of confirmations and elaborations are few. It is considered that this is because such identifications are very easy to achieve such as reactivation needs a smaller amount of information than the first time activation.

It has been reported that descriptions in spoken-mode dialogs are relatively brief and contain a smaller number of spontaneous elaborations than in spoken-mode monologs (Oviatt and Cohen, 1991). This report contradicts ours. We could not see much difference in the number of elaborations and the amount of information conveyed between dialog situations and monolog situations. One possible reason of this contradiction is that in our experiments the same expert explained in several modes. S/he could estimate how much information was appropriate without apprentices' feedback through the experiences gained in the dialog situations.

6   Summary and Future Work

We empirically studied what kinds of information are appropriate for referent identification requests in multi-modal dialogs, and how that information should be communicated in order to achieve that requests. Our findings include that there is a close relationship between the information conveyed via different communicative modes, and that in dialogs, especially in spoken-mode dialogs, the speakers realize identification requests as series of fine-grained steps, and try to achieve them step by step. This is true for a wide variety of communication aspects, such as confirmation and elaboration. We showed a sketch of a model that determines what kinds of information are appropriate. In the model, information cannot be divided into the semantic content conveyed and the communicative modes employed, and is treated as the primitive unit for consideration. Pointing is considered as information in this sense.

A lot remains as future work. We have to confirm if the characteristics we reported here are observed in other domains such as route-explanation using map or explanations of charts and graphs. We also have to make our rough sketch of the model more concrete and operational. It will allow us to implement some multi-modal dialog systems for evaluating our framework.

References

André, E. and Rist, T. (1994) Referring to World Objects with Text and Pictures, In *Proceedings of COLING '94*, 530-534.

Alshawi, H. (1987) *Memory and Context for Language Interpretation*, Cambridge: Cambridge University Press.

Appelt, D.E. (1985) Planning English Referring Expressions, *Artificial Intelligence, 26*, 1-33.

Clark, H.H. and Wilkes-Gibbs, D. (1990) Referring as a Collaborative Process. In *Intentions in Communication*, Cohen, P.R., Morgan, J. and Pollack, M.E. (eds.) The MIT Press, 463-493.

Claassen, W. (1992) Generating Referring Expressions in a Multimodal Environment. In *Aspects of Automated Natural Language Generation*, Hovy, R.D.O. Stock, D.R. (eds.) Heidelberg: Springer-Verlag, 247-262.

Cohen, P.R. (1984) The Pragmatics of Referring and the Modality of Communication, *Computational Linguistics, 10(2)*, 97-146.

Feiner, S.K. and McKeown, K.R. (1990) Coordinating Text and Graphics in Explanation Generation. In *Proceedings of AAAI-90*, 442-449.

Grosz, B.J. and Sidner, C.L. (1986) Attention, Intentions, and the Structure of Discourse, *Computational Linguistics, 12(3)*, 174-204.

Ishikawa, Y. (1984) Communicative Mode Dependent Contribution from the Recipient in Information Providing Dialogue. In *Proceedings of ICSLP '94*, 959-962.

Levelt, W.J.M. (1983) Monitoring and Self-Repair in Speech, *Cognition, 14*, 41-104.

Maybury, M.T. (1993) Planning Multimedia Explanations Using Communicative Acts. In *Intelligent Multi Media Interfaces*, The AAAI Press / The MIT Press, 60-74.

Neal, J.G. and Shapiro, S.C. (1991) Intelligent Multi-Media Technology. In *Intelligent User Interfaces*, Sullivan, J.W. and Tyler, S.W. (eds.) ACM Press, 11-43.

Oviatt, S.L. and Cohen, P.R. (1991) Discourse Structure and Performance Efficiency in Interactive and Noninteractive Spoken Modalities, *Computer Speech and Language, 5(4)*, 297-326.

Wahlster, W., André, E., Graf, W. and Rist, T., Designing Illustrated Texts: How Language Production is Influenced by Graphics Generation. In *Proceedings of EACL '91*, 8-14.

Walker, M.A. (1992) Redundancy in Collaborative Dialogue. In *Proceedings of 14th COLING*, 345-351.

Walker, M.A. (1994) Experimentally Evaluating Communicative Strategies: The Effect of the Task. In *Proceedings of AAAI-94*, 86-93.

Studies into Full Integration of Language and Action

Carla Huls[1] * and Edwin Bos[2]

[1] Informaat, P.O. Box 789, 3740 AT Baarn, The Netherlands
carla_huls@informaat.nl
[2] 532 Forest Ave #2, Palo Alto, CA 94301, USA

Abstract. In this paper we argue for conducting empirical studies into the actual use and usefulness of multimodal user interfaces. We have started formulating some important questions and attempting to answer three of them using the prototype multimodal user interface EDWARD. We investigated questions concerning efficiency, experience, speed, and error for multimodal and unimodal interaction. The preliminary results indicate that multimodality is indeed a useful approach.

1 Introduction

The combination of natural language (NL) and direct manipulation (DM) is so interesting that numerous papers about multimodal systems have been approved of by reviewers of human-computer interaction (HCI) journals and conference proceedings (e.g., Huls, Bos, and Dijkstra, 1994; Allgayer et al., 1989; Stock, 1991) even though they lack proof that this approach actually is useful to the user. Although it is valuable to know that multimodal interfaces can be made, we maintain that for HCI their main value lies in their benefit to users. Analytical approaches to support the claim of usefulness of multimodality are numerous (Desain, 1988; Walker, 1989; Hutchins, 1989; Cohen, 1992; Claassen, Bos, and Huls, 1990; cf. Sect. 3), but actual empirical tests and comparisons of unimodal and multimodal interfaces can not be found in the literature.

In this paper we use the term *mode* to refer to the distinction between the use of language to interact versus the use of action. Interaction *style* is used for different instantiations of these modes, e.g., natural language, command language, and menus for language mode interfaces, and direct manipulation for action mode interfaces.

A *fully integrated multimodal interface* combines the benefits from both modes by offering a series of interaction styles for one task and combining the language and action modes. Fully integrated multimodal interfaces allow the user to choose, at any time during the interaction, the interaction style that suits best at that moment. Consequently, there is no distinction between the availability

---

* The original version was written while both authors were working at the NICI, University of Nijmegen, PO Box 9104 HE Nijmegen, The Netherlands.

of interaction styles in different situations. In such an interface, all interaction styles are available at all times.

In order to examine the usefulness of multimodal user interfaces, we first describe EDWARD, a fully integrated multimodal user interface. Next, we present some theoretical analyses of the advantages of combining language and action in such a user interface. In Sect. 4, we then show some results of several user studies with EDWARD: What do the users actually do? Do they make use of the freedom of interaction style usage? Do they like it? Finally, we describe the conclusions and provide some more research questions.

2 Overview of EDWARD

EDWARD integrates two subsystems, each providing unimodal interaction , sharing a dialogue manager and knowledge sources (Huls and Bos, 1993; Huls, Bos, and Dijkstra, 1994; Bos, 1993). EDWARD is implemented in Allegro Common Lisp and runs on a DECstation. EDWARD is a generic, domain independent interface. Its current domain is a hierarchical file system consisting of various types of reports, email messages, directories, etc., but its knowledge sources have been designed such that switching to another domain is easy.

The user can manipulate the objects in the domain in four ways: by mimicking actions on selected objects, by selecting actions from menus, by entering commands in a command language, or by keying in Dutch sentences. Each of these ways can be used individually, but two of them can also be combined in one multimodal expression, e.g., by typing expressions like *"put them there ↗"*. The manipulation of the objects in each way results in an update of the model world as well as in an update of the internal knowledge base. In our example domain, this usually implies an operation on the file system.

Figure 1 illustrates how the user can interact with EDWARD. The computer screen is divided into two areas. The area occupying most of the screen is the graphics display: a window called Modelwereld (Model World). The tree shown in Fig. 1 represents a hierarchy of directories (depicted as bookcases), and files (e.g., reports, papers, email messages, and books). The viewport shows only part of the model world, which, in principle, extends indefinitely. In the bottom right corner of the viewport, a garbage container and a copier are displayed. The bear icon, at the bottom in the middle, represents the system itself (i.e., EDWARD). The OK button in the bottom left corner was added for use during our experiments only. Using a mouse, the user can manipulate the graphical representation of the domain objects. At the bottom of the Model World window, a mouse documentation bar is presented. Object-specific menus appear also in the Model World window at the user's request. In the bottom area of the screen is the language interaction window labelled Dialoog (Dialogue), where Invoer and Uitvoer mean 'input' and 'output', respectively. Here the user can enter natural and command language expressions and the system displays its linguistic output.

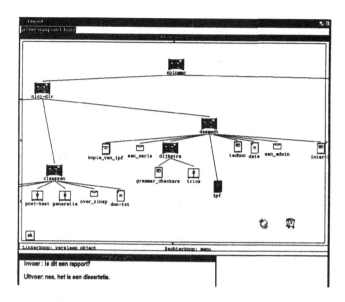

Fig. 1. Snapshot of a session with EDWARD; the user has selected the file icon labelled ipf, and subsequently entered: *"Is dit een rapport?"* (Is this a report?) EDWARD replies: *"Nee, het is een dissertatie."* (No, it is a dissertation.).

3   Theoretical Analyses of the Usefulness of Full Integration of Interaction Styles

3.1   Comparison with Real Life

In everyday life, people achieve their goals either by doing the appropriate tasks themselves or by delegating them to others. Although the nature of a task usually provides a reasonable clue for deciding whether to delegate or not, the context in which the task is performed also plays an important role in this decision. People usually, for example, prefer to delegate search tasks, but when they search on the Internet for information about a broad topic they might prefer to search themselves. Moreover, each type of means has its own virtues and limitations. For example, it sometimes takes longer to explain to somebody what you want than to do it yourself. Although, however, mostly both types of means are available, people do not seem to have major difficulties in selecting a way for achieving their goal.

Unlike in daily life, however, users of computer applications are often only offered one means for achieving their goal. In command language interfaces, the user always must describe the task he wants to delegate, regardless of, for instance, the length or difficulty of the command. In action mode interfaces, however, the user has to do everything himself, including the (sometimes very tedious) search for a particular object. Fully integrated multimodal interfaces always offering the user both language and action to accomplish his goals seem an obvious improvement making the interaction between a user and a computer more like normal day to day human interaction.

3.2 Advantages of Fully Integrated Multimodal Interfaces

Adding a model world to a language mode interface resolves problems with respect to maintaining a mental model of the system state and with respect to laborious referential expressions. Adding language to an action mode interface aids in resolving the following four inherent problems of action mode interfaces.

First, action mode interfaces have problems guiding the user's attention to changes in the world. In a multimodal environment, language in combination with simulated pointing gestures can guide attention. EDWARD, for instance, simulates the arm and hand movements which occur in human pointing behaviour. EDWARD animates a growing arrow simultaneously with printing the pronoun of a noun phrase (NP), for example, simultaneously with "this" in "this ↗ file". In this way, EDWARD mimics the strategy that Marslen-Wilson et al. (1982) observed in human pointing in real-world situations.

Secondly, a model world does not allow for the possibility to abstract from the 'here and now' of it (Walker, 1989). Objects outside the current viewport are not directly available; neither are objects in states prior to the current one. They can only be accessed (if at all) by additional actions (e.g., scrolling). Offering language for the user's input as well as the system's output enables both the user and system to refer to objects and actions that are not present in the current model world.

A third problem of action mode interfaces addressed by full integration of modes is the limited capacity of representation systems. For example, not all attributes of a file can be revealed by its icon. In contexts of high information density, it is impossible to design representations such that all types of information are immediately accessible. EDWARD generates linguistic descriptions of the user's activities in the model world. We call this part of EDWARD the Supplemental Linguistic Output (SLO). It provides additional information, that is, information that is not already visible. SLO is particularly useful to prevent the user from making reference errors. When a user hears (or reads) the NL descriptions of his actions in the model world, he may notice at an early stage whether or not he is acting as intended. If he perceives the description "you are about to delete Koen's dissertation" while dragging a file icon to the garbage container, he may realise that he made a reference error and should in fact have selected another file icon.

A fourth problem of action mode interfaces concerns the interpretation of the meaning of objects and actions. In many desktop interfaces, for example, icons can not be dragged off the desktop. However, these systems fail to inform their users why their action is constrained. Furthermore, the meanings of icons are not always clear for everyone. Icons which are normal in our culture may be unclear to other cultures. Language adds the possibility for the user to ask questions about the objects and the possible actions in the specific domain and for the system to generate descriptions of these.

4 Empirical Data

The analyses presented above overlook the fact that the user over and over again has to decide how to accomplish the present goal: drag and drop icons, use natural language, or select menu items? It should be investigated empirically how taking this decision, either consciously or unconsciously, affects the interaction. Many questions concerning among others the usefulness, pleasure and speed of using fully integrated multimodal user interfaces should be answered.

We can not pose nor answer all these possible questions. Several of these questions have been investigated, e.g.: Does style selection slow the user down? Does the user feel a cognitive burden? Does the user make use of the freedom of interaction style usage? Does the user like the freedom? Does the user select the most efficient style? What interaction styles are chosen? What influences the selection of interaction styles? Do users choose the same interaction style in the same situation? Does the interaction behaviour change over time? Does supplemental linguistic output help to make the interaction faster and less error prone? The results of these studies are presented below.

4.1 Efficiency and Speed

Although full integration of language and action provides the user with the possibility to interact very efficiently, it may also lead to inefficient or slow interaction. Huls, Bos, and Damen (1993) have investigated whether two factors, object name length and object visibility, influence the efficiency and speed of interaction style use.

They defined the efficiency of an interface style for a particular task in terms of the number of actions (keystrokes, mouse movements etc.) the user has to perform to complete that task, relative to the number of actions needed in an alternative style. The more actions the user has to perform to complete that task, the less efficient the style[1]. For example, the efficiency of linguistic input relative to action input increases as the number of characters to be typed becomes smaller. The tasks chosen for this experiment were all purely routine tasks. In the experiment the efficiency of styles was manipulated in terms of two variables, that concerned characteristics of the target object in the task.

The first variable was object name length (NLE). The longer an object name, the more key strokes it takes to refer to it by name. Language will thus become less efficient. The effect of NLE on the efficiency of action is expected to be only marginal. There might be an effect of NLE on object discriminability (because a larger name is spotted much easier than a short name, when displayed between short names) but this effect was assumed to be negligible.

The second variable was object visibility (VSB). An object in the experiment could either be in the current viewport, i.e. visible, or outside the current view port. Off-screen objects require one or more scrolling actions in order to be

---

[1] The users were asked to perform routine tasks; therefore we did not include mental effort in the operationalization of efficiency.

manipulable, while on-screen objects do not. The efficiency of action therefore increases with the visibility of the target object. On the other hand, the efficiency of the linguistic style is not influenced by visibility because naming the object requires the same number of actions irrespective of whether the object is visible or not[2]. Therefore the efficiency of the action style, as compared to that of the linguistic style, is maximal when the target object is visible.

In this experiment, the multimodal interaction style combining language and pointing in one expression, was never the most efficient style, therefore the use of this style was expected to be rare.

In addition to the efficiency question, Huls, Bos, and Damen (1993) tried to answer the question whether users who had a free choice of interaction style were actually faster in completing the tasks than those who were restricted to only one interaction style. The independent variable in this analysis was whether or not users were allowed to use different interaction styles for completing each task. The dependent variable was the amount of time needed to complete all twenty tasks.

Procedure. Eighty-eight randomly selected first year students were randomly distributed over the four conditions. They had little or no computer experience; some had experience with the word processing package WordPerfect, none were frequent computer users or had experience with more than one operating system.

EDWARD's model world was presented comprising a hierarchy with four levels of directories and files. It was three screens wide. The total number of objects in the model world was 34: 12 bookcases, 7 files with a long name (more than 8 characters), and 11 files with a short name (3 or 4 characters); the remaining files had names of medium length. Only the 18 files with long and short names and some of the bookcases were used as target objects.

All subjects received the same tasks: copying, deleting and moving files to another directory (bookcase). There were five groups of four tasks each, presented in randomized order:

1. ON screen objects with a LOng name   (ON-LO)
2. ON screen objects with a SHort name   (ON-SH)
3. OFF screen objects with a LOng name   (OFF-LO)
4. OFF screen objects with a SHort name   (OFF-SH)
5. Objects referred to by POsition ON screen   (ON-PO)

The subjects were instructed about the methods they could use to manipulate files. Depending on the condition, they were told that they could only use a fixed set of sentences (no paraphrases), a fixed set of mouse-actions, or a fixed set of combinations of these. For instance, when moving a file to another directory, the only type of command allowed was "move *file name* to *directory name*". An utterance such as "put *file name* in *directory name*" was not allowed, even though the system would have interpreted this utterance correctly.

---

[2] The names of the objects were printed on the task form; it was assumed that the users had no difficulty remembering them.

The subjects in the RESTRICTED conditions were familiarized with one interaction style only. Furthermore, only one expression was allowed for each task, e.g., only the phrase *delete this*, combined with a mouse selection, was allowed when deleting an object in the M-condition. In the L-condition, subjects were instructed to key in the commands. In the A-condition subjects were confined to the action style (object selection and manipulation). In the M-condition only the combination of keying in commands and graphical selection was instructed.

During a practice session the subjects were trained to produce all utterances in all three styles. The practice session ended as soon as the subjects were fully aware of the possibilities and no other than the prescribed utterances were generated.

Finally, each subject received a task form containing a list of the 20 tasks. The subjects were requested to complete each task with one of the utterances they just had been practising, as accurately and as fast as possible.

Results. The frequencies of the interaction styles used for the 16 tasks in the FREE condition are presented in Table 1.

The results of a MANOVA indicate that the subjects applied the action style more readily if the object is visible on the screen (F= 24.93, significant on the .01 level). Visibility, however, does not affect the choice of the multimodal interaction style (F= .21) . Furthermore, long object names caused the subjects to select the language style less often than short names did (F= 18.71, significant on the .01 level).

Table 1. The frequencies of interaction styles in the FREE condition (8 tasks in every cell, 22 subjects).

		Long Names	Short Names	Total
On Screen	A	46	33	79
	L	25	52	77
	M	17	3	20
Off Screen	A	23	9	32
	L	50	76	126
	M	15	3	18
Total	A	69	42	111
	L	75	128	203
	M	32	6	38

In order to determine whether the subjects in the FREE condition were faster than those in the RESTRICTED conditions, Table 2 shows the times the users needed to complete the 20 tasks in the four conditions. A one-way ANOVA shows a significant difference between the mean execution times ($p < 0.0005$). The RESTRICTED-Action group is significantly faster than the FREE group; the RESTRICTED-Multimodal group is significantly slower. The small difference between the Language and FREE condition is not significant.

Table 2. Means, standard deviations of time needed per group, and t-values for contrasts between RESTRICTED groups and FREE group.

Groups	mean completion time (seconds)	standard deviation	t- values RESTRICTED-FREE	Significance level (2-tailed probabilities)
RESTRICTED (L)	498	123.49	.340	0.732
RESTRICTED (A)	395	86.12	3.53	0.001
RESTRICTED (M)	629	128.47	2.99	90.005
FREE	512	129.47		

Conclusion. The data of the experiment with EDWARD showed that the users are inclined to use efficient interaction styles. Long object names induce subjects to prefer the action style where objects are selected by pointing and mouse clicks. Furthermore, when it is difficult to locate an object on the screen, subjects tend to prefer the language style. However, it was found that this does not make the interaction faster.

4.2   Supplemental Linguistic Output

Linguistic conveyance of information that can not be provided through graphics may prevent many errors in the interaction with these interfaces. Huls, Bos, and Dijkstra (1994) have presented an empirical study of SLO which generates natural language descriptions of the objects the user is manipulating and the actions he is performing. These descriptions can be presented both in the visual and auditory channels.

Thirty-three psychology students participated in the experiment. The subjects were counterbalanced between four different versions of EDWARD. These versions differed in that the linguistic descriptions generated by the SLO were either absent (No Output Condition), typed in the 'Description' window (Typed Only Condition), spoken by the speech synthesizer (Spoken Only Condition), or simultaneously typed and spoken (Typed and Spoken Condition). In the No Output Condition and the Typed Only Condition, the elaborate descriptions that could be requested from the menu by all users, were typed in the Description window. In the Spoken Only Condition and the Typed and Spoken Condition they were both typed and spoken.

The content and form of the typed and spoken descriptions were exactly the same. The descriptions were given whenever a subject performed an action in the model world, e.g., selected or copied an object. If for example a subject selected the report labeled grammar_checkers in Fig. 1, SLO immediately presented supplemental information about this object, in this case the file type, the author and the topic: "het onderzoeksrapport van Alice over grammatica" (the research report by Alice about grammar).

Procedure. At the beginning of the experimental session, each subject was introduced to EDWARD and received a short instruction (10 min) in which the basic operations including the DESCRIBE option were presented. The function of automatic SLO was not mentioned.

Twenty-five tasks were presented one by one in the window at the bottom of the screen. Every time the user clicked the 'ok' button, the next task was presented. The tasks comprised copying, moving, and deleting files. The files were referred to either by name or by definite description, e.g., "Move the letter OVER_SPIN to DESMEDT", or "Copy the research report by Wim about interaction". The referential definite descriptions were chosen such that they resembled the file names: e.g., the research report by Wim about interaction was named INTER-2. However, to induce errors, in ten cases there were two or more file names in the system that were very much alike. For instance, there was also a research report written by Edwin about interaction which was called INTER-1. In order to correctly execute these tasks the subjects had to make use of the information conveyed to them through the SLO, or obtain that information by calling the DESCRIBE-function from the menu.

The subjects were asked to complete the tasks accurately and fast. A background computer program logged all user actions, scored the number of errors (i.e., the number of times the subject manipulated files that did not correspond to the description), the time the subjects needed for each individual task and the overall time to complete the twenty-five tasks. After completing the tasks, the subjects filled out an evaluation form.

Results. Table 3 shows, per condition, the mean number of errors, the mean time to complete the experimental tasks in seconds and the mean number of times the DESCRIBE-option was selected in the menu. At the bottom row (Total-SLO) the data of the SLO conditions are combined.

Table 3. The mean data per condition.

	mean number of errors	mean number of seconds	mean number of selection of the describe option
No Output n=8	1.1	1717	22.9
Typed and Spoken n=8	2.25	1599	3.6
Spoken Only n=8	0.75	1772	9.6
Typed Only n=9	2	1384	5.5
Total-SLO n=25	1.67	1585	6.2

Unfortunately, some of the subjects in the Typed Only Condition did not use the descriptions provided by the automatically generated SLO, and some of the subjects in the Typed and Spoken Condition totally ignored the spoken descriptions provided simultaneously (or in fact a little later) with the typed descriptions. Consequently, it was decided to adapt the data in such a way that they would reflect the actual behaviour of the subjects (cf. Table 4). The data of three subjects were transferred from the Typed Only Condition to the No Output Condition, and the data of four subjects were transferred from the Typed and Spoken Condition to the Typed Only Condition.

Table 4. The adjusted data.

	mean number of errors	mean number of seconds	mean number of selection of the describe option
No Output n=11	2.27	1665	19.27
Typed and Spoken n=4	1.75	1620.5	3
Spoken Only n=8	0.75	1772	9.6
Typed Only n=10	1.4	1419	3.8
Total-SLO n=22	1.3	1604	5.5

From this table it shows that the time it took for the subjects to perform their task was the shortest for the Typed Only Condition, followed at a distance by respectively the Typed and Spoken Condition, the No Output Condition, and the Spoken Only Condition. The smallest number of errors was found in the Spoken Only Condition followed by respectively the Typed Only Condition, the Typed and Spoken Condition , and the No Output Condition. After adding the scores for the three conditions in which the automatic SLO was available (Total-SLO in Table 4), it showed that the subjects who did use the SLO were faster and made less errors than those in the No Output Condition. As could be expected, the subjects in the No Output Condition used the DESCRIBE-option in the menu most frequently, followed respectively by the Speech Condition, the Typed Only Condition, and the Typed and Spoken Condition.

Conclusion. The results show that linguistic descriptions provided by automatic SLO indeed help the subjects to perform the experimental tasks. The subjects that have the SLO at their disposal use less time, make less errors and have to perform less actions. When information is provided through the visual channel only, the interaction is fast and not many errors are made. Unfortunately however, subjects sometimes do not notice the SLO descriptions. When information is presented through the auditory channel only, the least number of errors is made, but on the other hand the rate of interaction slows down importantly. When the information is conveyed through both channels, speech coerced the subjects into reading the typed descriptions. In this condition, however, subjects made more errors than when the descriptions were only typed or spoken.

4.3   Experience

The users we saw thus far were all novice users of the EDWARD system. They did not have any prior experience with the system nor any experience with the freedom of interaction styles. In a third experiment we looked at the influence of experience on interaction style usage. We have investigated whether the use of interaction styles will change after a few elaborate training sessions.

Procedure. Thirty-three subjects participated in a Pretest, three training sessions, and a Posttest at the end. In the Pretest, the experimenter briefly described and demonstrated the four different interaction styles the users could use:

Action A brief description of the method for manipulating objects, selecting and dragging, was given.

Menus The experimenter showed how an object could be selected, how object specific menus could be displayed, and how to make a choice from their options.

Language The experimenter pointed at the dialogue window and told the subjects that normal, natural Dutch sentences could be typed in in order to ask questions and to give commands to EDWARD. He told the subjects that the system would also respond in Dutch. Additionally, subjects were explicitly instructed to move the mouse cursor to the dialogue window before typing a command.

Multimodal input The experimenter instructed and showed how language and pointing could be combined in one expression. The order of the pointing action and the deictic reference in a multimodal utterance was told not to be important.

The order of these instructions was randomized between subjects. The short introduction to EDWARD was followed by eleven task instructions (see Table 5). A style was scored as being language, multimodal, menu or action. Additionally, some comments, made by the subjects, were noted down.

After the Pretest each subject participated in three training sessions. These sessions took about 45 minutes each and were held on three consecutive days. During each session, elaborate instruction and training was given on how to operate the various interaction styles. The language style was extensively demonstrated with emphasis on the words and syntactic structures that could be employed in a linguistic utterance. The subjects were allowed to experiment with

Table 5. The task instructions

1. Determining the contents of a certain closed bookcase.
2. Formatting the screen.
3. Getting information about the author of a certain file.
4. Deleting a file or a bookcase.
5. Searching a file about ...
6. Creating a file or a bookcase.
7. Moving a file to another bookcase.
8. Scrolling the screen.
9. Copying a file.
10. Moving a file.
11. Getting information about a file.

different styles and with different expressions. The various types of feedback by the system were shown. Special attention was given to the error reports from the system and to methods for correcting errors, for instance, how to replace words unknown to the system by known ones. Furthermore, we showed the effects of all selectible menu options. We also demonstrated all methods for changing the system state by manipulating the icons on the screen. Each time a new style or a new explicit expression was shown, the subjects practiced the new style or expression and their alternatives. At any time the subject could ask questions. The order of instructions and demonstrations of different styles and expressions varied between subjects.

The last ten minutes of the last training session were spent on an evaluation test. The subjects were given a number of tasks and asked to complete these tasks in as many ways as possible. This evaluation test was not standardized. Its goal was to provide an indication as to whether the subjects had acquired the desired capabilities. All subjects proved to have mastered the desired level of expertise.

During the sessions we never mentioned any advantages or disadvantages of the interaction styles. Moreover, we did not provide any guidelines as to which interaction style was the best one to choose.

Two days after the last training session a Posttest took place. The procedure for this Posttest was identical to the procedure of the Pretest. The tasks were the same, but they occurred in a different order and affected different objects (files and directories).

Results. On both the Pretest and the Posttest the interaction styles used were scored. The results are presented in Table 6. The results show that experience does hardly change the number of times the users use language or menus. However, the number of times action is used decreased with almost same amount as the multimodal interaction style increased. Furthermore, action is the most used interaction style, while menus and multimodal interaction are used less.

Table 6. Total number of times each of the interaction styles was used in the Pre- and Posttest.

Interaction Style	Pretest	Posttest
action	37	26
language	24	21
multimodal	5	18
menu	11	12

Conclusion. We conclude that experience does make a difference in interaction style use. Especially the number of times action and multimodal interaction are used changes over time. Where action decreases, the usage of the multimodal interaction style increases with approximately the same amount. The data did not provide an indication why the interaction changed this way. We tentatively, conclude that full integration of interaction styles is beneficial because users can (and do) change their preferred interaction style.

5   Conclusions

Only a few questions into the actual use and usefulness of fully integrated multimodality have been investigated so far (and even those that have been investigated were of limited scope only). The experiments should be repeated with more subjects in real world tasks and other, more elaborate multimodal systems. Furthermore, the experiments described merely show a small part of the possible problems and advantages of these interfaces. The main question whether full integration of action and language in a multimodal user interface is indeed beneficial for each user in every situation can not be answered, yet. Many questions have not yet been addressed, and we think that finding empirical answers to many of them will require very complicated and laborious experiments.

However, we think the currently collected data described in this paper indicate that fully integrated multimodality is indeed a useful approach. In the first experiment, we found no negative effects of the freedom for the user, i.e. the interaction was not inefficient nor very slow. Secondly, we saw that SLO decreases the number of errors and the time needed. Finally, we have described an experiment in which we found that experience changes the usage of interaction styles. Further empirical research with more complex domains, with other tasks, and with more subjects, is required.

References

[1989]Allgayer, J., et al. (1989), 'XTRA: a natural-language access system to expert systems'. In *International Journal of Man-Machine Studies, 31*, 161-195.

[1993]Bos, E. (1993), *Easier said or done? Studies in multimodal human-computer interaction*, Doctoral Dissertation. Rijks Universiteit Leiden (NICI Technical Report 93-02. Nijmegen: NICI).

[1994]Bos, E., Huls C., and Claassen, W. (1994), 'EDWARD: full integration of language and action in a multimodal interface'. In *International Journal of Human-Computer Studies, 40*, 473-495.

[1990]Claassen, W., Bos, E., and Huls, C. (1990), *The Pooh Way in human-computer interaction: towards multimodal interfaces*, SPIN-MMC Research report 5, Nijmegen: NICI.

[1992]Cohen, P. (1992), 'The role of natural language in a multimodal interface'. In *Proceedings of the 5th annual ACM symposium on user interface software and technology* (UIST'92), New York: ACM Press.

[1988]Desain, P. (1988), 'Direct manipulation and the design of user interfaces'. In *Communication and Cognition - Artificial Intelligence, 5*, 225-246.

[1993]Huls, C. and Bos, E. (1993), 'EDWARD: A multimodal interface'. in *Proceedings of the Twente Workshop on Language Technology 5* (TWLT5), 89-98.

[1993]Huls, C., Bos, E., and Damen, H. (1993), 'Fully integrated multimodality: a case study'. In *HCI International'93*, Orlando, Florida.

[1994]Huls, C., Bos, E., and Dijkstra, A. (1994), 'Talking Pictures: An empirical study into the usefulness of natural language output in a graphical interface'. In *Workshop Notes of the AAAI workshop Integration of Natural Language and Vision Processing*, McKevitt, P. (ed.), 83-90.

[1989]Hutchins, E. (1989), 'Metaphors for Interface Design'. In *The Structure of Multimodal Dialogue*, Taylor, M.M., Néel, F., and Bouwhuis, D.G. (eds.), Amsterdam: North - Holland, 11-28.

[1982]Marslen-Wilson, W., Levy, E., and Tyler, L.K. (1982), 'Producing interpretable discourse: The establishment and maintenance of reference'. In *Speech, place, and action*, Jarvella, R.J. and Klein, W. (eds.), Chichester: John Wiley and Sons Ltd.

[1991]Stock, O. (1991), 'Natural language and exploration of an information space: the ALFresco interactive system'. In *Proceedings of the Twelfth international joint conference on artificial intelligence* (IJCAI'91, Sydney, 24-30 Aug.), San Mateo, CA: Morgan Kaufmann Inc., 972-978.

[1989]Walker, M.A. (1989), 'Natural language in a desktop environment'. In *Designing and using human-computer interfaces and knowledge based systems, Proceedings of the HCI International '89*, Salvendy, G., and Smith, M.J. (eds.), Amsterdam, Elsevier Science Publishers, 502-509.

The Role of Multimodal Communication in Cooperation: The Cases of Air Traffic Control

Marie-Christine Bressolle[1], Bernard Pavard[1], and Marcel Leroux[2]

[1] ARAMIIHS, 31 rue des Cosmonautes ZI du Palays 31077, Toulouse, France
`ressoll@cenatls.cena.dgac.fr`, `pavard@jazz.matra-espace.fr`
[2] Centre d'Études de la Navigation Aérienne, 7 avenue Édouard Belin,
Toulouse, France,
`leroux@cenatls.cena.dgac.fr`

Abstract. In the field of air traffic control, the rapid increase of demands leads to considering major technological improvements. Our research takes place in the context of a global program aiming at the design and validation of cooperative tools for *en route* air traffic controllers; this program, called ERATO (En Route Air Traffic Organizer), is based on a specific approach starting from the identification of users' requirements on the design and validation of the set of decision aids.

This chapter concerns the analysis of user requirements; we will question the traditional theoretical framework of information exchange for the study of communication between human agents, and examine some of the methodological issues arising in the analysis of multimodal communication. One challenge is to identify the mechanisms of cooperation responsible for the efficiency of a team of controllers, and to decide what support tools may have a positive effect on the cooperation between human agents.

The results that we will present concern the analysis of communication in the situation of control (reproduced in dynamic simulations); our aim was to identify the part played by multimodal resources in informal communication mechanisms which could be modified or changed by the introduction of a new technological environment. The results emphasize the impact of the verbal and non-verbal resources, used in an opportunistic way by team members, on the efficiency of the communication, especially with respect to the need to reduce the risks of miscommunication. Some of the implications are discussed for a general design method based on an assessment of the multimodal wealth of the working environment.

1 Introduction

As shown by numerous studies in the domain of CSCW, the study of cooperative processes between agents is essential when considering and validating choices of new technologies or new modes of interaction between human agents. The design of new working environments brings up questions such as what information about the activities performed by other agents should be presented to a given agent (for example, partially shared information, respecting confidentiality), and what operational procedures are required to support implicit or explicit exchanges between agents. For example, different approaches and their consequences for human coordination required in specific fields have to be examined (Dourish and Belloti, 1992). Understanding the cooperative dimension in work activities is complex because of the interaction between social and cognitive dimensions and because of the nature of the processes involved in intention recognition, which call upon different modalities (writing, use of moving objects, pointing, etc.)

When examining different approaches, focusing on the cooperative nature of working practices in different areas, it appears that understanding cooperation between human agents leads to the consideration of *collective cognition* as socially distributed with respect to external artifacts used in practice. In the domain of London underground control, Heath and Luff (1991) found that controllers develop a practice of overhearing each other's conversations and overseeing each other's actions. This allows them to manage a flexible division of labour well adapted to solving difficulties. This flexibility seems to depend on the ability to manage implicit task allocation in the team. Some researchers in the domain of air traffic control (Hughes et al. 1992) take into account the artifacts used in such situations to highlight how division of labour is related to working practice using artifacts to organize activities within the team (for example, writing on strips is seen as support for cross-checking each other's activities). Hutchins and Klausen (1992) develop the idea that cognition is fundamentally distributed. The use of artifacts is analysed in order to identify their properties, highlighting the mental operations they support. So collective cognition and artifacts are not considered independently.

In accordance with such studies, we suggest that collective cognition has to be seen in interaction with environmental resources used by human agents. Cooperative activities imply that agents communicate in order to share their understanding and to recognize their intentions in face-to-face situations. The problem we address in this paper is to assess the roles of non-verbal and verbal communication in cooperation. The idea that non-verbal aspects in communication are informative may seem to be trivial, but identifying their role becomes an important issue when we are concerned with interface design. In studying interaction between experienced human agents, in a face-to-face situation, our hypothesis is that non-verbal resources are needed in addition to verbal ones to ensure successful communication. Communicating partners are faced with the difficulty of constructing and updating a common cognitive environment which enables them to cooperate. As shown by Sperber and Wilson (1986), communication is based on inferential and decoding processes, so the success of communication is uncertain, and the construction of a compatible interpretation of the situation implies that human agents continuously regulate and anticipate misunderstandings which can arise in interpreting the other's utterances and actions.

We assume that the part played by non-verbal resources becomes essential in time-constrained situations where verbal interventions, needed in particular to recover a failure in mutual understanding, appear for several reasons to be only partially adapted. Our purpose is therefore to examine the ways in which modalities of verbal and non-verbal communication are required in order to establish a shared understanding in symmetrical situations of interaction (both agents being experienced controllers).

2   Mutual Cognitive Environment

Communication is a co-construction process where achievement is not certain. In order to describe the process of building a shared understanding, two main models of communication can be mentioned. On the one hand, in the Shannon and Weaver studies (1948), communication is considered as a coding-decoding process. On this view, establishing common knowledge or beliefs implies that the agents share the same knowledge used to code and decode a message. A problem in this case is to determine the level of mutual knowledge required (agent A knows that agent B knows that agent A knows that agent B knows...).

Sperber and Wilson (1986), on the other hand, question the mechanical nature of this process and highlight the inferential nature of communication. Their model allows a more specific description of what shared information actually is, using the concept of *cognitive environment* and the *relevance principle*. The cognitive environment is an individual construction developed by each agent through information acquired in his/her environment according to his/her beliefs, personal theories, etc. and to his/her perceptive and inferential abilities. The *mutual* cognitive environment is based on the hypotheses formed by the agents. This model presents communication as a process based on an imperfect heuristic. The agents are not able to determine accurately the respective cognitive environments. Moreover, this model takes into account ostensive behaviour. Resources from the environment may support intention recognition and modify the cognitive environment. The heuristic nature of communication implies that the main problem faced by human agents is to ensure mutual understanding.

A major problem is that agents have to manage misunderstandings which can arise in the co-construction of a compatible view of the situation. Rogers (1992) shows that the causes of failure of coordination have to be examined in order to be able to develop resources which can facilitate the detection of misunderstanding. In the case of a networked environment, engineers need to know what others are doing on the network in order to manage communicative problems, which may be very time-consuming. In face-to-face situations, a variety of communicative resources can be used by participants to construct a compatible view of the situation.

2.1   The Establishment of a Mutual Cognitive Environment Using Verbal Resources

Assumptions about the other's knowledge and beliefs on the basis of verbal resources are needed to communicate. The establishment of shared knowledge is analysed by Clark and Wilkes-Gibbs (1990) in verbal tasks. Experiments show that to identify the reference of a given expression, the subjects base themselves on the representation they have of the other's knowledge, and their performance evolves in the course of a session. Krauss and Fussel (1990) point out how agents try to determine what is mutually shared in order to communicate. They evoke three interrelated sets of mechanisms which communicators use to establish the existence of common ground: direction knowledge (assumptions about the partner's ability to have the appropriate interpretative context, because of co-presence, for example); category membership (such as predictions about individual knowledge with respect to his/her social category); and interaction dynamics (for example, what has been said is assumed to be known).

The dynamics of interaction and, in particular, the part played by feedback has been developed by Clark and Schaeffer (1989), Krauss and Fussel (1990), and Clark and Brennan (1991). Clark and Brennan (1991) analyse the contributions of agents in conversation divided into two steps, a presentation and an acceptance phase. For them all collective actions, communicative actions in particular, are based on the assumption of a shared ground (mutual knowledge, beliefs and assumptions) which is constantly updated.

A major issue in time-constrained situations is how verbal and non-verbal resources will be used when verbal explanations, reformulations, etc., ensuring mutual understanding, are costly.

2.2   Establishment of a Mutual Cognitive Environment Using Non-verbal Resources

In the communication process, meaning emerges from the interpretation of verbal utterences, but also from non-verbal elements which contribute to modification of the cognitive environment of human agents. As Shapiro et al. (1989) and Hughes et al. (1992) have shown, the flight progress strip is essential in the social organization of the work in an air traffic control team, where activities and information are distributed and used among team members. Strips are updated according to the usual routes, with symbols and circles around relevant destinations, e.g. to represent climbing or descending aircraft, etc. (see further the presentation of the main tools used by air traffic controllers below). They represent an evolving history and a plan of the controller's intentions and decisions.

More generally, through studies of interaction between human agents co-present at the work station, it appears that external resources available at the work station provide support for collective cognition. Heath et al. (1993) show that the ways in which dealers coordinate their actions and participate in each other's conduct in the dealing room of a City of London international securities house, is linked to the co-presence which allows the operators to collaborate.

Initiation of mutual engagement, for example, is based on the direction of the operators' looks and their body postures. Other studies have shown how resources in the working environment are used to determine, for example, the availability of colleagues, which condition the dialogues between permanent staff and doctors in the SAMU emergency services (Benchekroun et al., 1993). Studying the grounding process in communication, Clark and Brennan (1991) show in the case of establishing referential identity (mutual belief that the addressees have correctly identified the referent) that several techniques are used, including indicative gestures (pointing, looking or touching). As indicated by Krauss and Fussel (1990), literature provides little support for the assumption that communication by visual and verbal channels is more efficient than by verbal channels only (Krauss and Fussel, 1990, p.138). However, their study in using refential communication tasks shows that inserting a delay and temporally displacing feedback responses is sufficient to demonstrate the extent of the communicator's dependence on feedback to formulate efficient referring expressions. Other experiments show that visible feedback (smiles, head shakes, nods) can compensate for the absence of verbal information, so with visible information available, the effect of delayed transmission decreases.

3   Multimodality and Communication

In time-constrained situations, an important question is which part could be played by non-verbal resources to obtain efficient and successful communication, and more generally what is the nature of the resources needed to support the communication. Communicating partners are faced with the tasks of constructing their common cognitive environment so that misunderstandings are resolved or anticipated (related to the uncertain nature of interpretation), and of managing their cognitive resources. Moreover, in such situations verbal resources like explanations, reformulations,.. used in natural conversation to establish mutual understanding, are time- and resource-consuming. In this respect, artifacts considered as environmental resources can be used to support the communication. A major problem is how non-verbal resources will be used to ensure successful exchanges Other questions arising include: Can non-verbal resources be trusted, in the sense that they are reliable for mutual understanding? and What level of mutual understanding can be reached by non-verbal communication?

   As an introduction, we discuss two dimensions of non-verbal resources: the status of non-verbal resources (contextual dimension versus specific modality), and the informative nature of non-verbal resources (versus 'communicative').

   One possible approach is to consider the non-verbal dimension of interaction as part of the context of interpretation of the verbal communication. This attempt to understand the part played by non-verbal resources entails identifying how they are used as a context in interpreting verbal utterances. A slightly different perspective is to consider non-verbal resources as a specific mode of expression, and to analyse their use with respect to the meaning they convey. In non-verbal communication studies, it appears that non-verbal resources cover several dimensions. The 'multi-channel' notion of human communication, discussed by Cosnier and Brossard (1984), characterizes face-to-face interactive situations and suggests that the agents transmit a heterogeneous total message, resulting from a combination of several elements (vocal-acoustic, visual and olfactory, tactile and thermic). These authors establish a distinction between two mimetic-gestural functions:

1. framing the interaction; the mimetic-gestural function is assimilated as indication of the context (in that it provides a situational context);
2. providing a 'co-text'; it then makes a dynamic contribution to the exchanges.

Similarly, Cadoz (1993) shows that some semiotic body expressions (e.g. informative messages to the environment) are actions combined with verbal expression and can be considered as part of the communicative structure and a specific mode of expression.

A different approach of non-verbal messages is along the informative vs. communicative distinction. The realization of collective cognition in working situations involves various modalities of communication; for example, an action (pointing to the radar scope) may be interpreted by co-workers as an act of communication, to emphasize relevant information. This action can be analysed from several points of view. On the one hand, the action is a means for each agent to organize information for him/herself. On the other hand, the action may be performed in order to communicate (for example, showing something to a partner and saying *"Have you seen this?"*; the deictic gesture is part of communication). A more extensive analysis of the intentional nature of behaviour in human communication leads us to distinguish two intentional levels, described by Sperber and Wilson (1986). The *informative* intention appears when a speaker makes elements of a situation manifest without showing the intentionality of making them manifest. For example, an agent, rather than asking his colleague for some help to repair his tools, displays the various components prominently. The *communicative* intention corresponds to an interactive situation in which the speaker addresses his interlocutor and manifestly shows the intention of requesting something.

4   Experimental Situation

The air traffic control team for a certain sector of traffic is an operational unit, composed of the *executive controller* and the *planning controller* in a face-to-face interactive situation. The controllers of adjacent sectors are in telephone contact with the planning controller, and pilots are in radio contact with the executive controller. Controllers use a variety of information sources: the flight progress board (including strips arranged in front of the executive controller, according to problems detected or to spatial disposition in the sector), the radar, the telephone, and the displays.

The executive controller's responsability is sectoral, including the maintenance of separation standards within the sector. The planning controller is in charge of coordination of the traffic passing in and out of the sector and acts on the stream of traffic received into the sector. The controllers organize the flow of traffic to avoid conflicts between flights, taking into account constraints like the need for flights to be expedited as soon as possible (to minimize fuel consumption) and constraints linked to the situation, such as meteorological conditions. The training of the two controllers is the same, both in the theoretical aspects (concerning, for example, procedures described in air traffic service manuals), in handling each sector of traffic, and in being trained in real situations under the responsability of an experienced controller.

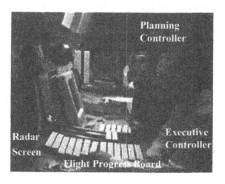

Fig. 1. The working environment. The strips of paper can be seen on the flight progress board.

Air traffic regulation is a complex task because it implies decision-making and resources management with time constraints, the processing of large quantities of information, which are both evolving and uncertain (Leroux,1992), and a functional and temporal coordination between actions performed by each agent. For experienced controllers, the problem is to define a strategy to resolve a conflict situation, to envisage the consequences of this strategy on the surrounding traffic (to avoid creating new conflicts), and to monitor the application of the strategy (acting at the right moment, checking that the aircraft did actually turn, for example). The monitoring of air traffic is complex and costly for the controller (Leroux,1992), one of the risks being that a conflict situation is not acted upon in time in a context where attention is shared between several simultaneous conflict situations. The complexity stems from the dynamic nature of the environment, where each decision has to be evaluated with respect to the evolving state of the traffic, requests from pilots and adjacent sectors, and unexpected events that have to be taken into account as soon as possible. Each agent has to take decisions under time pressure, some of which (negotiation with controllers from other sectors, for example) have consequences for the actions of others; communication may therefore be needed, but there may also be a need to wait until the colleague in question is available, to inform or negotiate with him/her.

5   Methodology

We have analysed how air traffic controllers resolve conflicts. A simulated air traffic control situation was set up, where six conflicts evolved over a period of about 30 minutes. Four teams of two controllers who had to regulate this traffic were video taped.

Verbal and non verbal communication were analysed in terms of exchanges. We consider as exchanges one or many turns focusing on the same object. A turn, corresponding to verbal or non-verbal action, is considered here as a basic unit of communication. In the analysis we distinguish four types of turns corresponding to:

1. verbal communication between controllers;
2. verbal communication between executive controller and pilots;
3. non-verbal communication related to strip handling (writing, moving or pointing to strips);
4. non-verbal communication related to radar scope (pointing to the radar scope).

Three considerations guide the collection of observations concerning the non-verbal element of the interaction: the nature of the observations selected, their description in reference to the activity, and their processing in relation to the action under way.

Taking into account the extreme richness of non-verbal and para-verbal elements, we focused on the behaviour related to the use of available environmental resources in the control environment and on the content of verbal communication (relating to, for example, the handling of strips, pointing to the radar scope). In addition, all these elements are described with a set of action verbs (e.g. "write", "give", "place", "point", "take", "shift", "move", etc.) The characteristics of this list are the observable nature of the selected behaviour (actions which can be described using the professional vocabulary) and the coherence of the list vis-à-vis the control activity (e.g., "shift" the strip out of line on the board has a distinctly different meaning from "move" the strip). Among the non-verbal actions taken into account are

1. deictics (indicating an object or some specific information such as flight level on the strip, possibly associated with comments such as "this one", "here", "there", and other illustrative gestures;
2. writing (making annotations on the strip, as controllers do);
3. handling of objects (organizing the strip board by moving the strips around).

In the analysis we will use the following abbreviations: Cp (planning controller), Ce (executive controller), Pi (pilot).

6 Results

6.1 Global Analysis

In face-to-face interactions between controllers, several communicative modalities can be employed according to the nature of the information communicated (diagnosis of a conflict situation, transfer conditions of an aircraft to an adjacent sector, etc.) and the status of the information (urgency of the situation, work context, etc.) At the worktation, the information is processed and memorized through the various supports, for example, the organization and handling of strips. Certain properties of the strips, such as their mobility and writability, and the visual accessibility of this information, have been discussed elsewhere; see Shapiro and al. (1989). The agents can also listen to radiotelephone communication and be aware of each other's activities. These elements will be considered through their implications for the communication in the team.

The results obtained through analysis of the four videotaped teams reveal that non-verbal resources are used in the majority of the exchanges. Communication between controllers mostly consists of a combination of verbal and non-verbal elements within a single exchange. This can be seen in Table 1, where the exchanges are categorized as follows:

- those consisting of only verbal contributions;
- those consisting of only non-verbal contributions;
- those consisting of both verbal and non-verbal contributions;
- those including a non-verbal contribution only relating to communication with pilots, which is a specific task in the domain (use of non-verbal communication supported by strip handling combined with use of verbal communication, in this case radio-communication with the pilot);
- other exchanges (including verbal radio-communication).

Table 1. Percentage of exchanges where agents used verbal, nonverbal or both verbal and nonverbal elements

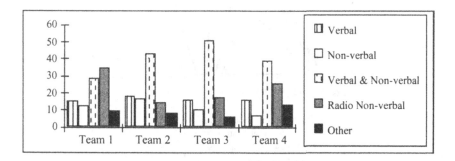

For controllers the use of non-verbal resources is most of the time associated with verbal communicative actions. In further sections, results will be presented of a study aiming at identifying the functional characteristics of the non-verbal elements in this activity, and examples will be given that highlight some of these properties.

6.2   A Case Study

In an scenario with three planes in conflict (MON1789, DHL498, SWR012), we can observe that the mutual cognitive environment is developed and updated almost every minute (see Fig. 2, solid lines). The dialogues concern the analysis of the potential conflict between these flights, the resolution (instructions for the pilots) and the reestablishment of the situation before the flights leave the sector. More significantly, the non-verbal resources are involved almost each minute (dotted lines indicating when this is not the case). Each minute several non-verbal resources may be used, for example one exchange at minute 2 (represented by single line 02) includes the planning controller pointing to the strip of flight DLH498 and pointing to the radar scope; the executive controller placing the strip of DLH498 close to the strip of MON1789 on the board, shifting the two strips to the link, etc.

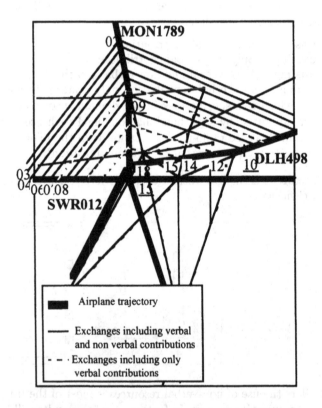

Fig. 2. A case study. In this figure, the exchanges are linked to the evolving state of the three aircraft in conflict (MON1789, DHL498, SWR012); nonverbal elements are distributed over the timespan of conflict detection and resolution.

This analysis of the dialogues between human agents in such face-to-face situations emphasizes the role of external artifacts in cooperation processes. It appears that the information sharing and retrieval is closely linked to the modalities offered for communication management in terms of use of complementary communication resources.

The role of non-verbal resources in mutual understanding can be considered from several points of view. First, we may consider the part of non-verbal resources according to the non-deterministic nature of the communicative events. Used in complementarity with verbal resources or not, non-verbal resources contribute to the interpretation process in reducing the set of hypotheses available (for the simplest example in its deictic function, to indicate the object referred to). It turns out that a large amount of verbal communicative actions are associated with non-verbal ones; in this sense they contribute to the augmentation of the mutual cognitive environment and serve as a basis for further interpretation. Moreover, the non-verbal resources may be used for other purposes than to give referring indications; for instance, they may highlight specific information (like the illocutionary value given to the information, for aspects such as urgency, which are not explicitly verbalized). Second, a major interest of the use of non-verbal resources lies in that they support having access to the information, used to augment the shared cognitive environment, with a minimum of interruption from the other team members. On the one hand, the information is distributed within the working situation in the course of the activity, so that several pieces of information become available for colleagues. The cooperating agents use these resources to organize their own cognitive processes, exploiting external artifacts as support for memory and problem solving, and at the same time to update their mutual cognitive environment. Also, these resources are used in different ways according to the current activity and the availability of each agent. Information may be communicated verbally with redundant or complementary information not verbally given, and especially information may be given using only non-verbal resources. This property appears critical; instead of making explicit verbal requests, each agent notices non-verbal acts by other agents as part of their cognitive activities.

We will now give some examples showing that non-verbal resources, including gestures as well as shared object handling, are critical for the efficiency of communication.

6.3   Non-verbal Resources in Mutual Understanding

The analysis of multimodal aspects of communication leads us to underline the importance of non-verbal acts for interpreting communicative events. As shown in the following example, verbal and non-verbal resources may be complementary in augmenting the mutual cognitive environment and deal with misunderstandings. This complementarity is used not only when misunderstandings occur, but also more generally to ensure mutual understanding.

Example 1: Strip pointing in communication regulation

In the following example, the exchange is based on the establishment of a reference flight, while two aircraft are present in the sector, SWR011 and SWR012. The executive controller's hypothesis is that the SWR concerned is SWR012, and the planning controller's contributions, both pointing at the strip and commenting verbally, allow him to make the flight explicit. This example underlines the richness of multimodal interaction, which helps to ensure successful communication.

Fig. 3. Strip pointing in mutual understanding. In the first picture, the executive controller wants to take the strip of flight SWR012; in the second picture the planning controller points to the strip of flight SWR011.

Team 3 -III

Cp-Ce: "watch out for the SWR eh?"
(...)
Cp-Ce: "We can transfer *the SWR* on frequency already"
      (Ce *wants to take SWR012 strip*)
Ce-Cp: "the SWR012"
      (Cp *points to SWR012 strip*)
Cp-Ce: "no, not that one"
Ce-Cp: "all right, *the SWR011* you mean at 280"
Cp-Ce: "no, no ...*011*"
      (Cp *points to SWR011 strip*)

Interaction associated with situation depicted in Fig. 3

The following examples illustrate the specific role of non-verbal resources in communicating: non-verbal resources are revealed to form a separate dimension of communication, dealing with types of information which are not verbally expressed, such as the urgency of the situation.

Example 2: Transmission of strip to mark non-routine character of information.

The planning controller receives the strips, several minutes before the aircraft effectively enters the sector, which he transmits to the executive controller. The gesture associated with the transmission of the strip is 'multiform (passing the strip from hand to hand, placing it on the edge of the board, using the strip to point to the radar scope, etc.). The strip can also be used for annotations, marking e.g. the evolution of the flight, or the airport of destination. In this example (see Fig. 4), it would appear that the planning controller transmits the flight IBE913 strip by placing it sideways on the edge of the board in front of the executive controller. The planning controller associates a verbal intervention with two non-verbal ones (underlining the strip and placing it on the board). These actions improve memorization of the requested level, and highlight for the colleague a conflict with another aircraft in the same sector at the same level. The act of it placing the strip sideways on the board can be interpreted by the executive controller as marking non-routine information which has to be taken into account quickly (the strip is not placed outside the board, which forces him to pick it up to visualize the strips which are integrated in the board).

Team 4 - V

Cp-Pi: "IBERIA takeoff, IBERIA 913 to Amboise OK?"
    (Cp *presents strip, writes on strip, places strip on edge of board*)
Ce-Cp: "OK"
    (Ce *writes on strip, keeps strip in his hand*)
Ce-Cp: "How many does he want that man there, he wants 330 too."
(...)

Interaction associated with situation depicted in Fig. 4

6.4   Verbal and Non-Verbal Resources in Dialogue Management

Our analysis of non-verbal acts leads us to consider, on the one hand, these actions as having communicative intentions (for example, handling the strip and simultaneously asking something), and on the other hand as a means of organizing information for oneself (which can be observed and interpreted by co-workers). In other words, informative actions and utterances (as distinguished from communicative ones) serve as a basis for inferences that agents make about their mutual cognitive environment, though they may not be intended to communicate. The co-presence in the same location clearly allows the construction of a mutual cognitive environment by using both verbal and non-verbal resources.

Fig. 4. An example of using non-verbal resources in communication to mark the non-routine character of certain information. In the first picture, the planning controller presents the strip of flight IBE913; in the second he writes on the strip, and in the last picture he places the strip on the edge of the board.

Where most of the exchanges between team members contain both verbal and non-verbal actions, we would like to point out that the non-verbal resources may be used to give information in an economical way. For example, if the executive controller is engaged in communication with a pilot, and doesn't find the strip of this flight, without speaking the planning controller may use strip pointing to communicate to him or her the flight concerned. In this case, overhearing the radio frequency and seeing the executive controller allows the planning controller to respond to a demand not formulated by the executive controller. The controllers may also use environmental resources to initiate an exchange. The cognitive effort required to interpret the meaning of an utterance which is initiated by the use of environmental resources, is less than if the controller had referred to another aircraft in the sector. Indeed, with respect to the relevance principle (Sperber & Wilson, 1986), the utterance expressed by the planning controller is relevant in the cognitive environment of the interlocutor.

Example 3: Strip pointing while forming a shared diagnosis of the situation

In the following example, the controllers initiate a common diagnosis of the situation. The planning controller acts on the strip, writing and moving the strip on the flight progress board. Two minutes later, the executive controller's first action can be interpreted by the planning controller as confirmation of his diagnosis concerning a problem at level 330 concerning DAN4446. One minute before the planning controller has passed the strip for AFR022, which is descending in the opposite direction. In analysing the situation, the executive controller shows that he does not find the flight on the radar scope, by tapping with his finger on the strip he is referring to, which is followed by the planning controller's engagement in this exchange. Therefore, such a non-verbal act can be seen as an implicit request in the sense that the planning controller is supposed to answer only if he is not engaged in an actf ivity which is difficult to interrupt.

In general, we see that verbal communicative acts are more or less linked to the use of environmental resources in the course of the action, for example to strip handling, which allows the controller to organize and process information related to each flight according to his/her diagnosis of actions concerning conflicts, and which is at the same time a medium of communication.

Fig. 5. An example of using a strip to initiate an exchange. In the first picture, the executive controller points to the strip of flight DAN4446, tapping it with his finger, and says: "That's the one I can't see"; in the second picture, the planning controller is engaged in this exchange, the two controllers point to the radar screen.

Team 2-I

Cp-Ce: "There's the 330"
   (Cp *underlines strip DAN4446*)
Ce-Cp: "Well yes... it's going to be hard"
   (Cp *shifts DAN4446 to the right*)
Cp-Ce: "We'll have to see (...)"
   (Cp *gives two strips, of AFR022 and FBJMG*)
Cp-Ce: "Here's a problem."
Ce: "There are lots of problems."
   (Ce *takes strips, places one in pos.4,*
   shifts it to the left and keeps the other in his hand)
Ce: "Ah yes"
(...)
Ce-Cp: "Yes there seems to be a lot of climbing to 330"
   (Ce *points to the DAN4446 strip, tapping it with his finger*)
Ce-Cp: "That's the one I can't see."
Cp-Ce: "Just a moment, yes, he is behind."
   (Cp *adjusts scope, points to scope*)
   (Ce *points to the scope...*)

Interaction associated with situation depicted in Fig. 5

The analysis of the exchanges between controllers reveals that verbal and non-verbal resources contribute to the establishing and updating of a mutual cognitive environment related to the current situation in various ways. With respect to the heuristic nature of human communication (see Sperber & Wilson, 1986), multimodality appears as a resource which is used by human agents to anticipate or regulate misunderstandings in face-to-face situations. As a consequence, the complementary use of verbal and non-verbal resources has to be examined with respect to the resource management within the team.

7 Discussion

The central issue in our approach is to capture and describe user requirements in terms of the 'cognitive model' which serves as guideline for the design of new decision aids. In the first step of this overall program, our research focused on the cooperation mechanisms which are critical for the reliability of the system.

The cognitive model developed addresses the issue of how cognition is distributed within the working situation. A fundamental aspect of human communication is its non-deterministic character, in part due to the inferential processes which enter into play in mutual understanding. The non-verbal resources which may be supposed unreliable because of the variety of interpretations they may allow, contribute to the efficiency of the team. The environmental resources play a critical part not only in interpreting locally the meaning of what is said, but they also more globally in augmenting the mutual cognitive environment, which is used to reduce the uncertainty inherent to communication.

In terms of requirements for information technology aiming at supporting human cooperation within the working environment, this analysis leads us to the conclusion that future systems should allow users to access, process and exchange information in several channels, singly and in combination. Coming back to the results presented, two levels can be distinguished in understanding the part played by environmental resources, and especially the complementarity between verbal and non-verbal resources: (1) the use of environmental resources for information processing and retrieval with respect to the requirements of the individual user, and for information sharing between users; and (2) the link between environmental resources and the modalities of their use according to dynamic resource management in the working environment. This applies to normal situations as well as to incidental situations where cooperation processes are under severe time pressure.

This work was performed in collaboration with the team involved in the global evaluation of a prototype of an electronic environment for air traffic controllers (Gaillard, Leroux, 1994). In the future, we aim at studying the effects of new media on cooperation mechanisms, firstly to evaluate these new media as support for cooperative activities, and secondly to further develop and validate a communication model of the users of the new media.

References

Benchekroun, H., Pavard, B., and Salembier, P. (1993) Design of cooperative systems in complex dynamic environments. In J. M. Hoc, P. C. Cacciabue and E. Hollnagel (eds.) *Expertise and Technology – Cognition and Human-Computer Cooperation*. New York: Academic Press.

Bressolle, M. C. (1992) Perception de l'intention et cooperation dans le cas du contrôle de la navigation aérienne. Premiers éléments d'analyse. Internal report, Centre d'Études de la Navigation Aérienne, Toulouse.

Cadoz, C. (1993) Le geste canal de communication homme-machine, la communication instrumentale. *Ecole d'Eté ARC/PRC CHM. Communication et Multimodalité dans les Systèmes Naturels et Artificiels*. Château de Bonas, France, 35–67.

Clark, H. H. and Wilkes-Gibbs, D. (1990) Referring as a collaborative process. In P. R. Cohen, J. Morgan, and M. E. Pollack (eds) *Intention in Communication*. Cambridge, MA: MIT Press, 463–493.

Clark, H. H. and Schaeffer, E. F. (1989) Contributing to discourse. *Cognitive Science 13*, 259–294.

Clark, H. H. and Brennan S. E. (1991) Grounding in conversation. In L. B. Resnick, J. M. Levine and S. D. Teasley (eds.) *Perspectives on Socially Shared Cognition*. Washington, D. C.: American Psychological Association, 127–149.

Cosnier, J. and Brossard, A. (1984) Communication non-verbale: co-texte ou contexte? In J. Cosnier and A. Brossard (eds), *La Communication Non-verbale*. Neuchatel: Delachaux et Niestle, 1–29.

Dourish, P. and Belloti, V. (1992) Awareness and coordination in shared workplaces. In *Proc. ACM 1992 Conference on Computer-Supported Cooperative Work*, Toronto, 107–114.

Gaillard I., and Leroux M. (1994) Improving air traffic control: proving new tools or approving the joint human – machine system? In J. A. Wise, V. D. Hopkin, and D. J. Garland (eds) *Human Factors Certification of Advanced Aviation Technologies.* Aviation Human Factors Series, Embry-Riddle: Aeronautical University Press, 275–287.

Heath, C. and Luff, P. (1991) Collaborative activity and technological design: task coordination in London underground control rooms. In L. Bannon, M. Robinson and K. Schmidt (eds) *Proc. Second European Conference on Computer-Supported Cooperative Work,* 65–80.

Heath, C., Jirotka, M., Luff, P. and Hindmarsh, J.(1993) Unpacking collaboration: the Interactional Organization of Trading in a Dealing Room. In G. de Michelis, C. Simone and K. Schmidt (eds) *Proc. Third European Conference on Computer Supported Cooperative Work,* Milan, 155–170.

Hughes, J. A., Randall, D., and Shapiro, D. (1992) Faltering from Ethnography to design. In *Proc. ACM 1992 Conference on Computer-Supported Cooperative Work,* Toronto, 115–122.

Hutchins, E. and Klausen, T. (1992) Distributed cognition in an airline cockpit. Report. Dept. of Cognitive Science. University of California, San Diego, Institute of Psychology.

Krauss, R. M. and Fussel, S. R. (1990) Mutual knowledge and communicative effectiveness. In J. Galegher, R. Kraut, and C. Egido (eds), *Intellectual Teamwork; Social and Technological Foundations of Cooperative Work.* Hillsdale, NJ: Lawrence Erlbaum Associates, 111–145.

Leroux, M. (1992) The role of verification and validation in the design process of knowledge based components of air traffic control systems. In J. A. Wise, V. D. Hopkin and P. Stager (eds). *Verification and validation of Complex and Integrated Human – Machine Systems.* Nato Advanced Study Institute, Vimeiro, Portugal, 357–373.

Rogers, Y. (1992) Ghosts in the network: distributed troubleshooting in a shared working environment. *Proc. ACM 1992 Conference on Computer-Supported Cooperative Work,* Toronto, 346–355.

Shapiro, D. Z., Hughes, J. A., Randall, D., and Harper, R. (1989) Visual Re-representation of database information – The flight data strip in air traffic control. Internal Report, Lancaster University, Dept. of Sociology, Lancaster University.

Sperber, D. and Wilson, D. (1986) *Relevance.* Oxford: Basil Blackwell.

Author Index

Lecture Notes in Artificial Intelligence (LNAI)

Lecture Notes in Computer Science